WHEN THE ROMAN BOUGH BREAKS

*A Fresh Look at
Roman Catholic Teaching in
Historical Context, Challenges for
Today's Church, and God's Perfect Grace*

Jeff Nottingham

When the Roman Bough Breaks: A Fresh Look at Roman Catholic Teaching in Historical Context, Challenges for Today's Church, and God's Perfect Grace
by Jeff Nottingham

ISBN: 978-1-953625-41-0 Trade Paperback
        978-1-953625-39-7 Hardcover
        978-1-953625-37-3 Ebook

BISAC: REL108020 RELIGION / Christian Church / History
        REL067050 RELIGION / Christian Theology / Ecclesiology

Cover design by Rick Turylo.

INTELLIGENT DESIGN PRESS
An imprint of Relevāre
Spokane, Washington, USA

Contents

A Note to the Reader

Throughout this book the term "catholic" (lowercase) is used in its original meaning to refer to the universal or singular early Church that spread from Jerusalem and the Mediterranean throughout the world. This early catholic Church existed prior to the institutionalized structures of denomination we know today. Capitalized as a proper noun, "Catholic" refers to the specific entity of the Roman Catholic Church and its members. The aim is not to confuse the reader with grammatical nuance, but to highlight the distinction and difference between the two.

Introduction

I have been a Christian for nearly fifty years, but it's only in the past two decades that I have come to understand the definition of grace and its true meaning. Grace is a term that is thrown around with other lingo in the Christian Church lexicon—such as reconciliation, justification, redemption, righteousness, and many more concepts—but that often has no contextual application for the average believer. The New Covenant is the ultimate manifestation of God's grace in defining these terms, but what is the New Covenant, really, and what was God up to by placing us under that system? What were God's real intentions when He initiated the greatest substitutionary sacrifice that has ever taken place?

We must acknowledge the context in which we attempt to apprehend the understanding of our Heavenly Father's plan. What was intended to be a movement to spread the news about the resurrection (the original Gospel) centering around one person (Jesus Christ) turned into a convoluted institution with ever-changing and supplemental doctrines that would drift away from the apostles' foundational intentions. This movement that would come to be known as the Church became a system that would ultimately blend the Old Covenant and New Covenant together in its doctrines, completely negating the plan God had to reconcile mankind back to Himself through the gift of grace.

Everything changed after the resurrection. God's will to make the Old Covenant obsolete was brought to bear, forever placing all of mankind under the canopy of the New Covenant, God's new promise and our new way to relate to Him on this side of the cross. However, time would prove that corruption comes quickly. Simple gatherings turned into religiosity and institutions promoting a system of self-effort and self-attainment toward right standing with God. The result was the creation of a legalistic web and a fatiguing list of duties to inherit eternal life.

This book will examine the Roman system and how much has changed since the first-century catholic Church and the teachings of the early apostles. Unlike similar Christian books that are written with the sole purpose of debating theological differences between Catholics and Protestants, this book looks at the fallout of wrong theology that puts man at the center, and what happens when a religious entity like the Roman Catholic Church is left alone for two millenniums with no accountability.

Beginning with an examination of the papacy, there will be hard and shocking explorations of what has remained behind closed doors for centuries, never discussed at Mass or in the living rooms of the average Catholic. This is not easy reading for the faithful attendee, but everything revealed in these chapters is public information that anyone can research, compiled here to show a full picture of what has transpired. The secrecy inside the Vatican will be unveiled as well, along with shocking information about the depravity of the priesthood, divulging realities of darkness in the heart and soul of the Holy See (the governing body of the Catholic Church).

If a choice is to be presented between the true New Covenant Gospel, and a human-centered Church system, then the two choices must be made abundantly clear for what they are. The beginning two-thirds of this book will present the realities of a Church system dependent upon a formal and dominating hierarchy and liturgy expanding outside the bounds of Scriptures. In the latter chapters, I will humbly attempt to present the amazing truth of the New Covenant.

Although this book focuses on the Roman Catholic version of the Church, an invitation is given to both Roman Catholics and Protestants alike to return to the original Gospel—to return to the original catholic Church—and in doing so, to forever define forgiveness, righteousness, and justification God's way, not by way of religious requirements with a fatiguing list. It is an invitation to come to the full understanding that Jesus was not a half-savior who only accomplished a portion of the mission to reconcile us back to God. He left mankind with the simple assignment to rest in His finished work by faith and trust in Him (Ephesians 1:7, Hebrews 4:9-11). This type of New Covenant faith is the motivating factor for a believer to walk in the Spirit, and to do so free from the bondage of Church requirements and institutional authorities.

The basics of the New Covenant are rarely taught in most churches but have been clearly defined by grace experts like Bob George, Steve McVey, Andrew Farley, and many others through their teaching and multiple books produced by their ministries. Even a cursory exploration of the New Covenant will reveal that the message of the Gospel and God's unmerited grace is graciously laid out for anyone to understand. Unfortunately, church traditions have replaced spiritual truths so evident throughout the New Testament, and the early apostles were willing to die to prevent heretics and the traditions of Judaism from slipping back into the equation and changing the Gospel and muddying the waters of such a simple message of redemption. The New Covenant is not a new teaching by any means but was the doctrine taught by the early apostles, and Christ set the platform for all future believers to be able to understand it.

A great exchange took place at the cross: our unrighteousness for His righteousness. This exchange not only permanently removed the penalty of sin, but placed God's holiness inside of us. It is an exchange that resulted in His only view of someone who has been born-again is "of the perfection of Christ." It is not because of any person's actions or behaviors, but because of His life inside of every believer. This knowledge leaves us with the choice between frivolously working our way towards salvation (the Old Covenant way) or believing that we could never do enough to satisfy God's righteous requirements, thus solely relying on our Savior.

Many Catholics I have met are some of the most genuine Christians I have known. This includes one of my best friends and many others I have met along the way. Regrettably, many spend their Christian lives participating in spiritual rituals and repetitions that would never be condoned by God, and never experiencing the freedom believers should have in the New Covenant.

This book is written in total love (tough love), and from a genuine heart to all the wonderful Catholics that help make up the landscape of Christianity. However, this book will shine the spotlight on what God initiated from the start, absent from pious and prideful human attempts to try to meet God halfway, and will take a hard stance challenging the Roman Catholic system and its initiatives to alter the original Gospel.

There is no meeting in the middle. There is only enjoying the Christian life, daily, because of the complete and saving message of the finality of the cross and the miracle of the resurrection, providing permanent forgiveness with no contingencies. There is no more guessing about our "salvation standing" on this side of the cross, as will be unfolded in the later chapters. Roman Catholics can finally have peace of mind and assurance of their redemption, with no fear of Purgatory and no fear of dying in mortal sin.

Through an in-depth look at the cornerstone sacrament of the Eucharist and the basic components of the New Covenant, the final conclusion will make a courageous call for Roman Catholics to shift from the trappings of institutional thinking and live primarily through the guidance of the Holy Spirit. The results of such a transition would be life-changing and could result in one of the greatest spiritual renewals in religious history.

Although tough love is seen throughout this book, its purpose is not "Catholic bashing," but to genuinely reveal a hidden history along with a current state of affairs. This is a must-read for everyone considering converting to Roman Catholicism, and a challenge for every cradle Catholic to re-evaluate their theological positions. Let me reassure every reader that there is no narrative or hidden agenda to have Catholics convert to Protestantism, but for all Christians to return to and embrace apostolic deposits and teachings.

If you are Catholic, there are going to be some shocking revelations uncovered in the first eight chapters that seem to be leading to a mass exit from the Catholic Church, especially in the United States. Are the facts disclosed in these chapters causing this catastrophic retreat? Will the new American pope (Pope Leo XIV) be the one who finally steps forward and concedes what has gone wrong? Will he be willing to take actions to correct it? This book will pull the curtains back and reveal the issues in granular detail!

You will hear about events you never dreamed possible—some enlightening, some disturbing and unsettling. This is going to be a hard ask, but if any Catholic is willing to make the commitment to journey through the entire book, not only will it be spiritually freeing, but you will never see Christianity the same again. Buckle up; it's going to be a jaw-dropping read!

PART I:

THE POPE AND THE PAPACY

CHAPTER 1

The Pope: How Did It Go So Wrong?

Roman Catholicism claims inauguration in AD 33 as, essentially, the original Church established by Christ with continuation through Peter, the apostles, and subsequent successors. Peter is known to have been the first pope in the eyes of the Church, and it claims that there has been a documented succession of popes ever since.[1] But there is not a clean line of succession regarding popes in the Catholic landscape, as we will see shortly, and many people will be surprised to find that the Bible doesn't even hint at this claim about the function of a papacy (office of the pope). There is no mention of a singular, assigned pope anywhere in the Scriptures, neither in the present first-century Church nor as a prescription for the future. A succession of a "created papacy" did take place, but much later than the Catholic Church would like to admit.[2]

Until about the sixth century, there were multiple bishops in the Catholic Church from the East and West of the European regions and they were in constant disagreement and conflict over whose view of theology was right and who would be acknowledged as the final authority. If you study the history, it was very chaotic (and that is an understatement). For several hundred years after the Church was established under Emperor Theodosius, the Church revolved around several powerful individuals, not an isolated pope. Bishops in some of the larger cities became archbishops, but in the very premier cities (Rome, Constantinople, Alexandria, and Antioch) they were all called "popes." Because of the constant East vs. West skirmishes (Roman Church vs. Constantinople Church), these popes (bishops) were often in opposition to each other.[3]

One would hope these leaders would want to represent Christ and have it as their sole mission to spread the message about the resurrection, but instead, many plotted against each other to secure the prizes of the Church: wealth and power. Gregory of Nazianzus complained, "The chief seat is gained by evil-doing, not by virtue; and the [Holy] sees belong, not to the more worthy, but to the more powerful."[4] It was, in short, a political power system.

The narrative projected by the Roman Catholic Church of a single pope leading Christianity from the time of Peter, with an almost spotless and unsoiled succession (and the teaching of a consistent message about the Gospel of Jesus Christ) is simply not candid and is not an accurate portrayal.

In Bruce Shelley's book *Church History in Plain Language*, he states:

> "The papacy is a highly controversial subject. No other institution has been so loved and so hated. Some Christians have revered the pope as the Vicar of Christ; others have denounced him as the Antichrist ... the concept of papal rule of the whole church was established in slow and painful stages. Leo is a major figure in that process because he provides for the first time the biblical and theological bases of the papal claim. That is why it is misleading to talk about the papacy before his time ... in theory, the bishops from the church were all equal ... Leo made his entrance into world history as the supreme head of all Christendom ... In the historic session on October 30, 451, however, the same council gave the bishop of Constantinople, as bishop of New Rome, authority equal to Leo's Constantinople became for the East what Rome was for the West ... Christianity acquired not one but two heads: the Roman church of the Western Empire and the Greek church of the Eastern Empire. Leo's representatives to the council immediately protested, but the council fathers would not alter their decision. It was an obvious reversal for Leo."[5]

It was hundreds of years after the church began that the Roman Catholic Church acknowledged a true, singular pope. This is far different from the Catholic Church's claim of a "succession of the papacy" from the inception of the Church, with all popes tracing back to Peter. The idea that leadership of the Church has always been held by only one individual can be very misleading.

Catholic apologists will deny this was the case and insist that there was only one recognized pope since the beginning, but that is simply not true. Roman Catholic Scholar Eamon Duffy, in his book *Saints and Sinners: A History of the Popes* (considered one of the most thorough single-volume histories of the popes ever written), states:

> "There is no sure way to settle on a date by which the office of the ruling bishop had emerged in Rome ... the indications are that there was no single bishop at Rome for almost a century after the death of the Apostles. In fact, wherever we turn, the solid outlines of the Petrine succession at Rome seem to blur and dissolve."[6]

In referring to Cyprian, an early third-century bishop and writer, Duffy concludes:

> "He himself, like many other bishops in the early Church, used the title 'pope', which only came to be confined to the Bishop of Rome [as we know today] from the sixth century ... but all the Apostles and all the bishops shared fully in the one indivisible apostolic power."[7]

The early church fathers and rulers simply shared responsibility for the duties of the Church and it would be completely foreign to the early church fathers to have one supreme, infallible teacher as the sole leader. Any "binding" (authority to make decisions) we see in Matthew 16 regarding Peter is reiterated again in Matthew 18 and 20, uniformly sharing responsibilities. Duffy states,

> "To begin with, indeed, there was no 'pope', no bishops as such, for the Church in Rome was slow to develop ... The visionary treatise, The Shepherd of Hermas, written in Rome early in the second century, speaks always collectively of the 'rulers of the Church' ... and makes no attempt to distinguish between bishops and elders."[8]

Duffy states that even by the fifth century, "regional churches governed themselves, elected their own bishops without reference to Rome."[9]

When there were multiple claims for the title (which happened often), each opposing pope would be called an "anti-pope" by the other, which became a common phrase in the Catholic Church. Many theologians in addition to Bruce Shelley agree that Leo (AD 451) seems to be the starting point for the papacy. A few even put Gregory (AD 590) as the actual starting point for a single pope. Catholic author Jerome Neyrey admits, "It would be wrong, however, to read back into first-century Rome the existence of the papacy as we know it today."[10]

Many scholars do agree that there seems to be a single bishop in Rome established by the end of the second century, but the proof is overwhelming that responsibilities were shared with other bishops, and supremacy—and especially infallibility—would have been adamantly rejected during that time. There was absolutely no universal papal jurisdiction for centuries. In fact, for approximately 1,000 years of church history, papal supremacy is not even demonstrative of what transpired. So, the primacy and supremacy that was proclaimed at the First Ecumenical Council of the Vatican (known as Vatican I) did not exist for the time period they claimed.[11]

Reformed theologian Gavin Ortlund states that the Church is not being truthful by declaring that Peter's Apostolic primacy (extending to the power of his teaching) has always been "the constant custom of the Church."[12] The early Church knew nothing about the coming infallibility of the pope that would be developed in time. Ortlund also reveals that:

> "None of the seven ecumenical councils were convoked [called together] by their own bishop, none of them were presided over by a Roman bishop ... For the first 1000 years, Bishops gathered at the councils considered themselves to have authority over and apart from the Roman Bishop. That's in contrast to the teaching at Vatican II [the Second Ecumenical Council of the Vatican] that says bishops [plural] have no power apart from the pope's consent ... A common argument and understanding in the early Church was: 'we are multiple; you are singular, therefore, we trump you in

power. We are in union with a group of bishops and therefore our authority surpasses yours.'"[13]

Ortlund proceeds to give a very specific example of the Pope not having the power that the Church claims that he had, and it was concerning Pope Vigilius in the sixth century:

"And with Pope Vigilius you have an ecumenical council and a pope in a standoff, but the bishops, in unity at Constantinople II, assert their authority over the pope's theological edict, even disciplining him and excommunicating him functionally."[14]

Shelly cites another historical situation to substantiate that a singular pope was not always common among the Roman Catholic Church, and the example summarized below takes place a staggering fourteen centuries after the start of the Church:

"In 1377 the aged pope Gregory XI reentered Rome. The joy over the reestablishment of the papacy in the Eternal City was short lived. Gregory's death within a year required a new papal election. The College of Cardinals, still heavily weighted with Frenchmen, yielded to the clamor of a Roman mob and chose an Italian. On April 18th, Easter Sunday, the new pope, Urban VI, was crowned. All the cardinals were present. The summer months, however, along with Urban's dictatorial ways brought second thoughts about his selection. In August the cardinals suddenly informed all Europe that the people of Rome had forced the election of an apostate to the chair of Peter and that the proceedings were invalid. A month later the "apostate" [pope] responded by creating practically a new College of Cardinals. For their part the French cardinals chose from their own number another pope, Clement VII, and announced this fact to the various civil and church authorities.

"Thus, with Urban ruling from Rome and Clement from Avignon, the murky chapter in papal history called the Great Schism of their papacy begins. It lasted for thirty-nine years. Each pope had his own College of Cardinals, thereby ensuring the papal succession of its own choice. Each pope claimed to be the true vicar of Christ, with the power to excommunicate those who did not acknowledge him. By 1409 a majority of the cardinals from both camps agreed to meet. They met for a general council at Pisa, on the west coast of Italy. They disposed both claimants to the papal chair and elected a third man, Alexander V. Neither of the two deposed popes, however, would accept the action of the council. So, the church now had not two but three claimants to the chair of Peter. Three popes at a time are too many by almost anyone's standards. Especially so when one of the popes preaches a crusade against another and starts selling indulgences to pay for it. At length in 1417 the council got one papal incumbent to step aside, deposed the other two, and chose a new vicar of Christ, Martin V."[15]

Right when you would think three popes at the same time was enough, along comes a fourth! This is additional proof that there has never been a "clean" line of succeeding popes. Other conflicts include Pope Gregory the Great's dispute with John the Faster, the dispute between Callistus I and Hippolytus, Damasus and Ursinus, Cornelius and Novatian, Cyprian and Stephen, and so many more. All these reveal that there is nothing that resembles a unified, single authority. There were even long gaps of vacancies in the papacy (AD 250 onwards), for those who defend the ideology of popes from the very beginning.

Well into the third century, Christianity was very turbulent, had competing theological slants, and was prone to split in the blink of an eye. In fact, the biggest rift in the Roman Catholic Church in Rome was in Constantinople in the East, where they did not acknowledge the Roman Bishop as being supreme over Christendom beginning in the early fourth century. This eventually led to the "Great Schism" in 1054 which resulted in today's Eastern Orthodox Church. This was the largest split from the Roman Catholic Church until the Protestant Reformation. It's important to recognize that multiple groups of Christians have broken away from the Roman Catholic

Church over the centuries because of either corruption or significant differences in theological interpretations.

It is also critical to take a look at exactly who controlled the pope throughout the centuries. Based on evidence that is known from history, many kings and feudal lords interfered in ecclesiastical affairs, even to the point of controlling the election of popes. An example would be King Phillip IV arranging for a French cardinal to be elected pope around the fourteenth century. In other words, the Church didn't elect popes for a long period of time, the kings did. Another example is a German king named Otto in the tenth century who controlled the papacy because the Church looked to him for protection. Kings enjoyed the freedom of interfering and controlling ecclesiastic affairs since they provided protection for the Church. It might come as surprise to many Catholics that popes did not call the shots for many centuries in the Roman Church. Popes, especially in the Middle Ages, were often mortifyingly subordinate to emperors and kings. In many situations, newly elected popes had to pay enormous sums of money to the ruler who had nominated them, and the potential for corruptness was very obvious.

We even see the Byzantine Empire controlling the popes for hundreds of years in the sixth, seventh, and eighth centuries. For several centuries after that, rich crime families selected popes to allow them complete control. The Medici, the Barberini, the Orsini, and the della Rovere all provided popes from their own ranks, but most notorious were the Borgias. Two of the popes placed in positions from these crime families were Calistus III and Alexander VI.[16]

After the fall of the Western Roman Empire around 476, the papacy was highly influenced by rulers of Italy; these periods were known as the Ostrogothic Papacy, Byzantine Papacy, and Frankish Papacy.[17] The papacy became a puppet office under the influence of these imperial rulers and was not even similar to the papacy we know today.

This blend of secular rulers, emperors, kings, and noble families having a pivotal role in papal appointments should concern every Christian. Duffy states, "By 1829, no fewer than 555 of 646 diocesan bishops of the Roman Catholic Church were appointed by the state."[18]

It was also very common for Italian noble families to appoint popes, such as the "Tusculan puppet popes" (Benedict VIII, John XIX, and Benedict IX).[19] In fact, for centuries, it was mandatory for popes to seek confirmation from secular emperors before they could be consecrated.[20] The ruthless politician Alberic II appointed five popes. Other popes were installed by local gang-bosses or corrupt emperors. Eamon Duffy states,

> "Of the twenty-five popes between 955 and 1057, thirteen were appointed by the local aristocracy [powerful noble families in political positions], while the other twelve were appointed by the German emperors ... and election to the chair of Peter, as we have seen, was frequently a commodity for sale or barter."[21]

Realistically, these facts alone start to cast a legitimate shadow on papal succession as a God-ordained event. I understand that Catholics are looking for a clean line of moral, "apostolic-like" successors dating back to Peter, but unfortunately, those who do the research are going to be gravely disappointed to find it simply doesn't exist. The point to grasp is that the foundational doctrines of the early, original, first-century Church were disappearing by the time the papacy started appearing with any semblance of a valid succession. Nevertheless, these facts about papal succession are just casual observations and a very small part of the overall story.

The Hallmark of Corruption

I want to be forthcoming in saying regardless of where it all began, in an effort to convince millions of followers of papal legitimacy, there seems to be a pattern in Catholic leadership of sweeping all the historical embarrassing stuff under the rug and pretending it doesn't exist. We'll see proof throughout this text, but the actions that are about to be uncovered are not an honest and ethical way to live or build Christ's Church, let alone advance the Gospel. But many Christians become mentally immune to the truth because there is no acceptable explanation for what went wrong. In all fairness, if today's Roman Catholicism were representative of the true, original catholic Church, it would not be logical to have numerous corrupt popes just a few hundred years after the Church started, continuing to be led with immorality and unscrupulous morals for almost 1,700 years. This is not referring to mere casual sin, but blatant, willful, unimaginable corruption on a level inconceivable to most Catholics or anyone.

The question has to be asked, is it even possible to have a person who is immensely immoral and ungodly as the "head of the Christian Church" since God is involved in the process? It is imperative to pause and realize just what this title is implying: the "One" who is succeeding directly from Christ, the "Vicar" (standing in the place of Christ), and derived from the early apostles via succession of the papacy. Remember that these individuals allegedly have a special, assigned, linked-in position with the Creator of the Universe.

As we will see, this is not "Catholic bashing" because papal corruption is historically documented and verifiable—killing, molesting, stealing, and deceiving—and it doesn't fit well with the Catholic story. Anyone venturing out to do the research can only logically conclude the "succession of the papacy" (the Catholic definition of divine continuing leadership since Christ founded the Church) does not seem very legitimate. This blatant accusation might come across as very condemning and offensive, as many Catholics have adored various popes. However, this story, tradition, and belief system about popes and their position over the Church that many cling to and defend with adamance seems to be massively flawed and misunderstood. There are critical elements that have been completely ignored or, at best, dismissed with unacceptable explanations.

Only a small portion of Catholics I have interacted with have ever scrutinized their faith because they are generally discouraged from questioning it. However, many inherently feel something is wrong. They just can't bear to look at it, and feel ashamed to bring it up. The notion of past popes having sexual relations with prostitutes, mistresses, and even children is very disturbing. When you learn that popes killed other cardinals to obtain this high position of the papacy, you know in your heart that is not a holy succession, and it looks nothing like Christ.

Although I hate to be the bearer of bad news, the truth is that the papacy was fairly warped from an early stage and became even worse during medieval times. Not corrupt in the sense that, "Yes, these guys made a few mistakes—they might not have been the best leaders—they probably sinned as we all do." In our search, we cannot dismiss these behaviors I'm introducing so easily. We are talking about corruption in the most sinister terms during certain periods of time. I think it is critical for Catholics to comprehend what really happened without being dismissive and accepting deficient excuses from Catholic spokespeople or the Church, which tends to dumb down and diminish the impact. It's only honest and responsible to hear what Roman Catholic scholars and theologians have to say about historical accounts concerning past popes, but that many Catholic apologists seem to want to hide, as we will see in Chapter 2.

Many popes were extremely irreverent and depraved individuals. Many committed capital crimes, as seen throughout the next chapters. Yet, unknowingly, these men are from whom Catholics get a big portion of their spiritual theology and direction. The original intent of the early Church, established after Christ ascended into Heaven at Pentecost, was intensely subverted and became distorted and self-focused after the first 300 years. Self-righteousness and "salvation-earning" developed in stark contrast and competition with the simple grace of God that Jesus taught, and scriptural principles took a sharp left turn when these bad popes emerged onto the scene.

This is not simply hearsay. This is basic, common knowledge among all Catholic theologians and even the clergy; however, it is rarely discussed. Many detailed books have been written divulging these devious popes long before this book was published: *The Bad Popes, The Sack of Rome, Sex Lives of the Popes, Sacred Betrayals, A Dark History: The Popes/Vice, Murder, and Corruption in the Vatican, Lives of the Popes, The Medieval Papacy, Holy Warriors/The Crusades, Absolute Monarchs,* and *Saints and Sinners,* along with endless articles and documentaries that corroborate the history.

Simple, cursory research can unveil the true nature of this highly coveted position and the unbiblical idea of the office and succession of the papacy. A common theme that emerges in papal history is that many popes killed others and leveraged their political and military power to steal the papacy, purchase it, or inherit it deceptively. The malicious intent from the Vicars of Christ is quite appalling.

Although no one can say they have a perfect interpretation of spiritual theology, the primary purpose of this book is to encourage Catholics to reconsider doctrinal positions and theological holdings from past popes (and their surrounding clergy) who developed a fraudulent system saturated with criminal acts and swimming in sexual and other perversion. In short, much of Roman Catholic theology the popes put forth was not sourced in the Scriptures or from apostolic teachings, but from a self-serving desire to preserve their power and gratify their flesh.

In examining the critical components of Christianity, the truth is seen that believers should not necessarily form their belief system strictly because of the Church they are attending. Instead, we should be looking at the original Gospel espoused by Christ and the early apostles as the very best understanding of biblical truth and correct doctrinal positions. Not that we can't learn from legitimate teachers within the walls of the Church, but the Bible clearly says that the Holy Spirit can teach us, and for us *not* to be so dependent on men. Hebrews gives a little window into this truth as it introduces the New Covenant (the "New Way" we relate to God on this side of the Cross). The truth of the New Covenant is the original Gospel:

> "...I will put my laws in their minds and write them on their hearts. I will be their God, and they will be my people. No longer will a man teach his neighbor, or a man his brother, saying, 'Know the Lord' because they will all know me, from the least of them to the greatest" (Hebrews 8:10-11).

> "And I will ask the Father, and he will give you another Counselor to be with you forever—the Spirit of truth. The world cannot accept him, because it neither sees him nor knows him. But you know Him [Holy Spirit], for he lives with you and will be in you" (John 14:16-17).

> "You show that you are a letter from Christ, the result of our ministry, written not with ink but with the Spirit of the living God, not on tablets of stone but on tablets of human hearts" (2 Corinthians 3:3).

> "For who has known the mind of the Lord that he may instruct him? But we have the mind of Christ" (1 Corinthians 2:16).

The inspired authors of the Scriptures are not speaking of the Old Covenant law. God did not write the Jewish, Levitical, or Sabbath law on our hearts. God has written a new command on our hearts from when Christ arrived on the scene. After the cross, God established a new way to relay information to us, to guide us, to speak to us, to reveal to us various instructions and directions for us to live out the Christian life. Surprisingly, this new way is not listening to man-made doctrine or tradition from a magisterium. In contrast, God tore the veil—He just unzipped the minds and hearts of genuine believers and came on in via the indwelling Holy Spirit to reveal His truth directly.

If you think otherwise and are a professing Christian, I'm sure you can remember numerous examples when you did something sinful and that inner voice suddenly let you know just how wrong that action was. You may also remember dozens of times when you were looking for direction and the Holy Spirit gave you peace and the proper focus in your situation, and it may have felt inexplicable. You may also remember something that seemed like a coincidence but would have been almost impossible without the Holy Spirit's intervention.

Welcome to the true Christian life. I think this is an extraordinary arrangement: God, Himself, living inside the believer, guiding us on how to live and intervening when He chooses to. What a source. Not religion, not a system, not from a hierarchy. Not useless repetition. Instead, a direct relationship with the Heavenly Father.

In defense of most Catholics, almost all Christians, including those within Protestant denominations, have adopted their belief system from what they have always heard or have been taught growing up. I do not denounce or condemn this in any way. In fact, it would be expected. Accepted theology is often a force of inertia, with a strong influence from family and a religious institution with powerful, convincing leaders. Many Catholics simply grow up in the system, encouraged never to question the teachings, or at the very least, never informed of the vast chasm between the Roman Church's doctrine and tradition and the original Gospel. So, very rarely does anyone branch out individually and do investigative research on the truth of where the Church they attend derived its doctrines. If they do, it is often with the goal of assuaging their fears and doubts, but they seek out biased material to do the fact-checking. Wolves never do a good job guarding the chickens in the coop!

I've learned many principles over the years, but one that has stuck with me is that you cannot be objective about something you have been steeped in and buried under your whole life, especially when it comes to spiritual matters. Objectivity requires stepping entirely away from an institutional system—even a church you have attended all your life—allowing the Holy Spirit to "wash" your mind, clean the slate, and start over again with Christ. In doing so, you can be released from the bondage of a religious system and have a fresh start with your Heavenly Father. I have personally experienced how refreshing this can be. Still, very few can ever experience this freedom because they are cemented into their churches and denominations.

This is not to make light of the work ahead of us—spiritual growth and understanding take time. However, it is a sobering reality that even earnest believers—with the Holy Spirit living inside of them—often place more trust in the Church, a priest, pastor, tradition, and the Church's dogma and statement of faith than the Bible and the guidance of the Holy Spirit for renewing their minds and discovering truth, along with accurate theology. It is widely acknowledged that pursuing truth is an important objective as a Christian, but how do we arrive at that truth? Should we consider interpretations of early Catholic popes and clergy as the "true" Gospel? If so, do we accept interpretations from those who have exhibited gross misconduct and who demonstrated ulterior motives? We must consider whether we should shape our theological perspectives for the rest of our lives based on popes who obtained the papacy through nefarious means, engaged in immoral acts, and initiated attempts to change the original Gospel.

If you are Catholic, I invite you to honestly consider the following challenge:

- If individuals like Ted Bundy, John Gacy, and Bernie Madoff had been the early leaders of Catholicism, would you still adhere to your same doctrinal beliefs?

- If, despite learning of their involvement, you chose to maintain your beliefs, at what point do you think your theology loses its credibility?
- If you discover that mass murderers, child molesters, and master deceivers occupied the position of pope and were instrumental in shaping the theological foundations of much of your belief system, would you be willing to pause and do some deeper research?

The reality seems to be that the character of many of the popes we will examine bears striking similarity to that of leaders of cults over the decades. When we consider figures like David Koresh, Warren Jeffs, Marshall Applewhite, or, for those familiar with distant history, Jim Jones, most of us react with a mixture of anger and disbelief toward such egocentric villains, and astoundment and grief at the vulnerable who were tricked into following them.

With the exposure of these cults, it was deeply disturbing to witness the aftermath of individuals permitting their spouses and children to enter into marriages and engage in sexual relationships with these manipulative leaders, eventually succumbing to mass suicides, all under the guise of "Christ". The point is that it is enraging to watch these leaders perpetuate the role of a messiah or prophet "directly appointed by God," knowing that God is totally absent from the equation. I want to be clear in stating that I am not labeling the Roman Catholic Church a cult, but I do want to show some similarities to cult leaders in how some of the Roman pontiffs operated.

Unfortunately, too many times in the past, popes have deceived the vulnerable and misled their followers into believing the falsehood that they are the head of the entire Christian Church—that they are the vicars of Christ—they are infallible in proclaiming dogma, and therefore should be treated like "little gods"—all while committing grievous acts of abuse and immortality. Over the years, we've seen videos of popes being carried on thrones, adorned in robes and towering triple crowns made of gold, consumed with self-importance, with followers gazing at them adoringly. Have popes been guilty of robbing God of His glory? The evidence seems to suggest so.

The Unfortunate Reality

Let's embark on the journey of exploring some of these successors at a time when the papacy was really off base from the biblical expectation of Christian leadership. This veering off course started happening intensely during the Middle Ages, but was prevalent from very early on. As we move forward, we have to keep in mind that popes are regarded as the "vicars" of Christ—the individuals who stand in place of Christ, claim to act in His stead, boast the throne of Peter, and when in power, have full, supreme, and universal authority over the entire Church, an authority that can be exercised without hindrance, and whose authority is sustained by our Heavenly Father.[22] When reviewing the popes listed throughout these chapters, in fairness, honesty, and humility, consider taking a look at where Catholic theology developed and determine if these popes and the surrounding magisterium are reliable sources on which Christians can be comfortable basing a belief system on.

In full disclosure, I want to warn readers that the following two chapters are going to be shocking and disturbing, but it's imperative for Catholics to understand what really happened in the history of the papacy. These events and characters were likely never disclosed in training classes at Church. The information that is going to be revealed is a very small sample of what actually happened with Catholic popes. There are dozens and dozens of popes, not mentioned for the sake of space, from the same time period referenced below who exerted similar behaviors. In fact, many times, the actions of those popes not mentioned was just a continuation of what had transpired with their predecessors. There is a distinct and disturbing pattern that will emerge as we near the end of this section after examining these papal selections. The following divulgences will require discipline and patience to get through, but Catholics will never see the papacy the same again.

Pope (Bishop) Marcellinus (296-304?)

Under pressure and persecution from the pagan Roman Emperor Diocletian, Marcellinus caved and surrendered copies of the Scriptures, and in full submission, offered sacrifices to the "gods." He died shortly afterward, and the Church had no desire to acknowledge him after these occurrences.[23]

Pope (Bishop) Damasus (366-384)

Damasus's election was contested by a rival pope (Ursinus), so in defiance, Damasus decided to "get rid of him with the help of the city police and a murderous rabble".[24] This was the start of an unfortunate pattern in the papacy of eliminating those who would interfere or compete for Peter's throne. Eamon Duffy states that many popes came and went during the fourth and fifth centuries who were described as "potentates" (monarchs so powerful that they do not have to follow any rules). Ultimately, many during this time were ruthless rulers full of pride and worldliness.[25]

Pope Vigilius (536-537)

Vigilius, likewise, needed to address a problem with an existing pope and took extreme measures to do so. The story is quite outlandish: After joining Theodora (the wife of an emperor), and "Laden with bags of Theodora's money for bribes," he raced to Rome to manipulate and buy his way into the papacy. Upon his arrival, he realized a gothic king had already "installed" a pope (Silverius). Vigilius was not happy about the appointment, and he bribed an imperial general to have Silverius arrested on a trumped-up charge and banished to a small town. Vigilius was then elected to the throne. However, that small town took it upon itself to help Silverius return to Rome, but Vigilius had him arrested again and exiled him to an isolated island where he died of malnutrition shortly thereafter.

Vigilius was known as being a fraud, and as he left office and boarded a ship, the crowd threw stones at him from the dock for all the misfortunes he had caused the city and the dishonest means he used to become pope.[26]

Pope Pelagius (556-561)

Duffy describes Pelagius as a pope "determined to become pope by hook or crook." His actions and means of operating the papal office were universally denounced in the West as "self-seeking treachery," leaving the papal reputation in ruins.[27]

Pope Stephen II (III) (752-757)

It is almost certain that Stephen or part of his entourage was behind the fraudulent document called "Donation of Constantine". This was a Roman imperial decree where the fourth-century Emperor Constantine supposedly transferred all-encompassing power and authority over Rome (and the whole Roman Empire) to the pope. With this declaration, the pope would inherit special privileges as well as the Lateran Palace. This forged document was a way to elevate popes to a level of supremacy over other bishops, especially those associated with Constantinople.

The goal also seemed to be to boost Roman ecclesiastical politics and power, especially to use the Church as a weapon against emperors and anyone not acknowledging papal authority and supremacy. This false document was used for hundreds of years—all the way through the Middle Ages—until it was finally exposed as a forgery in the fifteenth century. Countless popes fed off of this forgery to their benefit.

"Donation of Constantine" was not the only fraudulent document in the Church's possession. Another false decretal emerged called "Pseudo Isidore", which was a series of letters from early popes, all forged, which happened to include the Donation of Constantine. Effectively, these letters and false claims were used to establish the papacy as the real source of power in the Church. They ultimately made the collection one of the most often cited reference books of the medieval Church despite being completely fabricated.[28]

Pope Paul I (757-767)

Pope Paul I, along with Stephen III, was challenged by anti-popes and was "sucked into a sordid whirlpool of internecine violence and betrayal, punctuated by blindings, torture and judicial murder."[29]

I think it can be safely assumed that most Catholics are probably not aware that popes engaged in murderous activities, but this was actually very common, and the stories get much worse.

Pope Bonifacius VI (896-896)

Bonifacius's papacy lasted for only two weeks before he was murdered by Pope Stephen VI. Bonifacius did not have the opportunity to achieve any notable accomplishments during his brief time as pope, but became another murderous victim of "pope against pope."

Pope Stephen VI (896-897)

Pope Stephen VI decided he was so set on proving his position on a controversial issue, he had the late Pope Formosus exhumed from the grave, dressed him in papal attire, and put on trial for violating Church rules. Yes, Stephen put his rival's lifeless body on the witness chair and continued with questioning. A deacon, reluctantly, spoke on behalf of Formosus' dead body and answered all the questions. He was found guilty, and Stephen had three of Formosus' fingers cut off, then he was stripped naked, dragged through the streets, and reburied in a mass grave.[30]

Stephen also engaged in brutal politics and was only promoted to the position of pope to seize control of Rome. His actions and behavior during his papacy indicate that he was not a "holy successor" in the truest sense. It is important to recognize that throughout history, there have been a huge number of instances where leaders within the Roman Catholic Church exhibited problematic behaviors or suffered from mental disturbances. Stephen VI is one such example. These, and many more cases to come, make a strong argument against God divinely appointing a leader of a central Church or ever allowing one individual to stand in the place of Christ.

Stephen was later imprisoned and ultimately strangled as a result of his actions.[31] This is an undeniably shocking narrative, particularly when considering the subject is the pope—regarded as the highest position in the Roman Church that can ostensibly be traced back to Peter, and ultimately, Christ Himself. Their role is supposed to involve spreading the message of the resurrection to all future generations. Given these circumstances, it's understandable that a sense of unease might arise.

Over the twelve months following Steven's death, four potential popes hastily vied for "the bloodstained throne," with some occupying it for mere weeks or even days before meeting their demise. In a span of approximately six years, seven popes emerged. In fact, by the ninth century, the popes were virtually meaningless pawns for the noble families that controlled them. Shockingly, there were twenty-four popes between 872 and 904.[32] It would not take a renowned theologian to conclude something was terribly wrong with the Roman Church having twenty-four popes in a span of thirty-two years. Considering the belief that God is perpetually involved in the direct selection of the leader of the entire Christian Church, as He sustains this top position, one cannot help but question how things unfolded during that tumultuous period. One should start to wonder, what is really going on here?

Following these years, the Holy See entered a period called "The Dark Age of the Papacy". This era dove the Roman Catholic Church even deeper into depravity with papal leadership.

Pope Sergius III (904-911)

Another questionable pope, Sergius III supported the horrendous act that Stephen VII did to Formosus. In a shocking continuation of a similar event, Sergius had the late Formosus exhumed a second time, ten years after the first, and put him on trial again. As anyone can imagine, Formosus didn't do too well at this court show, either. One can only imagine the smell in the courtroom. Sergius III, like Stephen VII, had three more fingers cut off Formosus' dead body, then had him beheaded and dumped into a river, where his body was eventually caught in a fisherman's net.[33]

Despite this speechless spectacle, Sergius had two primary agendas after entering this coveted, holy, "vicar of Christ" position: to strangle and murder his predecessors (Pope Christopher and Pope Leo V) and spend "quality" time with a fifteen-year-old girl and her mother (both prostitutes). These prostitutes (Theodora and Marozia) highly influenced the papacy for decades. It is hard to grasp and comprehend that two prostitutes influenced the holy "office of the papacy" for this long, but that is simply what happened. It has been called the age of the "pornocracy popes,"[34] naming a period of sixty-eight years of extreme immorality among the vicars and spanning the reigns of fifteen popes. Stories like these are obviously not told during Mass at the Catholic Church.

> "These Roman amazons [Theodora and Marozia] combined with the fatal charms of personal beauty and wealth, a rare capacity for intrigue, and a burning lust for power and pleasure ... They turned the church of St. Peter into a den of robbers, and the residence of his successors into a harem. And they glorified in their shame. Hence this infamous period is called the papal Pornocracy or Hataerocracy."[35]

Sergius had lusted after Marozia since she was six years old, and her mother gave her to the pope when she was fifteen, and they had a son (the future John XI).[36] What a story, but part of papal history.

Cardinal Baronius, one of the first papal historians, concluded about Pope Sergius III that a monster had been unleashed against the church. He stated:

> "A wretch, worthy of the rope and of fire ... flames could not have caused this execrable monster to suffer the punishments which he merited."[37]

Author James S. Packer says of Sergius III that he was malignant and ferocious, slaughtering his enemies with a private army. Additionally, Jewish scholar Walter Ullmann, an authority on medieval political thought, describes this pope as a typical representative of the House of Theophylact, concerned with power and sexual liaisons.[38]

Sergius attempted to seize the papacy forcefully but was ultimately driven out and expelled from Rome. It is perplexing to try and understand why God would unleash a monster against the Church if you accept papal succession and divine appointments. However, unleashing a "monster" would not be accurate. Monsters (plural) would be far more factual, as we will soon see. The truth is that God does protect His Church, but one has to understand what the precise definition of "Church" really is in God's economy. As discussed in Chapters 4 and 5, Christians have to question whether today's Roman Catholic Church still should be labeled the sole, "one, holy, catholic, and apostolic Church of Jesus Christ" matching God's original intention. The early catholic Church, for the first 250 years (maybe less), certainly seemed much more aligned with apostolic teachings.

Pope John XII (955-964)

Pope John XII acquired his special appointment at the ripe old age of seventeen or eighteen. Undoubtedly, he lacked the maturity to lead the Church the way God would have intended (were that God's intent.) He acquired the title of being "the most immoral Pope in Catholic history."

John shunned his mandate to advance this "one, holy, catholic, and apostolic Church of Jesus Christ" by turning his papal residence into a brothel, and would even rape women in the cathedral. In addition, he had a habit of calling out to pagan gods while gambling at parties flooded with alcohol and was accused of homicide, perjury, and incest.[39]

There seemed to be no sin John XII would not commit. He slept with his father's mistress and even his own mother. He stole from the church's treasury, rewarding his lovers after nights of passion. Women were warned to stay away from the cathedral as John was always on the prowl for new women. He was extremely violent, blinding one cardinal and castrating another, causing his death. A Holy Roman Emperor actually wrote a letter to John, stating:

> "Everyone, clergy as well as laity accuse you, Holiness, of homicide, perjury, sacrilege, incest with your relatives, including two of your sisters and with having, like a pagan, invoked Jupiter, Venus, and other demons."[40]

In spite of John's threat of ex-communication, the emperor Otto deposed John, and Pope Leo VIII was put in his place. This enraged John, who returned to Rome, threw Leo out, and carried out vengeance on all responsible for his exile. John had the skin flayed off one bishop, cut off the nose and two fingers of a cardinal and gouged out his tongue, and decapitated sixty-three members of the clergy and nobility in Rome.[41] Once again, it's truly hard to imagine a pope qualifying as a torturer or murderer, but John XII was one of many.

John was able to draw upon the revenues of the Papal States to maintain armed gangs and was successful in terrorizing the citizens of Rome. The dark element of his nature allowed him to test the utmost extent of his corrupt power.[42]

Pope John XII was eventually killed by the husband of one of his lovers. This would not be a leader that the Church would be proud of or want to lay claim to. He was an absolute train wreck as a holy father but the Roman Catholic Church still considers him to have been the vicar of Christ.

Pope Benedict V (964-964)

Benedict V, yet another contentious pope with a brief reign, abruptly fled to Constantinople after seducing a young girl and stealing the church treasury. When he ran out of money, he returned to Rome, reverting to his previous pattern of maintaining multiple mistresses. Eventually, he met a gruesome end at the hands of a jealous husband, who mercilessly stabbed Benedict more than a hundred times.[43]

Pope Benedict VIII (1012-1024)

Benedict VIII worked in close harmony with Emperor Henry II to attack Byzantine southern Italy, breaking off the fragile relations between the Churches of Constantinople and Rome.[44]

Pope Benedict IX (1032-1044)

As if John XII had set a good example of a mature Christian leader at age eighteen, Benedict IX took over the top position for the entire Christian Church at the age of just twenty.[45] (Though some historical reports have Benedict at just fourteen when he acquired the papacy!)[46] His father paid off some officials of Rome in order for him to become pope. Barely an adult, possibly just a child by some accounts, he found himself in a vicar role, and it turned out to be quite a spectacle. Two of his uncles preceded him in holding the papal position, and he had a family with plenty of political, military, and papal muscle.[47]

One can only wonder about his ability, fortitude, leadership, and experience to shepherd millions of Christians as an immoral youth. Most individuals that age are still navigating the fundamental aspects of life, barely out of puberty, and do not possess the capacity to govern anything, much less an entire religious system. He would certainly not carry the wisdom to interpret, scrutinize, theorize, and assimilate biblical truths to influence your theology or the theology of hundreds of millions of Christians in the future.

Benedict IX held the papacy three separate times.[48] He even sold the position to his godfather during one of those reigns, who later became Pope Gregory VI. Later, this transaction drained the Church's treasury. Benedict set off for a life of leisure and pleasure at one of his castles in the country and had no interest in spreading the news about the resurrection of Christ.[49]

Is it logical to think that God was distracted around 1032-1044 in allowing him to acquire this position three separate times? As with all papal selections, I believe many will see it is safe to conclude God was not involved. Nevertheless, Benedict got in, so let's continue and see how he did.

Labeled "a demon from hell," described as "feasting on immorality,"[50] and a known homosexual, Benedict IX was recognized for his extreme cruelty and debauchery.[51] It even stunned the citizens of Rome, who were used to all types of depravity and degeneracy. He was accused of rape, murder, adultery, and sodomy (bestiality to be more specific, but no desire to envision).[52] There was an array of wickedness every place he went. He held multiple orgies in Rome, as sexual perversion was a common theme with the vicars of Christ back then.

He was finally driven out of Rome by a group run by Pope Sylvester III. A few months later, however, Benedict returned with an army and recaptured the papacy, reinstating himself on the throne. He then decided to sell the papacy to his godfather so he could officially marry his second cousin.

Benedict's imminent marriage didn't materialize, so once again, he marched back in with an army in order to get the papacy back, but Sylvester III did not let go of the title. Although there were three simultaneous claims for the papacy, Clement II got the coveted position before he died suddenly. Benedict tried to get the papacy again, but the title was denied. He was finally excommunicated, which in some respects is ironic, considering that excommunication was a constant and imaginary card played by popes to childishly get their way and maintain control. What a crazy story! What a papal mess!

As an obvious and repetitive reminder, the Roman Catholic Church claims this super important, critical leadership position of the papacy is a succession from Jesus Christ, succession from Peter, the holiest of positions, the head and authority of the Church, the holy father, part of the Holy See, and in authority over every Christian on the planet, with God right in the middle of these "divine" appointments. The Church holds the position that the pope is the actual vicar of Christ who stands in place of Christ and acts on behalf of Christ with complete supremacy.

God clearly does not seem to be even remotely visible regarding the office of the papacy, and there is a reason Jesus never addressed the topic, or made this Roman Catholic claim. There was never a plan for a God-ordained papacy or papal succession. Although this position is so highly regarded in the Roman Catholic Church, the papacy is simply not substantiated anywhere in the Scriptures. Here is a critical, but simple, historical observation: the papacy was not part of the original catholic Church.

To claim that these popes were advancing the simple Gospel of Jesus Christ is truly hard to imagine. A holy succession instituted and governed and sustained by God seems virtually impossible based on the track records of the popes that have been examined so far; and not surprisingly, there are more to come.

Pope Nicholas II (1058-1061)

Nicholas had the backing of the German court which allowed him to have access to imperial troops. This, along with lavish gifts he gave to the population of Rome drove Pope Benedict X out of town.[53] The competition to obtain the Roman throne and exert power over the population was intense. The rivalry for the papacy has always been, even from the very beginning, as "cut-throat" as political contentions have been. Duffy states, "Every new pope had to spend huge sums on lavish gifts to the citizens to ensure acceptance of his election, a use of Church funds which brought bitter criticism."[54] This common practice of purchasing one's way into the papacy is in total conflict with Jesus Christ having someone stand in His place. Those actions are irreconcilable with the true Gospel, yet this was a customary practice in the Roman Church. Should this give a Catholic reason to pause and consider that maybe the pope is not the Vicar of Christ? What have been the motives of so many that have sat in this Vicar position?

Duffy confirms this level of corruption by saying, "From Innocent IV [in the thirteenth century] onwards many of the popes forfeited moral credibility by using some of the most solemn spiritual weapons of the reform papacy for purposes which were blatantly political."[55] Of course, as we have already seen, the forfeiture of moral credibility has always existed in the papacy. There are many more disclosures to come.

Pope Boniface VIII (1294-1303)

Boniface VIII was another pope obsessed with power who constantly used his throne to acquire personal wealth. He demanded everyone acknowledge him as the ruler of the whole world and would retaliate against anyone who opposed him. He consistently used threats to get his way, as he did against the University of Paris in stating that he would use the power of Rome to destroy them if they continued to prove uncooperative.[56] He even took revenge on a previous pope (Pope Celestine) and sent armed guards to bring him back to Rome where he could imprison him. He was successful in doing so, and Celestine died a few months later.[57]

Like many popes of the past, he engaged in the crimes of simony and nepotism, determined to use the wealth of the Church to fund his family fortune. He had a terrible temper and on the news of the death of his brother and his nephew, he burst into bitter accusations, cursing God for bringing these things on to him.[58]

He had a fascination with being showy and being publicly admired. He appeared several times in robes yelling out, "I am Caesar; I am emperor." The crown that he wore contained forty-eight rubies, seventy-two sapphires, forty-five emeralds, and sixty-six large pearls. He had a ceaseless hunger for gold and would boast that he presided over kings and kingdoms in all affairs, deeming himself a god on earth.

Boniface wasn't exactly beloved. After his election in 1294, he erected statues of himself all over Rome and said that sleeping with women and boys was no more problematic than rubbing one hand against the other. His most flagrant offense? The entire city of Palestrina was destroyed on his orders—all because of a personal political feud.[59] Boniface VIII was another executioner among the vicars of Christ. In a separate incident, he absolved his followers of sin for those who sacked the Colonna property in Rome to steal their possessions. He was part of the Crusades (discussed later) and when he attacked the Colonna people, women and children were not spared but were executed or sold into slavery.

Excommunication was often exercised by any pope to maintain power. Boniface VIII, as an example, threatened any ruler who tried to tax the clergy. He demanded absolute and humble obedience, otherwise, he would inflict the utmost injury on their citizens and merchants, causing their property to be pillaged and confiscated in all parts of the world. According to many, the god that the world saw Boniface worship was the god of power. Even cardinals, who came into contact with him daily learned to hate him with personal bitterness.[60]

In the middle of controversial leadership and the motive to control all kings and emperors, Boniface made the most extreme papal claim: "It is altogether necessary for every human being to be subject to the Roman Pontiff."[61] He was opposed, however, by King Phillip and the pope fled like a coward into hiding. Phillip found and imprisoned him until he died a few weeks later.

This false papal claim by Boniface that every human being be subject to the Roman Pontiff (The Pope) is a window into the minds of these godless leaders who have sat on a throne that was never meant to exist. However, this claim becomes another chapter in Rome's desperate attempt to usurp authority over every Christian, when Christians are only subject to our Heavenly Father. Even today, the pope is treated like a little god on earth and it is expected that every Christian is under his authority (CCC 937). It's the worst type of dupery.

Urban VI (1378-1389)

The Roman Catholic historian and diplomat Ludwig Von Pastor summarized the character of Urban VI:

> "He lacked Christian gentleness and charity. He was naturally arbitrary and extremely violent and imprudent, and when he came to deal with the burning ecclesiastical question of the day, that of reform, the consequences were disastrous."[62]

After a controversial election to the throne, he had a conflict with the French cardinals who invited Urban to an ancient city near Rome with the intention of having him imprisoned and murdered. Urban avoided the capture and the cardinals proceeded to overthrow him and elect a militant pope (Clement VII). Urban did what he had threatened to do for a long time: he created his own set of cardinals, in effect erecting another Sacred College to take the place of that which had abandoned him.

Urban also excommunicated Queen Joan of Naples and had her murdered shortly after. He was later imprisoned by King Charles III in Nocera, where he daily and furiously declared damnations on his captors. With help, he escaped to Genova where he had six cardinals seized, tortured, and put to death. Urban later complained that he did not hear enough screaming as they were being tortured.

The cardinals' wealth was enormous during those days. Acquiring gifts from European monarchs, the cardinals were directly connected to a system which sucked gold from all over Europe. Boniface was jealous of this wealth. Petrarch commented on the great wealth of these cardinals living in their palaces:

> "Instead of the Apostles who went barefoot we now see satraps (governors of provinces) mounted on horses decked with gold and champing golden bits and whose very hoofs will soon be shod of gold if God does not restrain their arrogant wealth. They could be taken for kings of the Persians ... who demanded to be worshipped and into whose presence must no man come empty-handed."[63]

Throughout the centuries, popes and cardinals thrived on power and wealth and conquered lands to increase their territories and enhance their families' affluence. They murdered and pillaged and used spiritual threats to accomplish their mission. The vision that most Catholics have of a godly, honest, ethical, holy, religious Roman Catholic Church—occupied with the successors of Peter and the apostles—does not seem to be the actuality. This religious institution, instead, has historically paralleled the conquests of many militant leaders with the same unethical motives for dominance and power.

Urban VI fit this role as well. He was extremely violent and disrespectful to his cardinals, once yelling out, "I can do anything, anything!" Nobody knew what his mood might be when they came into his presence. He would launch into fits of rage at any moment and his verbal attacks steadily worsened, culminating in physical attacks upon the cardinals.[64]

Pope Julius II (1503-1513)

Thecollector.com describes Julius II:

> "Also known as the angry or Warrior Pope, Julius II did not choose his papal name in honor of Pope Julius I, but rather wanted to emulate Julius Caesar. A fiercely efficient pope, he spearheaded the Italian Wars, the creation of the Vatican Museums, and the reconstruction of St Peter's Basilica. Although he is remembered for his patronage of the arts, he had characteristics that were very un-Christian. He had a violent temper and treated his subordinates and servants very badly. He fathered several children before becoming pope and was accused of sexual misconduct."[65]

Philosopher and Dutch theologian Erasmus wrote a satire called "Julius Excluded from Heaven" that focuses on his sexual misconduct. In it, Julius II is described as a drunken pope trying (and failing) to persuade St. Peter to open the gates of Heaven for him. Julius II tries to bribe him with money, and when that does not work, he resorts to threatening him with armies, just as he had done on Earth. St. Peter is disgusted and ultimately turns him away.[66]

Having become a cardinal through the nepotism of his uncle, Pope Sixtus IV, Julius was known as a violent and harsh pope. At one point twenty-five members of the Sacred College met in a conclave and were unanimous as to the type of pontificate they desired—the exact opposite of Julius II. They were tired of marching and counter-marching across the face of Italy. They simply wanted someone who ruled in a civilized manner. Julius II hated the French and Spanish as well, although that hatred didn't seem to measure up to the character expectation of a pope.

In 1506, Julius promised indulgences to people who paid money to him to construct St. Peter's Basilica. Preachers were sent out by the Roman Church with the intention of scaring Catholics into giving their money so that they might get loved ones out of Purgatory faster. This was a despicable practice and played a big part in prompting the Great Reformation in the 1500s.

Indulgences are a "remission before God of the temporal punishment due to sins whose guilt has already been forgiven, which the faithful Christian who is duly disposed gains under certain prescribed conditions through the actions of the Church" (CCC 1471). Indulgences do not exist in the Scriptures, were not part of the early Church, and started to formally develop in the eleventh century as a con to get followers to go to war. It has to be noted that Jesus never set up a system of indulgences or Purgatory because His sufficiency at the cross eliminated our need to have to be purified before we enter Heaven. God already sees every Christian as righteous because He sees Himself inside of us. He took our place on the cross. He took the punishment in our place. He left nothing for us to reconcile. This topic is addressed extensively later in the book.

It's very sad and disappointing theology to have the Church offer indulgences as a salve for the consequences of sin when Jesus already "paid in full" the penalty for all of them and eliminated the eternal consequences of sin. Yet, the Roman Catholic Church hangs onto a shocking list of things that yield an indulgence, including the useless muttering of dozens and dozens of phrases, prayers, and songs on specified days. This is something that would never be condoned by God, and the apostles would be appalled at such accretions (developments over time) in the Church.

Julius, like so many others, had accumulated massive wealth from his nine years as the papal leader. He fathered a child out of wedlock before his pontificate and was alleged to have been a bi-sexual. He drank a lot and was accused of spilling Christian blood to increase the temporal power of the papacy. He by all accounts neglected spiritual matters and was focused on military control. An editorial on a book by Christine Shaw called *Julius II: The Warrior Pope* states:

> "Shaw succeeds in presenting a portrait of 'a plain spoken, short tempered, vigorous, impetuous, man of action', but a prince warrior rather than the religious leader of a Christendom in need of a renewal."[67]

One report about Julius II states:

> "By far his worst feature was his severe case of Syphilis, contracting it via prostitutes. It was documented that on Good

Friday, his feet were so covered by sores that no one was able to kiss them."[68]

Pope Sixtus IV (1471-1484)

Historical records indicate that Sixtus IV was involved in homosexual activities, which is so prevalent among popes that it is reminiscent of the influence social media has had in normalizing and promoting homosexuality among young people today. Unfortunately, the reign of Sixtus was just one of *many* questionable periods in papal history. During this era, popes seemed to be more preoccupied with family affairs and political ambitions than fulfilling their spiritual responsibilities as leaders of the Church, and as a result, nepotism was no problem for Sixtus either.

On the website Vaticancitytours.it, it is revealed that he taxed prostitutes and priests with mistresses. He did little for the Church, but made time to have six illegitimate children, with one being conceived by his sister![69]

He was pope during a time of the inquisitor's quest to be rid of witches, and although he had a change of heart because of the brutal torture methods that were used, King Ferdinand blackmailed Sixtus and reapplied the pressure to continue, so he caved in and withdrew his papal bull that attempted to stop the Inquisitions in Spain.[70]

He tried to instigate numerous wars, but his primary focus remained the enhancement of his family. His numerous relatives were given high offices, and his nephews constantly solicited the pope to attack and siege other cities. He had some of his nephews and nieces marry into the great Italian dynasties to gain political control and wealth.

Innocent VIII (1484-1492)

Innocent VIII made no attempt to hide the fact of his numerous illegitimate children and had no qualms about loading them up with riches. Offices and pardons of every description were frankly and openly for sale.[71] He engaged in nepotism as we have seen with many popes, and as part of a business deal made a fourteen-year-old a cardinal.[72] His spending habits were disastrous for the Holy See and reduced Rome to anarchy after his death.

In his papal Bull *Summis desiderantes* in 1484, Innocent VIII ordered harsh measures to be taken against witches and magicians in Germany. Even if individuals denied charges of heresy or witchcraft this would prove the charge to be true. It was a no-win situation for those who were accused. This insane policy even applied to bishops, theologians, and other church officials as much as it did to the lowliest serf or peasant.

This witch hunt became nothing short of a massacre that would be led by two Dominicans specifically chosen for the task by the pope himself. They published a manual called *The Witches' Hammer* that would be used for identifying and punishing witches. This manual could actually be found in courtrooms and was used by judges and magistrates well into the eighteenth century. The whole topic of witchcraft depended on gossip and superstition, particularly at the height of the campaign of hunting and burning witches.[73]

In his book, *A Dark History: The Popes*, Chamberlain states what happened as a result of the two Dominicans being unleashed by Innocent VIII in a vicious assault against witchcraft:

> "Armed with ideas like this and with a brief from Pope Innocent giving them the power to do virtually as they pleased, Kramer and Sprenger set off across Germany to root out witchcraft and heresy wherever they could find it. This was a no-holds-barred expedition and the inquisitors used lies, maltreatment and psychological pressure along with physical torture to get the convictions they wanted. They flogged their victims until the blood ran. They used the rack, thumbscrews and crushers of various kinds. But these were just the preliminaries. ... The real refinements, which came later, were listed on a tariff of tortures drawn up by Herman IV of Hesse, Archbishop of Cologne. One option involved cutting out a victim's tongue and then pouring hot metal into their mouth. Another entailed cutting off a hand and nailing it to the gallows, presumably before the condemned witch was hanged."[74]

Innocent VIII finally realized the error of his ways and was unnerved by the savagery and cruelty he had unleashed and tried to put the manual on a list of prohibited books, but the witch hunts continued and the damage persisted. This pope became a deranged killer fitting the title given to almost too many popes to count. After coming to this realization, Catholic attendees of Sunday Mass would certainly understand why the true history of popes could never be discussed. In fact, some Catholics leave the Church after they are informed of this appalling history and learn about the atrocities that have been committed. Individuals who convert to Catholicism are never told about this heritage, either, and have no idea how bad the Church's past has been.

Alexander VI (1492-1503)

The next pope and espoused role model for the Catholic Church—someone who is not perfect, not sinless, but at the very least is expected to have accountability and ethics, morals, and a good heart—was Alexander VI. Instead, he used bribery to work his way into the papacy and was a member of the notorious crime family, the Borgias. He was known for being a sex addict and being flashy with his affairs—fathering at least seven illegitimate children by three or four mistresses and supporting them from the Church treasury. One of his affairs included his daughter, and he celebrated his sixties by having an affair and cohabiting with a teenage girl.

Alexander VI was probably the most controversial pope ever to have reigned and remains infamous today. He obtained the papacy dishonestly by using his great wealth. He was able to dispense enormous bribes that could buy the vote of cardinals to win the position. One example was a bribe he offered Cardinal Ascanio Sforza, to whom he offered his position as Vice-Chancellor; but more importantly, a fabulous palace by the River Tiber opposite the Vatican. The cardinal managed to resist the offer for about five days but finally succumbed. The dilapidated palace still stands today.[75]

Rodrigo Borgia, now Pope Alexander VI, despite all the bribes barely won the election. He stood on the balcony of the Vatican and proclaimed, "I am Pope and Vicar of Christ ... I bless the town, I bless the land, I bless Italy, I bless the world."

This claim to stand in the place of Christ could not be further from the truth based on his character. Case in point: according to one of his ceremonial staff, the noted chronicler Johann Burchard, the Vatican occasionally hosted parties that were ultimately deemed "unrestrained orgies."

"On the last day of October, [the pope's son] Cesare Borgia arranged a banquet in his chambers in the Vatican with 50 honest prostitutes, who danced after the dinner with those present, at first in their garments, then naked. After dinner, the candelabra were taken from the tables and placed on the floor and chestnuts were strewn around, which the naked prostitutes picked up, creeping on hands and knees between the chandeliers, while the Pope, Cesare, and [the pope's daughter] Lucretia Borgia looked on. Finally, prizes were announced for those who could perform the act [of sexual intercourse] most often with the courtesans, such as tunics of silk, shoes, barrettes and other things."[76]

A pretty shocking activity for a pope to engage in, but behaviors like these seemed quite fitting for many popes in those days. Alexander's wasteful finances put the Apostolic See on the verge of bankruptcy, but he resolved to accuse wealthy citizens of crimes to extort money from them and to supplement that, he and one of his sons poisoned cardinals and took over their assets. This "leader" (a Catholic vicar) actually poisoned his own cardinals to steal from them.

For Alexander VI, the papacy was a business to be milked and exploited for gain, and a great deal of it. A historian and another contemporary wrote of him as pope:

"There was in him and in full measure, all vices both of flesh and spirit ... There was in him no religion, no keeping of his word. He promised all things liberally, but bound himself to nothing that was not useful to him. He had no care for justice since, in his days, Rome was a den of thieves and murderers. Nevertheless, his sins meeting with no punishment in this world, he was to the last of his days most prosperous. In one word, he was more evil and had more luck than perhaps any other pope for many ages before."[77]

He was also responsible for a war between France and Portugal and had a role in another war between France and Naples.[78] He was another profane individual, but a Roman Catholic vicar. In fact, Alexander VI and all the popes from the mid-fifteenth century on represent what was called the "Renaissance Papacy." Duffy describes the popes from this time period:

> "The Renaissance papacy evokes images of a Hollywood spec-
> tacular, all decadence and drag. Contemporaries viewed Renais-
> sance Rome as we now view Nixon's Washington, a city of
> expense-account whores and political graft, where everything
> and everyone had a price, where nothing and nobody could be
> trusted."[79]

In discussing Alexander VI specifically, Duffy states,

> "The bribery at his election was not much worse than at many
> others ... That such a man should have seemed a fit successor to
> Peter speaks volumes about the degradation of the papacy."[80]

So, it becomes very difficult to have confidence and trust in Catholic theology and tradition when the head of the food chain is dishonest, shady, and
unholy like the popes that have been mentioned. Obviously, one cannot conclude that all 266 popes have been corrupted on the level that has been mentioned so far; however, almost 40% of them will be referenced throughout
this and the next two chapters and this will only cover a fraction of the true
story. All this while keeping in mind that the Vatican has always been laced
in secrecy: one can only wonder about the actions of popes not mentioned
and what else occurred among those who have been.

Too many popes fit a profile of totalitarianism, greed, power, monarchy,
and sexual deviancy to be dismissed. Most would agree they should have
never been allowed to rule over any religious institution, and critical thinkers
have to question where their theology, traditions, and interpretations of the
Scriptures really come from. It is a valid question for an honest Catholic to
ask if they are willing to set their pride on the sidelines while seeking out
the truth.

Defending the Papacy

Incidentally, when you hear Catholic leaders like Scot Hahn, Jimmy Akin,
Brian Mercier, Bishop Baron, and many more defend the papacy at all costs,

and casually discuss these popes who have been profiled (when directly asked), they simply excuse them with the admission that popes can be sinful too, and make objectionable assertions that God will override fallible popes and make them infallible.[81]

Imagine if a man was charged with a bunch of crimes, hauled into court, and responded like this: "Good morning, Judge, I know you are not happy that I murdered that group of people and kidnapped all the kids, but God has overridden these acts and has made me perfect. There should be no consequences for my actions. Am I free to go?"

Everyone would demand justice to be served for these actions. The excuses put forward by Catholic defenders in an attempt to justify or downplay the level of corruption are unacceptable. Their efforts to defend a title, position, or leader that lacks legitimacy in the eyes of God are evident, and one can observe the embarrassed expressions on their faces as they try to conceal the extent of the corruption. For those who do the research, it becomes clear that there is no validity to the notion of the office of the papacy, but where does that leave the Catholic Church?

What are the implications for its dogmas, doctrines, beliefs, and traditions that have been passed down through the centuries if a divine papacy has been false all along? Yet the truth is that many of these teachings have been shaped and influenced by individuals who were simply not credible, using their power to advance their own agendas and fulfill their financial interests.

The Catholic List

With just a glimpse into the truth of the Catholic papacy out in the open, it warrants a few questions to Catholic attendees. First, when was the last time you attended Mass and the priest spent any significant time chatting about the extensive historical corruption of the Roman Catholic Church? Not in the sense of merely casual references, or unacceptable apologies from representatives and spokespeople for the Catholic Church, like Archbishop Piero Marini, who stated: "Given the number of sins committed in the course of twenty centuries, [reference to them] must necessarily be rather summary."[82]

When were you instead told the factual, verifiable truth regarding the corruption of the priesthood, cardinals, and popes on a massive scale—leaders who adversely affected the lives of hundreds of thousands of people and caused irrefutable damage to countless others?

The facts show that popes with little nobility were part of the "theology" handed down from generation to generation. Wouldn't it be fair to Catholic devotees to discuss, in detail, that the "Christ-oriented," perpetual flow of authority was often controlled by ungodly authoritarians that have little resemblance to the original Church leaders or our Savior?

If priests and other leadership did discuss this in their messages, would that dialogue destroy and debunk the credibility of the claim "one, holy, catholic, and apostolic church" and the entire office of the papacy? Maybe it would even allow them to question why the Roman Catholic Church looks very little like the original catholic Church of the first century.

If priests did inform the parish of the massive corruption and taught honestly about criminal popes and Church corruption, it seems the question that follows is, "What will you do with that truth?" After all, Catholic teachings have been changing and evolving since its opening day, and there must be some logical explanation for why today's Roman Catholic Church has doctrines and dogmas that look nothing like what Paul and the other apostles taught in the primitive Church.

Maybe the fear is that when all the pieces are put together, you'll realize that today's Roman Catholic Church far more resembles the results of a secular institutional history than a Christ-centered history; or at the very least, a blend of the two.

Could there ever be a Catholic priest or official (even one) who was honest enough, when finally realizing that today's Roman Catholic Church is not in alignment with the early Church and that most of the traditions, man-made doctrines, and dogmas are not accurate, would immediately teach that a reversal should be made? A reversal of everything falsified since Constantine (around AD 315) threw Christianity, politics, and paganism into one blender (something we'll look at more closely in Chapter 5).

I would be completely sympathetic with most Catholics, who would be downright fearful ever to entertain that perhaps the theology, doctrine, dogma, and Rome's interpretation of Sacred or Ecclesial Tradition passed on from generation to generation (trickling down from the leadership of some of the popes who have been mentioned) must be drawn into question. Yet, the truth has to be shown. At the risk of being offensive to many Catholics, against that backdrop it's impossible to ignore that these practices on the "Roman Catholic List" below are institutionally manufactured, not in alignment with the Scriptures, not glorifying to God, and were not practiced by the original catholic Church:

1. The perpetual, unbiblical role assigned to Mary (Queen of Heaven/ Queen of the Universe and much more)
2. An unhealthy obsession with Mary
3. Attempting to introduce Mary as a Co-Redemptrix
4. Mary as a mediatrix
5. Statues of Mary
6. Mary depicted on the throne with God in Catholic art
7. Mary titled "The Mother of God"
8. Mary's Immaculate Conception
9. The Assumption of Mary
10. The Perpetual Virginity of Mary
11. Aspirations of Mary
12. Mariolatry
13. The Rosary
14. Tradition and magisterium being equal authority with the Scriptures
15. The Office of the Papacy
16. The authority of the pope
17. Infallibility of the pope in the matter of faith and morals
18. Kissing the pope's foot
19. The priesthood
20. Penance dictated by a priest
21. Confession to a priest in a dark booth
22. The forced celibacy of priests
23. Infant baptism
24. The veneration of icons and images
25. Beautification
26. Canonization of a deceased person

27. Participating in Lent
28. Aspects of the Mass
29. Transubstantiation
30. Withholding communion from the laity
31. Purgatory
32. Masses for the dead to reduce time in Purgatory
33. Indulgences (especially the selling thereof)
34. Treasury of Merit
35. The Doctrine and Dogma of the Sacraments as a necessity for Salvation
36. Ex-communication for political purposes
37. Monks, nuns, convents, and monasteries
38. Unbiblical systems and procedures
39. Behaviors, works, and obtainment of graces to be in right standing with God
40. Fish Day
41. Meat Day
42. Saint Celebration Day
43. Blending Judaism with Christianity (Old Covenant with the New Covenant)
44. The Catechism
45. Canons
46. Military force to spread the Gospel (Crusades)
47. Utilizing torture methods to get confessions (Inquisitions)
48. Forced baptism upon cultures
49. Self-seeking motives to dominate Christendom
50. A fatiguing list of requirements and human effort to maintain salvation (yet, still with no security)

To mention just a few, referred to often in this book as "The Catholic List".

These proclamations and manifestations were not a part of the original Gospel, first-century Church, or patristic teachings, and have no biblical support. This might come as a surprise to many Catholics. However, Jesus and the early apostles would never have given a second of attention to anything on the list above and these practices, doctrines, dogmas, and ecclesiastical laws are not found when looking at the history of the early Church, especially in the first two centuries.

The Shocking News

The shocking and revealing news is that nothing on The Catholic List above came from our Lord and Savior, Jesus Christ. Instead, these doctrines and practices resulted from religious leaders who ventured far away from keeping the focus of Christianity solely on Christ. This list is in direct opposition to God's plan for believers and the original apostles, who were specifically assigned to spread the good news that Jesus was the Christ, Jesus was the Son of God, Jesus came to save the world from the penalty of sin, Jesus came so we could never thirst or hunger again, Jesus died on a Cross, Jesus rose again, and the assignment was and still is to spread the good news of the resurrected Jesus to every part of the world. This assignment came as He appeared to hundreds of eyewitnesses, with scripture after scripture saying not to add anything to this original Gospel. Jesus alone was the focal point of the early Christian Church. It was entirely about Jesus fulfilling all the righteous requirements so we would not have to.

"I warn everyone who hears the words of the prophecy of this book: if anyone adds anything to them, God will add to him the plagues described in this book. And if anyone takes words away from this book of prophecy, God will take away from him his share in the tree of life and in the holy city, which are described in this book" (Revelation 22:18-19).

"See that you do all I command you; do not add to it or take away from it" (Deuteronomy 12:32).

"Do not add to his words, or he will rebuke you and prove you are a liar" (Proverbs 30:6).

"I am astonished that you are so quickly deserting the one who called you by the grace of Christ and are turning to a different gospel—which is really no gospel at all. Evidently some people are throwing you into confusion and are trying to pervert the Gospel of Christ. But even if we or an angel from heaven should preach a gospel other than the one we preached to you, let him be eternally condemned" (Galatians 1:6-8).

In Galatians, Paul is adamantly saying that even if you are awakened in the middle of the night and an angel is standing at your bedside with wings that expand the width of your master bedroom with a spiritual proclamation that differs even the tiniest amount from the Gospel we have preached, you better roll back over and go back to sleep! The Gospel we are teaching right here, right now, will never, ever be changed. Don't add to it, don't take away from it, don't come up with your own system—everything you need for salvation is *already* contained in these pages, and it's not changing.

The original Gospel was not the good news about Mariolatry, not the good news about confession to a priest, or adoring a pope, or standardized procedures, or working your way into the kingdom, or participating in the salvation process. It was not about sacraments, penance, or indulgences. On the contrary, life, hope, peace, salvation, righteousness, justification, unconditional love, and forgiveness (all being a one-time gift) come from the unexplainable, undeserved, unmerited, sustaining Grace of our Heavenly Father, through Jesus Christ, with perpetual guidance from the Holy Spirit.

Our *only* focus should be Jesus and nothing on The Catholic List above. That's the original Gospel. Religious leaders came with personal agendas, added erroneously to the original Scriptures, and handed them down to subsequent generations by sinister popes and clergy for centuries without any accountability.

This includes many, if not most, Protestant churches as well. Protestants are not off the hook. For those denominations that have changed the original Gospel with a substitutionary, deceitful Gospel as we see with the "name it and claim it" prosperity Gospel, or a Gospel that teaches just to sign on the bottom line, pray this prayer, and you are good to go—and many other examples that could be used—the consequences to the abandonment of the original Gospel will be dramatic.

For those denominations that are driven purely by emotions, running the aisles speaking in tongues, wildly dancing, and collapsing on the stage, you will not be in the same ballpark of replicating the original Church. For those who embrace a secular, feel-good, cotton candy, "positive thinking" gospel absent of any New Covenant teaching, you would be following a wide path going in the wrong direction.

Whether Catholic or Protestant, who do you think Jesus really is and what is His message? The Jesus promulgated by the Roman Catholic Church or many of the Protestant denominations in existence now is not the Jesus of Scripture who simply said, "Follow me."

Chapter 2

The Pope: Murder, Deception, and Denial

If you are Catholic and could transport back to the time of Pope John XII, the eighteen-year-old who housed prostitutes in his quarters, or any of those mentioned in the first chapter, and you came across them in Vatican Square, would you feel compelled to bow down and kiss their ring or feet? Would you smile and get fuzzy feelings as you looked at your family standing beside you, relishing the moment? Would you shed any tears of happiness by simply being in their presence?

Or, by contrast, would you be willing to set your pride and preconceived ideas aside and denounce these popes for who they were: papal leaders with minimal trustworthiness? Would you, instead, be repulsed by being in their presence?

The Roman Catholic Church, left alone with no accountability for almost 1,200 years after Constantine legalized Christianity, had become so dishonorable, with degenerate popes and false theology, that Martin Luther and others broke away from the institution. Many are familiar with the Great Reformation in 1517. It was a huge blow to the Roman Catholic system (as was the Great Schism of 1054), and they did everything in their power to stop it, but it transpired regardless. Luther launched his attack against corrupt papal leadership and teachings, stating:

- Rome's Sacrament of Penance was without basis in the Scriptures and the early fathers.
- Indulgences are pious frauds.
- The pope is not the vicar of Christ.
- It's not up to the pope to decide on articles of faith and morals.
- Purgatory cannot be proved from sacred scripture.

- Heretics being burnt is against the will of the Spirit.[1]

With the context of Chapter 1, and keeping in mind that Luther was Catholic, was it warranted that he stepped forward and made such proclamations? The truth is that depravity was so rampant in the Roman Catholic Church under papal direction that something had to be done, and the Reformation would ultimately be the shakeup that was needed. God's people in multitudes set aside the false man-made traditions, teachings, practices, corruptions, and atrocities of Rome, and returned to the scriptural and primitive faith taught by the early catholic Church. Many Christians were finally liberated from Roman control and manipulation.

The extent of the Reformation was so impactful that over 500 years later, there are almost a billion Christians not part of the Catholic Church, many refusing to be part of an institution that has strayed so far away from the original Gospel by embracing theology derived from an untrustworthy magisterium with personal agendas to maintain power and wealth.

It should be acknowledged that Protestants have their own set of problems, as corruption invaded these movements as well, and only a few denominations have stayed true to something that would be considered "in close alignment" with the original Gospel. However, the purpose of this book is not to defend or promote Protestantism, but to have *all* Christians return to teachings accurately proclaiming the original Gospel. Satan never ceases from contaminating and counterfeiting legitimate Christianity, and he is certainly not absent in the Protestant arena.

The sole focus of this book is to appeal to Roman Catholics (and those Protestants that want to read along as well) to return to theology that embraces the original Gospel espoused by Christ and the early apostles and taught by the early catholic Church. It's a call to step away from religious establishments and return to a place that allows believers to fully understand the New Covenant that Christ ushered in as part of the plan to reconcile, justify, and extend grace to all of mankind, acknowledging there was nothing we could do to bridge the gap by human effort. The aim is for every reader to fully understand what type of forgiveness Jesus really offers us, and how one can know that they are in right standing with God. This will be discussed at length in Chapters 9 and 10, but until then, we must continue to dismantle the man-centered institutionalization theology of the papacy that relies on self-effort, causing everything to get off track.

Continuing the Legacy of Depravity

Most are not aware that the Catholic Church decided it needed to have its own reformation in the sixteenth and seventeenth centuries after being so rattled by the Protestant Reformation. The Roman Catholic Church violently lashed out at the Protestant revolt by forming the Council of Trent which would proceed to issue 151 canons condemning anyone who didn't follow Church teaching. Unfortunately, this "Catholic Revival Movement" didn't last very long under Pope Leo X or Pope Paul III (and many more). Once again, despite the Protestant Reformation, the Roman institutional leaders strayed back into the previous immorality that had existed for centuries.

Pope Leo X (1513-1521)

Leo X was made a cleric at age seven and a cardinal at age thirteen,[2] and is famous for his lavish spending during his pontificate. He had acquired his own wealth but then inherited a vast treasure from his predecessor Julius II who faithfully handed it on.[3] It was still not enough for Leo because of his frivolous spending. During his reign, he commissioned the rebuilding of St. Peter's Basilica, but struggling financially (despite his vast wealth) he deceitfully created one of the most heinous scams in all of religious history. He convinced believers that they could buy their way into Heaven quicker, selling "indulgences" that would reduce their time in Purgatory due to their sins.[4]

As a side note, in an effort to downplay and minimize Church corruption, apologist Trent Horn states in his book *Why We're Catholic*, "Indulgences do not forgive sins and the Church has never sold them."[5] Of course, this is entirely untrue, and Leo was just one of many who did sell indulgences. Keeping in mind Horn's quote denying the sale of indulgences, consider what Roman Catholic scholar Eamon Duffy says about the sale of indulgences and the sale of positions in the Vatican:

"Nevertheless, the mounting cost of papal wars, and the lavish building programs of successive popes, made the search for new sources of revenue unending. The most notorious of these was the sale of indulgences, especially the indulgence for the rebuilding of St. Peter's ... The preaching of this indulgence, however, was riddled with corruption ... More significant still, however, was the growing dependence of the popes on the sale of office ... Devout minds everywhere were revolted by this sort of stuff ... All good men recognized that something would have to be done about the popes ... By the time of the death of Leo X in 1521 it was calculated that there were more than 2,150 saleable offices in the Vatican, including the highest offices."[6]

This is an imperative place for a pause, because these are facts that cannot be dismissed and brushed over. Here is a Roman Catholic scholar with evidence that the Church sold indulgences, but Catholic apologist Trent Horn untruthfully claims that "the Church has never sold them." To subscribe to the narrative that the Church did not sell indulgences would be like aligning with people who think we have never landed on the moon or that it was a missile that hit the Pentagon on 9/11. It's quite embarrassing. It's an incredible insult to the intelligence of those who know otherwise. Roman Catholic scholars and theologians, Protestant scholars and theologians, secular historians and authors—all of these sources know that it is common knowledge that the Roman Catholic Church sold indulgences.

Why is this an important point to bring up? Two reasons: First, because Catholic apologists seem to be purposely evasive (in multiple areas) to hide the history of the Roman Church and to find ways to justify why theological positions changed from the first-century catholic Church. We'll see more of these diversions and deceptions from multiple Catholic apologists regarding papal corruption later in this chapter.

Second, it is critical for Roman Catholics to understand that the corruption was so deep in the Roman Church (not just the sale of indulgences, but the sale of offices in the Vatican, sexual perversion, torturing and murdering in the name of religion, and more) that it was only appropriate for Catholics like Martin Luther, John Calvin, and many others to put a stop to this madness. The Protestant Reformation had to take place to stop the unethical inertia of the Roman Catholic Church and to try to return to doctrines that were more in alignment with the apostles and the first-century catholic Church. The primary focus of this book is an appeal to do this.

Duffy states that Martin Luther viewed the St. Peter's Indulgence as "a cruel and blasphemous con-trick, taking money for empty promises." Luther stated,

> "Good works, penance, indulgences, contributed nothing to sal-
> vation. Faith, a child-like dependence on God, was everything ...
> If faith was everything, and faith came from the Word preached
> and the scriptures read, then reliance on priests, sacraments, hier-
> archy, was all in vain."[7]

Many Catholics were starting to realize that these false promises of spiritual blessings and incentives were fraudulent, whether it was Boniface's declaration of the first Jubilee year in 1300 (when tens of thousands of pilgrims converged on Rome) or again in 1450 when it was repeated all over again. Sadly, a plague ravaged the area during this second Jubilee journey, leaving graveyards full and roads lined with corpses.

The sale of indulgences, introduced at the Crusades, remained a favored source of income in which the absolution of sin became an economic transaction.[8] The humorous phrase that was around at the time was: "As soon as the coin in the coffer rings, the soul from Purgatory springs."[9] Another quipped, "Place your penny on the drum, the pearly gates open and in strolls mum [mom]." All of the "Avignon popes" (a series of popes who lived in Avignon, France, rather than Rome during a 72-year period) sold indulgences to raise money for war, bridges, and buildings. They were also wildly extravagant, according to Duffy, and most of the money they raised was spent on retaining mercenary armies and the manipulation of Italian politics. Pope John XXII spent 63% of his income on warfare.[10] Even Paul III wanted to take action and make reforms because of the sale of indulgences despite his own moral issues. Let's be frank and call out that it's highly deceptive for

Horn to deny the Church's sale of indulgences because it is well known to have been common practice.

Leo X had already led a costly war to secure power, but as with many popes in the past, power and wealth go hand in hand. Indulgences were falsely advertised to provide for sins to be lessened in exchange for good deeds, donations to charitable organizations, praying specific prayers, and certain pilgrimages to significant places. Leo, along with subsequent vicars, abused this practice and lined his pockets with the funds donated.[11] This deceptive pope even made the claim that the purchasing of these indulgences would allow a dead relative to get out of Purgatory much more quickly (a place that does not exist in the Scriptures and never was condoned by the early catholic Church). This "pay-for-penance" scheme angered many, ultimately sparking the Great Reformation.[12]

The construction of St. Peter's Basilica, an enormous project, progressed significantly under the guidance of Leo, however, the sanctioning of these indulgences ultimately resulted in devastating consequences for the Church. Martin Luther, a German monk, challenged Leo's papal authority and in so doing took the very first step in the Great Reformation. As expected, Leo retaliated with the "ex-communication card" in 1521, but the vast numbers of departing Church members (because of extensive corruption) would eventually create the biggest schism yet.[13]

Over the centuries, the Roman Church has disguised the indulgence scam (that Leo initiated) by focusing on the meaningful cultural achievements and the flourishing of the Renaissance within the Vatican. Yet, the truth will always be available to those who do the research to find that greed within papal leadership showed its ugly head, and Leo will forever be known for contaminating the Gospel with disingenuous promises through the selling of indulgences that God would not honor or condone. This snake oil hoax is an embarrassment for the Roman Church that can never be erased.

For those who pilgrimage to Rome and stand in awe observing St. Peter's Basilica, a slight pause can only be appropriate to reflect on the dishonest funds collected to construct this great structure. Rest assured, it was funded by one of the worst scams in religious history by one of the most fraudulent popes in Church history.

Pope Paul III (1534-1549)

The Catholic Church would like to focus on Paul III as a patron of the arts and specifically for persuading Michelangelo to finish "The Last Judgment for the Sistine Chapel", but this would be a gross misrepresentation of his character. He had multiple illegitimate children before his pontificate and was a determined enemy against the Protestants, offering Charles V an army to exterminate them.[14] In 1536, the Portuguese Inquisition began, and people who practiced Judaism were killed, expelled, and forcefully converted. Several years later, around 1542, the Supreme Sacred Congregation of the Roman and Universal Inquisition (a.k.a. the Roman Inquisition) began under Paul III. This Inquisition was a system of courts and tribunals established to prosecute anti-Catholics and combat Protestant heresy in Catholic territories. The Roman Inquisition was extremely brutal in its methods.[15] We add Pope Paul III to the ever-growing list of executioners among the vicars of the Roman Catholic Church.

Paul III is recognized by the Roman Catholic Church as a pope who became a big proponent of change and reforms because of corruption throughout the institution. He formed the highly recognized Council of Trent in 1545 to carry out "reforms." However, right when one would think a pope, the "head" of the Christian Church, would want to bring peace, harmony, and reconciliation as a result of this council, he fully aimed to suppress and attack the Protestants who were fracturing the Church with their own concept of Christianity.[16]

In other words, Paul III's primary goal was to attack "heresy" that was so erroneously defined as any viewpoint different from that of the Catholic Church. The Council produced multiple canons declaring damnation to anyone not following the beliefs of the Roman Church. Paul III was willing to torture and murder people to carry out his plans. That is how Paul III defined "reform". Paul supported Cardinal Caraffa's solution to the Protestant Reformation: "and the right way to deal with obstinate heretics [Protestants] was not to talk to them, but to hunt them down and eliminate them."

This type of mindset is definitely worth pondering for all Protestants and especially for Catholics. What do these intentions remind most people of today? Of course, that was the same purposeful intent Hitler had in his plan to exterminate all Jews. This was certainly not the approach of every pope who's come down the pipeline, but it's the direction that many would have taken if not stopped.

The Roman Church viciously fought back against the Protestant reformers (who were now considered enemies and not just "separated brethren"), although the Protestants simply wanted to return to the practices of the original catholic Church and have the freedom to worship as they pleased. The threat of damnation for not believing canons set forth by the Council was not enough, and Protestants became subject to the infamous methods of brutal torture and death by being burned at the stake.

And therein lies the irony: corruption was running rampant like a raging river throughout the Roman Catholic Church, yet the reforms focused on theological differences. Effectively, rather than attending to its own mess, the Church insisted on sponsoring the pursuit, torture, and murder of anyone with a different belief system. It is shocking that the "infallible" Roman Catholic Church, under the leadership of "infallible" popes, did not see the error of condoning the torture and murder of men and women, and often children as well, but saw defiance of the Catholic Church as the only real problem. This is appalling and something you might think would have happened in prehistoric times with cavemen, but this happened in the one, holy, catholic, and apostolic Church of Jesus Christ just a few hundred years ago.

Although Inquisitions had occurred since the Middle Ages, under Paul III they became an institutionalized part of the Church. Paul imposed excessive taxes on the faithful and when cities refused to pay, he often sent an army to enforce his policies. He believed in astrology and built himself a magnificent palace in Rome. He also used his power to appoint family members to various positions. In a move of nepotism, common throughout the history of the papacy, he appointed two of his grandchildren to the cardinalate.[17]

Pope Julius III (1550-1555)

Like others, Julius III claimed he would continue reforms in the Church, but his useless and reluctant efforts eventually gave way to licentious parties and sex with young boys. Unfortunately, he was yet another pedophilic and homosexual papal leader. He mostly devoted himself to a life of personal pleasure. As a fan of glitter and glamor, the pope indulged in banquets and entertainments. Ample evidence shows he spent little time at the Vatican, but instead stayed at an expensive villa in Villa Giulia he had built with Church money to maintain his alternative lifestyle.[18]

His reputation, and that of the Catholic Church, were greatly harmed by the scandal-ridden relationship with his nephew, Innocenzo Ciocchi Del Monte. Innocenzo was picked up on the street by Julius when he was around fourteen years old and eventually made a cardinal. During one period, when Julius was waiting for his nephew to arrive from Rome, people in Italy described him as a "lover awaiting a mistress." Julius even boasted about how good his nephew was in bed.[19] Innocenzo was eventually banished after he murdered two men who insulted him and also following the rape of two women.[20]

Pope Paul IV (1555-1559)

One of the worst and most hated popes in the sixteenth century, Pope Paul IV was known for his horrific acts of anti-Semitism. Opposite of simulating any semblance of being a Christian role model, Paul IV created a Jewish ghetto in a section of Rome, forcing Jewish citizens to identify themselves by wearing yellow hats (the same color of the prostitutes during those days). The citizens so hated this pope that after his death, his family quickly buried him to avoid the decimation of his body, but the citizens still managed to tear down all statues of him throughout the city.[21]

Paul IV, also known as "the evil," strengthened the Roman Inquisition and supported a faction to block the spread of Lutheran ideas in Italy. Many actions implemented by Paul embittered the Jews, including the burning of the Talmud (the central text and spiritual writings in Jewish faith), and of course, the establishment of the Jewish ghettos. However, he was also responsible for burning twenty-four Portuguese converts in a province in Italy,[22] thus extending the list of papal mass murderers.

He introduced the first modern *Index Librorum Prohibitorum* (a list of prohibited books). This index of prohibited readings was active from 1560 to 1966, and it included multiple editions and translations of the Bible.[23] After a 400-year span, it was only a few decades ago that the Church saw the error of its ways and lifted the ban, demonstrating the fallibility of the Roman Church in plain view.

Paul IV was a key figure in developing policies for renewing the war between France and the Habsburgs.[24] He was excessively violent and bad-tempered, and the people of Rome suffered greatly under his pontificate. He relished in his papal supremacy and thrived on the power it afforded him.

Pope Sixtus V (1585-1590)

Sixtus V was a violent tempered, ruthless pope who "ruled the Papal States with a rod of iron ... encouraging the force of Catholicism in France, Poland, and Savoy to throw the weight of their armies behind the campaign against the Reformation ... and attempted to impose the death penalty for adultery."[25]

The List Goes On

The dark popes who have been listed represent just a small sample of the overall landscape of individuals who have held the papacy and who gave no legitimate representation of Christ or Christian values. However, many more demonstrated adverse behaviors as well. Here are a few more examples of some of the vicars of Christ who have led the Roman Church:

Pope Honorius is known to have compromised the doctrinal purity of the papacy.[26]

Pope John VIII was bludgeoned to death by his own cardinals.

Pope Gregory II claimed that Peter was a "god on earth" and used military force against anyone opposing Roman Catholic theology.

Pope Leo III was a soldier by training; he made a disastrous decision to force the baptism of Jews.[27]

Pope Clement V became a puppet of King Phillip of France who dominated him throughout his pontificate. The outcome was the torture, imprisonment, and burning at the stake of numerous members of "the Templars".[28]

Pope Calixtus III excelled in nepotism and packed the Vatican with relatives and placed them in lucrative Church posts. In 1453, he called for a crusade and financed it with the unethical sale of indulgences.[29]

Pope Alexander IV received money from Henry III of England to have his son Edmund declared king of Sicily.[30]

Pope Paul V had St. Peter's Basilica decorated with an immense and vulgar inscription which seemed to claim the Church for himself rather than the apostle Peter.[31]

Pope Gregory IX established the papal Inquisition in 1231 and continued the witch-hunt, giving the inquisitors wide-ranging powers and an extra edge to the atrocities they would later commit.[32]

Pope Innocent IV likewise participated in the Inquisitions and even made torture official papal policy. The pope's inquisitors would seek out older women who were ugly or had crooked physiques and accuse them of being witches.[33]

Pope John XXII issued a series of papal bulls increasing witch hunts as part of the Inquisition. He was superstitious and thought his opponents were using sorcery to kill him. He ordered the inquisitors to pursue sorcerers and magicians and had 600 burned at the stake.[34]

Pope Gregory XVI believed that all modernity (in all its forms) was evil. This included gas-lit streets and even the railway system, which Gregory viewed as the works of the devil.[35]

Pope Leo XIII could not tolerate any contradiction to his point of view. It was his way or no way. One recorded incident happened where he snapped at his secretary of state on a very minor matter, and saturated with a raging ego, tapped the table and said, "I am Peter!" Duffy states, "He surrounded himself with the trappings of monarchy, insisted that Catholics received in audience kneel before him throughout the interview, never allowed his entourage to sit in his presence, never in twenty-five years exchanged a single word with his coachman."[36] He rejected equality and unconditional freedom of thought as unsuitable for ordinary people who, he believed, were too immature and undisciplined to handle them properly.[37]

Pope Pius IX was responsible for the kidnapping of Edgardo Mortara, a six-year-old taken by force from his Jewish family. In 1857, Pius's inquisitors had heard that Edgardo was secretly baptized when it was thought that he was going to die. A department of the Roman Curia held the view that the action irrevocably made the child a Catholic and, because the law of the papal states forbade the raising of Christians by other faiths, it ordered that he be taken from his family and brought up by the Church. He was kidnapped from his home the next evening. International protests mounted, but Pius would not budge. This became the most significant event of his pontificate.[38]

Pope John XXIII, although regarded as an anti-pope by the Catholic Church, he sat on the papal throne for five years. He was tried for heresy, simony, and immorality and found guilty on all accounts. The eighteenth-century historian Edward Gibbon wrote, "The more scandalous charges were suppressed; the vicar of Christ was accused of piracy, rape, sodomy, murder, and incest."[39]

Pope Gregory VI and Pope John XIX both purchased the office of the Papacy.[40,41]

Pope Clement VII has been described as a disastrous pope, and hopelessly indecisive. When the French invaded Rome, he fled the city like a coward with his white robe disguised by a purple cloak.[42]

Pope Gregory VII, in addition to his celibacy mandate and his disgust for the presence of married men in the Sistine Chapel, plunged the papacy into a disastrous war with Spain. Europe looked on in disbelief at a pope who would take such actions in the name of religion.[43]

Pope Urban VIII was extremely secular and the prestige of the papacy eroded under him. He was someone "who consulted no one and exercised the papal office as though he were oriental Khan."[44]

Pope Clement XI made extremely poor decisions and plunged the papacy into conflict with Spain and effectively destroyed Christianity in China.[45]

Pope Pius VII went out of his way to oblige Napoleon Bonaparte, granting him the right to appoint bishops and oversee the Church finances. Pius received lucrative compensation for extending this right to Napoleon.[46]

Pope Pius XI, like so many, had an insatiable thirst for power and control, and top officials who visited Rome quickly came to realize that the keyword in the Vatican was "obedience".[47]

There was even a story of a female pope (Pope Joan) who tricked her way into the papacy. This narrative lasted for over 400 years and was believed by many! A myth or truth, who knows, but nothing seems to be beyond the antics of the Roman pontiffs.

One of the most shocking periods in papal history was called the "Midnight of the Dark Ages". A few of the most notorious popes have already been mentioned from this era, but during this period of almost 200 years (858 to 1046) approximately forty popes came and went, most with corrupt reigns. It was one of the blackest chapters in the whole history of the Church because of the bribery, corruption, immorality, and bloodshed that was wrought by these pontificates. Some of the most heinous crimes ever committed in the name of religion took place, all with papal sanction.[48]

As we have already seen, cardinals were not exempt from corruption over the centuries either. Many plotted to poison and murder the reigning pope when they were not carrying out his orders of criminal activity. They were also fierce rivals in trying to obtain the papacy themselves. Most cardinals were conscious of their own power and often times bolstered that power against the seated pope by being extremely hostile and obstructive—even to the point of plotting assassinations. These facts have to be considered (as we will see later on) when considering the magisterium as a valid, equal authority to the Scriptures.

At the time of this writing, Pope Francis has passed away and a group of cardinals have gathered in conclave to elect another pope. However, unlike the projection in the media of a formal, official, religiously mature election of a new pope, if one looks at the historical past, it would not be unusual to envision the cardinals jockeying for position, acting like grown kids yelling out, "I'm the next Vicar!" "No, you're not, I am! I'm more qualified!" Then hours or days later, after the smokestack spews out its white smoke, a cardinal emerges with a serious expression and announces, "We have a new pope," and the world is in awe. The shocking reality is presented in Chapter 8 on just who compromises the cardinals that choose the pope.

The facts about past popes seem very harsh to write about, but this is simply the history of who they were. It's also a revealing history proving who they were not: the vicars of Christ. The popes who have been listed so far, in honest evaluation, could not have stood in the place of Christ or be considered to have sat on Peter's throne, because "Peter's throne" simply does not exist in the Scriptures. Instead, after gathering and examining all of the evidence, this papal position seems to be a Roman Catholic concoction designed to protect the power of corrupt popes.

Catholics have become so accustomed to hearing phrases like "Peter's throne," "Peter got the keys to the kingdom," and "Christ built His church on Peter, 'the Rock'" that they often miss Jesus's true message to Peter (discussed in Chapter 3), and totally fail to see what actually transpired with these pretenders who wanted to claim a position of authority but were poor representatives of Christ.

The inventory of characterless popes is quite lengthy. There seems to be an endless list, and likely they will continue well after the publishing of this book. Chapter 8 will even implicate Pope Francis and find this same unacceptable behavior in the modern era. So far, only a handful of popes have been discussed, and only chosen because of the prolificness of their crimes and atrocities. Complete books have been written on many of these unimaginable popes with detailed reports of their brutalities. However, this book will only serve as a mere introduction to their corruption and focuses far more on how a departure was made from the purity of the early catholic Church and the simplicity of the original Gospel.

The Crusades and Inquisitions

Central to much of the depravity popes have engaged in since the inception of the Roman Catholic Church is the death and destruction wrought in the name of Christianity during the Crusades and Inquisitions briefly alluded to earlier. Much of the worst was focused around the twelfth century, but the Inquisitions extended for over 700 years. Hundreds of thousands (by some estimates well into the millions) of men, women, and children were murdered, raped, and tortured, and countless were burned at the stake at the behest of the Roman Catholic Church or the civil authorities they gave the green light to do so. Many Catholics who discover the complete and graphic nature of what the Church did during this long period of time (all sanctioned by the reigning popes) make a decision to leave and never return to this institution. The acts committed by the Church are so horrific and went on for such a long period of time, that for many it becomes almost inconceivable to ever be connected to the Catholic Church again after discovering what transpired.

In his book *God's Jury*, author Cullen Murphy talks about the Inquisitions being "a 700-year trial." Kept secret until 1998, the archives in the Vatican containing millions of documents—filling twenty rooms in the palazzo's western wing—were off limits to outsiders (with the exception of Leo XIII opening them to historians in 1881). Murphy states,

> "But the record preserved on the millions of pages in these rooms is mainly grim: a record of lives disrupted and sometimes summarily put to an end; of ideas called into question and often suppressed; of voices silenced, temporarily or forever ... It is a record of actions taken in the name of religion, though the implications go beyond religion ... a set of disciplinary procedures targeting specific groups, codified in law, organized systematically ... exemplified by severity, sustained over time, and justified by a vision of the one true path."[49]

When Cardinal Ratzinger announced the *partial* opening of the archives, making records from prior to 1903 available for review, he stated, "We know all the sins of the Church."[50] Pope John Paul asked historians not to "overstep the boundaries of their discipline and give an ethical verdict."[51] Two years later, the pope led a procession through the streets of Rome to apologize for the errors and misdeeds of the past. However, in expected fashion, he pointedly referred to the bad deeds done during the Inquisitions as the actions of the "followers of the Church" rather than of the Church itself.[52] Historians know this not to be true.

It would take years of research to fully comprehend the extent of the violence done as a result of these popes issuing papal bulls to incite attacks against anyone with different beliefs, and numerous books cover the atrocities in great detail. The history of the Crusades and Inquisitions is a complex one. However, it is critical for Catholics to be exposed to these realities that are quietly swept under the rug by Catholic leadership who, if confronted, minimize the tragedies.

The enemy, according to the Roman Church, was anyone who expressed and maintained a different religious belief, and anyone who was not subject to papal authority. As a result, a genocide branded as "Holy Wars" was launched against these groups. Muslims, Jews, Protestants, and lesser-known groups like the Cathars, Waldensians, and many others were targeted in the massive assaults.

The Crusades were kicked off by Urban II giving a speech at the Council of Clement in 1095 that led thousands to believe it was God's work to slaughter anyone who did not recognize papal authority or who had a different belief system than the Roman Church. Urban stated:

> "I speak to those who are present, I shall proclaim it to the absent, but it is Christ who commands. Moreover, if those who set out thither lose their lives on the journey, by land or sea, or in fighting against the heathen, their sins shall be remitted in that hour; this I grant through the power of God vested in me."[53]

Urban offered spiritual incentives to anyone who would participate and threatened excommunication on anyone who did not fulfill their vow. The initial purposes of the Crusades included bringing the Greek Church under Roman control and reclaiming Jerusalem and the surrounding area from Muslim rule. Eventually, the pagan tribes in Northern Europe, heretics (those with different beliefs than the Roman Church), various cities, and many other groups became targets as well. Popes preached Holy War as a pathway to advance their cause, solidify their control, and fulfill their obsession for power. They used military power to do so. Greed was right at the center of the Crusades as well, and they brought an enormous increase of wealth to the Church. It was forced religion but with ulterior motives. For over 200 years, the Crusades remained a powerful movement headed by the popes.[54]

Here is a partial list of the popes who played a part in the Crusades besides Urban II: Paschal II, Eugene III, Urban III, Gregory VIII, Innocent III, Honorius III, Gregory IX, Innocent III, Innocent IV, Callixtus II, Gregory VII, Urban IV, and Martin IV.

Each one of these popes joins the long list of genocidal leaders among papal leadership, and these are just some of the key players in the Crusades and mass murders. Many more were involved as well.

Later, Crusades were even more coordinated, being organized by the armies of kings, all granted papal indulgences. Louis IV of France, Henry II of England, Phillip II of France, and Frederick II (king of Sicily, Germany, Italy, and Jerusalem) were just a few who advanced the Catholic slaughters, adapting the same military cause. This involvement of civil authorities and imperial powers greatly increased the casualties because not only was the Roman Catholic Church on the warpath, but they reeled in kings and other leaders with false promises of indulgences and other benefits.

One source states that approximately 1.7 million people died as a result of these Holy Wars and bloody assaults.[55] Some historians have that number much higher and some lower, but the undeniable truth is that it was extensive. Many of the deaths came as a result of the warfare, but also due to disease, starvation, and robberies caused by the complete mayhem.

The Crusades were ultimately a failure for the Roman Catholic Church and the politicization brought discredit upon the Church and the popes who ordered them. Many people simply saw through the horrible intentions of these popes and realized they were using their authority to enhance their own personal well-being and that of their families. Pope Gregory IX, because of the dwindling motivation behind the Crusades, in 1233 offered additional indulgences to those who would "take up the cross" and continue the murderous rampage.[56]

However, Islam did not go away, the Jews did not go away, the Protestants did not go away, heresy (by the Catholic definition) continued to spread, many lost interest in spiritual matters, holy orders were ignored, and the conquest for power and to gather stockpiles of gold did not materialize as planned.

The Crusades were military campaigns organized by the Roman Catholic Church to stop the expansion of Islam and accomplish other agendas, and the Catholic Inquisitions were no less evil. These Inquisitions were "judicial procedures" that began in the twelfth century, running parallel with the Crusades, and comprised one of the bloodiest periods in Europe's history. The intent was to persecute or force conversions of anyone with a different belief system than the Roman Catholic Church. The Church aimed to enforce religious conformity. The investigations conducted on all who opposed the Church were harsh and unfair.

Church officials pursued heretics, blasphemers against the Church, alleged witches, and essentially anyone who was not in total surrender and obedience to the Roman way. These Inquisitions were known to be extremely brutal, and widespread death and suffering occurred, especially among Jews and Muslims. Like the Crusades, the Inquisitions were "spearheaded" by the reigning popes at the time.[57]

Although there were multiple formal Inquisitions that took place, the Medieval and Spanish Inquisitions are two that come front and center for their atrocities.

The Medieval Inquisition

In his documentary "The Errors of the Roman Catholic Church", Keith Thompson talks extensively about the tragedies of the Inquisitions. The Medieval Inquisition has its roots in 1179, when the Lateran council condemned and pronounced damnation on a group of gnostic Christians called the Cathars that had risen up in France. They believed that the Catholic Church's sacramental system was evil and that its teachings did not line up with the Scriptures. This group had grown to over 4 million people across over 1,000 cities and was seen as a threat by the Catholic Church that had to be eliminated. However, it was not a threat in the sense of military invasion or violence by any means. The Cathars were peaceful people who desired to maintain lives of holiness. Yet, the Church saw them as a threat because of their spiritual beliefs. The Roman Catholic Church, with evil intent, set out to murder every Cathar they could find if they did not renounce their opposition to the papacy and to the Church.[58]

In 1208, Pope Innocent III launched a vicious crusade against this group by pronouncing: "O most mighty soldiers of Christ, most brave warriors; Ye oppose the agents of anti-Christ, and ye fight against the servants of the old serpent ... fight for God."[59]

Like many other popes, Innocent III offered his soldiers fabricated spiritual rewards in the form of indulgences for the murder of these believers. In one incident, somewhere between 10,000 and 20,000 Cathars were slaughtered, 7,000 of whom were put to death in St. Magdalen's Church. They were also ruthlessly tortured. Approximately 140 clerics were burned alive after having their noses, lips, and ears cut off. Pope Gregory IX set out to destroy those remaining by placing the Cathars in the hands of the Franciscans and the Dominicans. By 1244, the Cathars were basically wiped out, and the remaining 200 in France were finally murdered.[60] One can only guess how many of the 4 million Cathars were directly killed as a result of actions taken by the Roman Catholic Church. What history does show about the Roman Church is that its relentless pursuit of wiping out entire groups of people with different theological viewpoints was the norm to "spread" Christianity.

Another group that the Roman Catholic Church sanctioned to be hunted down like animals were the Waldensians—Protestant Christians who rose up in Italy around the twelfth century. This group of Christians believed that the Scriptures were the ultimate source of authority and opposed the Church's positions on Purgatory, the veneration of saints, and other areas. In 1184, Pope Lucius III issued a bull to condemn the Waldensians and similar sects:

> "To abolish the malignity of diverse heresies which are lately sprung up in most parts of the world, it is but fitting that the power committed to the Church should be awakened, that by the concurring assistance of the Imperial strength, both the insolence and mal-pertness of heretics in their false designs may be crushed …[we] likewise declare all entertainers and defenders of the said heretics be liable to the same … sentence."[61]

Of course, to no surprise, Lucius III declared that all goods and money of these "heretics" be turned over to the Roman Church. The Church's intention seemed to be to destroy all who opposed Rome and confiscate all their wealth and integrate it into their system. Sadly, Lucius III's bull to exterminate the Waldensians in the twelfth century was just the beginning; it is worth diverging from medieval times for a moment to understand the breadth of the inquisitions across the centuries. In 1487, Innocent VIII issued a similar bull of extermination against the Waldensians, but it was under the reign of Innocent X that the most disturbing event took place. To enforce Catholicism in his territories, the Duke of Savoy (Charles Emmanuel II) led one of the most disturbing massacres in religious history: the Piedmontese Easter Massacre of 1655 in the northwestern part of Italy. Dr. Paul Chappell describes the unimaginable event:

> "In January of 1655, the Duke of Savoy forced a cruel choice upon the Waldensians ... either attend Catholic mass, or move out of the valley within three days. In the dead of winter, some two thousand people journeyed across swollen rivers, snow-buried valleys, and ice-covered mountains with traces of blood marking their trail ... But the worst was yet to come ... In April of the same year, the Duke of Savoy sent an army to the upper valleys ... he ordered a gruesome slaughter. Saturday, April 24th, 1655 at 4:00am, the signal was given ... the horrors of this massacre are indescribable. Not content to simply kill their victims, the soldiers and monks who accompanied them invented barbaric tortures: Babies and children had their limbs ripped off their bodies by sheer strength. Parents were forced to watch their children tortured to death before they themselves were tortured and killed. Fathers were forced to wear the decapitated heads of their children as the fathers were marched to their death. Some of these Christians were literally plowed into their own fields. Some were flayed or burned alive. Many endured worse."[62]

Because of this savage attack, the remaining Waldensians fled for the mountains to seek shelter in caves. The soldiers in their relentless pursuit found them and hurled both mothers and their infants down onto the rocks below in a finishing act. Pope Innocent X did not denounce this event in any manner, and in fact, the massacre was instigated by the New Council of Propagation of the Faith and the Extermination of Heresy, an institution of the Roman Catholic Church established five years prior, in 1650. The Waldensians were targeted by the Roman Catholic Church across almost 500 years. It's another shocking example of the Church's attempts to force its version of Christianity upon the masses. Pope Francis finally apologized for the persecution of the Waldensians after 350 years, but one can only question why none of the other popes would step forward and admit the atrocities committed against the Waldensians.

Returning to medieval history, in 1229 the Council of Telus issued a decree sanctioning burning at the stake for the punishment of heresy. Pope Innocent IV authorized brutal torture as a means of getting confessions from "heretics" and Bible believers. Popes Alexander IV and Clement IV, likewise, confirmed and followed through with the same plan. Priests were to oversee the torture and the burning at the stake. In a disturbing gesture, the Roman Catholic Church even went after the dead: "The inquisition made war upon the dead, and exhumed the bodies of those found to have died in heresy and burned them."[63]

Some Catholic apologists will argue that the Church never engaged in murderous acts, but after interrogation and torture, prisoners were turned over to civil authorities who proceeded to burn them at the stake (since according to canon law, the clergy could not put someone to death). However, to accept that logic is to buy into deep deception. Most people understand that if someone hires an assassin to commit a murder, if caught, the mastermind gets the full weight of the law too. In fact, in most instances, the initiator gets the stiffer penalty. The Roman Church turning over individuals to civil authorities to be burned at the stake does not eliminate their culpability. This would be considered a Catholic diversion to protect a reputation of an "infallible" church that simply doesn't exist. History shows that the Roman Catholic Church sent out its own armies to murder thousands of people during the Crusades. It's a useless attempt by the Church to project clean hands during the Inquisitions and Crusades and to fabricate a narrative that there were only a small number of executions; historians and theologians know the truth.

For example, it is a historical fact that in 1572 between 5,000 and 30,000 Huguenots (French Protestant Calvinists) were brutally murdered by those embracing Catholicism in the St. Bartholomew's Day Massacre.[64] That is only one event in the middle of the civil wars between the two groups. These civil wars resulted in the death of 2 to 4 million people (both Protestants and Catholics). The wars began as the result of the Catholic League convincing King Henry III to issue an edict outlawing Protestantism.[65] To buy into the distortion that the Roman Catholic Church is not responsible for the slaughter of an untold number of people is not being intellectually honest.

Thompson shares the story about Conrad of Marburg, who was one of the most sadistic Roman Catholic inquisitors of them all. He gave accused heretics the choice of speedy confession or to be burned at the stake. One of the few archbishops who had a heart wrote to Pope Gregory IX in protest of this cruel method that was being used. Gregory's response was to identify Conrad as a champion of the Christian faith and encourage him to continue. Shockingly, many of Rome's "saints" came out of these Dominican and Franciscan groups: St. Thomas Aquinas and St. Albert the Great, to name two.[66] How the Vatican would canonize and exalt men who condoned the torture and death of a massive number of Bible believers and others is beyond comprehension.

Thompson tells about the evil during this era that continued under Innocent VIII, who issued a bull authorizing inquisitors to find, try, and murder alleged witches. It was believed by the Catholics that a witch could not cry from pain. But since those tortured cried, the papal inquisitors claimed the devils must have made them cry as a trick to convince everyone they were not witches. The inquisitors would often shave the bodies of alleged witches, including their private parts, since Catholic superstition at that time said that witches would hide objects of witchcraft in their hair or private parts and that witches had a birthmark or scar which would function as a teat to feed milk or blood to imps or the devil himself. Inquisitors would therefore stab alleged witches on their scars or birthmarks with needles since they claimed a witch would not bleed if their witch's teats were pierced. However, when the women did bleed, the torturers claimed Satan allowed the bleeding to make it appear the person was not a witch. They then resorted to torture, such as putting hot boiling fat in the women's eyes, underarms, and thighs, which many times led to infection or death.[67]

In Germany, alleged witches who were tortured into confession then had hot irons put on their breasts and arms, their right hands cut off, were burnt at the stake, and their ashes thrown into the river. Most of these accused witches were simply social outcasts the community did not like or women who were poor, unmarried, elderly, pale, or wrinkly. Tens of thousands of alleged witches were murdered in the Inquisition.[68] On reflection, one can only ponder, "Does the Roman Catholic Church look anything like the original catholic Church?"

The Spanish Inquisition

The Spanish Inquisition was directed primarily at Jews and Muslims who had converted to Christianity but were thought to be reverting back to their heritage. This Inquisition was extremely brutal and was prompted by Queen Isabella and her husband, who appealed to Pope Sixtus IV to establish an Inquisition regarding whether or not converted Jews and others were secretly continuing to practice their original religion. As a result, Sixtus issued a bull which promulgated the investigation. Historian Williston Walker states:

> "The Spanish Inquisition especially concerned itself with rooting out those Jewish and Muslim converts who had supposedly lapsed from the faith and with maintaining purity of blood in all offices of state and church. It was also to deal harshly with Spanish Protestants and all those suspected of 'Lutheranism.'"[69]

Any civilian could level an accusation of heresy or immorality against another, which would result in a tribunal. Even if no citizen accused anyone, inquisitors could freely accuse citizens. Abuses quickly crept in: the wealthy were often targeted by inquisitors since their wealth would be confiscated to fund and further the Inquisition.

Thompson shares the tedious process: Once accused, a person was detained and their property was seized temporarily, pending the outcome of the tribunal. Detention often lasted months, and families of the detained were not informed, which often resulted in the wives and children of the accused not being able to survive without the man of the house around.

After detention came interrogation. The goal was to gain a confession and pass a sentence. There were many methods of torture used to gain a confession: There was the *garrucha*, or *strappado*, which was a suspension system of ropes, weights, and pulleys. The victim's arms were tied behind their back, they were hoisted in the air, and then they were dropped. They were stopped in mid-air right before hitting the ground so that the weights tied to their ankles caused great pain and dislocation. There was also the *toca*, which was basically waterboarding. A cloth was put over the victim's mouth and water was poured in, resulting in the victim feeling like they were drowning. Also utilized was the *potro* or rack. The victim was placed on this device and their arms and legs were severely stretched, causing excruciating tearing of the muscles and dislocation.[70]

After interrogation through torture came hearings and trial and then sentencing. Acquittals were very rare in the Spanish Inquisition. When found guilty, the victim was handed over to the secular authorities for burning at the stake. Burnings were usually like festivals where Catholics in the community would watch and be entertained. The ritual began with a Mass and then a public procession of the victim. Instances of burning heretics during the Spanish Inquisition lasted into the late eighteenth century.[71]

In his 2007 work, *Inquisition: The Reign of Fear*, Toby Green remarks on the statistics of the Spanish Inquisition: "The Inquisition was at its most severe in Spain during the first fifty years after its formation in 1478, when it is estimated that 50,000 people were tried and a significant proportion as *relajados* burnt at the stake ..."[72]

Because these Roman Catholic-sponsored Inquisitions went on for so many centuries under a large number of popes, it would be impossible to know just how many individuals were tortured and murdered at the hands of the Church. The carnage was widespread. All across Europe bishops burned people at the stake—one in Switzerland burned 500 people in three months, another burned 600 in Bavaria, and another pope in Bavaria burned 900. During the Spanish Inquisition, torture and murder even transpired in a public place while holding Mass. They also killed thousands of black cats and dogs during this time in fear of them being associated with the devil.[73]

There were multiple other Inquisitions that happened over this 700-year period. Although some Inquisitions were controlled by the state, the Church was not exempt in its responsibility for the atrocities. During the Roman Inquisitions in the sixteenth century, the tribunal was controlled directly by the papacy, and the Church and the state were essentially the same entity.

An aftershock of the Reformation, the main focus of these Inquisitions was Protestantism, "but it did not spare Jews, homosexuals, people accused of practicing witchcraft ... In the latter half of the sixteenth century, no fewer than three grand inquisitors went on to become pope."[74]

If you are Catholic, it's undoubtedly disturbing to understand that the longest-running church institution in history—a Church you follow and are affiliated with—is responsible for the destruction, murder, and torture of so many human beings. Total massacres were conducted, killing every person in multiple cities, including children in many cases.

Catholics who do the research will be astonished at the history of a Church that has adopted doctrines from militant popes and clergymen who were responsible for the murder and torture of hundreds of thousands with different beliefs. The details are horrific, but make no mistake: these brutalities are hidden from the flock.

False and Misleading Doctrines

For those willing to accept mere "apologies from the Catholic Church for the behaviors back then," one will still have to reconcile in their hearts what historically transpired. Apologies from the Church only reveal the horrendous acts they engaged in.

Many popes used the papacy as a business to be milked and exploited for gain via bribery, scheming, and murder. The whole system was completely out of control. In some sense, the papacy has been a colossal disaster. Yet, most Catholics are still told:

"The pope can be traced back to Peter."

"The pope sits on Peter's throne."

"The pope is infallible when he speaks from the chair in certain situations," (ex-cathedra).

"The pope stands in the place of Christ."

"The pope is our leader."

"The pope is the vicar of Christ."

In hearing these familiar refrains, the average, uninformed Catholic attendee is convinced that their Church, belief, ideology, and theology are grounded and rooted and anchored right from the grassroots, right from

Jesus Christ. They accept that the multiple popes in their faith history are the original genealogy of God-fearing, Christ-following vicars, starting with Peter; and "There is only one true Church, established in AD 33, and we are it. We were first. The pope is our leader."

The problem is that thinking is incorrect, untrue, and naively misleading. The truth is that succession of the papacy, the legitimacy of the papacy, the office of the papacy, or the papacy having anything to do with a role ushered in by Christ is simply false. You cannot escape history. Too many were heinous, poisonous, and diabolical and had zero integrity as Christian leaders. The reality is Jesus Christ is the only one with a throne—not Peter or any successors. We have scripture after scripture revealing that Jesus alone is the rock and cornerstone of the Church. The Roman Church, however, chose its own path.

Emperor Constantine legalized Christianity (as will be discussed in Chapter 4), and afterward, the true, original catholic Church streamed off into believers who followed the Roman Catholic, governmental, legalistic, institutional, pagan-influenced church, governed by the popes who have been featured so far. The outcomes are the false dogmas, doctrines, and traditions of today's Roman Catholic Church (The Catholic List) that aren't part of apostolic teachings. One simply cannot ignore the source of these teachings or the result of adding to or changing the pure Gospel.

Prime examples of these false doctrines that started to emerge were Purgatory (a place to get "cleaned up" before entering Heaven) and indulgences (where the debt of sin could be erased by money, good works, or credit for various pilgrimages to select places). These doctrines started emerging and gaining ground in the corrupt Medieval times from popes with devious ulterior motives. Popes simply crafted systems to fit personal and financial agendas at the time. Some bishops would even offer forgiveness of sins to the faithful if they worked free of charge on building massive cathedrals.

The popes over the centuries, who controlled almost all of the revenue from Rome, channeled most of it into their basilicas and their personal family wealth. Bishops would accept financial compensation to reduce believers' time in Purgatory or to purchase a dead loved one's release from Purgatory.

The hierarchy sold certificates to trick parishioners into believing they could buy their way out of one spiritual state and into another. Sadly, people desperate for rightness with God and eternal security bought into the scam. It was a deceitful system created by popes with greed running through their veins at a river-raging speed.

Although done away with for a while, the Catholic Church has brought these false indulgences back after Pope Pius VI abolished them in 1567, but this time not to be sold.[75] Pope Francis even declared a plenary indulgence to those who participated in the National Eucharistic Pilgrimage in 2024,[76] but it's a deceptive theological hoax. Any promise to remit sin of any kind is no different than the lie Satan told to Adam and Eve that "you will not surely die" if they were to eat from the tree in the middle of the garden (Genesis 3:4,).

In a similar scheme, Clement VI (1342-1352) announced he had control over something called "the treasury of merit," an accumulation of all the good deeds contributed by saints and Mary in the past. As crazy as it sounds, this "special account" even has the excess blood of Christ leftover.[77] One has to wonder about this "account" that is not mentioned in the Scriptures and ask: What's the balance? Does anyone see a monthly statement? Quarterly reports? Year-end summary? No doubt, it's not apostolic, it's not even true Tradition—it simply was created by a deceptive pope. Clement had full authorization to disburse from the "treasury" in order to forgive sins and buy salvation.[78] One can only imagine his manipulative control over the people with this brilliant trick. What was the method of obtaining and tapping into this "treasury of merit" that could cancel sin, accelerate the salvation process, or reduce the time spent in Purgatory? It's an obvious answer and motive: Money.

Under the system of degenerate popes, you could acquire indulgences, buy your way into Heaven, buy your time away from Purgatory, and buy loved ones out of Purgatory. Money equaled accelerated salvation. By almost anyone's standard and wisdom, it was nothing more than a creative swindle.

It would be beneficial to take a brief intermission from Innocent III and expand on the topic of Purgatory for the sake of context. In general, Purgatory, like indulgences, has definitely been an accretion of the Church. We start to see this development in the sixth century under Gregory the Great, but it's not until almost 1,000 years later that the Council of Trent attempts to formally define it. The saddest part for those that embrace this dogma (that is not part of the Bible, apostolic teachings, or part of the early catholic Church) is the total disregard for what Christ accomplished on the cross. He removed temporal and eternal punishment from a believer's ledger. We never have to fear condemnation from a Holy God "who was reconciling the world back to Himself, not counting men's sins against them" (2 Corinthians 5:19). Here are a few realizations and considerations for those Christians who have fallen victim, who live in fear, and are held hostage and entrapped by the idea of this place called Purgatory:

1. Purgatory completely denies the sufficiency of Christ. It communicates that Jesus's wonderful sacrifice was not enough to eradicate the punishment from sin, according to the Roman Church.

2. Christians are forced to "atone" for their venial (less serious) sins.

3. Jesus's blood cannot perfectly cleanse one under this teaching.

4. For those who embrace this myth, there is no finished work on the cross, therefore never any peace or assurance.

5. No time period is defined for how long one will be in Purgatory (it could be five minutes or one million years).

6. Other religions teach about a similar fictional place, including Islam, Hinduism, and Buddhism.

7. Pope John Paul II and Benedict XVI recently redefined Purgatory, capriciously, from a place of suffering and fiery purging to a "condition of existence" (essentially, floating in space waiting to go to Heaven). So, which is it? A fiery furnace or just a place to hang out? There's a big difference, and the definition keeps changing in the Roman Catholic world.

8. Purgatory denies the "Great Exchange": Jesus exchanging His righteousness for our unrighteousness on the cross.

9. Purgatory blasphemes the true Gospel of Christ.

10. This belief system was formed and developed centuries after the apostles. In a desperate attempt to justify its validity, the Roman

Church grabbed a small handful of scriptures out of context to make the narrative fit (1 Corinthians 3:11-15, Matthew 5:25, 2 Maccabees), yet there are hundreds of verses that indicate that our faith and trust in Christ eliminates the need for interim purification to achieve holiness. Jesus achieved our holiness for us.

11. Make no mistake, Purgatory is not the "good news" of the Gospel, and it's not good news for a Christian.

12. Purgatory completely contradicts the teachings of Paul and the other New Testament writers.

13. Sacramental systems in the Roman Catholic Church attempt to control grace. "We are in charge, you need us, we dispense grace and the sacraments necessary for salvation." Purgatory was developed out of necessity to control the Church's followers and is directly tied to the deceptive popes that are listed throughout these first two chapters. That alone, should be the deciding factor to question this dogma.

14. The fear of this horrifying place called Purgatory was developed to empty the moneybags of anyone who fell for its scheme.

15. According to the Greek Orthodox Archdiocese of America, "Both Purgatory and indulgences are intercorrelated theories, unwitnessed in the Bible or in the Ancient Church, and when they were enforced and applied, they brought about evil practices at the expense of the prevailing Truth of the Church ..."[79]

16. It is a historical fact that the church fathers throughout the centuries were extremely mixed in their view of any type of Purgatory, and mixed on what exactly it conceptualized.

In the second century, Tertullian, a theologian, and considered the father of Latin Christianity said:,

> "This place, the bosom of Abraham [referenced in Luke], though not in Heaven, and yet above Hell, offers the souls of the righteous an interim refreshment until the end of all things brings about the general resurrection and the final reward."[80]

Does this sound like a place of purging or fiery penance or that any "remission of sins" is taking place? Does this sound like a place that Catholics need to atone for venial sins to escape? Does this sound like a situation where the masses need to conduct sacraments to "spring" mom out of this horrible abode? Does this sound like a place where indulgences will minimize the dwelling time? Or does this sound like a refreshing waiting place?

The patriarch Cyril of Alexandria from the fifth century says,

> "The souls of Saints, when they quit their earthly bodies, are, by the bountiful mercy of God, almost, as it were, consigned into the hands of a most loving Father, and do not, as some infidels have pretended, haunt their sepulchers [tombs], waiting for funeral libations; nor yet are they, like the souls of sinful men, conveyed to the place of endless torment, that is, to Hell. Rather, do they hasten into the hands of the father of all, by the new way which our Savior Christ has prepared for us ..."[81]

With a full understanding of the message of grace that is conveyed later in Chapters 9 through 13, Christians can certainly look forward to Cyril of Alexandria's opinion of the destination for all Christians: into the loving arms of our Heavenly father.

John Chrysostom, who served as archbishop of Constantinople and is a famous church father stated,

> "And to die is gain. Whereof? Because I shall more clearly be present with Him; so that my death is rather a coming to life; they who kill me will work on me no dreadful thing, they will only send me onward to my proper life, and free me from that which is not mine."[82]

Jerome, Ambrose, and many others expressed similar perspectives. Theologian Gavin Ortlund says that some of the church fathers expressed a "language of fire," but it was always in describing Hell, not Purgatory. Most believed that the rewards of the righteous were immediate and that deceased believers are enjoying the presence of God in Heaven.[83] There are so many other examples that could be given, but this is some compelling evidence that

Purgatory, as taught in the Middle Ages and as taught today by the Roman Catholic Church, would be a complete mystery to Jesus, the apostles, and the majority of the church fathers.

Here is the appeal to all Catholics: Please do not allow Purgatory, as defined by the Roman Church, to rob you of the peace and assurance that is so evident in the Scriptures. Jesus paid all of the penalty for our sins. He left none for us to deal with. We have to stop trying to override Him. Just imagine a "teaching" (not biblically based) where you are going to be in some mystical place of torment and purging, and you have no idea for how long. I just want to say how sorry I am that Roman Catholics have had to endure such mental anguish and entrapment. So many Catholics have an overwhelming, unwarranted fear of Purgatory. Fear just so the Church can maintain and control behaviors (and in the past, finances). It's a sad and depressing deceit that has to stop.

Why is the Roman Catholic Church so protective of this teaching on Purgatory, and why is it defended so fiercely by Catholic apologists? The answer is quite simple. When Purgatory, and especially the supremacy of the papacy is rebutted (the theme of these two chapters), all the other doctrinal positions start to collapse. Transubstantiation, confession to a priest, penance, and the Church's pathway to salvation and many more make no sense without a Vicar of Christ and without Purgatory. When this happens, what is left? What remains when The Catholic List disappears? Roman Catholics are simply left with the catholic, universal, primitive, original Church of the first century, and the teachings of the Scriptures put forth by the Holy Spirit through the apostles. That formula results in true freedom in Christ.

Let's return to Innocent III. Another sample of the distorted view of inflated ego and fantasy power was when Innocent said, "The successor of Peter is the vicar of Christ: he has been established by God and man, below God but beyond man; less than God but more than man; who shall judge all and be judged by no one.[84]

Coincidentally, this conceited disposition from Innocent was happening during the time when the government was becoming more controlled by the papacy. Most historians agree during the end of the 12th century and onward the "pope's government was fully a universal monarchy, and rapidly growing to become centralized.[85]

Not coincidentally, Innocent III, because of the "vicar of Christ" false claim, began to implement spiritual penalties. As Shelley states in his book:

> "Thus the pope's first weapon in bringing peasants and princes to their knees was the threat of excommunication. He could pronounce their anathema and they would be 'set apart' from the church, deprived of the grace essential for salvation."[86]

These orders and proclamations came from the Catholic vicars of Christ.

The stage was set for an unlimited amount of papal abuse during these Middle Ages. They had announced themselves as the vicars of Christ and that all instructions coming from their mouths were essentially coming from God. The abuse of the "ex-communication card" not only extended to individuals but was applied to whole nations. Instead of it being called ex-communication, in this application, it was called an "interdict". Pope Innocent III used it eighty-five times, including against England because of a disagreement with King John.[87] The king bought into the papal lie and gave into the threat with enormous amounts of money.

It is beyond the scope of this book to discuss all the history associated with this false, delusional power the popes possessed, but it is extremely important to understand the roots of this office if we are to understand popes of the modern day. This abuse over the centuries included authority over the souls of men and women, even in eternity. It's the worst type of dictatorship, the worst type of leadership, the worst type of barbarous, wicked, and deceptive ruler to use a fake religious pretense to try and rule over others even into eternity. Chapters 6, 7, and 8 will expose much about the current scandals that are so widespread in today's Catholic system, substantiating the consequences of nefarious popes and religious institutions.

As we have seen in the past two chapters, many Catholic popes were extremely dishonest and ungodly. Many used trickery and schemes to deceive followers. They thrived on greed, power, and control. Their lives and pronouncements discredit their interpretations of Christian theology because they had drifted so far away from original catholic teachings. These teachings that emerged on The Catholic List disprove any legitimacy of the papacy and call into question everything practiced in today's Roman Catholic Church.

Whitewashing the Problem

I think it is important to look at some comments from highly respected Catholic leaders minimizing the problems with the papacy. Below are thoughts from a few well-known names; however, many others express the same sentiment, downplaying the severity of the damage done. See the glaring difference in the truth about past popes that have been examined in this book so far from what these spokespeople say.

Bishop Robert Baron, a well-known Catholic author, speaker, and theologian: "Oh, it's just the doctrine of original sin—people go bad, and that doesn't exclude popes. The pope's infallibility when under very strict circumstances, articulated in the church's teaching—that's a whole different question from his moral rectitude. He (the pope) could be the worst person in the world, but still playing the role the pope should play ... To me, it's just in line with our doctrine of original sin. People go bad ... that doesn't exclude popes."[88]

I feel that it's a stunning comment to defend a pope's continued role regardless of his behavior. This rhetoric seems to be reflective of attempts made by some of today's American political leaders to make something evil appear good, forming their entire political platform around fraud, lies, and deception—all while claiming their legitimacy by declaring that they have the people's best interest at heart. Bishop Baron says the pope can be, "the worst person in the world," but he still has a job to do.

Can you convince a jury of millions of Christian believers that popes who have engaged in some of the worst acts in human history still have a job to do, and that job is to lead the entire Christian Church? This would not be a logical conclusion.

What credibility and believability do popes have with the type of exploitation that has been exposed so far? Wouldn't a better conclusion be that many popes have been wolves in sheep's clothing—predators cloaked in religious overtones—according to historical truths? Is this being too critical based on the evidence given in the past two chapters?

It is sad and concerning that many Catholics have missed this glaring truth. Millions more have said, "No recognition of the pope, no recognition of a singular Church claim." Many Catholics may think, "Well, we disagree with the pope sometimes;" however, accepting the whole of the papacy while only disagreeing on trivial matters dismisses the atrocities over the centuries. Many consider, "Yes, the pope sins also, but he just goes to confession like all of us." However, that would not be an accurate assimilation of the actions these popes have engaged in, and popes going to confession just disguises the consequential results of their actions.

The popes that have been mentioned were not just "sinners" who would pop into confession and strive to do better. They were criminal men with no affiliation whatsoever with a succession from Peter. Any assertion otherwise is not exercising critical thinking. In many, if not most, instances they were not Christ followers at all, yet they were leading the Christian Church. An objective jury would come back with a guilty verdict: the office of the papacy is not ethical or legitimate.

The Catholic Narrative

After two chapters of appalling revelations about the popes of the past, what does the Catholic Church have to say about these immoral popes? How do they account for all the atrocities over the centuries regarding the actions of the Church? How do they reconcile the papal sanction of the murder of hundreds of thousands of people? Let's continue to look at some of the most recognized Catholic theologians and apologists and see how honestly they respond.

Scott Hahn, a leading Catholic theologian, when asked what he thought about the bad popes and whether this level of evil disapproves the office of the papacy, responded by saying:

> "You have to distinguish what you mean by bad popes, because starting off with Peter, in choosing Simon Peter, Jesus is showing that a chain is only as strong as its weakest link...Peter denied Jesus three times. Pope Honorius, as one pope, who was cowardly in the most important area, and that is doctrinal teaching, and

that's why the ecumenical council condemns him, for not teaching heresy, but for not suppressing it. You have Pope Alexander VI who, famously, was much more of a military leader in war than he was the successor of Peter in Rome ...

"... The worst, bad pope was Benedict IX in the 11th century ... around the age of 20, looks as though the office was purchased for him by family members, he left it, and then he basically purchased that again, and by all accounts he was extraordinarily immoral, perhaps both ways—I'll leave it at that point for the sake of discretion. But He was probably too busy sinning ... and everybody recognized that this is a hellacious person on the throne of Peter, but what it did was set into motion the subsequent reform ... but one century later the Gregorian reforms ... set into motion, establishes not only the papacy, but the Catholic Church; it sets it up for one of the greatest periods of doctrinal, liturgical, moral, evangelistic renewal that its ever seen and so just as the darkest hours before dawn—so the most corrupt popes are usually coming right before reform and renewal ... You see that Christ is sustaining them (bad popes) in despite themselves ... There is this whopping disproportion between good popes and bad ones. You need two hands to count the bad ones, but you got over 200 good ones ... some are good, some are fair, some are great, some are saints, most are not ... it's a mixed bag, but I would say it's one that Christ is not ashamed to say, you know, 'I'm the one who sustains them; I'm the one who established that.'"[89]

There is a lot to digest in those comments, and several key points worth mentioning within Scott's interview and his subsequent statements above. First, comparing Peter with some of the popes that have been listed in the past two chapters is highly dishonorable and disconcerting. One of the original apostles, Peter had extraordinary faith in Jesus and witnessed the resurrection. Was it a scary proposition to suddenly watch Jesus arrested (knowing the ramifications of this event) and be confronted with questions on whether Peter knew Jesus? Absolutely. He was probably scared to death when he denied Christ.

Peter's denial before the cross does not indicate Peter's life after the crucifixion, especially after Jesus showed up in the upper room a few days after He was put to death, confirming that He was the Son of God. Just a few chapters later, Peter was no longer denying Christ. He stood on the stage at Pentecost and proceeded to deliver the very first sermon ever preached by Jesus's followers. The message was not complicated, and Peter was no longer in denial mode. Anyone reading the book of Acts will quickly realize that Peter—along with James, John, Paul, and others—risked everything to spread the simple message of following Christ as the pathway into His kingdom. Peter was thrown in jail and is thought to later have been crucified, as were many of the other apostles.

Here is what we know: Peter's life and death glorified God. He devoted his whole life after the resurrection to spreading the good news about Christ and doing what was requested of him by Jesus, and that was telling everyone to "follow Him," sharing what He accomplished at the cross and resurrection as Jesus instructed: "Make disciples of all nations, baptizing them in the name of the Father and of the Son and of the Holy Spirit" (Matthew 28:19). There was no Catholic list.

Sometimes, Jesus's messages were not very long because what He said spoke volumes: "As Jesus went on from there, he saw a man named Matthew sitting at the tax collector's booth. Jesus said, 'Follow me,' he told him, and Matthew got up and followed him" (Matthew 9:9).

To compare the incredible, dedicated life of Peter (an apostle, not a pope) to popes who were not only dirty and diabolical, but who were not even Christ-followers is disparaging and disappointing theology. It's like comparing a child throwing a temper tantrum with a Nazi executioner. It's an embarrassing analogy given by Hahn.

One of the most shocking revelations from Hahn's comments is his total omission of all the truly evil popes except one. As you can easily see from these first two chapters—information that anyone can research and that has been repeatedly confirmed by Roman Catholic scholars and theologians—the situation is much worse than he alludes to. In fairness, was it honest for

Hahn to hide the truth through omission? What would be his motive in hiding this historical evidence?

Catholics who are truly seeking the truth about the history of the Catholic Church and want legitimate answers surrounding papal corruption should really take note of what these defenders of the faith state. Most Catholics are very familiar with Scott Hahn and his Protestant background before his conversion; he is one of the leading supporters of the Catholic faith. In addition to what has already been mentioned, there are a few more revealing comments that he made, and fact-checking certainly should be a part of someone's due diligence on this topic. Hahn's comment, "You have Pope Alexander VI who, famously, was much more of a military leader in war than he was the successor of Peter in Rome," was his whole assessment of Alexander VI. However, a quick review of Alexander VI (see Chapter 1) reveals horrifying details that Hahn chose not to discuss. Would anyone agree that this avoidance was honest? Hahn is an expert in his field; he certainly knows the truth.

Let's expand on what he says, specifically about the number of bad popes that have come along: "You need two hands to count the bad ones." In this one comment, he is declaring that when you examine the history of the papacy, there were between six and ten bad popes. However, as we have seen so far, when you take into account the ones involved in the Crusades and Inquisitions and all those who have been discussed in detail, the bad popes far exceed eighty, and many of those were mass murderers. Can anyone be coaxed into believing that torturing and raping and murdering thousands isn't worth mentioning as examples of black marks on the papacy that need to be acknowledged by Hahn?

Is he purposely misleading the audience, or does he have his history wrong? Why only mention a couple of bad popes? What is the reason for his inadvertence? I believe inside the hearts of ethical and sincere Catholics, the Holy Spirit will certainly reveal the truth about the correct answer.

Hahn also comments on what happened after the horrendous reign of Pope Benedict IX: "But one century later the Gregorian reforms ... set into motion, establishes not only the papacy, but the Catholic Church; it sets it up for one of the greatest periods of doctrinal, liturgical, moral, evangelistic renewal that its ever seen and so just as the darkest hours before dawn—so the most corrupt popes are usually coming right before reform and renewal." However, not only is Hahn's comment incorrect, but the truth is the very opposite of what he states. Benedict IX served from 1032-1048. One century later, around 1150, began one of the darkest times in Catholic history, not the magical reform and renewal espoused by Hahn. The latter twelfth century marks the start of the Crusades and Inquisitions through which the Catholic Church, under direct orders from the popes of that period, launched a 700-year massacre facilitating the murder of hundreds of thousands of people. This is how Hahn is describing "reform and renewal"?

When you purposely mislead your audience once, they might turn a blind eye; the second time, you sit up a little straighter in your seat and start to really pay attention; the third time, however, (in the same interview with Hahn) you must begin to ask if there is a cover-up going on, a fraudulent scheme in the works, or are you simply dealing with someone who is not truthful? Have leaders like Hahn simply been misled by their own institutional rhetoric?

As a side note, I think it is also very important to acknowledge, when reading books by Roman Catholic scholars, the words "renewal" and "reform" are listed over and over and over again, stretching century after century. A reform was necessary at so many junctions of Catholic Church history. Why is that? Examining the framework of the papacy certainly is a good starting place to answer that question.

Would God really be proud of saying that He sustains these popes based on the past two chapters, as Hahn implies? Or might God grieve over what has transpired allegedly in His name? Regardless, something is definitely amiss here. One will be hard-pressed to accept a theological path that is viable, authentic, logical, and that follows after the pattern of Christ when the truth is not being told.

Most would agree it is embarrassing to have a long history of unscrupulous popes affiliated with the one and true Church, a Church that attempts to convince billions of people of its legitimacy. But more than embarrassment, it ruins the story of papal authority being divinely appointed. It is no longer believable. Conversely, to think that Christians are incapable of doing the research and seeing the horrifying historical events of these popes is both insulting and degrading. How can one protect the papal narrative without minimizing the corruption? It's virtually impossible without these purposeful omissions.

How do you convince Catholics that the office and succession of the papacy is a legitimate spiritual and biblical plan? Maybe you never discuss how deep the perversion has gone and keep the average attendee in the parish so busy with regiments, requirements, good works, confession, penance, sacraments, and endless, repetitive rosaries that they never discover the truth.

You simply cannot find any pope, especially in the Middle Ages, that even closely resembles the exemplary models of Jesus Christ, the early apostles, or the leaders of the first-century Church. The original Gospel was not practiced by any of the past popes that have been mentioned so far. If you look to popes for direction, authority, correct theology, infallibility, and ethical leadership, you might have gazed in the wrong direction. These papal leaders dressed like kings overwhelmingly demonstrated a false Christianity.

In addition to Scott Hahn's apparent dishonesty through misinformation and omission, and Bishop Baron's justification of papal bad behavior, let's look at another top leader and spokesperson for the Catholic Church, Trent Horn, who wrote the book *The Case for Catholicism*. In Horn's 342-page book, here is all he had to say about bad popes:

> "Every pope has been a sinner, and a few were notorious for the grave sins they committed during their pontificates."[90]

Horn only lists one sentence in 342 pages about bad popes. Being completely objective as a Catholic, how honest is an author—whose sole intention is to convince the reader the Catholic faith is the correct faith—when brushing past 1,700 years of papal corruption with one general sentence about it, referencing the bad ones as "a few"? "A few" would indicate to the reader that there were maybe three or four bad popes. Horn using one sentence to cover the brutal murders of hundreds of thousands of men, women, and children, a magisterium saturated with sexual immorality, greed, power, and unforgivable crimes certainly cannot be sufficient. Once again, the omission of critical information is dishonest. Firsthand, we seem to have Horn adopting the exact same false narrative as Hahn and others.

Why would Horn completely neglect to inform his readers that for hundreds of years, popes leveraged their power by falsely promising forgiveness to get participants to murder, rape, and plunder cities and villages? Why would he not disclose the atrocities that have been highlighted so far in these chapters instead of trying to generalize 1,700 years of damage in one sentence? Is that an honest portrayal of what really occurred?

In reading the title of his book—*The Case for Catholicism*—one would assume Horn is setting a goal to make a case that everyone on the planet should convert to Roman Catholicism. But his omissions beg the question: why would a non-Catholic want to convert to Catholicism when the dark history of the Catholic Church has been hidden from the seekers?

Why would a non-Catholic want to convert and accept tradition that was developed and adopted into Church dogma and doctrine that came from the Catholic popes who have been disclosed? How does any Catholic liturgy have credibility when one does the research and can clearly see the truth? How can logical, educated, practical individuals ever accept something like papal infallibility or the title, "vicar of Christ" being attached to popes who exhibit such callousness and cruelty in contrast to Christ?

Let's take a look at one more top apologist with the Catholic Church, Jimmy Akin, and put his transparency to the test regarding bad popes. In a YouTube interview, Akin was asked, "What about an immoral pope—what is one of best examples of a scoundrel pope?" Akin replied, "So, two spring to mind. First one, I want to say, is Alexander VI ... the worst was Benedict IX."[91]

In the video, he professes to have to really search his mind to even come up with the bad pope's name: "I want to say ..." and says absolutely nothing about the depth of the depravity that has gone on in the papacy for centuries. Akin chose not to address the extent of the problem by *only* referencing two bad popes, and as a result, we seem to have another case of blatant dishonesty through omission. Anyone can objectively see that there is something very suspicious going on with these key Catholic apologists and leaders.

In addition to Catholic spokespersons being elusive on this topic, Internet websites are full of writers doing the same. The Just Measure, a popular Catholic blog by Father Justin Huang, states this about bad popes:

> "Every pope has been a sinner, and always will be ... So, we're not out to prove they're all saints. But they're not all bad either. In fact, there have only been about 10 corrupt popes, which is 3.7%. Yes, some did kill, some had mistresses and children ... Today, we hear in the gospel that two of the first bishops, James and John, were seeking glory for themselves, and the other ten got mad at them."[92]

At first glance, there are two glaring problems with this statement. First, once again, is the dishonest representation of how many bad popes there have truly been. And then a comparison is made to something as trivial as James and John seeking glory for themselves, which is in no way like the total depravity of popes we have seen so far.

The late Richard Bennett was a former Roman Catholic priest and a cradle Catholic for forty-eight years. He left the Catholic faith after discovering the true message of grace that salvation is in the person of Christ, not in a church. As an author, he formed a ministry to reach lost Catholics and people trapped in false Protestant beliefs. He counts at least seventy-five popes from Innocent III to Pius VII (1179-1800) who endorsed the torture, murder, and burning of individuals at the stake in his research.[93] Of course, this does not account for all the immorality of popes discussed in the last two chapters. The papacy has not represented Christianity properly, and these quotes from Catholic apologists and websites do not match the reality.

Still, the majority of Catholic apologists state that there have only been a few bad popes. Is there an internal conspiracy to cover up, dismiss, and mislead Christians about how many bad popes there have actually been? Are the actions and atrocities of these popes so horrific that leaders feel compelled to maintain secrecy? I think the generous conclusion is that subsequent speakers and writers just feed off of the same information that was previously provided by recognized representatives of the Catholic Church. Regardless of the motives, the reader will have to decide if they consider these Catholic spokesmen to be forthright with their lack of disclosure and the apparent omissions. Can anyone trust what they say based on the evidence that has been presented?

Although these first two chapters have allowed Catholics to peer into the window of what really happened in the history of the papacy, the Church keeps this information out of sight from the average parishioner and still sticks with the description of the pope from the First Ecumenical Council of the Vatican, or Vatican I, in 1870:

> "... the primacy of jurisdiction over the universal Church of God was immediately and directly promised and given to Blessed Peter ... Thus, whoever succeeds Peter in this Chair, obtains, by the institution of Christ Himself, the primacy of Peter over the whole Church ... in virtue of which all the faithful of Christ must believe that the Holy Apostolic See and the Roman Pontiff possessed primacy over the whole world ... and is the true Vicar of Christ, and the Head of the whole Church, and Father and teacher of all Christians ... This is the teaching of Catholic truth, from which no one can deviate without loss of faith and salvation. If anyone, then, shall say that the Roman Pontiff ... [is] not the full and supreme power of jurisdiction over the universal Church, ... let him be anathema [cursed]."[94]

It is interesting that Pope Pius IX, who kidnapped a six-year-old boy from his family, also formed the Vatican I council for the primary purpose of defining papal infallibility, declaring that the position he held was over everyone in the world, and if anyone defied his proclamations, they would lose their salvation and be forever cursed. I believe most people would admit it's the ultimate self-centered tactic to call a council together to proclaim and ratify that you rule the world and that any defiance of that viewpoint would result in condemnation. These actions clearly demonstrate tyrannous behaviors. How many false leaders have come along in different religions with similar messages to, "I am the one, I am a prophet. God has chosen me to deliver His message and be in ultimate power"? A countless amount. Contrast that with true shepherds of Christianity whose character traits include humbleness, modesty, meekness, lowliness, and purity—the very opposite of, "I am in control, I have the highest authority, listen and obey or be anathematized and excommunicated." We see that Christians have such freedom in never being subject to domineering pontiffs, or any pontiffs for that matter, but instead solely relying on the finished work of Jesus Christ, and His definition of what secures our salvation (discussed in Chapters 9 and 10).

This study into the papacy shows there were never divine successors, only successors instituted by a political and religious entity whose purpose was to be drenched in wealth and power, creating a monarchy that operated as a dictatorship at times, and that would ultimately and unscrupulously control the masses. Popes became officials consumed with self-importance and dominance. James, Peter, John, and the other apostles did not have that agenda. You cannot use Peter in the same sentence, in conjunction with, or in comparison with the Roman Catholic popes of the past, and expect educated Christians to listen and adhere.

CHAPTER 3

The Pope: Never Bow Down

I t is critical for all Christians to understand that the head of the Church is Jesus Christ. A single verse can be plucked from its context and misinterpreted, as is often the case with Matthew 16:18, in which Jesus gives Simon the name Peter: "the rock". Or, you can see the undeniable truth that the central theme of the Scriptures is about Jesus. There is no mistaking that Peter was a fantastic apostle, and not a single pope in the Roman Catholic Church can compare to an apostle like him. However, the Bible is about the story of Jesus. Jesus is the story. Jesus is the Gospel. Jesus is the Rock. He's the whole thing: the only kingdom and the only foundation. No one individual stands in His place.

"And he [Jesus] is the head of the body, the church; and he is the beginning ..." (Colossians 1:18).

"Christ is the head of the church, his body, of which he is the Savior" (Ephesians 5:23).

"They all ate the same spiritual food and drank the same spiritual drink; for they drank from the spiritual rock that accompanied them, and that rock was Christ" (1 Corinthians 10: 3-4).

"Jesus looked directly at them and asked, 'Then what is the meaning of that which is written: The stone the builders rejected has become the capstone?'" (Luke 20:17).

"As you come to Him, the living Stone—rejected by men but chosen by God and precious to him" (1 Peter 2:4).

"For no one can lay any foundation other than the one already laid, which is Jesus Christ" (1 Corinthians 3:11).

I highly admire Peter, but Catholics have been misled by Rome in the belief that he was the cornerstone of the Church. God explicitly chose Jesus to be the cornerstone in the construction of the Church. I know it's been traditionally passed down to Catholics for generations, but one must dig a little deeper to see Peter's true role in the Church. Like the Eastern Orthodox and hundreds of millions of Christians worldwide, Catholics have the option to *refuse* to accept erroneous titles given to popes and embrace the One who Christianity fully centers around: Jesus Christ.

Was Peter the First Pope?

Although the aim of this book is not to fully examine or debate the argument of whether Peter was a pope, or what it means that he was referred to as "the rock," I believe it is worth noting a few critical facts. Trent Horn, in his book *A Case for Catholicism*, tries to answer theologians who have obviously concluded that the Scriptures never refer to Peter as a pope or a vicar of Christ. Horn responds by stating, "The answer is Peter can be a pope even if scripture does not use that title for him."[1]

Horn equates this to the fact that the word trinity does not exist in the Scriptures, but it is commonly known among most Christians that the trinity exists. Horn makes a weak argument with this analogy because the "completeness" of the Trinity is mentioned in multiple places and is a verified concept. We see it throughout chapter one of 1 Peter: "Praise be to the God and Father of our Lord Jesus Christ ...Which the Spirit of Christ in them ... It was revealed to them ... by those who preached the gospel to you by the Holy Spirit." We also see it in 2 Corinthians 13:14: "May the grace of the Lord Jesus Christ, and the love of God, and the fellowship of the Holy Spirit be with you all." The whole Trinity is listed. Other places, likewise, talk about the different persons of God (Ephesians 4:4-6, Matthew 3:16-17, John 10:30). The biggest failure in Horn's comparison, though, is that the central theme of the New Testament revolves around aspects of the Trinity, regardless if the word "Trinity" is absent, but never discusses the office of the papacy in concept, or the authority of the Church being centered around one individual apostle. There is a big difference in these two scenarios.

If we apply the logic that Horn is trying to use, then anything or anyone can qualify for any supernatural title simply because an institution says they do without any factual justification. We cannot say that Paul was "Superman" (even though the Scriptures do not use that title for him) and argue that it's equal to the doctrine of the Trinity regardless of the Scriptures never using that title for God. There would not be a logical argument for it unless we had events and evidence supporting such a silly claim. We have the evidence about the Trinity. We have no evidence about the papacy.

Ambrose, an early catholic Church leader from the fourth century, states:

> "God, then, is One, without violation of the majesty of the eternal Trinity, as is declared in the instance set before us. And not in that place alone do we see the Trinity expressed in the Name of the Godhead; but both in many places, as we have said also above, and especially in the epistles which the Apostle wrote to the Thessalonians, he most clearly set forth the Godhead and sovereignty of the Father, the Son, and the Holy Spirit."[2]

Horn makes another fragile argument for why Peter is the authoritative apostle, saying, "And [Peter] is placed first in every formal list of the Apostles."[3] In other words, when the Scriptures state a list of the apostles, Peter is listed first. Yet, there is no basis for the claim that a list is synonymous with authority. If someone were to ask me who I went to lunch with from work, and I replied that I went to a business lunch with Rob, Haley, Bill, and John, it would not be logical for me to have listed their names based on majority member, CEO, or senior partner. This argument Horn makes simply does not stand up. On the contrary, we even see in Galatians 2:9 that Peter is listed second: "James, Peter, and John ..."

Horn states in his book that Peter did hold a place of prominence in the early Church but admits, "It's true that prominence does not equal primacy, but it does provide evidence for Peter's primacy."[4] Even in acknowledging the fractures in his reasoning, Horn still will not let go of the idea of Peter's sole leadership of the Church (as a pope) and tries to support a biblical papacy that simply does not exist.

James, John, Peter, and Paul had critical roles in spreading the original Gospel. I cannot emphasize enough that the early apostles, all equal in authority, had the shared responsibility for one mission: to spread the news about the resurrection of Jesus. The early apostles would never have condoned The Catholic List and would have never recognized Peter as a pope.

In his documentary, Thompson makes the point that we never see Peter in his epistles ever mention the office of a papacy or formulate any formal plans to have a succession of any sort. There are multiple opportunities for the authors of the New Testament to mention the papacy, the succession of the papacy, the infallibility of the papacy, and clear everything up, but it is simply not there. We only have the Roman Church taking a few verses out of context and creating a narrative that is not well substantiated. Apologist Gavin Ortlund sates, "the biblical evidence for the papacy is slender and ambiguous."[5]

Here is what Catholic author Richard P. McBrien wrote about papal succession:

> "From the New Testament record alone, we have no basis for positing a line of succession from Peter through subsequent bishops of Rome."[6]

German Theologian, Wolfhart Pannenberg confirmed this as well when he wrote:

> "Today theological exegesis of the NT, including Roman catholic exegesis, has reached widespread consent that these NT sayings about Peter, no matter how else we might assess them, refer only to Peter, not to any successors in his office."[7]

Eamon Duffy says that Peter actually fades out in the book of Acts and states that the New Testament books do not "even hint that the special role of Peter could be passed on to any single 'successor'. There is, therefore, nothing directly approaching a papal theory in the pages of the New Testament."[8]

Ortlund observes that there is "no proof of the transfer of power from Peter to Roman Bishops; the evidence is not there."[9]

Research shows a lot of compelling evidence that reveals not only was there not a papacy in the Scriptures or in the early Church (or any individual with supremacy), but there were no apostolic plans to pass on any type of authority or official papal office. This confirmation comes from Roman Catholic scholars and theologians. Yet all the leading Catholic apologists, so prominent and well known on social media platforms, will not concede this fact.

Peter, without any absolute power or jurisdiction over anyone, had the assignment to spread the message about the resurrection, as every Christian believer should want to do. In his documentary mentioned earlier, Thompson concludes if there was any meaningful evidence that substantiates that Peter functioned as the first Bishop of Rome, one would think we would have numerous proofs for it. However, we don't. When one examines the historical record of the early Church, we see the opposite. The Bible and the apostolic fathers do not affirm it, and the patristic apologists and the early Christian writers before the third century do not either.[10]

Likewise, theologian Herman Bavinck confirms the same observation:

> "It is clear from the bishops' lists in Hegesippus, Irenaeus, the Muratorian Fragment, Hippolytus, Tertullian, and Epiphanius that at the end of the second century and even in the beginning of the third, Peter was not yet considered a bishop of Rome."[11]

Catholic author Jerome Neyrey states:

> "... there is solid support for his eventual travel to Rome and martyrdom there ... There is less evidence of how Peter functioned while in Rome. It would be wrong, however, to read back into first-century Rome the existence of the papacy as we know it today ..."[12]

Catholic leadership has long cited Matthew 16:18 in an attempt to prove that Christ built His Church on Peter, "the rock". However, that doctrine is in the minority view among the patristic fathers. In fact, according to Ortlund, there are three primary positions regarding exactly what Jesus meant by the word "rock":

1. The rock is Jesus.
2. The rock is Peter's confession.
3. The rock is Peter, individually.

In a work called *Retractions,* Augustine, one of the famous Latin fathers of the early Church, offered an alternative interpretation by stating, "The rock was Christ."[13] The logic is that if Jesus had been referring to Peter as the rock in this particular scripture the verse could have easily been worded as, "You are Peter, and upon you, the rock, I will build my Church."

Augustine stated:

> "Peter, called after this rock, represented the person of the Church which is built upon this rock ... For, 'thou art Peter', and not 'thou art the rock', was said to him. But the rock was Christ ..."[14]

Notice the nuance in that Peter "represented" the Church. He was a "symbol" of the Church. Not the head of the Church. Many church fathers were convinced that Jesus was referring to individuals having faith in Him as the foundation of the Church. Matthew 16:16, "You are the Christ; the Son of the living God," frames the context of Matthew 16:18 just two verses later. In other words, they thought that the Church was built on Peter's confession of faith. The gates of hell could wipe out Peter, but cannot destroy Christ, the Son of the living God. The early church fathers confirmed this to be true. John Chrysostom, a great theologian in the fourth century wrote:

> "And I say unto thee, Thou are Peter, and upon this rock I will build My Church; that is, on the faith of his confession."[15]

Cyril of Alexandria, a famous patriarch in the fifth century, also wrote:

> "Now by the word 'rock', Jesus indicated, I think, the immovable faith of the disciple."[16]

Basil of Seluecia confirms this perspective too:

"Now Christ called this confession a rock, and he named the one who confessed it 'Peter', perceiving the appellation which was suitable to the author of this confession ..."[17]

Ortlund makes the observation that many Catholic apologists quote Ambrose out of context when they say that "where Peter is, there the Church is", and in doing so they totally miss the point that can be derived by reading further into his quote:

"When he [Peter] heard, 'But who do you say I am,' he immediately, not unmindful of his station, exercised his primacy, that is, the primacy of confession, not of honor; the primacy of belief, not of rank ... Faith, then, is the foundation of the Church, for it was not said of Peter's flesh, but of his faith, that 'the gates of hell shall not prevail against it.'"[18]

Jerome, like many others, was also convinced that Peter only represented the Church by his confession and faith in Christ, and he clearly states that the Church is built on Christ; He is the Rock:

"The one foundation which the apostolic architect laid is our Lord Jesus Christ. Upon this stable and firm foundation, which has itself been laid on solid ground, the Church of Christ is built ... for the Church was founded upon a rock ... upon this rock the Lord established his Church; and the apostle Peter received his name for this rock ... The rock is Christ, who gave to His apostles, that they also should be called rocks."[19]

Jerome, in this quote, seems to be saying that not only is Jesus the Rock, but Peter, along with all the apostles, were rocks also. In other words, every Christian is a rock and shares this responsibility of spreading the message about the resurrection by the foundational proof of "faith in Christ."

Thompson states that these same views about Christ not actually building His Church on Peter, individually, as a supreme leader are likewise expressed by such major fathers as Ambrose, Cyprian, Origen, Tertullian, Hilary of Poitiers, Ambrosiaster, Jerome, Eusebius, Basil the Great, Gregory of Nyssa,

Athanasius, Ephraim Syrus, James of Nisbis, Victor of Antioch, Epiphanius, Aphraates, Theodoret, Cassiodorus, Asterius, Basil of Seleucia, Palladius of Helenopolois, Paulinus of Nola, Isidore of Seville, Bede, and many others. Other theologians have made these same observations. The book that has one of the most comprehensive patristic interpretations of the "rock" in Matthew 16:18 is called *The Matthew 16 Controversy: Peter and the Rock.*[20]

The early church fathers were not supportive of the modern-day Roman Catholic interpretation of Matthew 16:18. This would be a shocking revelation to most Catholics, and assumedly never taught in the parish, and especially not to those growing up in the Roman Catholic faith. Think about the implications of Peter not being a pope for the Roman Catholic institution. They have built their whole platform, organization, and monarchy on these inaccurate assumptions. However, one more perspective on Peter *not* being the foundation of the Church comes from Joann Joseph Ignaz Dollinger, the most renowned Roman Catholic historian of the nineteenth century, and who taught Church history for forty-seven years. He states:

> "Of all the Fathers who interpret these passages in the Gospels (Matt 16:18, John 21:17), not a single one applies them to the Roman bishops as Peter's successors. How many Fathers have busied themselves with these texts, yet not one of them whose commentaries we possess—Origen, Chrysostom, Hilary, Augustine, Cyril, Theodoret, and those whose interpretations are collected in catenas—has dropped the faintest hint that the primacy of Rome is the consequence of the commission and promise to Peter! Not one of them has explained the rock or foundation on which Christ would build His Church of the office given to Peter to be transmitted to his successors, but they understood by it either Christ himself, or Peter's confession of faith; often both together ..."[21]

In summary, Ortlund says,

> "I don't think anyone would doubt that Peter is foundational for the Church along with the other apostles, or that Peter has

a leadership role among the apostles, but in terms of identifying Peter as the rock in some way (that would lead to the doctrine of the papacy) I would go so far as to say this: if our interpretation of Matthew 16 follows the cues of the church fathers, then we will not arrive at an interpretation that is favorable to the papacy—to the Roman Catholic interpretation of Matthew 16. We just don't have a strong exegetical base for this massive doctrine … There has to be more than just leadership. There has to be proof for universal jurisdiction and the evidence is not there; it's always 'shared' responsibility."[22]

In fact, Eamon Duffy makes a revealing observation about the early catholic Church in the first couple of centuries:

"Till the reign of Stephen [mid third Century], the Roman Church's primacy had been gladly conceded, rooted in esteem for a Church blessed by the teaching and martyrdom of the great two Apostles [Paul and Peter]."[23]

In other words, primacy was not the priority of the primitive Church. Supremacy was not the priority of the early Church. A hierarchy was not the priority of the early Church. Instead, the Church relied on the Scriptures alone—the apostolic deposit (foundational teachings of the Apostles)—which only taught the simplicity of faith in Christ, not an overpowering hierarchy with supremacy, and not anything on The Catholic List.

By using good spiritual judgment and sound logic, one can only conclude that Jesus never assigned an individual to have His Church built on, when Jesus is the obvious foundation of everything. These are just observations and not nearly as striking as the proof after Peter's death that would cause anyone to conclude that God was not involved in a papal selection, as we saw in the first two chapters.

The Westminster Confession of Faith, written in the seventeenth century and later adopted by millions of Christians, sums it up with clarity: "There is no other head of the Church, but the Lord Jesus Christ. Nor can the Pope of Rome, in any sense, be head thereof."[24] I do not think it takes a lot of theological knowledge or advanced apologetics as a Christian to simply accept that Jesus Christ is the head of the Church. I shudder when an institution tries to diminish Christ and elevate man. Doing so is clearly an anti-Christ decision.

Peter and all the apostles were instrumental in maintaining the original Gospel with any authority they had to "bind and loose" and keep anti-Christ messages from entering the arena. This authority was never meant to add to the original Gospel or original practices, but to preserve it as emphasized in the verses warning not to change the original Gospel. It's a sobering reality when one observes that neither Paul, Peter, James, John, nor any of the other apostles ever proclaimed anything that is on The Catholic List practiced in the Catholic Church today.

Multiple scriptures show the apostles jockeying for position to see who was the greatest among themselves (Mark 9:34; Luke 9:46; 22:24). Jesus did not answer these arguments with, "Peter is the pope. He is the greatest, and you must acknowledge him as your leader." Instead, Christ in His perfection emphasized the importance that a leader is to be humble, a servant, and must not inappropriately exercise authority over other individuals. Here was Jesus's response when directly asked who was the greatest among them:

> "Jesus said to them, 'The kings of the Gentiles lord it over them; and those who exercise authority over them call themselves Benefactors. But you are not to be like that. Instead, the greatest among you should be like the youngest, and the one who rules like the one who serves'" (Luke 22:25-26).

To answer the question of who was the greatest, Jesus did not name one individual. In fact, the critical takeaway was that any leader in the future should be unlike a king who lords their authority over another. Yet, the whole history of the papacy—especially in medieval times over a period of over 1,000 years—shows that the popes in command ran a religious power-house using all kinds of manipulation tactics to get their way. They "lorded their authority" over everyone. This history is indisputable and can never be erased, but there seem to be erroneous attempts to cover it up.

It's a useless attempt for the Catholic Church to try to win the argument that there is a centralized pope recognized by God when so many popes ran an unethical, authoritarian monarchy. Most abused their authority in service of greed, power, and corruption—*exactly* what Jesus said not to do. And to reiterate, we are not referring to one bad pope or a handful that were just "sinful" as Catholic representatives would like the audience to believe, but a saturation of maliciousness by more than eighty popes documented here (and many more that were not discussed).

Further undercutting the idea of Peter being in an elevated position over the other apostles, we see Paul rebuking Peter in Galatians 2:11-14. This situation does not prove a case against a papacy, but it does provide a window into the fact that Peter struggled like all of us do and was reprimanded. I am a big fan of Peter and all the early apostles. I think they were simply amazing in their quest to spread the Gospel in dangerous situations, but there is no papal office established in the Scriptures. Peter was not a pope, but just an awesome leader. He was just like one of us!

Peter was simply an early apostle with a big mission to tell everyone what he had witnessed (the resurrection) as all the other apostles were doing, and what most believers were doing at the time. Other scholars note that Peter, although a remarkable Christ follower, wrote far fewer epistles than Paul, and in 1 Peter 5:1-2 we see Peter referring to himself as a fellow elder—not as the pope, not as the leader of the Church. Acts 8:14 tells of the apostles "sending" Peter and John to Samaria. It would be Peter doing the sending if he was exercising the authority of a pope. These are casual observations, but facts worth mentioning that have been observed by theologians.

The final piece of evidence we look at takes place during a critical meeting of many of the apostles and elders in Acts 15. Paul found out that some teachers in Jerusalem were teaching that believers had to be circumcised in order to be saved. This was the first sign of church "add-ons" to achieve salvation instead of faith alone in Christ, a trap we'll look at more closely in Chapters 9 and 10. Paul traveled and met with the council to clear up the confusion. While there, Peter stood up to address the group and proclaimed the original catholic message: that the grace of God and faith alone (not faith plus works) in Christ saves.

"Peter got up and addressed them ... 'Brothers, you know that
some time ago God made a choice among you that the Gentiles
might hear from my lips the message of the gospel and believe.
God, who knows the heart, showed that he accepted them by
giving the Holy Spirit to them, just as he did to us. He made no
distinction between us and them, for he purified their hearts by
faith. Now then, why do you try to test God by putting on the
necks of the disciples a yoke that neither we nor our fathers have
been able to bear? No! We believe it is through the grace of our
Lord Jesus that we are saved, just as they are'" (Acts 15:7-11).

Peter proclaimed the message of the early catholic Church: faith alone in
Christ saves because of God's grace. The Roman Church eventually added
other necessities to that message, but those who wanted to get back to that
same teaching prompted the Reformation in the sixteenth century. Who gave
the final word in this council meeting on the correct theology that was to be
taught? It was not actually Peter or Paul, but James just a few verses later:

"It is my judgment, therefore, that we should not make it difficult for the Gentiles who are turning to God" (Acts 15:19).

The early apostles understood that you cannot add anything to the original Gospel, and would strongly condemn today's Catholic List. They put an
immediate stop to even one addition to the Gospel (circumcision). The early
apostles, as we read in Peter's message, taught that faith alone in Christ saves.
And, when you look at this critical council meeting, you do not see Pope
Peter. You see the apostles acting in unison with James giving the final word,
making clear the falsehood of today's Roman Catholic claims.

One of the primary purposes of this book is to simply make Catholics
aware that what they have been taught for generations cannot be truthful in
the context of the Scriptures, history, and proof presented by Roman Catholic scholars and theologians. The evidence presented in these chapters, at
the very least, warrants a shift from an "institutional" relationship with Jesus
(and all the unbiblical, man-made dogma that has emerged from an unholy

magisterium) to a personal relationship with Jesus and the Heavenly Father, unburdened by all the Church add-ons.

The purpose of this book is *not* to try to encourage Catholics to immediately exit the Church and head for the closest Protestant structure. There is not a sentence in this book that recommends visiting your local Episcopal, Baptist, Methodist, or Pentecostal Church, *promptu*. The call is to pledge loyalty, solely, to the true head of the Church: Jesus.

Papal Infallibility

Many would conclude that just the mere mention of the word "infallibility" with regards to the pope or any individual is almost a blasphemous term, as we know Jesus was the only infallible person to have ever walked the Earth. Here is the official definition of the term according to Catholic dogma:

> "The Roman Pontiff, head of the college of bishops, enjoys this infallibility in virtue of his office. When, as supreme pastor and teacher of all the faithful—who confirms his brethren in the faith—he proclaims by a definitive act a doctrine pertaining to faith and morals (CCC 890-91)."

Just to clarify and avoid confusion from the terminology and other inaccurate Catholic rhetoric, the pope is not held to be infallible. The claim is that the pope is only infallible when he definitively proclaims a doctrine or makes a statement that relates to "faith and morals". The Church admits that this papal infallibility does not extend to the Church having all the correct decisions for the problems they face.

I find it interesting that the Church declares that the words that come out of the pope's mouth are absolutely perfect and divine—straight from God Himself—when he is speaking from the chair ("ex-cathedra" is the term); however, when it's time to make an absolute, critical, super important decision regarding the Church, well, the pope is on his own there.

In his book, Trent Horn agrees: "Papal infallibility is not a positive protection that guarantees the pope will always have the right answers."[25] Here is a presentation of an omnipotent God that exists outside of space and time, creating a universe and life as we know it, with absolutely no limitations, who easily has the ability to convey a message to the reigning pope to declare doctrine or dogma regarding faith and morals, but does not seem to have the ability to lead the pope in making correct decisions regarding Church matters. That is really bad logic and bad biblical exegesis that would not be accepted by any critical thinker. It's like trying to sell ocean-front property in Kansas. You can convince some, but others can see right through the swindle.

Horn further states, "Catholics simply believe that, as the leader of the Church, neither Peter nor any of his successors ever bound the Church to heresy or error."[26] In fairness, though, let's put Horn's comment to the test and evaluate whether any "succeeding" popes have ever bound the Church to error. Once again, we're asked to accept that when the popes of the past declared edicts to initiate and carry out the Crusades and the Inquisitions, killing hundreds of thousands of men, women, and even children; when the decisions were made to burn Protestants, Muslims, Jews, Cathars, alleged witches, and more at the stake; when the decisions were made to force baptism upon entire cultures; when the decisions were made for popes to engage in campaigning that would secure their political power and enormous wealth—all this was not leading the Church into error?

Most Catholics I have met are pretty smart individuals and it should not be challenging to evaluate the validity of Catholic excuses in protecting the Roman Church. The bad decisions made by the errors in the thinking of these past popes in the Catholic Church are immeasurable. One has to conclude from the evidence that popes have absolutely, emphatically, consistently led the Catholic Church in error for over 1,700 years.

If there is still any inclination toward accepting the concept of papal infallibility, consider that it did not exist, formally, until 1870. It was an accepted practice for a few hundred years prior until a carefully orchestrated business decision was made by Pope Pius IX to establish this pretentiousness as dogma to leverage even more control over the Church's followers and imperial leaders.

The notion of papal infallibility was not just to control followers, but to influence and control the political arena as well, as numerous popes and kings battled for prominence over the years. Fortunately, many individuals and kings rejected this papal infallibility nonsense and saw through the deception.

People outside the Catholic Church can easily see how convenient it is for the doctrine of papal infallibility to be invented, giving the pope a special grace from God that protects him from binding the Church into believing error, all while governing the Church in such unethical ways. Again, we see some parallels to cult leaders who convince their gullible followers that they are prophets, sent from God, here to proclaim this message from God, error-free, even if that message is, "I will proceed with having sexual relations with all your wives and all your kids." Many popes of the past did exactly the same thing: pursuing sexual relations with prostitutes and mistresses all while saying, "Listen to the words that are coming out of my mouth, as I am about to announce something regarding faith and morals." The disingenuous-ness is repulsive and disturbing.

It's particularly ironic that the official Catholic description of papal infal-libility specifies "a doctrine pertaining to faith and morals," yet there was simply nothing moral about any of the popes we have scrutinized. These popes are said to be able to open their mouths and make a declaration regarding faith and morals while being some of the most immoral individ-uals to have ever lived. This dogma is in opposition to the original catholic Church and simply cannot be found anywhere in the New Testament. Jesus knew nothing about papal infallibility, and to accept it is to be subjected to the control of fraudulent authoritarian leadership.

Trent Horn, in attempts to justify and substantiate papal infallibility, says that "we must proceed beyond the biblical evidence."[27] What Horn is saying is that we have to skip the Scriptures and try to find other sources to prove papal infallibility. Nobody as a genuine Christian should ever accept this reasoning. Even more disturbing is that Horn would emphasize the Catholic Catechism written in 1992 as an equal reference, as opposed to the Word of God itself as sole authority.

Papal infallibility is very convenient for the Church. What better way to convince millions of followers that what the pope says regarding faith and morals is an instruction from on high? No dispute. No arguing. This dogma came directly from God. These tactics are hard for Catholic followers to recognize as errors because it's long been taught, but papal infallibility is a man-made doctrine of deception. For over 1,800 years, it did not exist in the Church. Jesus never claimed it would happen, Peter never claimed it, and neither did Paul or the other apostles. Catholic spokespersons will argue that papal infallibility has not been exercised since 1950 in declaring the Assumption of Mary;[28] however, how often it has been used is not the point—it is an inaccurate dogma not condoned by Christ or the Scriptures. Interestingly, Eamon Duffy states about Mary's assumption,

> "The definition embarrassed many Catholic theologians, since it was unsupported in scripture and was unknown to the early Church, and it was a disaster for relations with other Churches ..."[29]

In fact, Pope Paul II wanted to "infallibly" promote Mary to Co-Redemptrix but cardinals discouraged it in lieu of the developing ecumenical movement.[30] The truth is that God could have chosen any of dozens of favorable teenage girls to be the physical birth mother of Jesus. To have a pope erroneously elevate Mary beyond biblical reference to a status similar to Christ is very disturbing theology, and should be rejected by all Christians. For parents who have had daughters, imagine your teenage daughter being exalted to a Co-Redeemer with Jesus Christ, promoted to be on the throne with God, and have millions of people go beyond veneration by praying to her and worshiping her. It would be preposterous to think of such foolishness. Mary had an awesome role in the Scriptures, along with dozens and dozens of other contributors (Abraham, Moses, Jacob, all of the apostles, and many more), but they would be horrified to discover themselves being placed on an exalted pedestal.

There are simply too many examples of popes promulgating incorrect theology and dispersing inaccurate doctrine over the centuries to affirm papal infallibility. One example is Pope John XXII and the erroneous view about the dead (that those who died in the faith did not see the presence of God until the Last Judgment) which he later had to retract because it wasn't official. An infallible pope was wrong, but not really, because it was not official. In fact, Pope Honorius was condemned as a heretic by the Third

Council of Constantinople. It's hard to imagine the Catholic Church condemning a pope, but they did. In fact, the more pertinent question might be, "Shouldn't there be a long list of condemned popes based on what has been unveiled so far?"

Here is Horn's explanation for a condemned pope: "But failing to lead the Church as one ought is not the same as infallibly teaching something that is false.[31]

There are other examples as well. We do know from history that Liberius, Zosimus, Vigilius, and Honorius—all earlier popes—did teach error, but Horn excuses the errors by stating that "none of them taught heresy in a way that was binding for the entire Church."[32]

One can only dance and trot around these fable statements for so long before the truth is out. Examples of common phrases that appear throughout this section of Horn's book are: "This case does not disprove the doctrine of papal infallibility," and, "This case does not refute papal infallibility."[33]

Another example is the appalling way the Church under Urban VIII treated the Italian astronomer Galileo when he put forward his conclusion that the sun was the fixed center of the solar system and Earth moved (heliocentrism). As a result of his discovery and opposition to the Church's view on the topic, he was put on trial and was forced to recant or face death. Galileo was threatened with torture and imprisoned, which later was commuted to house arrest. This was another major Catholic blunder of fallibility.

Pope Vigilius provided another example of teaching something regarding "faith and morals" and then changing his mind because of a conflict. It's a long and detailed story, but Roman Catholic scholar Richard Pride sums up the outcome:

> "It is unusual to have a debate in which two of the lengthiest contributions, arguing for diametrically opposed positions, are written by the same person. It is stranger still when both contributions claim to give the final and definitive ruling, closing the debate for all time."[34]

In other words, Vigilius spoke infallibly, but then changed his mind. This is the obvious problem with claiming a dogma not supported by the Scriptures. Even up to the eleventh or twelfth century, every single church father said that lending money at interest was immoral, but that later changed.[35] A doctrinal and moral proclamation was given, "but now we've changed our minds." We also clearly see a change of position regarding faith and morals with "no salvation outside our Church," and then there was a shift away from that thinking. A final example is what the Roman Catholic Church taught "infallibly" about capital punishment about 800 years ago, and then compare that with what it written in the Catechism today (CCC 2267). The bottom line is that when infallible teaching changes, it's not infallible; it did not come from God.

For Catholics to accept papal infallibility is to be entrapped by the Church's control. Even Roman Catholic scholars, like Brian Teirney, agree that this concept was never a part of the early Church:

> "There is no convincing evidence that papal infallibility formed any part of the theological or canonical tradition of the church before the thirteenth century; the doctrine was invented in the first place by a few dissident Franciscans because it suited their convenience to invent it; eventually, but only after much initial reluctance, it was accepted by the papacy because it suited the convenience of the popes to accept it."[36]

It is certainly worth appealing to Catholics who have been convinced of this unbiblical teaching to understand, as Gavin Ortlund put it, "the people of the Old Testament did not have an infallible teaching office, and yet they were able to discern and receive the Word of God given to them."[37] Ortlund proceeds to make the observation that popes did not pronounce infallible dogmas in the early Church and, in fact, did not even preside over the first seven ecumenical councils; emperors did. The popes were not consulted concerning these councils, and in some cases, not even invited (the First Council of Constantinople).

Other points of dishonesty come from Catholic authors who make blanket statements that the pope is infallible and end the sentence with a period before explaining the true meaning. Karl Keating, in his book *What Catholics Really Believe*, makes this mistake along with other sources like Catholic.com.

They later explain the limited scope of the concept. This highlights the fact that the use of the term at all is misleading. Infallible, by definition, means something or someone who is incapable of making a mistake. How then can it only apply at certain times? Here is the example in Keating's book: "The pope is infallible, but he isn't a know-it-all. His charism of infallibility, which he enjoys as the successor to Peter, is strictly limited."[38]

An uncanny number of mistakes have been made by the Catholic Church over the years, yet Catholic literature, websites, writers, and defenders often use the phrase "infallible Church" just as they do with "papal infallibility." The same logic applies here as well: "The Church is infallible ... well, that is they cannot be led to ever teach error." Yet, over and over again, the headline is "the infallible Church" as, once again, in Horn's book: "Christ founded an authoritative, infallible Church."[39]

It borders on deception to use the word "infallible" to advance an unbiblical ideology, and scholars know the Catholic Church has not been infallible, especially with respect to the teachings that have been proclaimed or its culpability in the murders of hundreds of thousands of people with different belief systems. All the evidence points to the Roman Catholic Church consistently leading its followers into error since its inception. These are patterns that should not be acceptable or condoned by honest Christians. The problem is the system, not Catholic followers. The fallacy is in the institution, not the hearts of the ones who follow their teachings. The system has overridden the simple Gospel of Christ because of its institutional nature and pattern of doing so.

When you override the simple message of Christ, you preach a different Gospel. When you introduce even a small amount of antifreeze into a savory pot of chili, all of it is destroyed, dangerous, and inedible. The apostles concluded not to add anything to the message that was already contained in the Scriptures. They knew that grace is Jesus plus nothing. Salvation is Jesus plus nothing. Forgiveness is Jesus plus nothing. Righteousness is Jesus plus nothing. Justification is Jesus plus nothing. The Catholic List changes, destroys, and desecrates the authentic, original, pure Gospel. You can't change or add or take away from the true Gospel and come away with anything beneficial.

Never Bow Down

I wish there was a kinder way to say this, but the deception inside the Roman Catholic Church goes deep, and the truth is the papacy and the surrounding hierarchy are unbiblical. It's all an illusion of spirituality, power, and prestige (the very opposite of humility), much developed and handed down by contentious popes as we have seen. It's a system that would be a complete enemy and opposition to the absolute truth of faith in Christ alone. The perversion and hypocrisy of all these past popes and the unfathomable number of priests and cardinals who practice homosexuality (revealed in Chapters 6, 7, and 8) are just swept under the rug to protect a false image and misconception of holiness.

The Roman Catholic Church boasts an "unbroken succession" which could not be further from the truth. The papacy is an unbiblical, broken system that Christ never intended. To read about the popes listed so far and call this an "unbroken succession ordained and initiated by Christ" is entirely deceptive and would require the complete denial of historical facts, the Scriptures, and the character of God. The early apostles would be astonished at the difference between what they taught and knew that Jesus wanted compared to what is practiced in today's Catholic Church, especially The Catholic List of rites, rituals, doctrines, and dogmas in Chapter 1.

When the blinders are taken off, you suddenly realize that it's all a facade, it's not real. Popes do not have any position sanctioned by God. It's a mirage, a front, a smokescreen, a pretense, a delusion; there is no vicar of Christ, there is no Peter's throne, there is no holy father (except our Heavenly Father). It's a system created by religious people with various motives, and as a result of parents trusting this system, thousands and thousands of kids have been sexually abused, destroying their view of Christianity, and misleading millions of individuals away from a simple Gospel. This difficult reality will be discussed more in Chapter 6 and 7.

As harsh as it sounds, the truth is that the Roman Catholic system is designed to indoctrinate and condition members from an early age to follow a theology that has little resemblance to the original Gospel. Instead, they promulgate a Gospel that has been ushered in by many problematic leaders.

Part of the indoctrination includes being told that every teaching is correct because of the Church's understanding of Sacred or Ecclesial Tradition, or because it's been around a long time. That conclusion, however, would not be using sound or reasonable logic. The early apostles had scriptural theology right and the original catholic Church had it right in adherence to the simple Gospel; the Roman Catholic Church has strayed away and developed its own accretions of dogma and theology.

Some natural questions emerge when validating a belief system based on the age of its origin and, separately, its mere size. Islam developed just a few hundred years after the beginning of Christianity and is still going strong today. Does that make it right? Do a long track record and a large number of followers make a good argument for the validity of any institution?

Joseph Smith ran out of the woods with a revelation from God almost 200 years ago, and now there are 17 million Mormon followers. Does that make it right? Does anyone think Mormonism or Islam will suddenly disappear? Of course, not. Tradition, age, and size are highly unreliable reasons to follow a teaching or to substantiate a doctrine. That is why it is beyond critical to always default back to the Scriptures, the original Gospel, and apostolic teachings. We are all responsible for spreading the good news about the resurrection and the teachings of Christ (Matthew 28:19-20, Mark 16:15-16, etc.).

It is very difficult for someone born into the Catholic system (a cradle Catholic) or any denominational situation to ever be objective about their belief system. Their family roots are just too deep. The solution is not complicated, it's extremely simple: Instead of being consumed and obsessed with a Church, we simply follow Jesus. We do this with no required attachment or bondage to an institution, although the right church can play a vital role in Christianity.

If you are an honest Catholic and you have sincerely examined the contextual roots of Catholicism and find that truths in this book and other similar sources are not ever spoken of at Mass, what do you do? Do you bury your head in the sand, sweep all the embarrassing stuff under the rug, convince yourself that what you have heard all your life about "succession of the papacy" and the doctrines and dogmas of the Catholic Church are true, and just accept the distorted reality? If you don't want to hear about what happened, if it's too scary to think you have been wrong this entire time, if you are comfortable with where you are spiritually—"Don't disrupt my peace; my mom, dad, and Church leaders know best."—I tell you, my friends, the risk is that you'll miss the true blessing of "following Jesus" and be completely burned out by religious requirements.

The truth, sometimes, is very difficult to hear, but it has to be revealed. The pope should not have salvific authority over anyone. He is just an ordinary man directing the glory and focus from Christ onto himself. The papacy has no place in the Christian arena, and the Church has no jurisdiction over someone's soul.

Some Catholics have expressed in forums about arriving in Heaven, seeing the Father, Jesus, and Mary on the throne, and just below them are all the popes from the centuries sitting on their thrones, the cardinals beneath them and a few angels hanging around playing harps. However, I would rather dash their hopes before they arrive; that will not be the layout. Many popes and cardinals might not be there; Mary is probably in the crowd with the rest of the genuine believers, bowing to and worshipping our Heavenly Father, but she is not on our Heavenly Father's throne. In fact, in a shocking statement, look at what Catholic apologist Joe Heschmeyer says about popes regarding Heaven:

> "It's possible for the pope not to be in heaven—only about a third of the popes are canonized—we hold out hope for the other two thirds."[40]

This statement truly substantiates all of the information that was revealed in the first two chapters about nefarious popes, and creates a crossroads for all Catholics. By mere common sense, wouldn't a logical conclusion be that if multiple popes are not going to Heaven—and they were the absolute leaders of the whole Christian Church—no Christian, at any time, should ever be under the authority of the pope? One can easily conclude that all Christians should look to Jesus Christ and the Scriptures as our only infallible authorities.

Popes "representing" Christ have accepted all the adoration, attention, superiority, and power given to them over the centuries. They have even welcomed tens of thousands of laypeople bowing down to them as if they were mini gods. Contrast that with what Peter said when someone came into his presence and fell to the ground in reverence and adoration of him:

> "As Peter entered the house, Cornelius met him and fell at his feet in reverence. But Peter made him get up. 'Stand up!' He said, 'I am only a man myself'" (Acts 10:25-26).

Translation: "What are you doing? Jesus Christ is the *only* one we reverence and worship. Please get up and never do that again. I am an ordinary man, just like you." Peter confirmed it. He was not any different than any of us who are genuine Christians. "Go spread the good news; Jesus has risen." Let's all go do this! That's the message. No hierarchy. Spread the good news at work, in your neighborhood, with people you come in contact with—no canonization, no calling one Christian a saint while others are not; we all have the privilege of being a part of the Great Commission. We are all part of a movement about Jesus. We are all a part of His story to let everyone know He has risen and accomplished His mission.

I think about the thousands of Catholics who have bowed down to popes of the past, kissing their feet or kissing their rings, thoroughly and unknowingly going against all biblical protege. Peter would have had no part in it whatsoever, but Roman Catholic popes allowed it. Peter knew he was called, just like every born-again believer on the planet, to spread the good news about Jesus without any title or superiority. This included not forming a strict hierarchy to do so by elevating people to a status they have no business holding. That simply did not occur with the early apostles.

In his book, Trent Horn reveals his biases and protection for the Catholic faith with regard to elevating popes: "Some critics claim that the humble bishops of Rome would have looked nothing like modern popes who move through throngs of people via the 'popemobile.'" I could not agree more with this initial presumption made by Horn; he continues, "In one sense that's true, but the first humble house churches would have looked nothing like modern Protestant 'mega-churches.'"[41]

Notice two avoidances Horn makes on that last statement which seems to be an attempt to deflect from the truth:

First, shouldn't Horn have included the massive, incredible opulent Catholic cathedrals in his critique of "mega-churches"?

Second, notice the deflection away from the self-absorbed image of a pope riding through throngs in the popemobile, being worshipped by his followers. Most Christians would agree that neither Peter, Paul, nor any other apostle would have been a spectacle riding in a popemobile. Of course, there were no popemobiles during that time, but the popemobile is the opposite of humility. Videos and historic writings give visual and written evidence of popes basking in the glory. It's very disturbing to watch and read about.

Although papal customs (a pope riding in the popemobile) or physical traditions (kissing the pope's feet) do not disprove Catholic theology, there is no disputing that they provide a window into actions that imitate pompous leaders, consumed with self-importance.

If you think the dubious popes were only in medieval times or the distant past (and most of the depraved ones were), be aware that pope errors and horrible decision-making still occur in modern times. Pope Francis called for the passage of civil union laws for same-sex couples and was caught covering up sexual abuse by Cardinal Theodore McCarrick, allowing him to continue to serve unpunished.

Pope Francis has formally approved the blessing of same-sex couples by Catholic priests, a flagrant rebellion against God's established model for marriage between one man and one woman. It's a decision that could never be condoned by God or established Scripture. In addition, Pope Francis appointed a close friend, Eugenio Raul Zaffaroni, to a Vatican position regardless of his support for abortion and the LGBT agenda.[42] Zaffaroni has been investigated and evidence shows that he owns numerous apartments in Buenos Aires that are being used for a lucrative prostitution business.[43]

The corruption in the papacy is certainly not limited to the medieval times or the past.

Joe Heschmeyer, the Catholic author of *Pope Peter*, says:

"The church right now is going through a period of crisis, at least in part because of bad papal and episcopal leadership. The household of God, which is the Church of the living God, is going through the roughest patch it's seen in centuries. Pretending, otherwise, is dishonest and sets non-Catholics up for disappointment."[44]

The Catholic Church would love to plead "not guilty" on behalf of the popes against the proven charges that have been brought against them over the centuries. Readers will have to decide for themselves just how guilty these popes are, but regardless of opinion, it will not change the historical evidence. Institutions like the Roman Catholic Church, which on the surface seem commendable and praiseworthy, eventually crumble under the facts preceding them.

The situation is similar to what is commonly seen in crime documentary programs on television. Defendants are shown videos of themselves at the scene perpetrating a crime, like rushing into a store full of people, guns drawn, opening fire, and killing people in the process. Later asked, "How do you plead?", they almost always claim "not guilty." It's just the dishonest and corrupt segment of the world we live in. The video evidence is not even enough. When there is a preponderance of evidence, there is always a shaking of the head and quiet laughter in the room when they plead "not guilty."

Catholic spokesmen along with attendees and defenders enter a plea of "not guilty" for past popes. Instead, a scapegoat is put forth, an individual pope who probably did a few things wrong—after all, "they're not perfect, just infallible ... well, sometimes." The audience in the room just quietly shakes their heads and laughs. History has spoken.

The reigning pope could clear out 1,700 years of heresy in one day by admitting that the Roman Catholic Church—via so many nefarious leaders with ulterior motives—changed the message of the early catholic Church and has been teaching altered doctrines ever since. He could have a major impact on Christianity by admitting that there is no basis for a hierarchy and that there is no God-ordained papal office or magisterium. Instead, and moving forward from this day on, the pope could pass along one instruction from the early Church and the apostles: "Follow Him. Follow Jesus and tell every-one you know about the resurrection, and that sins are no longer being held against mankind. Our platform changes today!"

But the train has been in motion for a long time. It's doubtful the pope will ever do it. He will probably not concede. It would be very difficult and embarrassing for any pope to swallow their pride and go back to the original Gospel. They know that the Holy Spirit is the vicar of Christ, not themselves. They know that Jesus is the only head of the Christian Church. They surely recognize that they have no infallible powers. However, all it would take is a return to the original Gospel, what Jesus taught and predicted, what the apostles carried forward, and what links every Christian saint together:

Christ died for our sins

He was buried

He was raised

He appeared

Reconciliation was complete

Sins are no longer counted against us

Follow Him

And when you get lost in theology, traditions, and false doctrines, you can end up burned out on religion and guilt. You may find yourself striving for something unattainable, living in fear about your eternal standing, and going through the motions of useless repetitions. In that moment, you can make a personal choice to leave the system and instead embrace, cling to, and follow Christ and the message of the one and only true Gospel:

Christ died for our sins

He was buried

He was raised

He appeared

Reconciliation was complete

Sins are no longer counted against us

Follow Him

That's the Gospel message.

Questions Catholics must consider

1. Based on the evidence presented in the past three chapters, does it still seem logical to consider the pope the head of the Christian Church?

2. Do the facts that have been disclosed about past popes match what you have always known to be true about the papacy, or is it far worse than you thought?

3. Were you aware that most of the popes that have been mentioned acted in their own best interest and not the interest of the Church?

4. Were you aware that corruption could be this extensive throughout the history of the papacy?

5. If so many of popes exhibited these types of immoral and self-interest behaviors, is it logical to conclude that it's only fair to question doctrines and dogmas that have been proclaimed by the Church as stated in The Catholic List at the end of Chapter 1?

6. In honest evaluation, do you think that the positive achievements of the Church override and should dismiss the papal depravity over the centuries?

7. Do you think it is possible to live the Christian life fully and completely separate from a pope and magisterium, relying solely on the indwelling Holy Spirit as your guide, and Jesus Christ as the only mediator to the Heavenly Father?

8. After looking at what scholars had to say, does it make sense to conclude that the papacy we know today did not exist in the primitive Church?

9. Being very truthful, based on the past three chapters, do you think that today's Roman Catholic Church very closely resembles the universal catholic (small c) Church of the first century, or apostolic teachings in the Scriptures?

10. Finally, if the primary goal in the Christian life, the primary priority in the Christian life, and the primary way to accomplish God's will in the Christian life is to lift Jesus up (He increases; we decrease), how do you think the popes score, based on the past three chapters?

PART II:

THE EARLY CHURCH

CHAPTER 4

The Early Church: A Movement, Not a Hierarchy

As we leave a disturbing history of Catholic popes, it's only appropriate to look at what the Church was originally supposed to be about. What was the original intention? What did Jesus have in mind for his followers moving forward after he ascended to Heaven? As we find ourselves in the middle of God's story here on Earth post-resurrection, what do we do now? What is the most authentic and purest definition of the Church?

I believe if you were to ask most Christians about the history of the Church from Pentecost until today, they would not be able to share many details about what happened during this 2,000-year span. For many, it's just too incomprehensible to think about. I have to admit, immersing oneself in multiple 600-page books about all that history would not be very exciting or motivating for the average person.

Nevertheless, to go back to the Roman Empire and watch the emperors' barbaric way of operating, and mingle that with early Christianity as it was trying to establish itself in the middle of Judaism that had been around for thousands of years, and couple that with the numerous pagan religions prevalent in the region, all the Church divisions, and various influential individuals coming along who had their own angles on theology—well, it creates quite a show.

The early Church was a crazy place to be. Even the first apostles were striving to get on the same page about *exactly* what was to be taught and proclaimed because Judaism and the followers of Mosaic law (obsolete after the cross) were trying to work their way back into the equation.

Although little detail of this 2000-year history is known by the average believer, most Christians are fairly adamant that their view of Christianity, their denomination, their church, their faith, their pastor, and their priest are the ones that have most of the details correct theologically; or at least the ones that are the closest. I guess we can all admit to having a certain amount of pride and confidence, and even a pinch of arrogance, when it comes to that type of thinking.

My challenge to the reader in these next chapters is to find a way to step out of the forest, out of predisposed, indoctrinated positions, release the attachment from a denomination or belief system or particular leader that you have been enamored with for decades, and take a fresh look at the original Gospel; and for many, to do that for the very first time.

What was God really trying to accomplish by sending Jesus to be the final sacrifice? And how did that simple message get so convoluted, contaminated, complicated, and conflicting over the centuries by the Church? Would we ever be willing to erase everything on the blackboards of our minds and start over again with just Christ? Is that too scary to think about?

If it's not too scary to think about, would it even be that easy? If you do take a step back, and somehow find a way to be objective instead of subjective, and realize that your belief system might not be quite right, will you actually be willing to shift your thinking, change your heart, and solely focus on the truth revealed by our Heavenly Father, through Jesus Christ, with the guidance of the Holy Spirit?

I am not suggesting changing your mind because of what is written in these pages. This book will barely scratch the surface of Christianity in 2000 years. But change as a result of your own self-reflection if you allowed yourself, unknowingly, to be molded or even brainwashed by a "system" as opposed to adhering to the pure, unadulterated, simple message of Jesus.

The Early Church

A fitting starting place would be to look at the basics of the early Church. One of the biggest misconceptions is that Jesus Christ started the Roman Catholic Church. However, that is not exactly an accurate assumption. Jesus started the Church (ekklesia), a gathering of people—mostly in the private homes of the wealthy, but also in rented halls in markets and public baths— without a single dominate officer.[1] The Church centered around one central event (the cross and resurrection), focused on one single person (Jesus Christ), and the simple message that God initiated a plan (without our permission, but on our behalf) to reconcile the world back to Himself, not counting men's sins against them.

This message was carried forth by the first apostles who called their movement "The Way". Later, at Antioch, the people that followed Jesus were called "Christians". After about AD 70, the apostles had all died, and the churches that were established by Paul and the main Church in Jerusalem were in the hands of others. This period began "the age of catholic Christianity" or universal Christianity.

This book attempts to distinguish between original catholic Christianity (what Christianity was like in its early inception), and Roman Catholic Christianity, which produced a major shift in doctrine and practices as the centuries went by. The Roman Catholic Church would like to believe that both are indistinguishably linked. The evidence seen so far and the evidence in the coming chapters, however, will show that not to be true.

First, what is Christianity? As Andy Stanley put it in his sermon series, "The Big Church":

> "The foundation and anchor of our faith is in a person—Jesus Christ. The historical, biblical, verifiable fact that Jesus walked on this earth, claimed to be God, gave us evidence supporting His claim, died for our sin, rose from the dead and ascended back to heaven in front of hundreds of witnesses. That is why we believe."[2]

This was the theme throughout the book of John and the other three synoptic Gospels (Matthew, Mark, and Luke), it was the message of the early Church, and exactly what Jesus said right before He ascended back to Heaven: Go into all the world and proclaim this message that you have witnessed.

What was the early Church like, compared to today's Roman Catholic Church and many Protestant denominations? What was opening day like—Peter's very first sermon? It was the most basic, simple message: believe Jesus was the Son of God, believe He died and rose again, change your mind about everything (repentance), and follow Jesus Christ. Christianity was a movement and not an institution.

In Acts 2, Peter laid out the basics of the Gospel (the cross and resurrection) before thousands of people, and at the end of the message had the very first invitation to begin the Christian journey, as described in Acts 2:38: "Repent and be baptized." Change your mind, change the direction of your life, believe that what we are telling you is true, trust and follow Jesus Christ, and you will receive the Holy Spirit.

There were no buildings, no stained-glass windows, no Mary veneration, no rosary, no pope, no traditions, no bands, no staff, no hierarchy, no confession to a priest, no penance, no Purgatory, no statues, no procedures, no institutions, no required behaviors, no participation requirements in the salvation process, no fatiguing list of things to do, and no required sacramental system.

The early Church and its message revolved around the simple fact of the resurrection, that Jesus was who He claimed to be, and a New Covenant is now in place, ushered in by God. It's absolutely like nothing you have ever seen or heard about and has no resemblance to the Old Covenant or the way of life you knew before.

After that first invitation in Acts 2, about 3,000 heard the message (in their own languages) and responded. This all happened about two months after the resurrection, and the message was so incredibly simple. It wasn't a process. It wasn't about massive cathedrals (there were no church buildings). It wasn't about tradition (Jesus came to do away with traditions and Old Covenant requirements). It wasn't about vain repetition. It wasn't about a hierarchy controlling you. It was about Jesus, the Christ, the Son of the living God, who rose from the dead, paid for the sins of the entire world (both past, present, and in the future), satisfying every single righteous requirement, and ushering in an understandable, perfect grace system, just as was predicted.

As you look at the early Church and how it so clearly defined its message around a single idea and a single person, you see a commonality among most Christians in our belief in the crucifixion, the resurrection, the payment for sins, and the desire to spread the message to the entire world (and both

Catholics and Protestants agree). Back then, Stanley notes, there was an excitement and enthusiasm around the simple Gospel; unfortunately, that later changed when a movement became an organization, anchored itself inside a building, and fell subject to a hierarchy and self-serving, monarchical abusers making up their own system and changing the message.

Amazingly, in the midst of a religious institution taking the message of Jesus and polluting it with man-made requirements and false doctrines of self-effort theology for centuries, there have always been groups of people, even since the opening day at Pentecost, that never got away from understanding the simplicity of following Jesus. They decided that they were not going to be controlled by an organization or system, that the Scriptures were for everyone, and they were willing to die to see to it that this would not be stolen away from them.

It was a resistance against going back to Old Testament Judaism where you have to approach God via another individual in a synagogue. They walked in the understanding that if you are a Christian, you are the temple of God— God lives and houses Himself inside of us as a result of His finished work.

> "... For we are the temple of the living God. As God has said: 'I
> will live with them and walk among them, and I will be their God,
> and they will be my people'" (2 Corinthians 6:16).

So, as believers, when we serve the poor, we are the Church. When we gather in a home for Bible study, we are the Church. When we go across seas to build an orphanage, we are the Church. When we teach the simple Gospel to kids and teenagers, we are the Church. When we exercise biblical principles in our workplace and businesses, we are the Church. The true Church is not a place. The Church is not a building with steeples or leaders wearing robes, a formal bulletin, banners, rituals, or repetitions. The Church is not the government. The Church is not an acknowledged magisterium. The Church is not an institution with a hierarchy.

The Church is us (2 Corinthians 6:16). God lives inside of us (1 John 4:12). Go spread the news: Jesus has risen, Jesus has forgiven us one-time and forever; we follow Jesus. The Bible sits in our home. As Stanley states, we don't have to attend Mass and have someone read it to us, or wait until we get to church to have someone read it for us. We have total freedom in Christ separate from an institution.

The Roman Catholic System

The Roman Catholic Church (a name, once again, distinguished and separate from the first-century catholic Church by principle), as mentioned in the last three chapters, brutalized and murdered and did everything in its power not to lose control of its followers. A history of religious aggression developed over centuries via military force to conquer anyone with different beliefs, leaving the original Gospel in a state where it was barely recognizable.

We see this type of immoral control in the political arena with authoritarians over the masses, we see it in families with domineering spouses who control and abuse, and we especially see it in the religious landscape. The modern-day Roman Catholic Church still holds power over its 1.4 billion followers. They will never relinquish that power, and their doctrines will never stop evolving on issues again and again as they announce, "This is what we believe now, this is what you do now, this is where we stand now— we are in control, we are sanctioned by Christ, we stand in the place of Christ. Listen to us, do not question us or our dogmas or you will be eternally anathema (formally cursed by the Church)."

Anytime a religious entity or institution tries to change the original Gospel and usurp authority over its followers, there is ample reason for concern. This is especially so when that institution pronounces endless damnations on those who do not follow their path. It is critical to understand, despite what is taught in the parish, that the pope, cardinals, priests, magisterium, liturgy, and dogmas should not have any authority over their members based on what has been uncovered so far; and especially what will be discovered in the chapters ahead. Those Christians who have a relationship with God through Jesus Christ, with the guidance of the Holy Spirit, absent of authority from their institution or hierarchy, enjoy amazing freedom.

When a system makes the decision to add to that simplicity (additions that comprise most of the Catholic faith, referred to in this book as The Catholic List), that is something each Christian will have to reconcile for themselves if they decide to adhere to that type of teaching. However, following The Catholic List can be like choosing to jump into quicksand—it's paralyzing and stagnates the Christian life.

The Roman Catholic institution is structured in such a way that its followers are often times bogged down in religious requirements and procedures, living in constant fear about one's eternity. When that happens, it ruins the freedom that the New Covenant established. Much more on the freedom we can have in Christ is presented in Chapters 9 through 11.

James, Peter, John, Paul, and many others were awesome, authentic, legitimate Jesus followers who risked everything to go into places where they were not welcome, carrying this New Covenant message that spelled out the new way we relate to God on this side of the cross. These early apostles were willing to die for that original faith—that original simple message, that life in the New Covenant—to continue the movement that Jesus started.

Saul (later known as Paul) was a primary perpetrator of the persecution of Christians before his conversion, and for about three years, he went door to door (because that's where the church met) looking for anyone belonging to The Way, dragging them into the streets to be tortured. Andy Stanley recognizes this amazing insight in Acts: Saul was on the way to Damascus to persecute more Christians and was suddenly blinded by a light from Heaven when he heard God's voice say, "Saul, Saul, why do you persecute me?" (Acts 9:4 ESV).

Saul was persecuting the Church, yet Jesus asked, "Why are you persecuting me?" The Church was never a building.[3] The Church was never a formal hierarchy. The Church is Jesus inside of us, and if Catholics can come to the understanding that their loyalty is not to their Church, not to Church leaders, not to institutional doctrine, not to a regiment or repetition or men in religious apparel, but simply to their Heavenly Father, everything changes. The dirty window of one's perspectives, with regard to how we relate to God, becomes sparkling clear.

We do not go through a religious system to get to God. The Church should never hold to a military-type structure with strict requirements and rigid instructions to make it into God's kingdom. We go directly to God, through Christ, absent of Mary, absent of a priest, a dead saint, or a sacramental procedure on a certain day with certain requirements. That liturgy is fabricated and has no spiritual validity. We have full access to our Heavenly Father 24/7, absent any intermediaries except Jesus Christ. He is the only One who qualifies.

True believers in the early Church, along with the apostles, were uncompromising and understood these critical principles to be true, but oppression finally came. Multiple books have been written just on the persecution of the early Church. It was horrendous and cruel. Most Christians today have never experienced anything that even closely resembles the torture of the martyrs of the early Church. These Christians died to preserve the original message and not surrender to an institution.

This type of faith continued for a few hundred years (James, Peter, and Paul were long gone by then), and the "inside" corruption started via the Roman Catholic Church that would go on to persecute and torture far more Christians than the early Church experienced from secular sources. Stanley describes the transition from a movement to a building:

> "Jesus launched a gathering around one simple idea, one simple mission, one simple focus. Then there was this transition from a movement to a "location"; from a "gathering" around an idea to a hierarchy; and if you know anything about history or medieval times, everything went embarrassingly wrong about "church". And that terrible time revolved around a misunderstanding of the word "church", and within 300 years, things were a mess. And instead of the simple idea of an "ekklesia" it transitioned to [a] Lord's House which could be any religious gathering; and this transition from a movement to a place (like a temple in the Old Testament) led to some horrible theology and before long the church was located in a building, and whoever controlled the building controlled the church, and whoever controlled the building controlled the Scriptures, and whoever controlled the building controlled the people. And in some places in Europe, whoever controlled the building and the Scripture and the people even controlled the government, and what began as a movement to distribute truth throughout the world became an "insider" focused, hierarchal, rit-

ualistic—and in some way a pagan and immoral—destructive and unethical movement with no reflection at all with what happened in the first century. All this happened in about 300 AD."[4]

The network of gatherings of people (the Church) meeting mostly in homes and a few public places (around a single person and a single event), along with small *ekklesias* that Paul was establishing, had some of its biggest changes right after Constantine legalized Christianity, blending politics and religion—Christianity and paganism—just before AD 315.

The Gospel centered around Jesus's goal to implement the New Covenant (God's new way of relating to mankind on this side of the Cross), centered around being transformed and born again with a renewed mind that has repented (choosing to cease following self, and simply doing what Jesus called everyone to do: follow Him). All this is done when an individual comes to these conclusions with genuine faith, trust, belief, and surrender absent from self-effort and self-righteousness. That is the essence of the original Gospel.

The Simple Gospel

The simple Gospel listed above is not an "ongoing" salvation process, not a striving to reach the kingdom, not doing just enough good works to tilt the scale, not crossing your fingers and hoping you get in. There's no complicated doctrine and no complicated theology that barely anyone can understand. The simple Gospel is not confessing to a priest in a dark room, no penance, no indulgences, no praying to a woman who has never heard a single word, no process of doing sacraments as a pathway to salvation, no performance-based system, no Purgatory and "getting cleaned up before you enter in." There is simply no "journey" to salvation.

Instead, simply believe that Jesus is the Christ, the Son of God, repent (change your mind) about the direction you were going, and follow Him. That was the message of the original Gospel. That was the message of Paul and the apostles. That was the message of the early Church.

We see this simplistic message in a couple hundred places in the Bible, including in Acts 9:15, shortly after Saul became Paul, where it was spoken of him, "This man is my chosen instrument to proclaim my name to the Gentiles and their kings and to the people of Israel." From there he simply taught in the synagogues and places he went that *Jesus is the Son of God*. That was essentially the whole message.

Paul headed out, away from Jerusalem to Turkey and Greece and throughout the Mediterranean, starting little *ekklesias* (gatherings of individuals) centered around that single message: Jesus is the Son of God. He wrote multiple books of the Bible during his journey (many from prison); some of those books were lost but many currently make up most of the New Testament. The central theme of Paul's message is summarized in 1 Corinthians 15:3-4:

> "For what I received I passed on to you as of first importance: that Christ died for our sins according to the Scriptures, that he was buried, that he was raised on the third day according to the Scriptures" (NIV).

Again, we see the message of the original apostles:

Christ died for our sins.

He was buried.

He was raised.

He appeared.

Will you follow Him?

And with all the different accounts, sometimes with verses that seem to say one thing, but a few verses later say something else, with all the different interpretations, theologies, scholars, and apologists, and especially institutions trying to take hostage the scriptures, everything still comes back to:

Christ died for our sins.

He was buried.

He was raised.

He appeared.

Will you follow Him?

Are you willing to believe this is true? If so, join the movement and follow Jesus. The foundation of all Christianity—the foundation of the Church—is encapsulated in those two verses above. That's the Gospel. No tithing, no system, no procedures, no hierarchy, no complicated process, no honoring a pope like a king, no going back to the old ways of Judaism and the priesthood. The Gospel is *only* about the story of Jesus.

Stanley describes how the first-century Church had its challenges, and one of the conflicts was over who should be a part of the Church.[5] Who gets in, how good do you have to be, how many rules do you have to keep, how holy do you have to be, how much of your lifestyle do you have to clean up before you can be accepted in the Church? The Jewish believers, with the primary Ten Commandments and an additional 613 laws that they were brought up to keep, thought Jesus was just an extension of Judaism, and that you had to be a follower of Moses before you could follow Jesus. Effectively, you had to become Jewish before you became a Christian. This point of confusion for the Church back then is critical to understanding the system that Christians are now under.

> "For the law was given through Moses; grace and truth came through Jesus Christ" (John 1:17).

Jesus came and confronted Judaism and brought in a different way to relate to God, a movement that shocked and angered the established religion. The New Covenant changed everything. Jesus marched onto the scene and openly violated the Sabbath laws and challenged religious self-effort and spiritual arrogance. The Pharisees were notorious for trying to project an illusion of holiness with their showmanship, standing and praying repetitious prayers, and trying to keep every single Jewish law as a way of working their way to the kingdom. But Jesus came along with His message of repentance, belief, faith, and grace and debunked their self-righteousness. Essentially, Jesus rejected the established, self-righteous system of that day.

As offensive as it may sound, it's a very similar parallel to the "illusion" Catholic leadership portrays and requires of their members today. The Pharisees are representative of many of the religious leaders we hold today in such high esteem—the leadership in many of our Protestant churches, but especially in the Catholic Church. These Pharisees were kind of "professional good people." They were the holiest and best people around during that day. They wore all the right clothes, said all the right things, and were all about following the law. In fact, they made up rules for following rules, inventing a system to keep "in good standing" with God (Matthew 23:2-26).

Stanley describes this in another series with a scene where Jesus was teaching His disciples one day and pointed out these Pharisees (the "good" people) and said they would never be good enough to make it into His kingdom. This was perplexing to the disciples, because if the Pharisees (the "best" law followers around during those days) were not going to Heaven, they questioned, "What about us?"

As the narrative progressed, Jesus approached all the "bad" people of that day who demonstrated just a little faith and said, "You're forgiven." The thief on the cross became a classic example. The disciples were baffled by His teaching that these "religious professionals" were not going to Heaven, but the worst of sinners were getting in all because of faith? Jesus's indictment carries to today's Catholic Church leaders—and those of many Protestant denominations—that their religious professionalism means nothing in His kingdom.

> "Woe to you, teachers of the law and Pharisees, you hypocrites! You are like white-washed tombs, which look beautiful on the outside but on the inside are full of dead men's bones and everything unclean. In the same way, on the outside you appear to people as righteous but on the inside you are full of hypocrisy and wickedness" (Matthew 23:27-28).

The message Jesus spoke when He walked the earth, and the message proclaimed by the early Church and apostles, was a simple message of faith centered around a single person (Jesus Christ) and a single event (the resurrection). Pious and showy religious orders, procedures, rituals, requirements, repetitions, allusions of holiness, and a "pathway to salvation based on human effort" were not what Jesus condoned—He condemned them.

That message changed a couple hundred years later, and it is down the road of that change that you now find today's Roman Catholic Church operating a system that looks very different from the original Gospel, preaching a message that Jesus or the apostles would not recognize. Today's Catholic Church could be better described as religion with Jesus still depicted hanging on a cross, a whole lot of Mary, and a long, complicated man-made list of obtaining and maintaining salvation through religious self-effort. Popes and Catholic leadership have promulgated a different Gospel for the past 1,700 years that only vaguely resembles Peter's ground-breaking message in Acts 2.

The Bible for All

In the sixteenth century, after about 1,200 years of an out-of-control religion with unbelievably bad popes and a Gospel that no longer reflected a clear picture of what Jesus or the early apostles intended, something incredible happened. William Tindale, an English author and linguistic scholar decided that the average person should have their own copy of the Bible. Anyone researching history (with no bias) will quickly learn this infuriated the Catholic Church.

The Roman Catholic Church had centuries to form their own doctrines, dogmas, and traditions unchallenged, and had become a powerful religious and political colossus. It was a machine to control the masses by initiating and instigating whatever would keep the followers submissive and dependent. Unexpectedly, Tindale entered the equation with the idea that every person had a right to the Scriptures.

Tindale recognized the insanity of a system in which believers had to go to the Roman Catholic Church and listen to a priest read the Bible in a language nobody even understood, providing random interpretations. Whoever controlled the Church controlled the Scriptures, controlled the interpretation, and controlled the people. Tindale concluded, "Enough of this nonsense." God's people had a right to have access to the truth of His Word with an actual copy they could hold in their hands, hold next to their heart as they slept at night, possess in their own home, and memorize in their own language—a copy not written in Latin (meaningless to just about everyone), but in English, translated directly from the Greek and Hebrew writings.

I can only imagine the excitement, the enthusiasm, the relief to finally not be in the dark anymore, to finally, *not* be dependent on a priest to understand the powerful words of Christ and the authors of the Scriptures. Imagine discovering verses that were never previously read, or never interpreted properly. Imagine the joy, peace, and freedom they must have experienced reading:

> "For God so loved the world that he gave his one and only Son, that whosoever believes in him shall not perish but have everlasting life" (John 3:16).

> "And if by grace, then it is no longer by works; if it were, grace would no longer be grace" (Romans 11:6).

> "For it is by grace you have been saved, through faith—and this not from yourselves, it is the gift of God—not by works, so that no one can boast" (Ephesians 2:8-9).

> "I write to you, dear children, because your sins have been forgiven on account of [Jesus's] name" (John 2:12).

> "But because of His great love for us, God, who is rich in mercy, made us alive with Christ even when we were dead in transgressions—it is by grace you have been saved. And God raised us up with Christ and seated us with him in the heavenly realms in Christ Jesus" (Ephesians 2:4-6).

> "See to it that no one takes you captive through hollow and deceptive philosophy, which depends on human tradition and the basic principles of this world rather than on Christ" (Colossians 2:8).

> "Know that a man is not justified by observing the law, but by faith in Jesus Christ. So we, too, have put our faith in Christ Jesus that we may be justified by faith in Christ and not by observing the law, because by observing the law no one will be justified" (Galatians 2:16).

One can only imagine reading and understanding for the very first time all the amazing verses above and hundreds more just like them after all those centuries of sitting on the pews listening to Latin being muttered out like a meaningless ritual of just doing what you are told to do, no questions asked.

It's the true definition of spiritual bondage and mind control. Many call that tradition; but in truth, it was a mystical religious prison.

For the average Church member to hold a copy of the Bible in their hand, to be able to read it, and have the Holy Spirit guide them to the truth was just remarkable. It was an incredible contrast to the old line: "Just trust us; no matter what we say, what we make up, what we require, just do as we tell you to do." That was the message from the Roman Catholic Church. Enough was enough.

Who could ever follow a Church that has been such an adversary to the freedom Christ intended? The answer would prove to be those individuals trapped in a building, trapped in a system, trapped in an institution, trapped by requirements and procedures, trapped by a formal, confusing process of obtainment to achieve a "salvation" that looks nothing like what Christ came to give through His grace.

I can also imagine those individuals who finally obtained a copy of the Bible, in their own language, reading verses like the ones listed above (along with many more) and thinking, "Wow, I have never heard this perspective before. This isn't exactly lining up with what we have been taught over the years." This was the first time someone pulled the curtains back and exposed the institution for what it was and showed the beauty of the Christian life outside of its prison walls. This was all happening in the 1500s.

Let that be the red flag, the bright flashing light, the bell that goes off loud enough to deafen you as a warning that when you are told what to think, told that an institution is in charge of forming your belief system, taking biblical themes and verses out of context and not allowing anyone to interpret for themselves under the guidance of the Holy Spirit. When you peek out the window and see the truth, you will inevitably want to leave the bondage of the building and run outside and experience that freedom.

This goes for any spiritual influence that holds your freedom in Christ hostage by making the claim that the only source of truth is coming from their faith perspective, their dogma, their doctrine, their statement of faith, their pulpit with messages proclaiming: "If you have been directed in any way other than what we speak, regardless if you think it came from the Holy Spirit or your personal quiet time studying and looking at the Scriptures, you are damned for even considering any of these other options." When you get that false message from a religious entity, my best advice is, "*Run, Forest, run!*" The best action would be to separate yourself from that influence, person, ideology, or institution.

Stanley shares and continues the story that Tindale became an outlaw because of the hatred the Catholic Church had for what he had accomplished, and he was forced to flee to Germany where he continued his English translation. Because of the incredible inventor and craftsman named Johannes Gutenberg (who developed a version of the printing press and the use of oil-based ink for printing books), translations of the Bible could spread across the world. This printing facility allowed Tindale to get a massive number of Bibles into print (finally, in a readable language), smuggled back into England, and distributed all throughout Europe. Was Tindale's and Gutenberg's combined effort a coincidence? Many would agree that God was right in the middle of directing these two amazing individuals.

Tindale was eventually betrayed and hung, but his mission had been accomplished. Finally, people had a translation of the Bible outside of church walls. During his trial, he was quoted as saying, "If God spare my life, ere many years, I will cause a boy that driveth the plow to know more of the Scripture than thou dost."[6]

He also said that he wanted every single person to be able to hold the Holy Scriptures in their hand. This drove the Catholic Church crazy because when he translated *ekklesia* (church), the context was a "congregation," a "gathering" of individuals who wanted to be a part of the movement about Christ, not a controlling entity.

Tindale's translation marks the beginning of the process to squeegee the dirt of deception off the windows so that people could understand that Jesus will build His *ekklesia*, His movement, His congregation, His assembly, and the gates of hell will not prevail against it (Matthew 16:18). Regardless of how many religious pretenders with illusions of holiness and false doctrines come and go, His movement (the message about the resurrection and His plan to reconcile mankind back to Himself) will continue forever.

True to nature, the Roman Catholic Council of Trent (1545-1564) placed the Bible on its list of prohibited books and forbade any person to read the Bible without a license from a Roman Catholic bishop. They prohibited anyone from reading the Scripture in a language other than Latin. The council declared: "That if anyone shall dare to read or keep in his possession that book, without such a license, he shall not receive absolution til he has given it up to his ordinary."[7]

The *modus operandi* of the Roman Catholic Church seems to be control: "Do it our way or you will pay the price." They made constant threats to achieve that agenda. They did it with the Bible, and they did it with anyone who had a different belief system. The Roman Catholic Church hunted individuals down, imprisoned them, tortured them, and even dragged civil authorities into their schemes to execute them. It's completely indicative of manipulation, but certainly not reflective of the love of Christ.

The most obvious question to ask when observing an institution trying to conceal the written Word of God is, "What truths are you trying to hide?" That question was answered when the Bible was finally obtained outside the Church walls, revealing that the Roman Catholic Church and its theologies simply didn't match up with the teachings of the early apostles.

It's worth noting that God gave us the Bible, not the Roman Catholic Church, or as J.J. Packard said, "The Church no more gave us the canon than Isaac Newton gave us gravity."[8] In the first few centuries, the early catholic Church (the original church) organized and agreed on criteria to select the Scriptures that would make up the Old and New Testaments. But even then, the Church didn't write the Bible—they simply organized the Bible. That was awesome. It's the Church anyone should admire and appreciate for the sacrifices that were made back then, including the martyrs of that time. Then came the Roman Empire, and subsequently, the Roman version of the Catholic Church. All bets were off after that. They hijacked the Bible and created a monopolistic institution and dynasty where the Scriptures remained primarily hidden until the 1,500s. In more recent times, the Roman Catholic Catechism was developed, shifting the focus and attention away from the Scriptures and onto secular interpretations and religious orders. It's a document that is masked in confusing, complicated doctrines, leaving the average parishioner to conclude, "Wow, I better just trust the Church to tell me what to do."

Many are also familiar with John Wyclif, an English scholastic philosopher, theologian, and Bible translator, and John Huss, a Czech theologian and philosopher, who both shined a spotlight on the flaws and corruption of the Roman Catholic Church in the fourteenth century. They stated that the Church was much more than just an institution headed by a pope. They held and understood the belief that Christians should have spiritual freedom, not remain trapped under the bondage of a system or a hierarchy. They believed that all Christians, whether priest, pope, or layman are viewed equally in God's eyes.

The Church was in desperate need of reform. Popes were even excommunicating other popes. Wyclif envisioned the pope's position as simply a shepherd over a flock; that he would be one who would simply share the Gospel and bring people to Christ, not a tyrant full of worldliness and luxury. Wyclif wanted to show just how far the papacy (and the Church) had departed from the simple faith and practice of Christ and his disciples and said:

> "Christ is the truth; the pope is the principle of falsehood. Christ lived in poverty, the pope labors for worldly magnificence. Christ refused temporal dominion; the pope seeks it. Christ alone is the head of the church. The papal institution is full of poison. It is Antichrist itself, the man of sin who exalts himself above God. Let judgment fall."[9]

Wyclif detested the trappings of power and the corruption of the papacy. He gave a reminder of just how far the Roman Catholic Church had strayed from the original Gospel, Christ, and the apostles:

> "Everything should be judged by Scripture, not the church. The New Testament is of full authority, and open to the understanding of simple men, as to the points that be most needful for salvation … Christ did not write his laws on tables, or on skins of animals, but in the hearts of men."[10]

He called out the doctrine of transubstantiation (discussed in Chapter 13), denying that Holy Communion was turned into the physical body and blood of Christ, holding that it was a symbol of Christ's body and blood. He also called for the Bible to be made available in languages for all to understand, and headed the movement to have it translated into English by a group of scholars in Oxford. Wycliff's premise was very simple on the two topics: transubstantiation originated from corrupt popes, and the Roman Catholic Church could no longer try to control the Scriptures.

As expected, and true to the Church's nature and character, they hunted down Wyclif followers (and there were many), demanding that they renounce their beliefs, and drove Wyclif out of the university. But it was too late—the message he spoke was clear and understandable. The Bible was translated and was rescued from the Church, but more than that, it started the process for Christians to find freedom from the Roman institution and called into question any doctrine or dogma that originated during corrupt medieval times under the leadership of papal authority.

Huss subsequently adopted the same teaching that Christ, not the pope, was head of the Church. He, likewise, exposed the abuse of power and corruption in the papacy. Author Bruce Shelly makes the distinction on the walls of the Bethlehem chapel: "The pope rode a horse; Christ walked barefoot. Jesus washed the disciples' feet; the pope preferred to have his kissed."[11]

Huss openly attacked the corruption of selling indulgences. He called the Church out for their corruption and was willing to die for his belief. He was quoted as saying, "I have said that I would not, for a chapel full of gold, recede from the truth; I know that the truth stands and is mighty forever, and abides eternally, with whom there is no respect of persons."[12]

In 1415, Huss was led to the courtyard to be burned alive (another Roman Catholic casualty). Before being murdered, he prayed that God would forgive his enemies and proclaimed:

> "God is my witness that the evidence against me is false. I have never thought nor preached except with the one intention of winning men, if possible, from their sins. In the truth of the Gospel I have written, taught, and preached; today I will gladly die."[13]

Reforming the corruption of the papacy was almost impossible, but the groundwork had been laid and Huss is an example of someone who was willing to die in order to see the Roman Catholic Church reformed from bad popes and clergy, and true to nature, the Church had him executed.

Dogma vs. Gospel

We get a little window into the intentions and motives of Catholic leadership and their obsession with power and control in a quote from the book *Dogmatic Theology for the Laity* by Matthias Premm:

> "The teaching of the office of the Church is more important than the Bible; only an infallible church can interpret the true meaning of Sacred Scripture; no one can do this for himself."[14]

Of course, we have already seen what the Roman Catholic Church looks like based on historic evidence. It is very dangerous when any one group makes the claim that they, and they alone, can interpret the Scriptures. Second, to place the teaching office of the Church on the same level of authority as the Scriptures is even more dangerous and deceitful.

The Church is referred to by Premm as infallible, but here again, what do we do with the Church's decision to destroy the lives of so many individuals? What do we do with 1,700 years of criminal acts? Can any intellectually honest Catholic accept and embrace the concept of an "infallible church" while knowing the term is dishonest, and that the Roman Catholic Church has been a collection of individuals with characters not reflective of Christ?

Earlier, we saw a stern warning from Paul regarding teaching a different Gospel:

> "I am astonished that you are so quickly deserting the one who called you by the grace of Christ and are turning to a different gospel—which is really no gospel at all. Evidently some people are throwing you into confusion and are trying to pervert the gospel of Christ. But even if we or an angel from heaven should preach a gospel other than the one we preached to you, let him be eternally condemned! As we have already said, so now I say again (must be pretty important): If anybody is preaching to you a gospel other

than what you accepted, let him be eternally condemned" (Galatians 2:6-9).

Paul faced heresy in his time and warned of it coming later as well. A look at the early Church reveals all kinds of heresies that the Church had to wrestle against. However, after Constantine, we see a shift from outside influences trying to pollute and corrupt the Church, to Church leadership itself becoming the source of the corruption. The Gospel that is preached today by the Catholic Church, 2,000 years after Paul made his warning, looks a whole lot different than the first-century Church. If you are a straightforward and curious Catholic, and willing to do the research, you will realize that the dogmas and belief systems of today's Catholicism were not part of the original Gospel.

Authors like Trent Horn, Scott Hahn, Jimmy Akin, Karl Keaton, Stephen Ray, and Bishop Baron all try to justify why today's Catholic Gospel looks nothing like the original Gospel, but it's a useless, dishonest, unethical, and futile attempt to enter that territory. "An acorn turns into a beautiful oak tree,"[15] is an example of an embarrassing analogy for why the original Church looks nothing like today's Roman Catholic Church. Another example used is that of a fully grown man who grew and developed and no longer resembles the little boy.[16] Yet, there has been nothing beautiful about the murder of hundreds of thousands of innocent civilians and the molestation of over 1 million kids (to be discussed in Chapters 6 and 7). Little boys can grow up and become mass murderers, and with the Roman Catholic Church that is, oftentimes, exactly what transpired.

The reality hits home quickly for the cradle Catholic by asking just a few basic questions regarding practices in today's Church. Did any of the apostles set the stage for a rosary or praying to Mary? Did any of the first Christians pray to Mary after she died? Did any of the apostles talk about Purgatory or indulgences? Did any of the apostles list sacraments in a structured form that had to be performed as part of the salvation process? Did any of the apostles talk about *anything* on The Catholic List? The questions can be endless, and very revealing.

Of course, the answer is, emphatically, "No," to all of the above and many more. It is sobering to realize that Paul's writings condemn many of the belief systems of the modern Roman Catholic Church. This is a very strong accusation, but a simple pause and evaluation—as objectively as possible— unfolds a different Gospel. Most of the actions, beliefs, traditions, doctrines, and dogmas practiced in the Catholic Church today did not exist in the time of the apostles. The Catholic List is an invention that would be totally foreign to all of the apostles. Should that be a concern for Catholics?

The Bible provides the best way to sum up false doctrines: if anything is claimed as a different doctrine, a different faith, a different Jesus, a different statement of faith that adds to the Gospel, changes the Gospel, or conflicts with the Gospel, it's to be rejected and condemned (Galatians 1:6-12). So, we have an obligation to examine any teaching that has been handed down from popes and clergy, many of whom were morally embarrassing, and evaluate how those doctrines stack up against the Bible. It will not take long to realize that what is found in these teachings is not in the Scriptures. Some of these teachings will be examined in detail later in this book.

Jude reminds the audience that a faith has already been delivered to the people and never needs repeating; the foundation has been established, no other foundation is needed:

> "Dear friends, although I was very eager to write you about the salvation we share, I felt I had to write and urge you to contend for the faith that was once for all entrusted to the saints (all Believers in Christ). For certain men whose condemnation was written about long ago have secretly slipped in among you. They are godless men, who change the grace of our God into a license for immortality and deny Jesus Christ our only Sovereign and Lord" (Jude 1: 3-4).

We see in the Gospel of John and the epistle of 1 John that we as Christian individuals test the spirits and test the doctrines coming our way to guard against false prophets:

"But the Counselor, the Holy Spirit, whom the Father will send in my name, will teach you all things and will remind you of everything I have said to you" (John 14:26).

"Dear friends, do not believe every spirit, but test the spirits to see whether they are from God, because many false prophets have gone out into the world" (1 John 4:1).

A magisterium doesn't do the testing. An organization doesn't do the testing. We as individual believers need to do the testing, not the one who guards the chicken coop. We can listen to pastors and teachers and authors (those who understand the New Covenant) for encouragement and for spiritual growth, but the ultimate test is in how any teaching aligns with the infallible Word of God, not the fallible words of a pope, pastor or magisterium.

As Christians, we have to conclude that the Scriptures are our guide and the Holy Spirit is our true teacher. What awesome peace it is to know that the Holy Spirit—God Himself—is living inside of us, giving us the ability to interpret the Scriptures, test the spirits, and not be held hostage by a magisterium or entity.

Our relationship with our Heavenly Father is personal, it's direct, it doesn't need a Church mediator, Mary, or dead saints. It certainly does not need wealthy narcissists at the pulpit with jets or mansions or secretive cities. What incredible freedom there is in not needing self-focused, self-righteous, organized religion, with all its bells and whistles and expensive cathedrals, mega-buildings, and stained glass—we just need Jesus Christ.

Christianity can never go wrong following the pattern of the early apostles, teaching and proclaiming, "Jesus is the Messiah."

"Day after day, in the temple courts and from house to house, they never stopped teaching and proclaiming the good news that Jesus is the Christ" (Acts 5:42).

Christianity can never go wrong following the simple instruction from Peter and the early apostles on how an individual can start a relationship with God and secure a place in eternity:

"'The time has come,' he said. 'The kingdom of God is near. Repent and believe the good news!'" (Mark 1:15).

"Peter replied, 'Repent and be baptized, every one of you, in the name of Jesus Christ for the forgiveness of your sins. And you will receive the gift of the Holy Spirit'" (Acts 2:38).

However, Christianity *can* go wrong when following a hierarchy that will tell you what to do from this day forward and following a system where if you are lucky and follow the rules you just might make Purgatory, and that's after following a system of self-effort, self-righteousness, and maintaining your own salvation. Christianity is about Jesus being the Messiah. He really did it; He really rose again; we can't stop talking about it. He is the Savior of the world. Follow Him, and your life will never be the same. Institutionalized religion has strayed from the simple Gospel into confusion and perilous terrain.

When we contrast the simple message of Jesus regarding repentance (change your mind and follow me) and grace (I am going to do everything on your behalf since you were not capable of fulfilling the requirements) with the self-righteousness of today's Catholic—and many Protestant—teachings, the landscape does not look the same. We essentially have two methods to choose from:

1. One method of trying to follow a system to obtain righteousness (the Jewish and Pharisaical way, but now continued by Catholics and much of modern religion).
2. Another method that rejects a self-righteous effort, and by simple faith, trusting in a God who has unexplainable grace and mercy, freely giving us His righteousness , announcing our justification (the true and original Gospel).

The apostles preached the resurrection, and instead of "no salvation found outside the Church" as falsely taught by Catholic liturgy (CCC 846-848), the apostles said no Gospel, no salvation, and no Church apart from the resurrection and the belief therein.

CHAPTER 5

The Roman Catholic Church: Endless Apologies

In 1517 the Age of Reformation started, along with the shattering of papal leadership, in time setting millions of believers free from Roman Catholic control. The reform became much bigger than anyone could have ever anticipated as Martin Luther attacked papal authority and exposed corruption and false dogma. The Roman Catholic Church continued its rampage of sponsoring the execution of anyone with different beliefs if they did not recant. These mass executions were carried out in a barbaric way: burning people at the stake. Author John Foxe, in his *Book of Martyrs*, reveals in horrendous detail accounts of these martyrdoms. Endless apologies would ultimately come from the Roman Catholic Church.

Burning people alive at the stake in front of their families is not something that took place thousands of years ago in the Old Testament. This is an activity that the Roman Catholic Church engaged in during the 1500s—just a few hundred years ago. The Roman Church instigated these terrors. Even reporting on the gruesome acts that the Church engaged in seems disrespectful today—almost as if there is an apparent attempt to bash and discredit its reputation, but these actions have to be recounted and Catholics have to factor this into the equation of their spiritual confidence in the Roman institutional system. As a result, Catholics are challenged in a contemplative way to consider whether the Roman Catholic Church is not really the "one, holy, catholic, and apostolic Church of Jesus Christ." *That* Church rests simply on the "message about the resurrection" through faith and trust in Christ with the guidance of the Holy Spirit and the inherent Scriptures for spiritual support.

As we think about a Church that would authorize murder as a tool to spread the Gospel, it's events like these, and hundreds of years of other atrocities, through which one starts to comprehend that the true *catholic*

Church, the Church built on spreading the news about the resurrection by the incredible, wholesome, character of the apostles (living genuine, spirit-filled Christian lives) had long set sail. Had the Roman Catholic Church—the institution, the monarchy, the governmental pagan-blended Christian Church—taken its place?

The very early Church, shortly after the apostles, taught the Gospel with accuracy; however, in a fallen world corruption came, and it came quickly. Within a few hundred years, power and political and financial motives had invaded the Church. What started out as a movement turned into a powerful imperialistic entity. Centuries later, after the Protestant Reformation, the Roman Catholic Church still had not properly reformed. Corruption invaded many Protestant churches as well.

Jesus knew His true Church would always be about a movement centered around the simple message of His final sacrifice, reconciling mankind back to God. It would be a movement absent of an obsolete sacrificial or sacramental system, priesthood, hierarchy, religious regiments, the Ten Commandments, Jewish laws, and man-made doctrines.

It would not be a system centered around self-righteous acts, or trying to jump a little higher to land on the moon, or a religious treadmill where you keep going and going but never get anywhere. It would be, instead, a movement of grace, an unexplainable love extended to every single person who would ever be born who would trust, believe, follow, and embrace Jesus Christ. He is a Savior who came to give, not require, as we see with Catholicism and a fair number of Protestant denominations.

Andy Stanley describes it best as a movement focused on spreading the news about Jesus that, unfortunately, finally got buildings. Then groups got control and realized they could leverage religion to control people. The leveraging of people meant power, and power meant wealth, and what was supposed to be the simple task of spreading the message of the resurrection became an institution caught in an immoral and corrupt religious landslide.

The original, simple message was contained, contaminated, and suppressed. It became overshadowed and consumed with doctrines and dogma and rules and regiments and requirements and distractions that would essentially allow an exploitation over the flock, with Jesus and the inerrant Scriptures barely visible on the sidelines.

The Catholic Church's Place in History

After Constantine and the power of imperial influence and control, the Church would never be the same again. We see the Church going from humble locations to luxurious palaces, almost overnight. With that change came the blending of politics and religion; Christianity joined the power of the state. The eventual results would be endless apologies from a Church to try and minimize centuries of destruction and devastation.

It's important to note how historians and theologians often classify the different chronological segments of Christianity:

6 BC – AD 70: The Age of Jesus and the Apostles

70 – 312: The Age of catholic (universal) Christianity

312 – 590: The Age of the Christian Roman Empire

590 – 1517: The Christian Middle Ages

1517 – 1648: The Age of Reformation[1]

The first Age is self-explanatory, but notice that the Age of catholic Christianity (the original catholic Church) had a transformation big enough to propel it to a different era: The Age of the Christian Roman Empire. It was a shift that will leave the Church forever redefined. This is where Constantine blended Christianity and politics, along with pagan practices. Imperial influence in the affairs played a major role in the direction of the Church, and the Roman Church became a political giant. This politicization is the distinction between the original catholic Church up to AD 312 and the institutional Church we know today as the Roman Catholic Church—especially in terms of its foundation, motives, and doctrinal teachings.

Although the emperor Constantine's reign highlights just the initial start of the numerous aristocratic changes that would ultimately transpire in Christianity, author Bruce Shelley notes his conversion to the faith is shown to have been purely a political move by how much paganism remained after he controlled the papacy. He not only carried pagan gods around with him the first five years after his "conversion," but he refused baptism until his deathbed.[2] Likewise, he conspired and murdered—not exactly a role model after the apostles we knew. This is a really important part of the history of Christianity that Catholics should not ignore because this is the start of the introduction of practices, procedures, doctrines, and dogmas that would have never been approved by either Christ or the early apostles. It was the opening of the door to The Catholic List.

Bruce Shelly describes the transition that took place after Constantine:

> "The advantages for the church were real enough, but there was a price to pay. Constantine ruled Christian bishops as he did his civil servants and demanded unconditional obedience to official pronouncements, even when they interfered with purely church matters. There were also the masses who now streamed into the officially favored church. Prior to Constantine's conversion, the church consisted of convinced believers who were willing to bear the risk of being identified as Christians. Now many came who were politically ambitious, religiously disinterested, and still half rooted in paganism. This threatened to produce not only shallowness and permeation by pagan superstitions but also the secularization and misuse of religion for political purposes. By 380 rewards for Christians had given way to penalties for non-Christians. In that year the emperor Theodosius made belief in Christianity a matter of imperial command."[3]

Theodosius commanded:

> "It is Our will that all peoples we rule shall practice that religion which the divine Peter the Apostles transmitted to the Romans. We shall believe in the single Deity of the Father, the Son, and the Holy Spirit, under the concept of equal majesty and of the Holy Trinity. We command that those persons who follow this rule shall embrace the name of Catholic Christians. The rest, however, who We adjudge demented and insane, shall sustain the infamy of heretical dogmas, their meeting places shall not receive the name of churches, and they shall be smitten first by divine

vengeance and secondly by the retribution of Our own initiative, which We shall assume in accordance with divine judgment."[4]

This quote from Emperor Theodosius was not only a prophecy of the horrendous crimes to come but would be on par with some of the Islamic extremist factions we see today. This was only the beginning. It was literally the introduction to the warpath the Roman Catholic Church would take in its harsh method to spread its version of the Gospel.

Church buildings in the Christian Roman Empire also took on a completely different appearance, recognizing not only Christ as the head at the top of the hierarchy but the emperor as well. Centuries later, the Roman Catholic Church would erroneously do the same with Mary. Shelly gives us a description of these buildings subsequent to Constantine from a Greek traveler at the time:

> "... a hall covered with a dome; the inside was adorned with sapphires sparkling with a celestial blue brilliance, and standing out against the blue background of the stones were golden images of the gods, glittering like stars in the firmament."[5]

One can scarcely imagine Paul and the other apostles ever condoning Christianity developing under such descriptions, especially "golden images of the gods" being portrayed. Yet, this is where the Roman Catholic Church took true Christianity with a sharp left turn from its roots, setting the stage for ecclesiastical corruption and papal perversion. Much of today's Catholic theology comes from the period after Constantine and during the dark Middle Ages. Unfortunately, Catholics have embraced it and adored it with little contextual understanding of its roots, and the malicious side has been ignored by modern Catholic leadership and hidden from parishioners.

How do you convince an average pew-sitting Catholic that the "one, holy, catholic, and apostolic church" is the only one to follow and believe? Once again, you hide the past. What we do know as historical fact is that imperial power took over the control of the Church, and true Christianity became a showy, outer covering.

The next era—The Christian Middle Ages—is significant in the length of time it lasted (almost 1,000 years), and this is the time period where the most intense papal corruption and papal fallibility took place. The misconduct was so deep that it sparked the Great Reformation in 1517.

The ensuing depravity and immorality of the Roman Catholic Church has run rampant for almost 1,700 years. For a moment, contrast the amazing early apostles, who went around the region proclaiming the Gospel and were arrested, beaten, thrown in prison, and martyred—with popes being carried on a throne, dressed in robes, glittering with jewelry, gleaming with political power and worshipped by duped followers. The difference in those two scenarios is an embarrassment to the Church. The true Church comprised groups of people whose only agenda was to spread the good news about Jesus.

With even a remote bit of intellectual sincerity after reviewing the history of the Church, it's very difficult for one to look at the Roman Catholic Church and feel confident that they are solidly on track with their theology. The very early catholic Church was right on track (with a few bumps in the road), and was basically the same from Jesus to Constantine. We see vast theological changes start to take place after AD 315. For example, Constantine had thousands of pagan priests he had to do something with, so he blended them into the Catholic system in a merging of Christian beliefs with pagan beliefs, which inevitably created an institution unlike anything that the early apostles would have ever envisioned. However, this is only one small example. Popes would later emerge and create the items on The Catholic List.

Endless Apologies

The Roman Catholic Church really came into power in AD 590 under Gregory the Great right at the beginning of the medieval period, and that began a 1,000-year span of the Catholic Church engaging in some of the worst acts in human history, as we saw in the first two chapters. I believe anyone can understand a religious organization going through a rough patch for a few years and then getting back on track, or one bad pastor or leader needing to be replaced, but that is not what happened here. There were 1,000 years of carnage so intense and corrupt and evil that the modern leaders of the Catholic Church go back and have a list a mile long to apologize for. Even the late atheist Christopher Hitchens called out the Roman Catholic Church for having to make these apologies:

1. Killing, slaughtering, and torturing the Jews
2. Killing, slaughtering, and torturing the Muslims
3. Killing, slaughtering, and torturing the Europeans
4. Killing, slaughtering, and torturing the Protestants
5. The Crusades and Inquisitions (murdering hundreds of thousands)
6. Injustice towards women
7. Forced conversion of indigenous people
8. The African slave trade
9. Violence and legalized torture, institutionalized by the pope
10. Religious wars against anyone with a different belief system
11. The inactivity and silence of most Catholic leadership during the holocaust
12. The rape and torture of orphans and children in Catholic-run schools in almost every country in the world
13. The horrible doctrine of "limbo" (another Catholic, made-up theology) upheld by St. Augustine and others—described by many as a "cruel and stupid disposal solution to a non-existent problem"—regarding the destination of the souls of children who died before baptism
14. The pronouncement of the damnation of all Eastern Orthodox Christians, heretics, and people dwelling outside the Church that was only lifted in 1964[6]

Pope John Paul II, during the year of Jubilee in 2000, presented ninety-four public recognitions of appalling crimes, error, cruelty, and offenses that had been committed by the Catholic Church over the centuries, as he offered up "apologies" for these actions. He apologized for serious criminal acts, including murdering hundreds of thousands of people (although specific numbers were not discussed), and the sexual torture and other crimes against thousands of children—all instigated by "the only Church that should ever be recognized as legitimate" according to Roman Catholic proclamation.

Jewish, Muslim, Protestant, and many other communities have never for-gotten what the Roman Catholic Church did in authorizing the murder and torture of so many men, women, and children over centuries. The popes of the day convinced their gullible Church members that they would receive full and complete forgiveness of all past sins, including the sins they were about to commit, as they ventured out to murder, destroy, and pillage vil-lages. Pope Urban II gave the word and put his devious plan into action. Shelly lists the historical facts:

> "The inception of the Crusades ignited horrible attacks against the Jews, and even fellow Christians were not exempt from rape and plunder. Incredible atrocities befell the Muslim foes. Crusad-ers sawed open dead bodies in search of gold, sometimes cooking and eating the flesh—a delicacy they found 'better than spiced peacock', as one chronicler chose to describe it. From the end of the eleventh century to the end of the thirteenth, Christian Europe, led by [200 years of pope leadership], launched seven major crusades, as well as various small expeditions."[7]

Shelly continues, sharing a contemporary account of what happened during the first of the seven crusades:

> "Some of our men ... cut off the heads of their enemies; others shot them with arrows, so that they fell from the towers; others tortured them longer by casting then into flames ... It was nec-essary to pick one's way over the bodies of men and horses. But these were small matters compared to what happened at the temple of Solomon [where] ... men rode in blood up to their knees and bridle reins ... At nightfall the crusaders' hands were still bloody when they folded them in prayer and knelt at the Church of the Holy Sepulcher, sobbing for excess of joy."[8]

It was during these Middle Ages that Urban II took the man-made tra-ditions of confession to a priest, penance, and Purgatory to a new level by offering indulgences. Anyone willing to go to Jerusalem to murder, rape, and plunder the city was granted a total remission of sin.

Shelly states:

> "It was only a slight step farther to confer like benefits upon those who were unable to go on a crusade, but who contributed to the cause. The wealthy could virtually buy a substitute. Thus, the possibilities for fundraising opened in all directions, including construction of a hospital here or a cathedral there."[9]

The apologies from the Catholic Church for the crimes they've committed are extensive. One could surely conclude how convenient it is for the Church to come along in modern times—in an Internet, information, and media-driven world that exposes the true nature of 1,700 years of the Roman Catholic faith—in a futile attempt to soften the impact and destruction of the reputation of the Church by offering "apologies."

Does the enormity of the actual apologies presented reveal that maybe the Roman Catholic version of church has been a gargantuan spiritual imitation the whole time? Only those Catholics with great humility and honesty might come to the proper conclusion. I think some can be misled that the egregious acts are offset by charitable acts and achievements, along with the spread of Christianity over the centuries. However, that would be similar to a murderer bragging to the surviving family of his victim that he'd been working in the soup kitchen at the homeless shelter lately, and hopes this has recompensed for his "mistake".

It may be easy to just gloss over these things and treat each heinous crime as a general topic because you, the reader, were not involved, or even yet born. However, in fairness, all Christians, especially Catholics, should reflect on what acts these apologies were for, because they were committed against real people with families, hopes, and dreams for their lives.

In his book, Trent Horn quotes and agrees with Pope Hormisdas as saying, "the Apostolic See the Catholic religion has always been preserved unblemished."[10] This quote took place in AD 517 and Hormisdas had no idea what was coming via the medieval period, malevolent popes, and the criminal acts that would be done by the Church. However, Horn lives in modern times and knows exactly what they've done. Yet, Horn seems to hide the truth and remains in denial with his teachings that he insists represent the Church.

Has the Roman Catholic Church remained unblemished? Before answering, I think it is important to define unblemished: "Not damaged or marked in any way; perfect, impeccable, flawless, without mistake, pure, spotless, stainless, untarnished, uncontaminated, unpolluted, blameless, incorrupt."[11] I would also like to also insert my own adjective: squeaky clean!

So, for a Catholic and someone who considers themselves honest, a person of integrity, with high morals and values, and accountable to the Heavenly Father, a couple of questions naturally emerge:

Was Hormisdas right in labeling the Catholic Church "unblemished"?

Was Horn honest in reiterating Hormisdas' unblemished claim to defend Church infallibility?

One can clearly see from the past few chapters that this is a religious organization very distant from being unblemished. You simply cannot declare that the Roman Catholic Church has remained unblemished when history shows there has been this much depravity. My opinion in voicing such a harsh statement can only be drawn from the historical and theological evidence. I have no personal vendetta against the Roman Church, and I have amazing, genuine friends who are Catholics, but this is the only obvious supposition to render after sincerely doing the research.

Considering the history of the Roman institution, one can only question Roman Catholic theology, tradition, and biblical interpretations and come to the realization that all these doctrines and dogmas that have been declared by the Catholic Church, logically, cannot be entirely trustworthy. The Catholic List seems to have been invented for corrupt agendas by an unreliable magisterium, and more recently relying mostly on a 1992 version of a Catholic Catechism with the Bible taking a subordinate role. Scriptures the Church does use are many times taken completely out of context to fit an ideology that doesn't match the original Gospel. Whenever a religious entity formulates and develops a doctrine and then seeks out biblical support for authenticity, the truth is traveling in the wrong direction. The only path for theological truth is in the reverse direction: coming from the Scriptures and traveling to the hearts and minds of believers through the teaching of the Holy Spirit.

The important point is this: for Catholics to rely on a twentieth-century book (Catechism) versus the protected, infallible Word of God is not sensible, and it would be an utter shock to the participants of the early Church. Tactics like that simulate the actions of other sects that have developed their own liturgy (The Book of Mormon, the Quran, etc.). It begs the question, who would want to follow a 1992 Catechism full of threats and inaccuracies, developed by the Church that has been described so far? Meanwhile, we have the complete and final message of the simple Gospel in the inherent original Scriptures!

Sola Scriptura

No other topic comes up for debate among Catholics and Protestants more than *sola Scriptura*, "by Scripture alone". One section in this book cannot comprehensively cover this topic, but it's important to address. The argument hinges on a question of authority; specifically, how many authorities are we under as believers? Most of the early church fathers and the original catholic Church affirmed that Scripture alone is our authority (through the guidance of the Holy Spirit). This understanding still allows for councils and teachings of Church offices to have positions of authority as long as they:

1. Are subordinate to the Scriptures, which has ultimate authority and the final say.
2. Do not teach things that conflict with the Scriptures or that cannot be proved from the Scriptures.

The Westminster Confession of Faith, formed as a result of the Reformation, confirms the perspective of *sola Scriptura*:

> "... the Supreme judge by which all controversies of religion are to be determined, and all decrees of councils, opinions of ancient writers, doctrines of men, and private spirits, are to be examined, and in whose sentence we are to rest, can be no other but the Holy Spirit speaking in the Scripture."[12]

Gavin Ortlund reports that at least twenty church fathers affirm that Scripture is at the very top of the pyramid when it comes to authority, so although the term *"sola Scriptura"* is a relatively new term, this understanding of the Scriptures being the final authority and above Church tradition and the magisterium did not first surface during the Protestant Reformation, but has been the absolute rule since the apostolic age. The Roman Catholic Church, as it spun off of Constantine in the fourth century with its blend of Christianity, paganism, and politics, embraced an entirely different system. The Roman Church acknowledges the Scriptures but equally acknowledges the magisterium (the teaching authority of the Church headed by the pope) and Sacred Tradition. Catholic spokespersons like to refer to their authority structure as a "three-legged stool." In other words, each has equal authority and no single source is more important than any other.[13]

However, the "three-legged stool" analogy is a Roman Catholic illustration and does not have biblical accuracy. It is very ironic that the Roman Catholic Church looks to the early church fathers when they are trying to substantiate that the primitive Church beliefs are in unison with today's Church on the subjects of tradition and authority. Yet, the early church fathers taught *sola Scriptura*, the very doctrine that the Roman Catholic Church discarded! The Roman Church hides this from their flock, but as with every area we have discussed thus far, a small investment of time reveals the truth. Let's examine whether the early church fathers accepted the magisterium and Sacred Tradition as equal sources of authority to the Scriptures, or if they were adamant about the Scriptures being the final authority. Keith Thompson, in his documentary, lays out the framework from many of the patristic fathers concerning *sola Scriptura*:

Hippolytus, a Christian theologian and Bishop of Rome in the second and third centuries, stated:

> "There is, brethren, one God, the knowledge of whom we gain from the Holy Scriptures, and from no other Source ... all of us who practice piety will be unable to learn its practice from any other quarter than the oracles of God ... But let him quote the passage as a while, and he will discover the reason kept in view in writing it."[14]

Theologian Cyril of Jerusalem from the fourth century affirmed *sola Scriptura* as well:

> "For concerning the divine and holy mysteries of the Faith, not even a casual statement must be delivered without the Holy Scriptures; nor must we be drawn aside by mere plausibility and artifices of speech. Even to me, who tell you these things, give not absolute credence, unless thou receive the proof of the things which I announce from the Divine Scriptures. For this salvation which we believe depends not on ingenious reasoning, but on demonstration of the Holy Scriptures ... For the indwelling Spirit hence forth makes your mind a house of God. When you shall have heard what is written concerning the mysteries, then will you understand things thou knew not."[15]

In the next three quotes, Irenaeus, an early church father from the second century, states that everything we need for salvation is contained in the Scriptures and, against all Roman Catholic belief, says that the Scriptures can be clearly understood by all. He also warned against deriving a belief system from anything but the Scriptures:

> "We have learned from none others the plan of our salvation, than from those through whom the Gospel has come down to us, which they did at one time proclaim in public, and, at a later period, by the will of God, handed down to us in the Scriptures, to be the ground and pillar of our faith."[16]

> "Such, then, is their [Gnostic] system, which neither the prophets announced, nor the Lord taught, nor the apostles delivered, but of which they boast that beyond all others they have a perfect knowledge. They gather their views from other sources than the Scriptures."[17]

> "... the entire Scriptures, the prophets, and the Gospels, can be clearly, unambiguously, and harmoniously, understood by all ..."[18]

The brilliant theologian and Archbishop of Constantinople, John Chrysostom, in the fourth century wrote:

> "I exhort and entreat you all, disregard what this man and that man thinks about these things, and inquire from the Scriptures all these things."[19]

Unlike the Roman Catholic Church's decree that scripture interpretation may only come from the magisterium that attempts to discount the Holy Spirit's role in revealing truth to a believer, theologian Athanasius of Alexandria in the fourth century declared:

> "... the sacred and inspired Scriptures are sufficient to declare the truth."[20]

Ambrose, another famous fourth-century church father, stated:

> "Further, that none may fall into error, let a man attend to those signs vouchsafed us by the holy Scripture, whereby we may know the Son."[21]

> "For how can we adapt those things which we do not find in the holy Scripture?"[22]

> "I do not wish that credence be given to us; let the Scripture be quoted."[23]

Bishop Gregory of Nyssa in the fourth century taught *sola Scriptura* as well:

> "We are not entitled to such license, I mean that of affirming what we please; we make the Holy Scriptures the rule and the measure of every tenet(dogma); we necessarily fix our eyes upon that, and approve that alone which may be to harmonize with the intention of those writings."[24]

On his podcast "Know What You Believe", Theologian and apologist Michael Horton gives additional proof of how the patristic fathers felt about the authority of Scripture alone:

"We understand the truth if we listen to Paul's words as the very words of God. Do not go beyond the canon even through teachers like me. If I stray from the canon, then I stray from the rule of faith" (theologian Clement of Alexandria, second century).[25]

"Therefore let God inspired Scripture decide between us and on whichever side be found doctrines in harmony with the Word of God in favor of that side will we cast the vote" (theologian Basil the Great, fourth century).[26]

"As to all other writings in reading them however great the superiority of the authors to myself in sanctity and learning I do not accept even their teaching as true on the mere ground of the opinion being held by them but only because they have succeeded in convincing my judgment of its truth from the canonical writings themselves" (Basil the Great).[27]

"I've learned to yield this respect and honor only to the canonical books of holy scripture—of these alone [*sola Scriptura*] do I most firmly believe that the authors were completely free from error" (Augustine).[28]

"The excellence of the canonical authority of the old and new testaments is distinct from all the books of later writers

"Whoever dissents [expresses opinions different from what was established before] from the sacred scriptures, even if they are found in all places in which the Church is designated, are not the Church" (Augustine).[29]

No doubt this is compelling evidence that is never discussed in Roman Catholic circles. I know there were a lot of quotes above to sift through, but so many Catholic apologists will insist that "Scripture alone" was never taught in the early Church and is simply a Protestant invention of the sixteenth century. This book has already uncovered the secrecy with Catholic apologists disguising how many bad popes there have been, and a similar pattern happens regarding the topic of *sola Scriptura*. The truth that will not be told to the majority of Catholics is that the patristic fathers were adamant about the Scriptures being top priority with regards to spiritual authority—over and above tradition and a magisterium.

Why aren't they told this truth? The answer always defaults back to control. When the Church makes itself an equal authority with the Scriptures, this allows for doctrinal deviations from the original Gospel. Its proclaimed authority solidifies its interpretations, whether truth or error. This has happened with papal infallibility, the immaculate conception, and assumption of Mary. These dogmas are nowhere to be found in the Scriptures, but the news flash from the Roman Church is: "Our authority matches Scripture, so we say it's true (even though there is no legitimate proof); do not question us; do not dispute our findings, or we will be quick to pronounce an anathema against you." This mentality should alert Catholics that have been sheltered in obscurity to start seeing through this maze.

Keith Thompson makes the point that Jesus himself confirms the truth of *sola Scriptura* and that it alone is materially sufficient for authority and truth. He used Scripture alone all through His life and ministry and never claimed authority based on an oral Word of God. Christ used the Scriptures as the final judge of tradition. In contrast, in the sixteenth century, the Roman Catholic Council of Trent developed their own version of Christianity in their anger toward the Protestant Reformation. Regardless that the apostles and the patristic fathers of the early catholic Church taught otherwise, they produced canon after canon attacking the very foundations of faith, proclaiming that "these truths and rules are contained in the written books and in the unwritten traditions."[30]

Sola Scriptura was the universal teaching of the church fathers and even for the Catholic Church as a whole up through the later part of the Middle Ages. In earlier chapters, we clearly saw the corruption of the Church that was happening in the Middle Ages, and unsurprisingly *sola Scriptura* got bumped out. The "rules" of the institution were declared as gospel. This opposition to Scripture alone as Christians' only infallible authority is still the view of Roman Catholic theologians today, and was expressed clearly by former Archbishop James Cardinal Gibbons in the nineteenth century:

"The Scriptures alone do not contain all the truths which a Christian is bound to believe ... The Scriptures alone cannot be a sufficient guide and rule of faith because ... they do not contain all the truths necessary for salvation."[31]

We see this same mindset from Pope Leo XIII:

"The sacred writings are wrapt in a certain religious obscurity ... no one can enter into their interior without a guide."[32]

Yet Scripture contradicts Roman Catholic exegesis:

"... and how from infancy you have known the holy Scriptures, which are able to make you wise for salvation through faith in Christ Jesus. All Scripture is God-breathed and is useful for teaching, rebuking, correcting, and training in righteousness, so that the man of God may be thoroughly equipped" (2 Timothy 3:15-17).

"For the word of God is living and active. Sharper than any double-edged sword, it penetrates even to the dividing soul and spirit, joints and marrow; it judges the thoughts and attitudes of the heart" (Hebrews 4:12).

"Now the Bereans were of more noble character than the Thessalonians, for they received the message with great eagerness and examined the Scriptures every day to see if what Paul said was true" (Acts 17:11).

Catholic Apologists will try to be clever, as they do in many areas regarding theology, and pluck an individual scripture out of context in a feeble attempt to make it fit their agenda and their Church position. The doctrine of Purgatory and papal infallibility are classic examples. They do this in trying to affirm that the Church is needed for interpretation. One example is in 2 Peter:

"Above all, you must understand that no prophecy of Scripture came about by the prophet's own interpretation" (2 Peter 1:21,).

At first glance, you might think, "Wow, I need help interpreting the Scriptures." This is exactly what the Roman Church would like for you to think, and they stop dead in their tracks after that verse. However, anyone who has ten more seconds can read the very next verse and get the truth:

> "For prophecy never had its origin in the will of man, but men spoke from God as they were <u>carried along by the Holy Spirit</u>" (2 Peter 1:21).

It's not the Church that interprets the Scriptures, but the Holy Spirit. As you can see, there are a lot of diversions inside the church walls with false proclamations and the taking of scriptures out of context.

All the Scriptures above confirm the truth, but Jesus said it best:

> "All this I have spoken while still with you. But <u>the Counselor, the Holy Spirit</u>, whom the Father will send in my name, <u>will teach you all things</u> and <u>will remind you</u> of <u>everything</u> I have said to you" (John 14: 25-27).

And we see Paul quote our Heavenly Father who tells of the coming New Covenant (discussed in detail in Chapter 11) and what God's new way will be in how He communicates to His saints (all Christians):

> "I will put my laws in their minds and write them on their hearts" (Hebrews 8:10).

The earlier quotes from Cardinal Gibbons and Pope Leo XIII sum up the current Roman Catholic position on *sola Scriptura*. The Roman Church is willing to go against what the Heavenly Father announced, what Jesus taught, what the apostles imparted, and what most of the early church fathers proclaimed for centuries. The authority of the Scriptures, through the guidance of the Holy Spirit, has no equal. Even Thomas Aquinas, in the thirteenth century, made the following comment regarding *sola Scriptura*:

> "The canonical scriptures alone are the rule of faith (*Sola canonica scriptura est regula fidei*)."[33]

Here are a few more observations that are brought by theologians and apologists when looking at the evidence of relying on the Scriptures alone as our sole authority

1. Interestingly, Catholics often speak of Sacred Tradition as not being the inspired Word of God—not God-breathed-or Spirit carried.[34]

2. Scripture is the speech of God; that which is not the speech of God is subordinate to that which is the speech of God.[35]

3. St. Augustine taught that Scripture is infallible but all post-apostolic productions and functions of the Church are fallible. This includes councils formed for the whole Christian world, yet Catholic apologists believe Sacred Tradition and early ecumenical councils are infallible rules of faith.[36]

4. Trent Horn states, "Most Catholic teaching has not been infallibly defined."[37]

5. Jesus explicitly told people of His time that the Pharisees (who had a lot of traditions) were teaching the people in error—it was known to be error because it didn't line up with the Scriptures.[38]

6. The problem with declaring tradition as an equal source to the Scriptures is the large number of contradictory proclamations. For example, "Outside of the Church there is no salvation," and then later going back and changing that declaration. This became true with the doctrine of Limbo (a place where unbaptized babies go). First they were proclaimed to be staying in a kind of "natural state of happiness;" changed later to "hope of salvation for all." Even Easter had conflicts: two different groups were proclaiming that the celebration be on the day they announced, and both positions claimed that it was established by apostolic tradition. The Church's view on the death penalty also had changing doctrinal proclamations. Tradition from the Church is not only unnecessary, but cannot ever be trusted as authoritative and infallible.

7. Tradition is simply not reliable. That is why people leave written wills, not just promises by "word of mouth" which there is no way to prove or disprove. The appeal of Jesus was always: "It is written ... "[39]

8. Paul refers to oral tradition and in the subsequent verses tells what those traditions were. All the oral traditions were eventually written into the canon. The canon was then closed.[40]

9. We have peace and assurance in the Christian life simply by taking God at His written Word, not the teaching of a fallible Church by fallible men.

10. The early church fathers were convinced that the Scriptures could be so clear as to be summarized for a child. The Roman Catholic Church does not think that the Word of God is that clear, but that it needs clarification by an infallible teacher.[41]

11. Because Christ is the central message in the Scriptures, it only stands to reason that the Scripture should be the central and sole authority.[42]

12. The argument can be made that if you adhere to *sola scriptura*, then everyone will become their own interpreter. But everyone, including Catholics, still take all the data that is provided into their minds and make personal decisions about what they believe. In fact, Catholics that have been interviewed have a huge variety of answers to the most basic questions concerning how, specifically, a person can have salvation, along with a variety of other topics. As believers, we have to realize that there is nothing more powerful than the Holy Spirit dwelling inside of us. When we read inspired Scripture and genuinely seek the Spirit of God, the pieces of the puzzle come together. This is still a process, and it takes time, but God is patient in revealing His truth. Man-made declarations from an institution, cloaked in unscrupulous authority, will surely keep one in bondage and spiritually depleted.

The final authority and sufficiency of the Scriptures has been under attack for centuries, not just from an outside secular source like atheism, but from the Roman Catholic Church. This should be cause for any Catholic to be concerned. Just to clarify, the Roman Catholic Church does not attack the Scriptures, but they do attack the Scriptures as the supreme authority. The Scriptures themselves teach that everything we need for salvation and the will of God is found within them, so we do not need any authoritative interpretation from a magisterium, but only the Holy Spirit. We need to realize, unless a declaration comes from the Scriptures, it has been invented by man. This is specifically true for doctrines derived from The Catholic List.

Failure of Interpretation and Doctrinal Issues

The Roman Catholic Church teaches that Catholics have been united in their doctrinal beliefs from the very beginning. Thompson further states in his documentary that Catholic spokespeople claim that there are tens of thousands of Protestant denominations teaching a variety of different doctrines, but claim the one, holy, apostolic, Catholic Church has always been consistent in its message. However, all of these assumptions are simply not true. Catholic theologian Karl Rahner, in discussing Catholic exegesis, interpretations, and doctrinal issues, admits that Catholics "are far from being unanimous ... We discover that there are innumerable questions of profound importance upon which we Catholics are far from being united among ourselves."[43]

Eric Svendsen, in his book *Evangelical Answers*, lists some common divisions among Catholic leaders over the years:

> "Among the smorgasbord of beliefs from which to choose in Roman Catholicism are: (1) Whether the creation account in Genesis 1 and 2 should be interpreted literally or mythically (2) whether or not we should believe that Jonah was really swallowed by a fish, (3) which brand of predestination we should subscribe to (there are as many as four), (4) whether or not we should believe that the Bible contains errors, (5) whether or not Mary is to be seen as a Mediatrix of all graces, and if so, (6) whether she should be viewed next to Christ facing the church or next to the church facing Christ (7) whether or not Vatican II is to be considered an infallible council (which invites exegesis, embraces Protestant and Orthodox churches as Christian churches, and displaces the use of force in the propagation of the faith ...)"[44]

Conflicts about the millennium, fallen angels, the immaculate conception and assumption of Mary, evolution, Peter's role in the Church, and many other topics have surfaced in disagreements across the Catholic landscape.

The conflicts about Easter, Limbo, lending money with interest, and the death penalty have already been mentioned. The Church has been far from unanimous on spiritual matters over the centuries. Most Catholics are only aware of The Great Schism in 1032 (when the Eastern Orthodoxy split away from the Roman Catholic Church) and the Protestant Reformation in 1517 (that was initiated by Martin Luther and others). However, apologist Gavin Ortlund makes the observation that there have been numerous times throughout Catholic history where every time there was another shift in doctrinal beliefs, there would be a split or a schism.[45] Catholic scholar Eamon Duffy agrees that "well into the third century Christianity in Rome would remain turbulent, diverse, prone, to split"[46]

The splits and conflicts did not even remotely begin to fade away—that was just the beginning. Even today there are the arch conservatives and the extreme liberals within the walls of Catholicism. The facts show there is as much division in the Roman Church as you see in a lot of Protestant churches. Ortlund further states that "the unity claim in the Roman Catholic Church becomes subjective."[47] In other words, they are claiming unity from the beginning, but the facts show a different account. They are as fractured as any other religious institution.

We know there was not unity in the Roman Catholic Church regarding doctrines from the beginning, but we also must look at the topic of scriptural interpretation. There are volumes and volumes of early Church commentaries where the Scriptures are interpreted in many different ways. But interestingly enough, in his documentary, Thompson makes the observation that the Catholic Church has barely interpreted many scriptures at all. Catholic writer Peter Stravinskas states:

> "The Church exercises great restraint in offering authoritative interpretations of individual pericopes (texts); fewer than a dozen such instances can be pointed to in her two-thousand-year history, most of them at the Council of Trent."[48]

Roman Catholic Scholar Peter Williams expresses the same opinion:

"... over the centuries only a handful of texts have been subject to authoritative interpretation by the Magisterium."[49]

Likewise, Apologist Trent Horn states,

"The Catholic Church only offers a handful of infallible interpretations of Scripture."[50]

And finally, the most disturbing comment comes from Catholic Apologist Jimmy Akin:

"The Church has not established the correct interpretation of the great majority of Scripture passages. It has taught that Scripture and the faith do not conflict, so if you know your Catholic faith well then that will help you discern what a particular passage of Scripture DOESN'T mean, but it normally will not help you identify precisely what it DOES mean."[51]

It is extremely perplexing that the magisterium of the Roman Catholic Church insists that only they are divinely appointed to interpret the Scriptures, yet after 2,000 years they've only interpreted a handful. This is not only perplexing, but not logical in light of the fact that they hold the magisterium in equal authority with the Scriptures. There are over 31,000 Bible verses and they have only interpreted a few? Notice that Jimmy Akin admits that your Catholic faith will not help much with biblical understanding, and mentions nothing about the Bible clearly teaching that the Holy Spirit is the one who teaches us. This blatant avoidance of the Holy Spirit's role in communicating truth to believers conflicts directly with the foundation of Christianity. It's a problematic quote from a leading Catholic apologist.

Apologist James White points out that Catholics will make the claim that Protestants have an array of different beliefs, but Catholics say, "'We can go to the pope and can find exactly what a text means.' Yet, in debates they say, 'Well, it might mean this, it might mean that, you can read this author of this book who says ... '"[52] So White concludes that there is less confidence in the interpretative authority than there once was.

On a side note, the question has often been posed by Catholic apologists in debates, "Isn't it OK for doctrine to develop over time?" James White and Gavin Ortlund conclude that there is no problem with that as long as it is an extension of topics from the Apostolic Age (a deposit from the apostles in the Scriptures in the first century). However, White points out that the doctrines regarding the papacy and the Marian doctrines (and many others on the Catholic List) happened many centuries later[53] and that's why they cannot be trusted. The motive and purpose behind these man-made doctrines have already been extensively discussed in earlier chapters.

In his film, Thompson goes on to state the claim that there are tens of thousands of Protestant denominations teaching an array of doctrines is a common debate tactic used to divert attention away from the conclusion that the Roman Catholic faith has not been consistent in its doctrines concerning faith. Although distorted teachings are rampant through both Catholic and Protestant denominations, this argument is not accurate and the numbers are extremely skewed. Thompson reveals that the source of these numbers is David Barrett's *Christian Encyclopedia*, where he discloses that there are 22,190 denominations as of 1985, but states that these are neither true denominations, nor are they all Protestant. Theologian Dr. Eric Svendsen, in his book *Upon this Slippery Rock*, explains:

> "In other words, if there are ten independent Baptist churches in any given city, even though all of them are identical in belief and practice, each one is counted as a separate denomination due to its autonomy in jurisdiction."[54]

So, there are not tens of thousands of Protestant "denominations" like Lutheran, Baptist, Methodist, Presbyterian, Reformed, etc.; most long-term Protestants can only name about ten or fifteen that comprise the majority. So, it becomes misleading for Catholic apologists to throw around these large figures without mentioning this truth, leaving the uninformed to think there are tens of thousands of different, true denominations, all believing different things.

When condensing all Protestant denominations and looking at the variety of Catholic denominations, Svendsen states:

> "... the true count of real denominations within Protestant-
> ism is twenty-one, whereas the true count of real denominations
> within Roman Catholicism is sixteen."[55]

This denominational count becomes a trivial topic and is only used by debaters to paint a narrative of "unity from the beginning," diverting the attention away from the fact that Roman Catholics no longer believe in *sola Scriptura* or faith and justification alone in Christ, and many other doctrines that were part of the primitive catholic Church. These meaningless arguments and many more are also front and center in Roman Catholicism because they distract from the centuries of crimes of the Church and the subtle changing of biblical precepts. They sidetrack attention away from The Catholic List that Roman apologists and theologians defend.

Purgatory, indulgences, transubstantiation, penance, sacraments, rosary, confession to a priest, focus on Mary, and sources given equal authority in addition to the Scriptures—it's all a diversion of man-made creations to control and cause followers to be dependent on the system. In reality, we go directly to God, we have the Scriptures to guide us, and we have the Holy Spirit inside us to finish the story God invited us to be a part of. We have no need to allow religious establishments to dictate their legalism, propaganda, and false theologies; and certainly, we do not need them manipulating their followers to drain their financial accounts.

"When you shuck it down to the cob,"[56] as one Bible teacher used to say, you have the Church that follows the truth of the Scripture and follows the teachings of the early apostles; and then you have the contra-Church— any institution, denomination, cult, or even individuals that have not only departed from the simple resurrection message, but have adapted man-made philosophies, man-made doctrines, man-made dogmas, man-made statement of faiths, and man-made theologies to fit their own agendas. Surprisingly, this latter group was even an issue while the early apostles were still around:

> "They went out from us, but they did not really belong to us.
> For if they had belonged to us, they would have remained with
> us; but their going showed that none of them belonged to us" (1
> John 2:19).

"For false Christs and false prophets will appear and perform great signs and miracles to deceive, even the elect—if that were possible" (Matthew 24:24).

"How is it you don't understand that I was not talking to you about bread? But be on your guard against the yeast of the Pharisees and Sadducees. Then they understood that he was not telling them to guard against the yeast used in bread, but against the teaching of the Pharisees and Sadducees" (Matthew 16:11-12).

"For the time will come when men will not put up with sound doctrine. Instead, to suit their own desires, they will gather around them a great number of teachers to say what their itching ears want to hear. They will turn their ears away from the truth and turn aside to myths" (2 Timothy 4:3-4).

"Keep watch over yourselves and all the flock of which the Holy Spirit has made you overseers. Be shepherds of the church of God, which he bought with his own blood. I know that after I leave, savage wolves will come in among you and will not spare the flock. Even from your own number men will arise and distort the truth in order to draw away disciples after them" (Acts 20: 28-30).

The Bible showed early on that there was going to be a separation. And not just a separation, but that the deception would be so convincing that those grounded in the faith would be deceived. One has to explore if the magisterium and its liturgy seem to come front and center with the "call out". The Roman Catholic Church has changed much of the Gospel message since the early apostles' teaching, and we know that clearly because of The Catholic List described in Chapter 1.

Even during the time of diabolical leadership in the Roman Catholic Church, there have always been groups of genuine Christian believers who set themselves apart from the hypocrisy of the Church. There have been individuals and groups of believers who always embraced the original Gospel preached by James, John, Peter, Paul, and many more—a Gospel not corrupted by an evolving theology instituted by questionable popes or a political Christianity, but a Gospel that kept everything simple.

They clung to an understandable and genuine faith, trust, and belief in the resurrection of our Lord and Savior, Jesus Christ, recognizing that His mission was to reconcile the world back to Himself, not counting sins against humanity. Complicated and made-up theology that almost no one can fully understand was not part of the plan; it was only instituted to have financial and political power to control the masses. This control was facilitated by creating "spiritual busyness": endless penance, confessions, repetitions, indulgences, and unbiblical systems that have been in place for far too long.

Apologies for all the wrongdoings over the centuries are no longer acceptable. A genuine apology would be to admit that the items instituted on The Catholic List (since the original Gospel was espoused by Jesus and the apostles) are not in sync with biblical theology. Then, repentance would mean moving forward with a return to the Great Commission, a return to simple faith in Christ, promoting the proper understanding of grace, and choosing to "follow Him."

Jesus did all the work. Jesus did everything for us to avoid a self-righteous, human-effort, religious path.

Anyone who gathers, as the original Church did primarily in homes with just a few people, to worship, acknowledge, and fellowship with God and other believers in a celebration of that single event, that single person, that single idea has found the biblical definition of "church" (*ekklesia*).

For Cradle Catholics

For many, your mom and dad are Catholic, your grandparents were as well; your family has been steeped deep in the Catholic faith, never entertaining the idea that something could have gone wrong in the 2,000-year journey. Maybe the theology they embraced is not right after all. Most older Catholics have never done the proper research on the early Church or studied any biblical theology. Not many have attempted to read lengthy books on the history of Christianity and the early Church, especially from non-biased sources. They certainly did not have the Internet to accelerate that process. They were faithful attendees, but they only went through the motions, caught in the inertia of a religious wheel; they were not theologians.

Like automation, generations parroted everything they were told to say and do from family tradition without ever stopping, walking across the street, looking back, and asking, "Is there anything wrong here?" I am not criticizing them at all. I admire their loyalty and faithfulness. I admire their intentions as well. However, I think if we are all honest, we're prone to believe that "the Church I am attending right now is accurate on spiritual matters. My parents got this right." However, a valid question that every Christian might ask is: how much humbleness is required and how much does pride have to retreat to admit, "maybe I have been wrong about my belief system over the years"?

For the Catholics who have done research and bring questions about what they find, they are simply taught to forget about all the bad events that happened over the centuries and claim God will always protect and preserve the Church Christ founded. This begs the question, though, is it ethical or wise to dismiss and ignore all the bad the Roman Catholic Church engaged in? Yes, we do know that God *will* always protect His Church. The irony is that today's Roman Catholic Church is not the Church God is protecting.

The true Church is not Roman Catholic, but it's not necessarily Protestant either; it might not be the denomination that you went to on Sunday; instead, it's any gathering of people meeting in homes, meeting at Starbucks, meeting in your car, or even meeting in a church building with thousands of others—any gathering of those who have not *abandoned* the original Gospel established by Jesus and preached by Peter on opening day in Acts 2.

There was an understanding by the early apostles that following Judaism would not get you into Heaven, nor would following the Old Covenant or following rules and regulations and the Ten Commandments. Good works outweighing evil deeds would not get you in, striving to obtain salvation would not get you in, keeping current on your confessions would not get you in, and following a long, fatiguing list established by a Church would not get you in either. You simply have to be born again by genuinely trusting that Christ accomplished His plan (through the cross and resurrection) and making a personal choice to respond to the call to follow Him. Trust

Him. Embrace Him. That's true Christianity. That's the Gospel. That's the true Church. God protects His Church for those who follow those simple provisions.

There is no mystery, guessing, or crossing your fingers in hopes that you've done enough to be a part of the kingdom of God. There is no system, no playbook, no journey to salvation or progressive obtainment. Instead, trust that God has reconciled the world through Jesus Christ, not counting men's sins against them (2 Corinthians 5:19).

Tell everyone you know that this is true, and let them see your fruit that stems from an inward change and a life that has transitioned from darkness to light, from spiritual death to spiritual life through the finished work of Christ, not by striving and earning and trying to achieve. Simply yield to the Holy Spirit's life inside of you. That was the message from the early apostles. The Gospel of Jesus Christ has not changed and needs no modification.

If you genuinely repent, believe, and trust this message about Jesus Christ, welcome to the Christian life. Now, let's show the whole world your life is defined by following Christ. Jesus is your Savior who came to give, not require. It's amazing. It's straightforward. It's not a system. It's not a list. It's not a process of procuration. It's not perseverance to the end by human effort. It's not a self-righteous system. It's entirely God's grace.

When you carefully look at The Catholic List in Chapter 1, the rejection of those Catholic concepts is logical because they never appear in the Scriptures. Those doctrines and dogmas that the Catholic Church has embraced in that list have been taken out of context, misinterpreted, or added erroneously. Many Roman Catholic beliefs are forced, coerced, and have trickled their way into a pure Gospel, corrupting it like broken glass in homemade garlic mashed potatoes: one bite causes devastating problems.

The Church as Christ Intended

Jesus started the *ekklesia*, any gathering of believers centered around Himself and what He accomplished at the cross and resurrection, absent of pretentiousness and self-effort or any obtainment process. The catholic Church in the first couple of centuries implemented and carried forward this simple Gospel; the Roman Catholic Church amended that.

Jesus lived out his ministry not in a cathedral, not in an institution or organization, not with a hierarchy that would turn into a regime or monarchy with imperialistic motives. Jesus did not start that system. We are in a fallen world full of corruption, full of Satan's attempts to jeopardize, confuse, and distort Christianity. So, the true Church that Jesus started is defined as one following the original Gospel.

The Church, as Jesus indicated before His ascension back to Heaven, had a simple goal: go spread the news of what you have seen and what you have heard by simple faith. The original catholic Church did that. The Catholic Church of the Roman Empire and the subsequent Middle Ages altered those instructions. Today, the message of Jesus's death on the cross and His permanent, one-time forgiveness, sacrifice, and invitation to follow Him and experience true life, surprisingly, can still be discovered in the Roman Catholic Church, as well as all Protestant churches.

How can that be possible since the Catholic Church and many Protestant churches teach a distorted Gospel? God is simply powerful enough to get His message across, not because of controlling, theologically inaccurate institutions, but despite those institutions.

Today, many genuine Catholics have incredible hearts for God and believe in His simple Gospel. That is the true Church. Those Catholics are genuine Christians. Today, we see Protestants who have incredible hearts for God and believe in His simple Gospel. That is the true Church. Those Protestants are genuine Christians. Is the Roman Catholic Church still an institution full of corruption, immorality, deception, and inaccurate theology from devious popes over the years? Absolutely. Can the same be said about many Protestant churches and Protestant theologies? Definitely. Does God still protect His Church? Yes, He does. One simply has to recognize what the term "His Church" really means.

I understand that there are some high-profile teachers (names most would know) who preach total condemnation for anyone in the Catholic faith because they have been sold a different Jesus and a different Gospel. These teachers claim that every Catholic has been misled and is on the path of destruction. Similar claims would be made by the Catholic faith regarding

Protestants and their failure to find any salvation outside the context of their assembly.

However, it doesn't take a lot of wisdom, experience, or spiritual intellect to recognize that both parties would be wrong. Some of the most genuine born-again Christians I have met have been in the Catholic faith. This is just the opposite of what one might expect I would say since I have called out the Roman Catholic institution for what they represent. Yet we would grossly underestimate God and His incredible power to reveal Himself to those who are still trapped and surrounded by a legalistic system if we were to just write off souls for showing up at the wrong address each week.

Does being trapped in the institution make it harder for someone to latch onto the simple message of faith, trust, and belief in Christ alone and follow Him? Are individuals more likely to completely miss the message and accept a system of checking boxes as opposed to a personal relationship with God, through Jesus Christ alone with the guidance of the Holy Spirit? Absolutely.

I have participated in enough Catholic forums to understand the confusion many have regarding their faith. It would not be unusual to get dozens of different answers when asking Catholic forum participants the most basic theological questions. The Roman Catholic Church is packed full of individuals who are not Christ followers because the message of Christ has been so contaminated. This tainted message deceives individuals into falsely assuming that if they check the Catholic boxes they are in the kingdom. These individuals miss the simple message of grace that will be unfolded in the later chapters of this book.

It is equally as hard to find the message of Christ in many Protestant denominations, but we have a God who extends grace that is unmeasurable in human terms. He is not peering out like a judge in a courtroom, but a Heavenly Father who wants us to be a part of His story. The gates of hell can never prevail against the Church Jesus started or the message of what He came to do. My appeal to all Catholics is to carefully read Chapters 9 through 13 and finally discover the Church Jesus truly started.

PART III:

THE CATHOLIC PRIESTHOOD AND THE VATICAN

CHAPTER 6

Catholic Priests: It's Worse Than You Think

A lot was revealed about the papacy in the first three chapters, and the consequences of the Roman system redefining the Church in Chapters 4 and 5. As we work our way down the hierarchy a few notches, we find Catholic priests. Most people have grown up seeing priests depicted on television and movies with their black robes and white collar, and mostly there is an illusion that these men are moral, virtuous spiritual leaders as they go through the rituals of the Church, dispensing the sacraments, and certainly many are.

The reality of what has gone on behind closed doors of the lives of many of these priests has been quite a controversial topic in recent years and has become a revelation of the gross error that has been made by the Church regarding the ecclesiastical law of celibacy. If one seeks to learn how the Roman institution got so far astray from the original catholic Church, there are two critical components to examine: the papacy and the priesthood. The papacy has already been exposed, but the reality of what is about to be revealed about the priesthood will leave readers aghast.

First, it should be acknowledged that the entire priesthood and sacrificial system of the Old Covenant has been abolished by Jesus. This will obviously be vehemently debated by Catholic apologists, but Christ became the fulfillment of the Jewish priesthood and now is the only mediator between God and man (1 Timothy 2:5). The idea of a mediating priesthood after Jesus is not biblical and conflicts with the New Covenant. There is no mention in the New Testament or early church writings of mediating priests for the first two centuries. Bishop and elder (*presbuteros* and *episcopos*) are interchangeable terms used for the same office according to the Scriptures. The New Testament does not use the Greek term for priest (*hiereus*) as a separate office.[1] However, instead of the two-tier system of the New Covenant, the Roman Catholic Church, in a reversal from the early catholic Church's teaching, chooses a three-tier system.

Thompson makes the point that the early church fathers like Clement and Polycarp only recognize bishops and elders, and in the Didache (a late first-century Christian manual written by students of the apostles), only a two-tier system is outlined: "Appoint yourselves bishops and deacons worthy of the Lord" (Didache, 15). We see multiple scriptures affirming this teaching as well (1 Peter 5:1-2, Acts 20:17, 1 Timothy 3:1-15, Titus 5:1-7, and more). Paul sends greetings to the bishops and deacons of Philippi, but omits the presbyters because they were included with bishops as the plural indicates (Philippians 1:1).[2] We even see from later church fathers like Jerome that a two-tier system was in place:

> "A presbyter, therefore, is the same as a bishop ... so let bishops know that rather by custom than by the Lord's arrangement are they greater than presbyters."[3]

Jerome understood that the priesthood was a later idea and not what was practiced by the original catholic Church. A priesthood is a leftover tradition from Judaism that Christ came to challenge. However, the priesthood worked its way into the Roman system and its legitimacy will continue to be proclaimed, so let's take a look at the results of that invasion.

The Celibacy Scam

It is important to recognize that there seems to be a divide. There are Catholic priests with good intentions, devotion to God, and the desire to serve and primarily focus their lives on heading a parish in a full-time ministry capacity.

There are also those men who seek out the priesthood seemingly with the sole purpose of indulging their sexual orientation and their insatiable desire to have sex with young men, and oftentimes, even younger boys. Because of the distorted and broken Roman Catholic system and the obsolete celibacy requirement, both paths ultimately end in destruction and disillusionment.

Most Christians are aware that Roman Catholic priests are required to take a vow of celibacy. The Roman Catholic Church sees this vow of celibacy as "a special gift of God by which sacred ministers can more easily remain close to Christ with an undivided heart and dedicate themselves more freely to the service of God and their neighbor."[4]

It's important to understand the origin of this harsh, Draconian rule that has created such havoc among the priesthood. This totalitarian structure of the Church, with its enormous wealth and secrets, involved an agenda to become more lucrative, and, like a script from the program *American Greed*, came up with another scam not too far removed from the indulgences scam discussed earlier.

This chapter is dedicated to exposing and shining the light on one of the worst ecclesiastical laws that has ever been generated by the Roman Catholic Church: the celibacy of priests. This, with many other man-made regulations and requirements, has resulted in devastation in whole communities and has shipwrecked the lives of not only the priests themselves but the hundreds of thousands of people they've victimized.

Although priests do make a vow of celibacy, this does not preclude them from having sexual relationships. Exercising chastity and celibacy are two completely separate ideas, whether a vow has been taken or not. Celibacy relates to remaining unmarried, and chastity is choosing sexual purity. We find that priests, cardinals, nuncios (ambassadors), and many members of the Roman Curia (the Vatican court system) have relinquished honoring any characterization of the word chastity (see Chapter 8). In addition, history has now shown that the system set up by the Roman Catholic magisterium paved the way for the most extreme sexual anomalies ever recorded.

Since it relates only to marriage, the vow of celibacy is not broken if a priest engages in sexual relationships. So, a "celibate priesthood" does not reflect the actual conduct or purity of the priests. However, in the Roman Catholic Church's distorted theology, when priests do engage in sexual relationships, even criminally with children, they just pop into confession for a pardon and their slate is cleaned for another few hours or days until they transgress again. It's a very dysfunctional system.

Author and pastor John MacArthur says about the Roman Catholic Church, "It absorbs its immoral, it absorbs its heretics, it absorbs everybody and perpetuates the system."[5] It's always about the Catholic "system", and MacArthur makes the point that regardless of the sexual deviancy of priests, their standing as a priest cannot be canceled, reverted, or rescinded. A priest is a priest for life according to Roman Catholic law. It's once and forever. Shortly before the election of Pope John Paul II, thousands of priests were trying to exit the Church and get married, but that changed after he came to power. Duffy states in his book that, "Priests might leave the ministry, but with difficulty, and the pope would not release them from their vows of celibacy." Why would the pope be so adamant that priests not leave the ministry? Instead of being disturbed about their departure, wouldn't someone caring (with even a small amount of empathy) want these guys to be able to get married and have normal families, if that is the pathway they have chosen to seek happiness? One can only speculate. Of course, this leaves the Church having no idea what to do with sexually deviant and pedophile priests.

MacArthur goes on to summarize that when you take men with raging sexual passions, priests who are driven by lust and restrain them with the false doctrine of celibacy, put them in monasteries and seminaries, locked up with other men with sexual frustrations—many of whom are homosexual—you have a recipe for disaster. To compound the problem, stick them in confession booths all day long listening to all kinds of immorality and perversion from confessors and the curse of celibacy is even worse. It produces a level of hypocrisy that is just astonishing. Nuns are not exempt from this perversion either. MacArthur states, "Priests and nuns are sexual ticking time bombs."[6] It's not *if* they're going to explode, but when.

And the Roman Catholic Church? They care more about priests remaining unmarried than the sexual abuse being done to innocent children. In the past, marriage threatened the Church's power and property. And yet, as a total hypocritical gesture, the Church holds that marriage is a sacrament—the "holy" sacrament of marriage that the alleged "most holy" priests and nuns are completely denied. It's a depraved system.

The sexual deviancy of past popes filtered over to priests on an enormous level centuries ago while implementing this devastating doctrine. The system that began to be put in place after Constantine in AD 315 bred and spread homosexuality and pedophilia at a rate never seen in human history. And most disturbing, pope after pope covered up these publicly announced sexual abuse cases. The popes of old were the sexual perpetrators themselves, and modern-day popes cover up and protect the current sexual predators (Pope Francis, Pope Benedict, and Pope John Paul II, to name a few).

Pope Francis issued a law requiring priests and nuns to report sexual abuse when they are the ones doing it! It's insanity on the highest level. The perpetrators and sexual predators *are* the priests—thousands and thousands of priests, all warped by a *colossal* mistake of the doctrine of celibacy, handed down by tradition, and which was never a doctrine of the original Church or part of the original Gospel.

How rampant is homosexuality in the priesthood? In 2019, *The New York Times* published an article titled, "'It Is Not a Closet. It Is a Cage.' Gay Catholic Priests Speak Out." In the article, author Elizabeth Dias highlights the hypocrisy that church leaders have driven gay congregants away in shame and insisted that homosexual tendencies are disordered while thousands of priests are gay. I do not believe that the average Catholic attendee fully grasps how widespread homosexuality is among the priesthood. Although less than a dozen have publicly come forward in the U.S., estimates have gay men making up over 40% of the priesthood, Dias states. Many priests that were interviewed have that number closer to 80%.[7]

According to Fr. Donald B. Cozzens, a PhD and president-rector and professor of pastoral theology at Saint Mary Seminary, "An NBC report on celibacy and the clergy found that 'anywhere from 23 percent to 58 percent' of the Catholic clergy have a homosexual orientation. Other studies find that approximately half of American priests and seminarians are homosexually oriented. Sociologist James G. Wolf, in his book *Gay Priests*, concluded that 48.5 percent of priests and 55.1 percent of seminarians were gay."[8]

One can just imagine the average Catholic family driving up in the parking lot of their parish and, before walking inside, they flip a coin: Heads our priest is gay; tails he is not. That would not be too far away from reality. To comprehend the hundreds of thousands of kids that have been sexually abused by a percentage of these priestly predators causes one to second guess their faith, and rightfully so. Only a portion of homophile priests have either acted on their urges, engaged in adult homosexuality, or pursued young people, but the reality is now known. The secret is out.

And popes and bishops, because they represent an entity, not anything ordained by God, cover all the abuse up; if not, the whole system is doomed and discredited. The entire system is exposed. The irony? The truth has already exposed the prevalent sexual perversion and predation in the priesthood and the subsequent cover-ups. It's too late to hide it now.

The arguments that Catholic leadership has given over the years, stating, "Well, there is sin in every Church, we always self-correct," is a weak excuse and unacceptable to any intelligent, objective person. The problem is systemic. And, to protect the system, the Church has its members so caught up in "regiments," "procedures," "a system of staying in good graces with God," and "staying so busy" that most Catholic attendees do not perform the research; they never take the time to realize something isn't right here. Grievously, molested kids are left to question, "If God is so loving, how could He ever have allowed these leaders of the Church to molest and destroy my life?"

This senseless doctrine of celibacy among priests is upheld despite opposition by most Catholic attendees, who know it makes no logical sense. More than 80% in one survey revealed that the Catholic population is in complete disagreement with the Catholic blunder of celibacy.[9] Of course, the Church will not rescind this policy because it would prove that the Church has been led into a grievous miscalculation and error that resulted in rampant perversion throughout the institution.

In 1 Corinthians, Paul encourages those who have self-control that it might be better not to marry so total attention can be given to the Lord, versus the care and concern and effort it takes to maintain a family. Just a suggestion, Paul disclaims. But that is not the whole story. The rest of the story is critical not to overlook. Paul says:

> "Now for the matters you wrote about: It is good for a man not
> to marry. But since there is so much immorality, each man should

have his own wife, and each woman have her own husband" (1 Corinthians 7:1-2).

"Now to the unmarried and widows I say: It is good for them to stay unmarried, as I am. But if they cannot control themselves, they should marry, for it is better to marry than to burn with passion." (1 Corinthians 7:8-9).

Although celibacy was around early on, Paul's exhortation is primarily what the Church taught until about the eleventh century. To make celibacy mandatory is completely unbiblical and naive. To advocate that Paul preached only singleness and leave out the verses above is dishonest. Some Catholic teachers, at times, have taught that Peter was unmarried, but scholars know this is untrue. Peter may have been widowed later, but he was definitely married since the Scriptures talk about his mother-in-law.

Since Peter, so highly revered in the Catholic Church, was married, wouldn't it be a logical conclusion to leave marriage up to the individual? In fact, look at what Paul says in 1 Timothy:

"The Spirit clearly says that in later times some will abandon the faith and follow deceiving spirits and things taught by demons. Such teachings come through hypocritical liars, whose consciences have been seared as with a hot iron. They forbid people to marry and order them to abstain from certain foods, which God created to be received with thanksgiving by those who believe and who know the truth. For everything God created is good, and nothing is to be rejected if it is received with thanksgiving, because it is consecrated by the word of God and prayer" (1 Timothy 4:1-5).

I think it safe to say that the Roman Catholic Church, which forbids priests to marry, is engaging in rule-making that God would never approve of. Celibacy existed in Buddhism and other pagan religions, but this requirement by the Catholic Church is devastating and destructive beyond comprehension, as we will see shortly.

Celibacy in Church History

To understand the roots and devastating effects of the Catholic Church's celibate priesthood policy, let's take a glance at the past. MacArthur states that there were many philosophies floating around during the first few centuries, one of which was Gnosticism, and it had a strong focus on the human body around the idea that matter (the human body) was evil, and the spirit was good. The belief formed that spirituality could be obtained by denying the body. Numerous vows were taken by Gnostics to align with this belief system such as vows of poverty, vows of silence, vows of chastity, and not surprisingly, vows of celibacy.

This group ate only meager meals and attempted to deny the body any pleasure whatsoever. Around the third century, celibate priests became common. By the time of Pope Leo in the fifth century, it was obligatory in the western Roman Catholic Church, while the Eastern Orthodox Church never bought into this doctrine.[10]

It wasn't until 1917 that celibacy became canon law for priests, but in the eleventh century, under Pope Gregory VII, the Holy See began to manipulate and capitalize on forced celibacy. Until then, it was well understood and documented that the housings of priests were "dens of corruption" engaging in orgies and strolling the streets at night for mistresses and male prostitutes.[11] This was the start of what would develop into one of the highest concentrations of homosexuals in modern history: the Vatican (the shocking truth will be revealed in Chapter 8).

It's imperative not to overlook the main motive behind the Catholic Church's hard-lined policy concerning celibacy: Money. Prior to the time celibacy was demanded, priests had families and were powerful people. They were married with kids and acquired great amounts of wealth from gifts that citizens would give them. Many priests owned land and passed this wealth on to their children. The Roman Catholic Church, in pursuit of financial gain, saw an opportunity. They required priests to separate from their wives and children and their property was confiscated.

This created a huge surplus in the Roman Church's treasury. One can only imagine the devastation resulting from a Church making a decision to kick wives and children into the streets to live in poverty, resulting in many becoming prostitutes and committing suicide at alarming rates.[12] A Christ-centered Church would have never made such a foolish and dishonest decision; a fallible institution would. And the Roman Catholic Church did.

The Fallout

To realize that the root problem of today's global sexual abuse of adults and minors, but mostly children, is the result of the Church forcing celibacy on its priests in a move to grab power, money, and control is quite shocking. This is hard to comprehend, but no other religious system or institution on the planet has caused more damage to children than Catholic bishops, cardinals, and priests. The sexual abuse of children at the hands of Roman Catholic priests is a global catastrophic crisis. And it is the outcome of a blatant Church error of the highest magnitude.

A good starting place to view the damage is right here in the United States. According to the Meneo Law Group, their database contains over 6,000 clergy members accused of abuse in the U.S. alone.[13] *The Boston Globe* had that number closer to 9,000 during previous investigations. Forty-one Catholic dioceses have not even released their lists of credibly accused abuse, with these dioceses covering the attendance of over 9 million Catholics.[14] The problem is far worse than the staggering 6,000 that have been identified.

New York, for example, has yielded a high source of identified abuse that has caused devastating results to these dioceses. The Meneo Law Group details the extent of the problem:[15]

Location	Amount paid to victims	Number of victims
Albany Diocese	$3,000,000	40+
Brooklyn Diocese	$90,000,000	Unknown
Buffalo Diocese	$17,500,000	100+
New York Diocese	$64,000,000	300+
Syracuse Diocese	$11,000,000	79

The approximate numbers above represent New York only, but they are significant. In fact, one-half of the Catholic dioceses in New York have filed for Chapter 11 bankruptcy due to sexual abuse allegations. This is an eye-opening, stunning fact! After followers recover from being speechless and angered, this should be a wake-up call for all Catholics, because attending Mass at your local parish, grabbing lunch afterward, and ignoring the truth of the corruption in the priesthood is simply imprudent.

Including the New York numbers above, the settlements paid to victims so far in the U.S. have reached a staggering $3 billion. This is an astounding figure.

After the pope visited the U.S. to speak to church officials and thank them for selling Church assets to pay restitution to the victims and address the sexual abuse problem, *The Guardian* reported:

> "The pope said that 'God weeps for the victims' but we believe that there would be many less victims to weep over if Pope Francis and other church officials would take action to protect the children,' said Barbara Blaine, who was sexually abused by a local priest in Ohio and founded an outspoken advocacy group called SNAP (Survivors Network of those Abused by Priests)."[16]

This sexual abuse started to come to the public attention in the U.S. in the 1980s, and by the 1990s Canada, Chile, Australia, Ireland, and many other areas of Europe and South America were experiencing the same priestly predators. It was in 2002 that everything erupted when five investigative journalists with *The Boston Globe* exposed the depth of Catholic sexual abuse in a report called: "Spotlight Investigation: Abuse in the Catholic Church". This exposure was dramatized in the 2015 film *Spotlight*.

In addition to the sexual abuse that was uncovered was the discovery that the priests accused of this misconduct were being shuffled to other parishes to work, even being moved to other countries. This report brought the attention to the national level in the U.S., winning these journalists the Pulitzer Prize for public service.

Sadly, bishops who were found guilty of breaking canon law for the sexual abuse cover-ups have been allowed to retain the title of bishop "emeritus", a signifier that confers continued prestige and power. The bishops who covered up sexual abuse and allowed it to go on for decades, destroying the lives of more and more children, continue to be allowed in the governance of the Church. That is disconcerting and should be disturbing to all Catholics.

What had first appeared to be isolated cases revealed by *The Boston Globe* became a nationwide scandal, then a global crisis for the Roman Catholic Church. It takes a few minutes to sink in when you realize that the sexual abuse so prevalent in the Roman Catholic priesthood is a worldwide crisis, and better described as a catastrophe. "Father" is an unsettling term for these sexual predators who have been duped into remaining single, have no kids of their own, and their only interactions with children consist of grooming and abusing them. It is extremely disturbing, but a reality.

Many sources cite Bernard Francis Law as a classic and all too common case of a cardinal who covered up the serial rape of children that was exposed in 2002 by *The Boston Globe*.[17] He served as Archbishop of Boston from 1984 until the time of his resignation in 2002. Law was proven to have ignored or concealed the molestation of numerous children. Church documents demonstrate that he had extensive knowledge of widespread child sexual abuse committed by dozens of Catholic priests within his archdiocese. Over a period of almost two decades, he failed to report these crimes to authorities. Instead, he just transferred these priests to other parishes, where the abuse would often start all over again.

Cardinal Law also participated in the cover-up scandal with a priest named John Geoghan, who raped and molested 130 children in six different parishes over a period of thirty years. The summary description of "father" Geoghan in the article "North American Man/Boy Love Association" is: "An American serial child rapist and Catholic priest in Boston, Mass., who was treated for pedophilia and was reassigned to several parishes where he was involved with children again."[18] This seems unfathomable but is actually true.

Two years after Cardinal Law resigned from his position in Boston (for covering up the serial rapists Geoghan and others), Pope John Paul II appointed him Archpriest of the Basilica di Santa Maria Maggiore in Rome in 2004. There are simply no words for the cover-ups conducted by Cardinal Law, or the disgraceful actions of Pope John Paul II being proactive in appointing this criminal pedophile protector to a position in Rome.

It is worth noting that one of the priests that Cardinal Law moved from parish to parish was a priest named Paul Shanley, another serial rapist of children. Later, it was discovered that Shanley had addressed a 1978 conference that led to the formation of the North American Man/Boy Love Association (NAMBLA). Here is a description of this perverted organization:

> "NAMBLA is a pedophilia and pederasty advocacy organization in the United States. It works to abolish age of consent laws criminalizing adult sexual involvement with minors and campaigns for the release of men who have been jailed for sexual contacts with minors."[19]

Cardinal Law saw no problem moving this perverted sexual predator from parish to parish to continue his rampage of sexual crimes.

In 2019, NBC News reported that 1,700 priests and clergy accused of sex abuse are unsupervised, but more disturbingly an *Associated Press* investigation found that those credibly accused are now teachers, coaches, and counselors and also live near playgrounds.[20] Some have gone to Disney World to work, others to orphanages, and many are still working for the Roman Catholic Church. In fact, many have moved overseas to places like Peru, Mexico, the Philippines, Ireland, and Colombia, where they are unknown, and have remained priests in the Roman Catholic system.

In 2018, a Pennsylvania landmark jury report named over 300 predator priests accused of abusing more than 1,000 children in six different dioceses in the state.[21] One of the biggest misconceptions among American Catholics is that the "Spotlight" news report in Boston is over twenty years old, is ancient news, and problems like that do not exist today. The prevailing opinion seems to be that the Catholic Church has cleaned up its dioceses. Unfortunately, that could not be further from the truth. In fact, worldwide, sexual abuse by priests is worse than it has ever been.

Trent Horn attempts to shield the Catholic Church with a statistic that is very misleading: "Most accusations of sexual abuse among priests come from incidents that took place between 1950 and 1980."[22] Not only is this comment entirely untrue, it is a well-known fact that sexual abuse is worse than it has ever been in the Catholic Church. We have only begun to peel a few layers off of what has been hidden from the parishioners for decades, and most of these cases have emerged after 1980!

Due to the secrecy in the Catholic system and the reluctance of victims to come forward, it is almost impossible to identify every abuser or get an accurate number of all the ones abused. Consider a young boy, molested and raped by a priest who he trusted and held in high regard, having to tell his parents and even friends that this horrible event occurred. First, he is told that he better remain silent—but if he does break that silence, it is humiliating to have to endure the strenuous and stressful legal process, which includes having to publicly testify on a witness stand, all while the pedophile priest is just a few feet away.

What percentage of those abused never come forward? It's not easy to get raw data on that number. Many do not speak of their abusers until they are adults well into their fifties or sixties, if ever. Even then, they are embarrassed for having to admit this to a spouse or others. We know that clerical abuse has not stopped anywhere in the world. According to pewresearch. org, almost 70% say that abuse by Catholic clergy is an ongoing problem, and news reports confirm this to be true. As a result of how prevalent sexual abuse among priests is, one in four Catholics claim to have scaled back Mass attendance and reduced the amount donated to their parish.[23]

We have only glanced at the sexual abuse in the United States. As we head overseas, the results are far more extreme and impactful. Many have likely only heard about the prevalent 2002 scandal in the northeast and are not aware of what is happening in other countries. The bulk of the sexual abuse problem involving the rape and molestation of minors has been in Catholic churches in European countries. It is critical to look at a broader global range of abuse by the priesthood to confirm and absolutely verify that these are not isolated issues with some "bad apples", but the widespread result of a horrendous error made by the Roman Catholic Church in mandating the celibacy of priests.

If the abuse seems bad in the United States, with its almost 17,000 documented cases (and anywhere from three to ten times that amount because of victim silence due to shame, intimidation, and threats from the Catholic hierarchy), we leave and travel to Spain to see it has become a national crisis there with a much higher number of reported cases.

VOA News states that as of October of 2023, a staggering 400,000 people are estimated to have suffered sexual abuse from Spanish Catholic clergy and lay people, according to an independent commission, with over half of those victims being children. A nearly 800-page report of the abuse was released to the Spanish Parliament Lower House. Spanish Prime Minister Pedro Sandez commented: "Today, we are a little better as a country, because a reality has been known that everyone has known for many years, but no one spoke of."

VOA further reports that the Catholic Church refused to carry out its own probe into the abuse, but Spain's Parliament in March 2022 overwhelmingly approved the creation of an independent commission. Following an eighteen-month independent investigation, reports were critical of the attitude of the Catholic Church, calling its response to sexual abuse cases "insufficient." All agree that something has to be done to stop the Catholic abuse of "defenseless boys and girls." The Church minimizes or denies the problem, and only responds and "apologizes" after something explodes into a national headline.[24]

Research done by France's National Institute of Health and Medical Research shows that 80% of the Church's victims were boys, and the Roman Catholic Church covered up its shameful, mass criminal secrets. One Spanish individual of abuse stated: "I think each victim experienced it as if they were the only one [victim], and that's part of this phenomenon involving control and secrecy—we are in a condition of submission ... in a mental captivity. So, we follow this person who suddenly takes power over us ... We are caught in a spider web."

Another victim said: "I perceived this person as someone who was good, a caring person who would not harm me, but it was when I found myself on that bed, half-naked and he was touching me that I realized something was wrong—it's like gangrene inside the victim's body and the victim's psyche."[25]

One convicted French priest admitted to sexually abusing more than seventy-five boys over decades. Right around this time, in May of 2019, Pope Francis issued a new Church law requiring all Catholic priests and nuns to report clergy sexual abuse and cover-ups, yet he is fully aware that the priests and the nuns are the ones committing the abuse. This is an example of the fox in the hen house, typical hierarchal problem solving, and fallibility at its worst.

It's really important for Catholics to realize that worldwide, with no exceptions, most sexual abuse is taking place because of homosexual priests. Almost unequivocally, here is the chain of events:

1. A homosexual Catholic priest sexually rapes and abuses children.
2. The victims are threatened and told they better not tell anyone.
3. Some victims eventually come forward and report the abuse.
4. An investigation ensues.
5. Catholic leadership denies the allegations, blames the victims, and protects the priests.
6. The abuse is found to be so prolific and widespread that it hits the media and explodes into a national story.
7. The bishops, and even the pope, step forward and humbly apologize.

This is a very revealing chain of events and is absolutely not acceptable. Apologies under this repeated sequence of episodes have no value or sincerity. The pope's willingness to meet with just a "few" victims, in the public eye, shed some tears, and offer a visual "let me bless you," is determined to be despicable by many people. The pope needs to fix the root problem by either abolishing the priesthood (since it is not applicable in the New Covenant) or allowing priests to marry. Only bold action will fix a significant amount of the abuse.

Worldwide sexual abuse of kids under the umbrella of the Roman Catholic Church will not change or be reduced until celibacy is finally abolished. Afterward, the Church can follow in their pattern of an apology, forever regretting this destructive Church law.

As we fly a few hundred miles to the northeast from Spain, we land in France and find another country saturated with Roman Catholic priestly abuse. Sylvie Corbert with *AP News* released documentation of 330,000 children abused in France over a seventy-year period. That is a staggering and unprecedented number in and of itself. The abuse was perpetrated primarily by 3,000 priests, and here again, Catholic authorities and leadership engaged in another cover-up, according to the president of the commission that released the 2,500-page report.[26]

What did the French Bishops' conference do? Asked for their forgiveness. It's the central theme in the broken country club of the Catholic priesthood—the hierarchy just offers apologies. In Chapter 5 we saw the long list of things that the Roman Catholic Church has had to apologize for over centuries of corruption, and as we come to the sexual abuse discoveries in modern times, we find the same prolific apologies.

Reuters reported on a commission that 4,815 children were sexually abused by members of the Portuguese Catholic Church—mostly priests— over a seventy-year period, stating that the findings were just the tip of the iceberg. The same abuse. The same narrative. The same cover-ups. The same denials. All followed by an apology.[27]

Although we have only scratched the surface in Europe, we navigate to South America to examine cases there as well. The findings are much the same: prolific sexual abuse and cover-up by the Catholic Church and Catholic schools with little justice or criminal convictions. As a reminder, "sexual abuse" and "cover-ups" seem to be used synonymously in all of these worldwide reports. There is never one without the other in the Roman system. María Hernández with *AP News* reports on the sexual abuse and cover-up of Catholic priests in Chile, describing a mother who spoke of her 12-year-old son who was abused at a Catholic school: "Soon after she learned what happened, Helmut Kramer's mother grabbed a pair of scissors and cut the priest out of photographs from her son's baptism ... she never attended Mass again. She says that she will never set foot in a church, and she does not trust the pope or any priest."

"What brought the sexual abuse in Chile to the forefront", Hernandez says, "is another priest, Fernando Karadima, which shook the Vatican itself and marred Pope Francis's trip to Chile in 2018. Instead of applause, he was greeted with unprecedented protests against a papal visit. The situation became worse when Francis accused Karadima's victims of slander, only to later admit, he made 'grave errors' in judgment and begged them for forgiveness." The "infallible pope" making grievous errors! The term would be humorous if it wasn't so offensive.

Hernandez reports that the confidence of the Chilean people in the Roman Catholic Church has gone from 77% to 31%, and shares the story of Jamie Concha, a 55-year-old doctor who was watching the news and became shocked at what he saw: a report about victims claiming clergy sexual abuse at the Mariest Brother's school where he had studied from the age of ten. It took him a few minutes before he turned to his wife and said, "That happened to me as well."

Hernandez shares another story of Javier Molina who said the priest was supposed to be his mentor, and from the very beginning of his family moving to Santiago, the priest showed interest in him and stated he was going to be his spiritual guide. Molina was fourteen and the priest was forty-eight. Here is Molina's description of what happened:

> "The priest showed up at our house and told my mom he was going to take me to his beach house. My mom worked at the parish, so feeling pressured, she agreed. I don't know how long I cried when the priest banged on the bathroom door and woke me up. We ate breakfast, he celebrated Mass and made me feel guilty. He said the devil tempted his faithfulness to God. On the way back the priest threatened me to never speak about this or he would tell everyone I was gay, and will make sure my mom would never find another job. It was shocking that people doubted my testimony."

A final story entails another victim of sexual abuse stating that he headed to the Archdiocese of Santiago and handed in his baptism certificate. When the employee on duty asked why he wanted to renounce Catholicism, he said, "Do you see the name of that priest? He raped me."[28]

Sadly, in many cases, the abused do not even get the consideration of an apology. Reuters.com reports about a group that was representing victims of child abuse in Argentina who had sent Pope Francis a letter to request to meet with him to start a dialogue about the sexual abuse problem, but after ten years, there had been no response. Ironically, Argentina is Francis' home country. Sebastian Cuattromo sent this letter because he, along with another student, was abused by a priest while attending a Catholic school in Buenos Aires. Pope Francis' response? He completely ignored the allegation (more on this story in Chapter 8).[29]

The stories are unending; it's a crisis in just about every country in the world. It's worse than an epidemic. Countless articles and publications have been written regarding meetings with past (and the current) popes about sex abuse cases from country to country, about scandals and cover-ups. Here is a very tiny fraction of some of the article titles out there:

"Pope meets with victims of sex abuse by clergy"

"Pope meets sex abuse victims: Vatican"

"Pope meets clergy abuse victims"

"Victim in Malta: Pope had tears in his eyes"

"My shame and humiliation: pope's emotional apology over 'unspeakable' child abuse as he meets five British victims"

"Pope meets with German sex abuse victims"

"Pope puts off punishing abusive priest"

"Benedict XVI, Munich and cover-up claims"

"Pastoral letter of Benedict XVI to the Catholics of Ireland"

"Pope and the sexual abuse—Pope Francis in Argentina"

"The Pedophile Paradise"

"The Silence"

"The History, the Unforgivable, and the Healing of North American Indian Boarding School"

"Northwest Jesuits to pay largest sex abuse settlement in US history"

"Future Pope John Paul II knew of sex abuse of priests"

"Polish TV report: John Paul II knew of abuse as archbishop"

"The shame of John Paul II: How the sex abuse scandal stained his papacy: The pope failed to take decisive action in response to clear evidence of a criminal underground in the priesthood."

There are hundreds and hundreds of reports in every part of the globe that would take years to research. Here are some of the countries that have documented sexual abuse cases involving the Roman Catholic Church: Argentina, Australia, Austria, Belgium, Brazil, Canada, Chile, Dominican

Republic, England, France, French Guiana, Germany, Guam, Honduras, Iceland, India, Ireland, Italy, Jamaica, Kenya, Liberia, Mexico, Netherlands, New Zealand, Nigeria, Norway, Paraguay, Peru, Philippines, Poland, Portugal, Puerto Rico, Scotland, South Africa, Switzerland, Timor-Leste, United States, Uruguay, Wales.

Anywhere you can find a Roman Catholic Church or school, anywhere you find a priest, bishop, or cardinal, anywhere you find a convent or monastery, or anywhere you can find Catholic clergy having to adhere to the obsolete and destructive requirement of celibacy, you find unprecedented sexual abuse.

It is important to not skip past some of the numbers presented so far, only seeing victims as a group or number. It is so easy to read articles and see the numbers of victims and abusers, but not let it register just how numerous the crimes are. First, the number of priests committing the criminal acts, and even more importantly, the number of victims that have been traumatized for life. So, let's think for a moment about the 6,000 priests that are on the watchlist in the United States. How many is 6,000? If you are Catholic, does that seem like a shockingly high number? How long would it take to drive across the country and find 6,000 Catholic priest pedophiles?

Hypothetically, you get in your car and you drive up to your local parish where there is one priest. You leave your local parish and head just slightly north to another town where you find one priest and a deacon. You leave there and head west for ten minutes, arriving at another parish where you find a priest. You spend half a day driving and have covered about fifteen priests, having only navigated a fraction of your state.

You realize that you have 5,985 priests to go, and you have to cover all fifty states. However, the revelation in the journey comes from the fact about every ten to twenty minutes, you arrive at another parish with another pedophile priest (statistically) adding to your numbers but realize you have just started this venture. How many is 6,000? You realize that if you want to accomplish your goal you have to come to the understanding that 6,000 corrupt, criminal clergy who are rapists is a gigantic number. Now, instead of 6,000 just being a number thrown around in an article, it represents an overwhelming number of criminals, all masquerading as Catholic priests that you have to go chat with. The problem is far more severe than you thought.

Then, you discover that you have only covered the United States. It probably took a couple of years to drive to thousands of parishes to find all those priests. Now, you have to head over to Europe where the number of perpetrators and victims there are far more than in the United States. In fact, the closer you get to the secretive Vatican City and the heart of Rome, the center of the Roman Catholic Church, the numbers are unimaginable.

I think the same consideration of recognizing the scope of the damage should be given to the victims as well. There are about 400,000 reported victims in Spain and unfortunately, it simply is too difficult to imagine driving to all of these individuals' homes to repeat the example used for the priests. Instead, a visual example might be a better option. You realize that a full football stadium might be the best analogy to depict wrapping your head around what 400,000 sexually abused individuals—mostly children—would look like.

The larger college football stadiums hold about 80,000 people. This would entail taking a look at five football stadiums full of people just to simulate the number of victims in Spain alone. What does that look like?

Now, you set out on a different journey, and that is to do a 10-minute interview with each victim to hear their personal, heart-breaking story—although their sexual abuse, on average, has lasted 4 years (1,460 days or 210,240 ten-minute periods). Yet, you are only covering one of those 210,240 ten-minute periods of pain they have experienced. Skipping lunch, you decide to work eight hours a day, seven days a week, 365 days a year until you hear at least ten minutes from each victim. You finally wrap up the interviewing process of all 400,000 victims after a staggering twenty-two years.

That is how many victims are in just one country. The worldwide numbers are astronomical, making it abundantly clear that the Roman Catholic Church has made the most damaging and devastating mistake in all of religious history by requiring priests to be celibate and not monitoring and taking action over the criminal priests spotlighted.

The number of worldwide victims that have been sexually abused under the Roman Catholic Church, its schools, monasteries, and convents is incomprehensible. Entire countries have been ravaged by cases of pedophilia and sexual abuse. This abuse has invaded the Catholic Church like a cancer. The Catholic sex abuse scandals became, and still is, the largest and most impactful scandal in all of modern-day Christianity. It should be mentioned that these horrific reports should not take away from acknowledging all the amazing, loyal, hard-working Christian teachers in Catholic schools who work tireless hours to educate kids and keep them protected. There is no bad reflection on them in any manner; in fact, most are probably not even aware of the widespread abuse that is written in these pages.

The reports we can primarily research today only go back about seventy years at the most, yet this abuse and perversion has gone on for centuries, as we saw in our examination of popes in the first two chapters. Documented reports of sexual abuse in the Catholic Church go as far back as the eleventh century. Martin Luther claimed that Pope Leo X vetoed a measure that cardinals should restrict the number of boys they kept for their pleasure, "otherwise, it would have been spread throughout the world how openly and shamelessly the Pope and the cardinals in Rome practice Sodomy."[30]

There are far more stories to look at and other countries to examine, but it would only serve the purpose of reporting the same pattern we have seen so far. What we know is that sexual abuse among priests is extensive—up to 50% of priests are homosexuals and/or pedophiles in some dioceses.

When looking outside the Roman Catholic system, the closest profession you can even find that might have the opportunity to engage in sexual abuse of children are secular teachers, and those instances consist of way less than 1%. Essentially, the Roman Catholic Priest is leading the pack with the sexual abuse of minors, and there is not even a close second. In addition, you don't have an "organized conspiracy" inundated with cover-ups and secrecy protecting the violators in the school system, or a system of moving the perpetrators to other schools just to hide the abuse. Only the Roman Catholic Church engages in such dishonest and deceitful practices.

What if we got this rare opportunity? A once-in-a-lifetime chance? What if Catholics and the public could beam up to Heaven for just a few minutes where it could be revealed how many priests are sexual predators and how many actual victims there have been (it's more than likely in the millions)? There would be such an outrage, a return to earth would certainly bring an inevitable change. In truth, the Catholic magisterium could make that change right now based on what they already know, but they won't. The dishonesty is too ingrained, and admitting the error is simply too embarrassing and humiliating for the one, holy, catholic, apostolic church.

By contrast, when genuine, born-again Christians have made mistakes and have participated in actions that have violated others, the Holy Spirit is constantly prompting us to make transgresses right—to make amends—and do the right thing. This common practice is how anyone should live the Christian life. Then, there is an institution like the Roman Catholic Church, a "Christian" Church by name, but the actions do not match any urging by the Holy Spirit to make things right.

Every reigning pope has been aware of the homosexual problem and sexual misconduct among tens of thousands of priests worldwide, and the devastating consequences involving children. However, not a single pope has had enough humbleness to say, "We have to stop this. We were 100% wrong. We have to let priests get married and have their own families. This will be our attempt to keep homosexuals from seeking out the Church with bad intentions, and not develop desires in those with good intentions to satisfy their sexual needs (because of an absence of marriage). It's a start." In fact, the laity would be far happier knowing their priest is married. This is the consensus of Roman Catholic members. One has to wonder, does the Church care what the laity thinks?

Because no pope has ever stepped forward to make a change (even after 1,000 years), this is a crystal-clear picture of a system that has developed other doctrine, dogmas, and laws not in alignment with the early apostles and not in alignment with the Scriptures. The movement about the resurrection and following Christ at the center of the original catholic Church has all but disappeared.

In like fashion to the pope, Trent Horn steps out to defend priests remaining celibate by stating:

"Some people say that if priests were allowed to marry there would be less sexual abuse in the Church and more men would want to become priests. But many pedophiles are married men, and being single doesn't cause someone to become attracted to children."[31]

This is an outrageous denial on Horn's part that celibacy in the priesthood has been a complete failure. Married men being pedophiles cannot be used as a diversion for what has transpired in the Catholic Church regarding sexual abuse among the priesthood. Horn's comments can only assume that the statistics that have been listed so far will only be discovered by a handful of people. Likewise, Horn does not address the flagrant homosexuality plummeting through the Church.

Celibacy in the Roman system shows no signs of ever going away. Catholic attendees should not tolerate it anymore. What has developed instead is a religious system centered around decisions that would only benefit that entity with liturgy developed according to the personal agendas of the clergy. The consequences have left millions with an altered Gospel and a religion that has policies that have damaged countless, but they refuse to correct course.

CHAPTER 7

Catholic Priests: Have the Talk

To dive a little deeper into the sexual abuse perpetrated by Roman Catholic priests, we must examine the homosexual connection. It is critical to note that the sexual abuse perpetrated by Catholic clergy primarily happens to boys eight to fourteen years old.[1] I know this is a sensitive topic to discuss, but the statistics revealed in the last chapter demand more dialogue and scrutiny—these truths have to be told. Why is that important? The priests perpetuating the abuse are obviously male. With some abusing as many as 150 boys or young men, many have proven to be uncontrolled and unrestrained predators. We should all recognize that a sexually abusive priest is exceptionally dangerous. There are even numerous, documented cases of two and three-year-old babies experiencing sexual abuse from Catholic priests. William Donohue of the Catholic League admits that the Church's child sexual abuse problem was really a "homosexual crisis."[2]

Acknowledging this is imperative for several reasons. We saw this same behavior with homosexual popes and clergy in the centuries past, and in the next chapter, we see this with the cardinals and priests in the Vatican today. When you place this stringent, prison-like law of celibacy on male priests and then house them in quarters with other men having access to young boys, they seek after the only sexual beings in their presence. The Catholic law of celibacy distorts their thinking and becomes mentally tormenting.

Once these sexual tendencies are developed through the perpetuation of Catholic policy (celibacy), and couple that with young boys pouring into a confession booth revealing intimate details about their flaws and struggles, you have a recipe for disaster and the results are devastating. Under the false illusion of absolution from a priest, vulnerable young boys become immediate targets.

Many priests that have this sexual persuasion will not stop until they are performing sexual acts on these young boys and coercing young boys into performing sexual acts on them. It's the worst possible violation of trust. And many unguarded Catholic parents are proud of their young sons for going to confession, yet, unknowingly, the parents have sent them into a compromising situation.

This false dogma of confession to a priest will be discussed in Chapters 9 and 10, but this is why the practice of these false doctrines and beliefs is so dangerous. They help to create the atrocities perpetrated under the Roman Catholic system. Confession should be to our Heavenly Father and openly and mutually with trusted believers (James 5:16), not in a private booth with (in many cases) a sexually-confused pillager who has been given an illusion of spiritual and emotional power over the confessor.

The Roman Catholic Church has shown many signs of being a malfunctioning system over the centuries, and the predatory nature of some priests is certainly one of those indications. Many crave and are obsessed with young boys. They are a huge threat to children and a huge threat to society. In fact, a number of books, such as *The Rite of Sodomy: Homosexuality and the Roman Catholic Church*, have argued that homosexual priests view sex with minors as a "rite of passage" for altar boys and other pre-adult males.[3]

Are there genuine priests in this false system whose sole desire is to honor God and serve the needs of the parish in an honorable way? Absolutely. Can the average parishioner distinguish the difference? They cannot. It's the "closet" and the secrecy of the Church that hides the offenders. Are all homosexual priests actively practicing? No, many use great restraint in this distorted system of celibacy. Are all homosexual priests child predators? Of course not. However, the potential to start the abuse begins through that channel.

Have the Talk

It is beyond critical for Catholic parents to find a way to have a conversation with your kids about what might have happened if you suspect anything is wrong. Of course, the first "knee-jerk" response from most parents would be, "Oh no, you do not know our priest. He would never do anything like that with our kids or any kids in the parish." Unfortunately, that thinking would be careless and misinformed. It would be a fatal mistake on any parent's part to dismiss this possibility. Catholic attendees do not know their priest behind closed doors. The thousands of priests that have been exposed so far have left their parishioners in utter shock.

It's a challenge, it's not going to be easy, but don't dismiss it. If you've thought something might be wrong besides the typical and expected hurdles of adolescence, please listen and take this critical advice: have the talk. Kids might deny it at first, but gently and firmly press the issue. Don't wait for your son to bring up the topic in his fifties. If your son, or daughter, has ever been alone with your priest, have the talk (just to make sure). Many would consider this "due diligence 101" for a Catholic parent because of what is now known.

In the midst of the prolific abuse among children in Catholic facilities by a countless number of priests, once again, we get an appalling comment from apologist Trent Horn: "According to journalist David Gibson, 'The Catholic Church may be the safest place for children.'"[4] This is an atrocious comment based on what has been uncovered so far. If Gibson could only interview the one million or so victims, how different his view would be. However, the takeaway here is the continual denial, contradiction, and inadvertence that comes from Catholic spokespeople. Horn proceeds to state:

> "... the Church as a whole should not be blamed for crimes committed by priests ... leaving the Church because a priest ... committed a serious sin would be like swearing off hospitals because a doctor committed malpractice ..."[5]

There are multiple problems with Horn's illustration. First, the Church as a whole *should* be blamed for the sexual abuse that has gone on for centuries, because the buck stops there. It's Church policy (celibacy), a failure to monitor, and the hierarchy repeatedly covering up priestly abuse that makes the Church responsible. Horn attempts to disguise the widespread abuse by saying in his example above that attendees should not leave the Church because *one* priest who commits a serious sin is just like *one* doctor who engages in malpractice—the hospital should not be abandoned, so the Church should not be abandoned.

However, we are not talking about a singular case or even a handful of cases—we are talking about 1 million victims or more under the Catholic roof. A better thought experiment would be whether an individual should choose to go to a hospital in which thousands of doctors injured or caused the death of thousands of patients, and it was all covered up by the administration. Of course they wouldn't. Who would ever feel safe in a place like that?

Psychologists and organizations that research sexual abuse have shown that predator priests make it a priority to approach the most vulnerable children: those who are passive, have little self-confidence, are easy to manipulate, often coming from dysfunctional families, and even those with learning disabilities. These kids are more apt to remain silent, even for decades. However, that is not always the criteria. Young people rarely have a lot of self-confidence anyway. According to Save the Children, here are common consequences after a priest has abused a victim: anxiety, hostility, aggression, PTSD, mistrust, guilt and shame, depression, low self-esteem, rejection of one's body, early or inappropriate sexual knowledge for their age, problems of sexual identity, socially withdrawn, antisocial behavior, sexually promiscuous behavior, suicidal tendencies, and even actual suicides.[6]

Catholics have to understand that this sensitive topic of celibacy and the devastation that it has caused worldwide could never be discussed at Mass. Even though celibacy has proven to have ravaged some communities, a priest would never take the liberty to divulge the facts that have been presented in these chapters because it would reaffirm that this canon law has been a tragic mistake.

One could come to the conclusion that sexual abuse happens in Protestant denominations, as well as other religions too, and that would be true. However, these cases are much more isolated cases and number in the hundreds, not over a million. There is no close second to the Roman Catholic Church. Any comparison that the Catholic Church could try to initiate would be useless—except as a complete diversion. Here again, diversions have been historically used as common tactics to protect the secrets of the Church.

To think otherwise is to be uninformed and choose to sweep the issue under the rug—which has been a common theme among the Catholic hierarchy. The Roman Catholic system is fragmented, the Church has made immense mistakes and has led its followers into error, yet it refuses to retract or change. As a result, it is responsible for destroying the lives of over a million individuals all because of one major blunder: celibacy.

Men and women go into monasteries under the illusion of being "holy" as they are so told by the Church, but it's a deception that ties back to the Middle Ages where so much vile corruption took place among the popes of the era. John MacArthur, in his teaching series "The Scandal of the Priesthood," talks extensively about the trap this medieval creation caused:

> "You know, the thing that is so sad about a priest is this. He's absolutely a blip on the screen, he has no past. Because when he came into the priesthood, or when she came into the convent, they gave up all their possessions and their relationships. They (the Roman Catholic Church) quote them, 'that if a man is not willing to leave father and mother and hate father and mother, for my sake, he's not worthy to be my disciple.' And so, there's a strong urge to hate everything that your parents stand for. So, you cut yourself off from the past, you have no present because you share life with nobody, and for sure, you have no future. Sad. And these kinds of unnecessary restrictions are no help to personal sanctity, let me tell you, they are a hindrance, a severe hindrance to it. So, the life of the monk and the life of the nun withdrawing from society, withdrawing from work, withdrawing from culture, withdrawing from the world, retiring into this cloister, losing themselves in mystic contemplation was thought to really be the higher life. Celibacy was a holy state. Some of them even emasculated themselves, thinking that would remove the temptation ... the Reformation came along and demolished all of this thinking with basically one theological fact: And that was in God's eyes, there's no difference between the sacred and spiritual and the

secular ... because in whatever you do, whether you eat or drink, you do to the glory of God.

"The Reformation understood you serve God, not by withdrawing from the world. And it may be safely said that there is far more of moral excellence and of true religion to be found in Christian households, than in the desolate homes of priests and in the gloomy cells of monks and nuns. Priests are broken, shattered, tragic, sad, disconnected people—no past, no present, no future. They are denied normal relationships and the friendship of marriage. They're victims of a terrible system with no biblical basis whatsoever. It is a soul-destroying process that leaves them in a situation of rampant temptation."[7]

The Trap of Legalism

Individuals seeking out the priesthood or desiring to become nuns falsely believe the perception that if you walk away from everything and decide to forfeit all material comforts, this elevates your spiritual position, and God is well pleased with your super-human self-effort. Many Christians do this to "gain points" with God but unknowingly drift into legalism (mimicking the Old Covenant Jewish system of following the law), which becomes a trap. The trap translates into never feeling like you do enough. Doing more is always required. The reason this is not spiritually satisfying is that Christians have inserted themselves into the equation of Salvation and have equated their position and right standing with God to "good works." It's a false theology, a false premise.

There is a sobering account in Matthew that all Christians take note of. Jesus is speaking:

"Not everyone who says to me, 'Lord, Lord,' will enter the kingdom of heaven, but only he who does the will of my father who is heaven. Many will say to me on that day, 'Lord, Lord, did we not prophesy [preach the Gospel] in your name, and in your name cast out demons, and perform many miracles? Then I will tell them plainly, "I never knew you. Away from me, you evil-do-ers" (Matthew 7: 21-23)!

These are a few scary verses until you understand what Jesus is saying. The theme of the New Testament, the theme of the New Covenant, scattered in hundreds of places throughout the text, is that your belief and faith in Christ is what makes you acceptable in the Father's eyes. In the verses above, you see a group of people who are taking credit for and boasting in their own righteousness ("look what I have done") rather than on what Christ has done. Religious institutions put their followers in great jeopardy when they preach a works-righteous faith system. Works righteousness will not save anyone. This is a message that has to be shouted from a megaphone: your good works will not get you into the kingdom of God. Jesus did not set up the system that way. Faith in Christ saves; human effort and good works (equally relied on for salvation) condemn, as we see from the verses above. A former Catholic, evangelist Mike Gendron makes the observation, "Religion wants to control, so they add requirements to the gospel of grace—holding people in religious bondage and deception."[8]

I attempted this "works based righteousness" in my Christian walk in my early twenties when I was saturated with legalism and trying to be the "Rambo" of Christianity. The thought was that I had to flood myself with religious busyness and constant work to measure up to God's expectations. Sunday included church in the morning and church in the evening. Monday was visitation day, where a group of us would drop by the homes of those who did not come to church that Sunday. On Tuesday was a Bible study in Atlanta consisting of about 2,500 singles, Wednesday night was church again, Friday night was a singles activity, and Saturday was often spent fasting, all to start the routine over again the next week. I felt "spiritual," but it didn't seem normal. It seemed forced. It seemed obligatory.

Not that any one particular thing on my weekly schedule was wrong, but it was the mentality of trying to live every minute striving to be in good standing with God. Forty years later, I've found it to be simply yielding to the indwelling Holy Spirit living inside of me and enjoying my freedom in Christ. That schedule in my twenties would have never lasted. I burned out.

Christians burn out. They become frustrated, and right when you hope that the busyness has a positive spiritual effect, it becomes a chore and a dread, followed by guilt. This is no way to live, thrive, or enjoy the Christian life.

Much of the Roman Catholic system is set up to strive to do good works instead of yielding to the Holy Spirit. It is a system of checking boxes, going to Mass, going to Mass again and again, repeating rosaries, repeating them again, standing up, sitting down, confession, giving up this, now it's time to give up that. It's hoping that God is just so pleased with my self-righteous striving for salvation, meeting Him halfway, a merited structure of endeavoring to accomplish something Jesus already accomplished on the cross. It's a system that does not work.

Christ released us from guilt, relieved us of spiritual obtainment, and gave us a new way to relate to God on this side of the cross, and we are barely part of the equation. Good intentions by many Catholics, and good intentions by many priests and nuns, result in disastrous spiritual emptiness for most. Even after all the boxes are checked, you have no idea where you stand with God and go to bed at night wondering how long you will spend in a Purgatory that doesn't exist. It's an organism of medieval manipulation, headed by a magisterium immersed in power, control, and supremacy.

Homosexuality in the Church

MacArthur goes on to call monks and nuns "inmates of monasteries"— essentially prisoners of the system. A group of unmarried men or unmarried women is a hangover from the Gnostic idea of "the flesh is evil, so just seclude yourself," which is very bizarre. In the fourth century, some went so far as to eat only grass, never bathe, and even live in trees to "achieve" this holiness state,[9] although God had already given them His righteousness at the time of their salvation. Martin Luther considered the monastic life to be pointless and anti-Christian (although monks did accomplish spreading Christianity in difficult times throughout European history).[10] Reports state that almost 50% of men are homosexual by the time they arrive at these strange monasteries, and the rest have little chance to remain heterosexual after any significant time is spent in such places.

I know this description sounds disrespectful, but it is a well-known fact that the priesthood, along with convents and monasteries, propagates the homosexual lifestyle, which unfortunately leads to a percentage becoming pedophiles. What is known to be true now is the fact these priests take whoever is available to them, and they have a lot of access to kids.

CBS *Sunday Morning* did a report that can be found on YouTube: "Gay Priests: Breaking the Silence". The report centers around homosexual priests who are starting to come out of the closet. "I just want to break the silence, I'm here," one priest declared. Another stated, "You cannot be homosexual and a priest—you have to hide one or the other."[11]

One interview that took place was with Father James Martin. He is the most high-profile advocate for LGBT Catholics, and in 2019 Pope Francis requested a meeting with him. A picture was posted in the Apostolic Palace (where pictures of presidents and diplomats are posted)—a strong sign of support. Martin said, "If you suddenly had all the gay priests in the United States come out, the Church would be forced to look at the question of homosexuality in a very different light. Martin states that Francis is the "most pro-LGBT pope ever." Martin guesses that 40% of the priest population is gay but would not be surprised if that number is closer to 80%.

The reason homosexual priests could never announce this sexual tendency to their superiors is that they would lose their income, their health insurance, and their pensions. As a result, they remain in the closet. They suppress their tendencies and continue to preside over the parish; the congregation is totally unaware. Many attendees are also not aware of the thousands of priests who leave the priesthood to get married. A recent CBS News report claims that the US faces a serious priest shortage, and that "between 1970 and 2024, the number of priests fell by more than 40%."[12] This mass exit happened profusely in the 1960s as well.[13] This topic is never talked about, as with many other Church secrets.

Average Catholic attendees are probably not aware of someone like Vincent Doyle, whose father was a priest. He launched a global website for the "children of the priests." The website got hits from 175 countries and he estimates, conservatively, that there are over 10,000 children from priests that are not recognized by the Church because of their secrecy, according to a special that was done by ABC Australia."[14]

According to the report, Doyle wants just one phrase to be uttered from the mouth of the pope: "Children of the priests."

Most Catholics are not aware of the internal battle that is going on inside the lives of these priests; even their local priest. They would be shocked if they could hear an honest confession from their priest of what they are not verbalizing to the parish. However, it is worth taking a look at some of these admissions. *The New York Times* article referenced earlier lists some quotes from some of these priests:

> "It really never was my shame. They're the ones that should have the shame for what they have done to myself and many, many other L.G.B.T. people" (Father Greg Greiten).

> "My family does not know that I struggle with this. I've never told them. I believe the Church's teaching on marriage, sexuality— just trying to understand what it means for me. It may sound kind of strange. I feel like, what I struggle with, I hope I can help other Catholics not lose their faith" (anonymous).

> "This is my life" (referring to homosexuality, Parish Priest in the Northeast).

> "It is not a closet. It is a cage" (Father Bob Bussen).

> "You can be taught to act straight in order to survive" (anonymous).

> "I was in my 50s when I came out. I entered the seminary at 18, A young, enthusiastic, white, male virgin who doesn't know anything, let alone straight or gay. There were years that I carried the secret. My prayer was not that, 'would God change me.' It was that I would die before anyone found out" (Father Bob Bussen).

> "When I was in the eighth grade, there were three things I could do. I could be a truck driver like my dad. I could be a

doctor; I wasn't smart enough for that. But I was gay, so the only other thing left was, I could be a priest" (anonymous).

"When I first came to my parish, I remember thinking, if I were to come out now, this would be the kind of place I could. That is far from my mind now. Obviously to my friends, it's nothing I hide. But the climate we are in, I'd never self-identify as a gay priest" (anonymous).

"There will be a time in your life when you will look back on this and you're going to just love yourself for being gay" (Catholic seminary professor, to a seminarian).

Author Elizabeth Dias tells the story of one gay priest, Father Greiten, who decided it was time to end his silence. At Sunday Mass, during Advent, he told his suburban parish he was gay, and celibate. They leapt to their feet in applause.[15]

This is not just unsettling in the realization of a homosexual priest in a leadership role, but in Catholic attendees being on board and excited for his announcement. The red flags are flying high with what is being bred, even among many followers.

These admissions from priests are just a small sample of the chaos that stirs inside the lives of so many priests. MacArthur shares an admission by the former Catholic priest, Emmett McLaughlin:

"The life of a priest is an extremely lonely one. He lives in a large rectory—he is still lonely. If he is the only priest in a solitary parish or desert mission, he is still more alone. As his years slipped by and the memories of seminary and its rigidity fade away ... The realization made that his life is not supernatural, but a complete mental and spiritual and physical frustration. He sees in his parish and his community a normal life from which he has been cut off, he sees the spontaneous childhood which he is denied. He sees the innocent normal companionship of adolescence which for him never existed. He performs the rites of matrimony as starry-eyed young men and women pledge to each other the most natural rights and pleasures. He stands alone and lonely at the altar as they turn from him and confidently, recklessly, happily step into their future home, family, work and troubles, and the success of a normal life. More than anything else, he seeks companionship, the companionship of normal people, not frustrated, disillusioned victims like himself. He wants the company of men and women, young and old, through whom he may at least vicariously take part in a relationship with others that he has been denied, and for which, at least subconsciously, the depth of his nature craves."[16]

That's the scandal of the priesthood. Priests who have heard other priest's confessions know that sexual activities are the common theme among priests as they try to fill the pain and void of a broken, obsolete system. And this is why we are finding, today, homosexuality has always been a large part of the priesthood. The Church has forced this unnecessary burden on priests and has been the cause of this dysfunction. The resulting sexual abnormality and its progression to pedophilia has been unprecedented.

MacArthur, in his examination of the priesthood, uncovers law enforcement's understanding of what happens with many priests who have become pedophiles:

"Pedophilia isn't the beginning of anything. It's the end of a long, long pornographic conduct trail. You don't start there, you end there. That's how it goes. At first, you just take what is there. And then the deviation demands more and more aberrant behavior, and it moves down younger and younger and younger. Pedophilia is the caboose on a long train. So, you see why this happens in this terrible, terrible system. And yet, they can't change it—the infallibility of the church. And as long as you don't get married, all you have to do is confess to another priest. Then, that perpetuates the power of the system. The immorality of the monasteries and the convents is legendary."[17]

MacArtur observes that it is well understood by priests that the recruiting process starts at a very young age for both men and women, as priests listen to the very hearts and souls of young confessors. Priests know the most opportune time to seize the opportunity and take advantage, especially for women who have had their hearts broken, often through the ending of a relationship; disillusioned, they are talked into going into a convent, wearing a ring, "marrying Jesus," having a chance to get away from an embarrassing situation. They are told that they can leave at any time, but the brainwashing is too intense to ever leave.

Not Just Priests

Helen Conroy (a former nun), in her book *Forgotten Women: In Convents*, talks about these women who are slaves to a system, and the horrible lives they are subjected to. She exposes how the Church leads them to these nunneries and how it discourages them from leaving. There is nothing more cultish than a Catholic convent, she states. Conroy points out that Catholicism adopted the idea of virgin women dedicated to the gods from pagan religions for its own purposes. The treatment of nuns in the past was horrendous. A nun becomes a "church possession"—the girls' minds are poisoned against their own mother who bore them, and against their fathers and siblings as well. It is dehumanizing.[18] Another book that unfolds the truth about life as a nun is *The Truth Set Us Free: Twenty Former Nuns Tell Their Stories*.

The Roman Catholic Church will argue that the lives of nuns are no longer like that, and certainly, in the past, it was much worse, but the root system is still in place. They will argue that priests and nuns serve an essential role in communities in hospitals and orphanages, and taking care of the poor—and that is not untrue. It is only the outside presence and projection of their involvement in these charities that most will ever see. However, what happens behind closed doors has been revealed. The truth is out.

Fortunately, the latest statistics show a drastic reduction in women becoming nuns. An ABC news report titled "America's nun population in steep decline" states, "According to a recent study, less than 1% of nuns in America are under forty, and the average sister is eighty years old."[19]

These men and women all need to be delivered from a prison system and into the arms of Christ. They are told they are going into the arms of Christ when they subject and attach themselves to this religious system, but in fact, it's bondage on the highest level. They need to be set free from the slavery, set free from a false self-denial, and fulfill the life God intended for every human being: freedom in Christ and Him alone.

As Christians, all of our hearts should go out to priests and nuns who are ensnared in a web, a clever trap, spun by the Church. It parallels all the schemes that have come along over the decades with followers tragically enamored with a false belief. MacArthur further states:

> "Some priests think they have this elevated position and fellowship with God in the dispensing of the sacraments. It's a lie. The true Christian life does not involve them at all. In many cases, they know it. They have a terrible plight in life and try to disguise it. They go in the closet. We know what happens in the closet. It's a scandal on the highest level. It's not an opinion. It's the life of a priest. We simply do not need any priests. We need one high priest—His name is Jesus Christ."[20]

At the ushering in of the New Covenant in the moment of Christ's death, the veil was torn (Matthew 27:51, Mark 15:38, Luke 23:45). Now we have direct access to the Heavenly Father not in a temple, not in a confession booth—we go into a private room with the Heavenly Father. Through Jesus Christ and no other way, we have a direct channel to God. And it's in the presence of God that we fellowship, we commune, we freely worship, we adore, we cry, we exercise humility, we surrender, we yield, we bond, we chat, and we confess any topic we want with no judgment, no checked boxes. It's absolute and complete freedom in Christ, alone.

All of this is available absent of an unnecessary priesthood which is still attached to the Old Jewish Covenant that not a single person has been under since the resurrection. It's past time to save the children and end the priesthood once and for all. At that point, priests can be allowed to marry and simply become pastors, shepherding and encouraging their congregations, but doing so without dispensing and performing magical sacramental accomplishments that were never part of the apostolic deposit. Jesus gave us a one-time sacrifice, forever eliminating the need for a priest and sacraments as prescribed by the Roman Catholic system. We are free to permanently yield to the one High Priest. These measures will precipitate the Roman Catholic Church, once again, becoming "a replica of" the one, holy, catholic, and apostolic Church of Jesus Christ.

CHAPTER 8

The Vatican: Behind Closed Doors

If you were to engage most Catholics in a conversation and discuss the fact that the Vatican has one of the largest percentages of gay men per capita in the world, there would be a lot of offended Catholics and some pretty mean stares. If you commented that best estimates have as many as 80% of the cardinals, nuncios (ambassadors), priests, and workers at the Vatican as being homosexual it would probably be perceived as a definite smear campaign.

To state that three of the last five popes were possibly gay, according to legitimate sources in the Vatican, would almost be unbelievable and incomprehensible. There have been a lot of shocking discoveries disclosed in this book so far (transpiring over centuries), but this could be the most appalling of them all.

In this chapter, we'll examine these claims and more, exposed by actual members of the clergy in a groundbreaking expose published in 2019.

Exploring the Vatican

Before diving in, however, let's take a quick look at what the Vatican is, especially for those who do not have a Catholic background. The Vatican, or Vatican City, is the headquarters of the Roman Catholic Church. It is the "White House" of the whole Catholic faith. It sits on a little over one hundred acres in Rome, Italy, and is actually the smallest country in the world (although the Church spent centuries trying to acquire much more territory than a mere 100-plus acres). It is often referred to as a city-state inside of Rome. Vatican City has about 1,000 citizens, a few hundred of whom live abroad. Citizens inside the Vatican include the pope, the College of Cardinals, members of the Roman Curia (the court system), clergy, the Swiss Guard (along with some of their children), and others.

Half of the geography comprises the Vatican Gardens, which contain a large number of sculptures, buildings, and monuments from the ninth century, with beautiful flower gardens and green lawns throughout the premises. The Vatican is also the home of a significant collection of ionic art, and money is made from many of the museums that are located inside. Thousands of tourists visit every year and contribute significant revenue.

Famous attractions are centered around St. Peter's Basilica, an impressive and beautiful cathedral, the Sistine Chapel whose ceiling features the famous painting by Michelangelo, the Apostolic Library, and multiple museums.

Although Vatican City does not have an airport or military, the Swiss Guard provides personal security for the pope and for the Vatican, and the Italian police also provide security, as the public has access to St. Peter's Square. The Swiss Guard's members are required to be Catholic, unmarried males, aged nineteen to thirty, and as we will see, those requirements fit in perfectly well with many of the clergy hidden inside the secret Vatican walls.[1]

Interestingly, Vatican City is often summarized as an absolute monarchy headed by the pope.[2] Vatican City being the only absolute monarchy in Europe confirms how much has really changed since the simplicity of the early apostles, when church was a simple gathering in the homes of Christian believers to talk about the resurrection and following Christ. In fact, there are only subtle differences between a dictatorship and a monarchy. Both rule with absolute power, with the distinction that dictatorships use military force to accomplish their agendas.

We saw this with Hitler, Stalin, Hussein, and many others; and even in modern times, dictators still rule. Of course, the popes in the past did utilize military power to accomplish ideology, as seen earlier with the Crusades and the Inquisitions, so this would have easily qualified Catholicism, theoretically, as a dictatorship during those specific times. A dictatorship certainly does not exist today, but that's undoubtedly something that the Church would like to sweep under the rug and not chat about during Mass.

Why is it important to recognize in the Vatican the dictatorship of the past or the monarchy of the present? One important answer is secrecy. It's worth questioning, who really has access behind the scenes at the Vatican? Who would be an objective source? If you were to call the Vatican up and request to bring a team of auditors and examiners into the Holy Palace, would this request be granted?

As a Catholic, if you were to book a flight to Rome, take the thirty-minute drive to Vatican City, knock on the front door of the Apostolic Palace, announce your loyalty to the Roman Church as a cradle Catholic, and demand an audience with the pope and full access to all the archives and secret files in the vault, would you be granted these permissions? Well, before shopping for tickets on Expedia, understand the answer is emphatically, "No."

There is just too much incriminating evidence for anyone to see or discover except a select few. Of course, as we have already uncovered, the public usually doesn't have to wait too long to see the majority of what would be in those hidden documents. The sex abuse cases alone are enough to win the argument of a concerning religious system, but although we may never have access to those records, there is much more that has been exposed from an unexpected source. Let's just say that "the beans have been spilt!"

What really goes on at the Vatican away from the public eye? Apart from video-recorded ordinations that you can access on YouTube, or national news about the latest visit from the pope, or a weekly message in St. Peter's Square, what's happening behind the scenes? What occurs in the dark of the night, inside the apartments and palaces of the cardinals and members of the Roman Curia, in the nightlife, and on the streets so active around the Vatican—what is life really like?

Well, the rarest opportunity in the history of the Roman Catholic Church has come along, and for the first time the closed curtains were pulled back and the blinds were opened, exposing what these "holy" people are doing when they are not parading around in their multi-color robes inside of St. Peter's Basilica, trying to imitate and be viewed as apostolic successors. A massive exposure happened in 2019, but not more than a handful of Catholics probably even know about it. Let's take a small journey through the story.

The Book that Unveiled it All

The book that ripped off the veil from the eyes of uninformed Catholic loyalists everywhere is, *In the Closet of the Vatican: Power, Sexuality, Hypocrisy* by Frédéric Martel.

The attention this book brought to the Vatican has been worldwide and eye-opening. A *New York Times* bestseller, the proof will leave Catholics and non-Catholics alike gasping about the homosexual presence in the Holy See. For those who knew something didn't seem right under the veneer of holiness in the congregation of men in robes, this perspective will change your view forever.

In 2019, this book was published in eight different languages in twenty different countries simultaneously. Frédéric Martel, a French writer, researcher, and author of ten books, undertook the most extensive investigation that has ever been done in the Vatican and Catholic facilities in thirty other countries. The investigation covered a four-year span and included in-person interviews of almost 1,500 people. Among them were forty-one cardinals, fifty-two bishops and monsignors, forty-five apostolic nuncios, secretaries of foreign ambassadors, eleven Swiss guards, and over 200 Catholic priests and seminarians.[3]

The book is 555 pages long and provides detailed accounts of the secret lives of those at the Vatican and of clergy in multiple other countries. In addition to the final published work, three chapters that were too long to include in the book can be accessed in a 300-page document available on the Internet. There has never been—and probably will never be another—exploration into the dark side of the Vatican as extensive and revealing as this one. It is almost a Catholic miracle (and not one that they would like to claim) that this information has been uncovered from such a secretive and guarded organization.

Before exploring some of Martel's findings, it is important to understand a few facts. He reveals that he never concealed his identity as a writer and journalist, yet these cardinals, priests, members of the Roman Curia, and other clergy welcomed him in and opened up in ways that were unimaginable. Why did so many open up and tell their stories? How was Martel able to insert himself into the Vatican for one week every month? The over-whelming theme was the frustration of these clergy having to stay locked in the closet with their sexual preferences since the Roman Catholic Church was so outspoken and adamant about its stance.[4]

These Catholic clergy were forced (or chose) to be extremely homophobic in the public eye and then retreated to their gay lifestyles when the doors closed at night. They confided in Martel because they knew he was not there to judge them, but simply to hear their story. Some remained anonymous, some did not. He was not there to "call them out" but to tell a hidden story of a system that keeps the gay community in the Vatican locked in a closet.

It is also important to make clear that Martel stated the purpose of his book was not to criticize the Church as a whole, but a very particular issue within the gay community in the Vatican. An example would be senior cardi-nals who screamed the loudest against homosexuality—while making public appearances and around other senior prelates—all while living as flagrant homosexuals in their private lives. Stereotypical hypocrisy. The main purpose of his book is to report on a system that created the problem through cel-ibacy and then suppressed homosexuality. So, the goal was not to rebuke them for their homosexuality, but to denounce the hypocrisy. Martel states:

> "Whether they are 'practicing', 'homophile', 'initiates', 'unstraights', 'worldly', 'versatile', 'questioning', or simply 'in the closet', the world I am discovering, with its 50 shades of gay, is beyond comprehension. The intimate stories of these men who give an image of piety in public and lead a quite different life in private ... Never, perhaps, have the appearances of an institution been so deceptive, and equally deceptive are the pronouncements about celibacy and the vows of chastity that conceal a completely different reality. The best-kept secret of the Vatican is no secret to Pope Francis. He knows his 'parish.'"[5]

Also worth noting is that Martel is not Catholic or Protestant. In fact, although he grew up in a Catholic environment when he was young, he does not now have any religious affiliation. Sometimes, those on the outside can provide the most objectivity to examining such a complicated institution as the Roman Catholic Church.

Obviously, in this chapter, I can only be "rather summary" in describing everything that was uncovered during his examination of the secret sexual orientation of the Catholic hierarchy. However, if any Catholic is proactive in reading Martel's book, it will change their perspective forever on this place they call "holy"—the headquarters of the "one, holy, catholic apostolic church", and the people who occupy its structures whom they hold in such high esteem. Martel's book, in fact, is not a smear campaign, but an insight into the reality behind the veil.

Behind the Veil

As the investigation began, the coded expression whispered in the ear of Martel, he states, came from an archbishop in the Roman Curia: "He's of the parish." It was a phrase describing one being a known homosexual. "The problem is that if you tell the truth about the 'closet' and the special friendships in the Vatican, people won't believe you ... they'll say it's made up. Because here reality goes beyond fiction according to another worker in the Vatican for a period of over 30 years."[6]

Many of Martel's meetings took place under the ceiling of the Sistine Chapel in the Apostolic Palace, the pope's official residence in Vatican City. It is ironic that Michelangelo, believed by most historians to have been homosexual, took great pride in painting young, muscular, naked boys, coincidentally sharing the same inclinations as those who would regularly pass under it.

Some of the insights that Martel discovered in researching the occupants of the Vatican for four years are:

> "One of the main engines and wellsprings of Vatican life is homosexual desire."

> "Being gay in the clergy means being part of a kind of norm. Being homosexual is possible in the Vatican, easy, ordinary, and even encouraged; but the word 'visibility' is forbidden."

"For a long time, the ecclesiastical career was the ideal solution for many homosexuals who found it difficult to accept private orientation."

"Homosexuality spreads the closer one gets to the holy of holies; there are more and more homosexuals as one rises through the Catholic hierarchy. In the College of Cardinals and at the Vatican, the preferential selection process is said to be perfected; homosexuality becomes the rule; heterosexuality the exception."

"The more vehemently opposed a cleric is to gays, the stronger his homophobic obsession, the more likely it is that he is insincere, and that his vehemence conceals something."

"[Chem Sex Parties] I had heard for a long time that parties like this were happening inside the Vatican itself, real collective orgies in which sex and drugs combined in a sometimes dangerous cocktail."

"It is not rare for a nuncio or a bishop to promote a priest who is also part of 'the parish' because he expects some favors in return."

"That cardinals and bishops who cover sexual abuse do it because ... they fear that their homosexual inclinations would be revealed if a scandal erupted or a case came to trial."

"'Don't ask; don't tell' which remains mantra number one at the Vatican."

"Pornography, essentially gay pornography, is such a frequent phenomenon that my sources speak of 'serious addiction problems among the Curia prelates.'"[7]

For those struggling with homosexuality in the priesthood, bishops and other priests advise them:

"To persevere in the priesthood to stop talking about homosexuality and not to feel guilty. He was very directly given to understand that he could live out his sexuality as long as he remained discreet and didn't turn it into a militant identity."[8]

A young priest named Francesco Lepore, who translated the pope's official documents into Latin and answered his letters, and who was also a favorite of Pope Benedict XVI, states his experience at the Vatican to Martel:

"We knew the names of the ones who had a partner or who brought boys to Saint Martha's [next to St. Peter's Basilica] to spend the night with them. A lot of them led a double life: priest at the Vatican by day; homosexual in bars and clubs at night. Often those prelates were in the habit of making advances on younger priests like me, seminarians, the Swiss Guard, or laypeople who worked at the Vatican."[9]

Martel asked Lepore to estimate the size of the gay community inside the Vatican, all tendencies included. Lepore replied, "I think the percentage is very high. I'd put it at around 80 per cent."[10]

Another ambassador to the Catholic Church warned Martel at the start of the investigation, "At the Vatican, as you will see, there are a lot of gays: 50 percent, 60 percent, 70 percent? No one knows."[11] In the very center of the Roman Church, these priests and hierarchy are hidden away in closets throughout parishes and apartments in the Vatican, although they are supposed to be a part of a Church community where they are expected to be apostolic successors and role models. As a side note, an obvious question becomes: Does the average Catholic attendee want a gay priest, cardinal, or pope to be the role model for their kids?

Lepore proceeds to tell Martell about the "mad gaiety" at the Vatican and admits several lovers he had among archbishops and prelates, along with being propositioned himself by numerous cardinals. Basically, there is an endless list of available homosexuals and free access to the way of life in the Vatican landscape.

Martel shares about numerous meetings he had with cardinals inside their apartments at the Vatican. One in particular, Cardinal Burke, seemed to have "drag queen" overtones. Someone who knew Burke well stated, "What strikes me when I look at Cardinal Burke's cappa magna, robes and hats topped by floral ornaments, is its overstatement. The biggest, the longest, the tallest; it's all typical of drag-queen codes. He has this extravagance, this boundless artificiality ... to those who want to parody themselves."[12]

As expected with those prelates who speak the loudest all while protecting their private lives, Cardinal Burke stated, "I think it's high time to acknowledge that we have a very serious problem with homosexuality in the Church."[13]

Investigations into this highly sensitive topic revealed that the Church, in general, always looked for scapegoats.[14] In other words, it's an excuse, blaming gays who "infiltrated the Church." But Martel revealed that not to be the case. Hundreds of interviews showed that Catholic cardinals, priests, ambassadors, and even some popes engaged in homosexuality because of the broken system—the canon law of celibacy.

Young men with raging hormones locked in the closets of seminaries, the prison of convents, the apartments of the Vatican, or the parish in a local community all lend themselves to the proclivity for sexual urges to be acted on with whomever is available. This is common knowledge about prisons throughout the world. When options are limited, those trapped take whomever is available. The "celibacy trial" has become one of the longest-running experiments in religious history. The results? A complete catastrophe of shattered lives and broken spirits.

This investigation of the double lives of cardinals, priests, ambassadors, and prelates reveals a worldwide epidemic. Catastrophe or epidemic are strong words used after a category four or five hurricane slamming a coastal city, or a viral outbreak claiming thousands of lives, or an army invading a territory killing thousands of innocent victims—but these are appropriate words to use when describing the homosexual problem in the Roman system that has harmed hundreds of thousands of victims.

Martel saw a pattern with many of his interviews when talking to heterosexual clerics. They would completely deny allegations about certain cardi-

nals, bishops, and priests being homosexuals, but after the evidence was presented, they just appeared to be shocked and almost speechless. But in truth,
Martel actually met some of the boyfriends of these cardinals and prelates
and had substantial evidence on some who had passed away and others who
had already been recognized in the media. He also had ample evidence on
current clergy in the Vatican that he had no intention of exposing. He was
not there for that purpose.[15]

Martel states that an archbishop in the Vatican who goes by the nick-
name "La Paiva" asked him, "Did you know that the pope was surrounded by
homosexuals? There are many gays, very many. Many being 'of the parish.'"
He confirmed that homophiles and homosexuals comprise the majority of
the College of Cardinals and that the presence of gay men in the entourage
has been consistent from John XII, Paul VI, John Paul I, John Paul II, Benedict XVI, and Francis.[16]

What About the Pope?

"Who am I to judge?" became a pretty infamous and controversial phrase
of the pontificate when Pope Francis uttered those words during an interview in 2013. However, what is understood among the higher-ups is that
Francis cannot go much farther than that without causing a war within the
College of Cardinals, Martel states. So, he is primarily an opponent of things
like gay marriage publicly (an expected spiritual stance), but is unable to do
anything about homosexuality in the Vatican and other places.

It would be a more lopsided battle than David and Goliath for Francis (or
any pope) to attempt to block homosexuality in the Vatican, much less in the
thousands of parishes around the world. It would be the Kansas City Chiefs,
with no compassion, going up against the county peewee football team. It's
not going to be pretty!

A bold pope would have to finally admit that their "ecclesiastical system"
was wrong, celibacy was wrong. And then after the admission, make a
change. This change would have positive long-term benefits.

Would it solve the whole problem of rampant homosexuality and predatory priestly rape of children? Inevitably, it would certainly reduce it.
However, a requirement of having married priests instead of celibate priests

would be a landslide victory over the current situation. It's a start in the right direction. Will the Roman Church ever admit its mistake? Maybe not. If so, it would start a landslide of admitting many other things that have been adopted in error—traditions and theological positions that were derived from leaders having no business changing the original Gospel.

It would be understandable to think this extensive research done by Martel into homosexuality in the Vatican is just an attempt to attack, dishonor, or discredit the legitimacy of the Church. However, the evidence Martel uncovers is verified over and over again from countless sources, even from the pope himself. Here is a quote from Pope Francis in 2017, when he condemned the cardinals of the Curia:

> "Like soap bubbles, [these hypocrites] hide the truth from God, from other people and from themselves, showing a face with a pious image to assume the appearance of holiness ... On the outside, they present themselves as righteous, as good: they like to be seen when they pray and when they fast, when they give alms. [But] it is all appearance, and in their hearts there is nothing ... They put make-up on their souls, they live on make-up: holiness is make-up for them ... Lies do a lot of harm, hypocrisy does a lot of harm: it is a way of life."[17]

Another revealing quote came from Francis: "Behind rigidity something always lies hidden; in many cases, a double life."[18]

Many of the Vatican members seem to be a flashback to the Pharisees that Jesus called out:

> "Beware of the teachers of the law. They like to walk around in <u>flowing robes</u> and love to be greeted in the market-places and have the <u>most important seats in the synagogues and the place of honor at banquets</u> ... and for a show make <u>lengthy prayers</u>" (Luke 20:46-47).

Outward appearances of righteousness, but empty inside, as Francis alluded to. This can be the drawback of a system that outwardly projects "holiness" but operates as a hierarchy controlling the masses—when all along, the Christian life was a movement about the resurrection and spreading the good news about the redemption of mankind and enjoying the simplicity of following Jesus and His life inside us.

Martel was informed that Francis stopped replying to letters from homosexuals (according to a gay priest who is one of Francis' secretaries) but then was proactive in protecting sexual abuse done by the clergy; not because he is pro-gay, but because of the embarrassment to the Church.[19] The bottom line: It's a complete mess within the walls of the Roman Catholic Church, and almost all of it is hidden from the view of Catholics who attend Mass and then go to lunch, clueless of a system that is ruptured and broken.

Because Catholic attendees have been taught from early on that this is the one, holy, catholic, and apostolic Church of Jesus Christ, the natural reaction is to think: "Whatever they say, we follow—this is the Church that Christ started." Some Catholics will admit that there might be problems—certainly, sin invades all churches, including the one true Church, but it's rare, and taken care of by the hierarchy. However, the hierarchy is not solving the problems. The hierarchy has been known to be the problem for centuries. Very few Catholics know even a fraction of what has already been discussed in this book. Many have suspected that something was off, but not to this extent. For the ones who have fully digested what the Roman Catholic Church has evolved into, there has been a mass exit from its doors.

In a rare admission, Trent Horn did a segment on his YouTube channel, shocking his followers with just how bad the departure from the Catholic faith has become. Horn quotes Eric Sammons with Crisis Magazine as saying,

> "A new survey shows that for every 100 new Catholics, more than 800 people leave the Church. As bad as that is, the news is actually worse when we look more closely at the numbers... only 19% of Americans self-identify as Catholic, down from 24% in 2007 ..."[20]

Even more revealing, Sammons states that the numbers would even be worse than that if it were not for immigration inflating the numbers on the positive end. He states,

"As the Pew Survey itself states, 'immigration has helped to bolster the number of Catholics in the United States' ... So, while millions are fleeing the Catholic Church, new migrants keep the overall numbers from looking horrific."[21]

Finally, Horn says that "there are seven times as many converts to Protestantism than there are to Catholicism, between the two groups ... but Catholics who say that America is becoming a Catholic country are having a major hallucinatory episode ..."[22]

These revealing statistics have left many leaders of Catholic parishes baffled and confused. Why such a mass exit from the Catholic Church? Is it because of the information that has been clearly defined and documented in the past eight chapters? Are Catholics starting to understand that the pope holds no superior power over anyone? Is it because of the atrocities that occurred in the past with holy wars? Is it because of the prolific priestly abuse of our kids? Is it because of Martel's book exposing homosexuality in the Vatican? Or is it that Catholics are starting to get exposed to the simplicity of the Scriptures that prove a different story than Catholic theology? One can only speculate, but it would be logical to conclude it's because of all these reasons and more.

To continue the story, *The Church: A Code of Silence* is a Java Film documentary that was produced by Luc Herman and Paul Moreira, covering the work of five journalists. Available on YouTube, the film documents an international coverup conducted by the high officials of the Catholic Church who moved pedophile priests from country to country. The Church calls it the "geographical solution" to the pedophile problem: simply move these perpetrators to another part of the region, or even to another country, where their offences are not known.

Any research into the sexual abuse problem so prevalent in the Catholic Church reveals the truth of what Father Joulain says from Paris, "The Church forgives the abusers but shows little compassion to the victims. What kind of system is that? A perverted system!"[23]

Pope Francis is implicated in this documentary as well. When he was bishop of Buenos Aires, he tried to influence the Argentinean justice system in order to get a convicted priest released from prison. As the journalists were investigating this allegation, another significant story unfolded in the Vatican. The journalists were able to obtain an interview with Father Hans Zollner, a member of the pontifical commission for the protection of minors appointed by Pope Francis. He advises the pope on sexual abuse issues.

When he was interviewed, he was shown a small poster-size picture of the pope and the ten most senior cardinals or "advisory board." It was pointed out to Zollner that four out of ten of these top cardinals are known to have covered up pedophile priests. It is highly revealing that almost half of all the chief cardinals covered up sex abuse cases regarding children and others. This is quite appalling. The four cardinals that are the closest to Pope Francis, the top of the hierarchy, that have covered up sexual abuse are Gerhard Muller, Oscar Maradiaga, George Pell, and Francisco Errazuriz.

In the filmed interview, you can see Father Zollner start to squirm, knowing what the follow-up questions would probably be. Here was Zollner's response when he was asked about these four top cardinals covering up criminal acts: "I have no particular knowledge of any of them."[24]

However, he spends the rest of the interview revealing very detailed information on all of them after being backed into a corner. There is a pattern of misrepresentations with Catholic leaders, followed by being exposed, followed by an apology or admission of guilt because the evidence is just too much. We saw this systemically in the past two chapters. Why didn't Pope Francis take action against these cardinals at the time of this interview? I think the reader can draw their own conclusions, but the case against Francis himself will be the most telling reason why he never acted.

Journalists in this documentary are led to Buenos Aires, the hometown of Francis, where at the time he was archbishop Jorge Bergoglio. In a book of interviews with Francis called *Sur la terre comme au ciel*, written by Robert Laffont, on page sixty-four the pope is quoted as saying, "[Sex abuse] never happened in my diocese ... On the holy father's name."

After arriving in Buenos Aires, the journalists quickly realized how famous Pope Francis is, his picture plastered everywhere from wall posters to coffee mugs, along with numerous statues. They immediately located and met with seven sexual abuse victims and were informed that Francis, when he was archbishop, was notified of their abuse but did nothing about it. All of them contacted him, but there was no reply. When the journalist quoted from Francis' book that, "There were no cases in his dioceses," the abused victims just looked at each other, shook their heads, but were not surprised. "He wants people to believe that, but it's a lie," one interviewee said.

One of the biggest stories in this documentary with regard to Francis is the Father Grassi case, which was the largest scandal ever in the Argentinian Church. He was the most well-known priest in the country and was regularly featured in local newscasts showing him at the orphanage he operated. Multiple children lodged a complaint against Grassi regarding the sexual abuse of kids, and in 2009 he was sentenced to fifteen years in prison. The Catholic Church did everything in its power to have him acquitted by providing the most high-profile attorneys and the power-backing of the Roman Catholic Church.

In 2010, after his conviction, the Church ordered a "counter inquiry" into the case called "Studies on the Grassi Case" by a renowned legal expert and criminal law professor at the University of Buenos Aires. It was a lengthy, 2,800-page argument to have Grassi acquitted! It can be summed up as, "the children are all lying and Grassi should be released on appeal." As the journalists dived deeper into the documents, they discovered a shocking paragraph: "This work was commissioned in 2010, by the Argentina Episcopal conference, notably by the then president Cardinal Bergoglio (now Pope Francis)." He tried to persuade and influence judges to have this convicted priest pedophile released. Francis actually ordered the "counter inquiry."

If you would like to witness Francis allegedly not being forthright, this video segment is one of the rare times you can see this happening. The scene begins around the fifty-minute mark of the video and proceeds for two minutes or so. A journalist inside Vatican Square secured a position so that when Francis stepped out of the popemobile and started greeting the crowd, the reporter was able to ask him about the Grassi case:

> Reporter: Your holiness, in the Grassi case, did you try to influence Argentinean justice?
> Francis: No.

Reporter: No? Then, why did you commission a counter-inquiry?

Francis: I never did.

Reporter: Never?

Francis: (Walks Away)[25]

The purpose in sharing this story is not about catching the pope in a lie, because lies, diversions, and cover-ups are simply part of the Catholic landscape among the hierarchy concerning anything related to sexual abuse. Did Francis lie on camera? It appears from understanding the background of the story that he did. Was it a more significant lie than just telling someone that you are busy right now and you really aren't? It was absolutely much more significant, since this involves going to severe lengths (a 2,800-page commission to influence judges) for the sole purpose of the exoneration of a child rapist.

Instead, the purpose of this report is to provide incredible insight into the Catholic hierarchy being unethical, dishonest, and absolutely guilty of protecting the Church, even above protecting innocent children. Incidentally, Francis did not get his way, and the Grassi conviction was upheld. Would there be any chance this story was shared in Mass around the world when it became public knowledge? One can only conclude that this story would never be revealed.

There is ample evidence to prove and confirm and verify that the cover-ups in the Roman Catholic system go all the way to the pope himself. What does this say about a person "standing in the place of Christ" and a Church that is supposed to be the "one, holy, catholic apostolic Church" when half the leadership are hypocritically and secretly embracing homosexuality, and the rest are covering up the crimes committed against children? It clearly reveals a historical pattern of being a suspicious entity with questionable undertones, yet disguised as Christ's Church.

Marcial Maciel

In continuation of Martel's account at the Vatican, although it is beyond the scope of this book to cover the hundreds of conversations and the unbelievable stories Martel and his team uncovered during their four-year investigation and subsequent book, there is one particular chronicle that is worth referencing that serves as an example of what happens outside the visual frame of the average Catholic attendee.

Martel shares the story about Marcial Maciel, a Mexican Catholic priest, as one of the most diabolical figures to have ever come through the Roman Catholic system. The head of numerous Catholic schools, universities, and charities, he was extremely wealthy and oversaw a sustained level of sexual violence during his time. Protected and fully supported by Pope John Paul II and others, he was the General Director of "Legion of Christ" from 1941-2005, a Catholic education charity in Mexico. He recruited thousands of seminarians who were told to give up all their goods, possessions, and money to the Legion of Christ organization. He was known as the greatest fundraiser of the modern Roman Catholic Church.

A long-term drug addict, Maciel purposely formed his inner circle from the smartest, most handsome young seminarians, who were often athletes. In the 1940s, Maciel was dismissed twice from the seminary by his superiors for troubling events relating to sexuality. He was even suspended by the Vatican. But in 1958 another cardinal at the Vatican wiped his slate clean. In 1965, Pope Paul VI even officially recognized the Legion of Christ, removing any doubt of their connection, linking them directly to the Holy See.

Maciel found himself the head of this powerful machine of the Catholic Church, virtually unsupervised. By the end of his career, he had fifteen universities, fifty seminaries and institutes of higher education, 125 religious houses, 200 educational centers, and 1,200 oratories and chapels scattered throughout Mexico. This was a powerful man with a formidable organization. According to *The New York Times*, Maciel had liquid assets of hundreds of millions of dollars stashed away in secret accounts."[26]

Paul VI and John Paul II were proactive in legitimizing this predatory priest and ignored the allegations that had poured into the Vatican. A stunning 200 sexual abuse victims of Maciel have been identified to date. He also kept as many as four mistresses, with whom he had six kids, and two of his kids are among his victims. Despite his predatory background, he was always welcomed as a humble servant by Paul VI and John Paul II. In 1997, a credible complaint was made by seven priests and many former seminarians of the Legion who said they had been sexually abused by Maciel. The letter was filed under "no further action" by the Catholic Secretary of State and the pope's private secretary, Angelo Sodano.

Martel states that it is not known if the pope ever saw the complaint. Cardinals have always protected priests at all costs just to keep division down in the Church. They have done this for decades and continue to do so. New allegations of rape committed by Maciel were brought to the attention of the Vatican in 1997, but under John Paul II it was again stamped "no further action." It was Benedict XVI in 2015 who finally put an end to the sexual rampage of Maciel and stripped him of all his duties.

However, Benedict XVI still went easy on Maciel, and he was not reported to law enforcement, ex-communicated, arrested, or imprisoned. There was not even a trial according to canon law. He would simply have to lay low, commit to a life of prayer and penance, and not be able to administer the sacraments until the end of his days. Of course, many readers would like to know why he wouldn't be convicted and sent to prison for life. Why didn't the Church take action against him? How can a serial rapist possibly be allowed to dispense anything at the end of their life? One can only look to the Vatican for that truth, but the truth is not revealed by anyone in the Catholic hierarchy.

Instead of a deserved prison sentence, Maciel went from country to country staying out of sight, and ended up in the United States. He died in Florida at age eighty-eight, living a life of luxury. Benedict XVI launched a posthumous investigation into the crimes that were reported against Maciel, and the Vatican finally acknowledged his offenses. He was one of the worst Catholic priest pedophiles of the twentieth century. In addition, thirty-five other priests with the Legion of Christ were implicated in the sexual abuse.[27]

It is important to note that American Catholics are barely exposed to what happens in the U.S. with regard to Catholic clergy sexual abuse. However, most have virtually zero knowledge of what happens in foreign ecclesiastical affairs. One of the most disturbing revelations is the length of time these predators are able to get away with raping children and sexually abusing young men under the umbrella of Catholicism. Maciel was in his predatory position for sixty-four years. The implications of the hierarchy in the Vatican protecting these criminals are unfathomable.

Guilty Beyond Doubt

The final information coming from Martel's book that is important not to skip is the collection of interviews that Martel did on the streets in Rome, close to the Vatican. He interviewed sixty migrant prostitutes who confirmed with great detail that priests, cardinals, and prelates are a big part of their business. These encounters happened in the Roma Termini area, as some were regularly summoned to the Vatican. In fact, priests were the main clientele of these male prostitutes. The male prostitutes revealed that they like going to the Vatican because they pay well.[28]

The Piazza della Repubblica is the central place where the priests would pick up the prostitutes in their cars. They communicate on private messaging apps like WhatsApp. In a strange irony, many of the prostitutes even claim the priests want to "save them." Much of this activity is confirmed by the police, as some priests even become victims of crime and rarely report it except for serious cases.[29]

Martel exposed the Vatican for being secretly inundated with sexual perversion. One Swiss Guardsman said, "It took me a long time to realize that we were surrounded, at the Vatican, by frustrated men who see the Swiss Guard as fresh meat. They impose celibacy on us and refuse to let us marry because they want to keep us for themselves, it's as simple as that. They are so misogynistic, so perverse! They would like us to be like them: secret homosexuals."[30]

Many Catholics might not even be aware that in the 1980s and 1990s AIDS ravaged through the Vatican and Italian Episcopate Conference. A number of priests and cardinals died of the effects of AIDS. There was even a statistical study carried out in the United States that revealed from the death certificates of priests that they were dying of AIDS four times more than the general population, corroborating the significant epidemic within the Vatican and worldwide. Of course, we are just now realizing that homosexuality is nothing new in the Vatican. This was not publicly known before. It is only recently that their secret lives have been exposed.

Martel quotes two significant medical sources regarding the attitudes and mentality of a lot of priests. The first is Professor Massimo Giuliani, a specialist in sexually transmitted diseases: "As a rule, priests are not afraid of STDs. They feel untouchable. They are so sure of their position, of their power." Second, a dermatologist stated, "Some priests tell us that they were infected by coming into contact with a syringe or an old blood transfusion; we pretend to believe them."[31]

The takeaway, however, and the more significant story and revelation is that we now have an overwhelming amount of evidence covering centuries of Catholic popes, Catholic bishops, and Catholic cardinals committing and covering up the crimes of serial sexual abuse. Even at the very center, at the very headquarters of the Roman Catholic Church, there is corruption and extreme immorality in the Vatican.

Is the Roman Catholic Church the pivoting centerpiece for Christianity it makes itself out to be? Instead, the evidence seems to point to the center of most of its leadership being sexually perverted and masked in religious accomplishments with imposing cathedrals, projections, and busyness on the outside and splattered with hidden atrocities on the inside.

For those who have done an extensive search into the inner workings of the Roman Church, the Vatican presents a "holier than thou" hierarchy. It governs and dispenses liturgy and Church policy and Church statements for the public to see with their rich history—an allure of righteousness—all while the naked men on the ceilings are much more revealing about the fundamentals of this institution.

However, the closet door is starting to crack open because the reality is that society is gradually accepting homosexuality as normal, giving hope to the Vatican cardinals, bishops, priests, and ambassadors, worldwide, to finally be "liberated" from their hiding. On the outside, we see the spiritualized stance against homosexuality, homophobic at its best, and on the inside, we see young boys coming and going. It's the ultimate embarrassment for the Church because it shows that a spiritual institution with a hierarchy should have never been in place, and its ecclesiastical laws and other false doctrines have become disastrous.

As a Catholic, there is almost no way to digest and assimilate the saturation of homosexuality in the Roman Catholic system. To understand that statistically half (if not more) of all parishes in America have a gay priest, to grasp that the highest Roman Catholic clergy in the Vatican are primarily gay, to look at all the names, all the corruption, all the convictions, all the hundreds of thousands of sexually abused kids—how does a Catholic even begin to perceive this? It goes against everything that they would have ever imagined. A true, genuine Catholic would be against almost everything that transpires behind the walls of the Vatican. Most Catholics have sincere and incredible hearts, yet they are forced to ask: do we serve a devious system?

There is simply too much that was uncovered in Martel's book to cover here—everything from the real reason Pope Benedict XVI retired in 2013 (in relation to the homosexual topic) to the massive egos and piousness uncovered in the private apartments of the cardinals. Martel's book should be mandatory reading for every Catholic. It's quite disturbing and unsettling.

Benedict XVI once stated, "The Church is filled with filth."[32] Even the very words coming out of his mouth would implicate his own brother, Georg Ratzinger, who found himself in the middle of a huge sex scandal of physical and sexual abuse against minors when he was in charge of operations at the famous boys' choir at Regensburg Cathedral between 1964 and 1994. Over 547 children were abused, and forty-nine priests and laymen were suspected. Georg Ratzinger denied any knowledge.[33] The same Catholic pattern. Martel reveals this insight and comes to this conclusion: the Vatican is one big "Kingdom of hypocrisy."

Remember the Catholic hierarchy formula that Martel discovered: the louder one cries against homosexuality, the more likely that they themselves are covering their own tendency (at least, in the Vatican landscape). Pope Benedict XVI cried out against homosexuality, but one priest at the Vatican stated, "And it's true that any gay looking at photographs of Benedict XVI, his smile, his gait, his manners, might think he is homosexual."[34]

According to Martel, one priest, Krzysztof Charamsa, who worked beside Benedict XVI for years, described him as "the gayest pontificate in history."[35] These assumptions are common among those interviewed, where three of

242 | WHEN THE ROMAN BOUGH BREAKS

the last five popes are said to have had homosexual tendencies. It would not be surprising with the evidence that has been revealed so far.

If you are Catholic, it warrants the questions: Based on the past eight chapters, is this a Church that looks like Christ? Is the Roman Catholic Church really the one, holy, apostolic Church that Christ intended? Was this the Church the apostles had in mind when spreading the good news about the resurrection? Would their Church include an institution responsible for murdering thousands of people in the name of religion? Would their Church include a central place like the Vatican where most of the hierarchy are homosexuals? Would their Church be a hierarchy that is considered a monarchy and, at times in the past, even a dictatorship? Would their Church have leaders who sexually abuse and rape and destroy the lives of over a million people (mostly kids) and then, regularly, cover it up? Would their Church alter the original Gospel and come up with its own liturgy? Can an intellectually honest Catholic hold that the institution that has unfolded in the preceding chapters is truly the place Christ built—His Church? Is this an apostolic Church or an apostate institution? These are the questions that have to be answered and not excused with Catholic apologies. Are the answers to these questions creating the mass exit from the Church?

Why is it hard for a cradle Catholic to read a book like this or to read Martel's book exposing the Vatican system? Because it is extremely problematic to let go. How do you take everything that you have ever believed about your Church being the divinely chosen one, the only one that is recognized by God, and realize that something changed over the past 2,000 years? But even if you did recognize that something is not right, how do you break the bondage of the Roman system in your life? There is no other way but by yielding to the Heavenly Father, through Christ, and allowing the Holy Spirit to speak the truth.

Why would God allow someone to stay in a system for decades without them finding out the truth? It's a difficult question to answer, but I believe it is simply because of a fallen world, and Christians stubbornly remaining in a state of prideful "tunnel vision" with the Church they serve. They never look outside of the context of this entity that has lured them in, cloaked in Christ, but saturated in dishonesty and deceitfulness.

For those Catholic families that have pilgrimaged across to the Vatican (hopefully not to be credited with indulgences that unfortunately have no value), and stood there in awe of the mighty St. Peter's Basilica (built with funds that were from a dishonest proclamation), walked around Vatican square, toured the multiple museums, adored the Apostolic Palace, observed the naked men on the ceiling of the Sistine Chapel—they were within walking steps of the highest per-capita homosexual population on the planet. I know this sounds critical. I know it's hard to comprehend. I wish this was not the case, however, the facts can no longer be ignored. It's a serious matter to assimilate.

If one were to venture a few steps further to the district of the Roma Termini and stumble across the nighttime prowlings of the aggressive priests and cardinals as they engage street prostitutes (not to save them but to pay them for sex), an appropriate question becomes: Could you ever have imagined this being a part of the itinerary of the pilgrimage? Even more so, although not allowed, if you could take a tour around the perimeter of all the cardinals' apartments—hypothetically observing the after-hours activities of these clergy—there would certainly be the booking of an early flight home, never to return again, never to embrace the Roman Catholic version of the Gospel.

I want to encourage Catholics not to keep the blinders on, pretend all the information revealed in this book isn't true, and assume that the atrocities that these chapters have uncovered apply to only a few bad apples, because that would not be the truth. As Christians, we can choose to follow an organization, a hierarchy, a monarchy, saturated with "developed over time" doctrines, or we can simply follow Christ. The choice is easy for those authentically wanting to embrace the original Gospel.

Based on the evidence in this book, what can you do personally as a member of the Roman Catholic Church? This book is not a call for you to abandon your local parish and find a Protestant congregation. It is true that in the United States, 800 members leave for every 100 that join the Church, and these first eight chapters shed some light on why that might be the case. In the remaining chapters, we'll turn our attention to the realities of grace and the truths of Scripture you might have been missing from a Church that is weighed down trying to justify unbiblical medieval doctrine, pervasive scandal, and the unwarranted burden of celibacy on priests. Before we make the transition, take a moment to consider what this means for you and your family. How have the actions of this institution impacted your faith and relationship with Christ? One can only speculate, but at the end of the day, each individual Catholic will have to search their heart, rely completely on guidance from the Holy Spirit through Scripture, and make a personal decision if they think that they have fallen victim to deception. God is surely not absent from the equation for those genuine Christians who seek out His wisdom on such an important matter.

Papal hierarchy or not, Catholic attendees who embrace their freedom in Christ can be set free from the control of an institution that changed the Gospel, and learn the simplicity of embracing and following Christ without adhering to a single item on The Catholic List. The possibility exists that this could be the greatest religious revival in human history and still allow parishioners to maintain the close relationships they have with other Church members, a vital part of the Christian life.

The preceding chapters have unfolded just a small fraction of the carnage associated with the Roman Catholic Church over the past 1,700 years. The full story is much more convicting. We've seen the unimaginable and prolific corruption of the papacy, the immorality of the priesthood because of celibacy, the true revelations behind the closed doors of the Vatican, and watched the foundations of the original Church all but disappear as a movement about the resurrection turned into an unbiblical hierarchy and monarchy, led by a significant percentage of questionable leadership. There is no doubt that letting go of The Catholic List, letting go of the Roman institution, and acknowledging the spiritual conditioning from unscrupulous sources will not be a simple task, but the power of the Holy Spirit, with no limitations, can set anyone free.

In the final chapters, let's journey together through the New Covenant—the way we relate to God on this side of the cross absent of an institution. Let's venture back to the original Gospel and embrace the way Jesus set the system up from the very beginning. Let's go back to the original catholic Church. Let's grasp the true definition of grace, the true definition of forgiveness, the true definition of righteousness, the true definition of justification. Let's journey into the beauty of total freedom in Christ because of His finished work and not our merited way. The story is absolutely one of amazing grace.

After three years of writing and research, it's probably not a coincidence that I enter these next chapters, literally, the day after Easter: the celebration of the cross, and even more exciting, the triumph of the resurrection. Easter marks the ushering in of the New Covenant that is in place today, applying to every single believer, forever bridging the gap between God and mankind, and fully reconciling the world back to Himself, not counting our sins against us. This amazing grace happens absent of institutional necessity and rests solely on Christ's fulfillment of every righteous requirement. Are you willing to travel back to what the apostles taught and once again become unified with Christ, the New Covenant, and the original catholic Church?

PART IV

THE NEW COVENANT

CHAPTER 9

Forgiveness: It Really Is Finished

I remember it was a beautiful Saturday afternoon at the lake, and I was fully engaged in my favorite hobby of water skiing when I got the call. Many people can relate to getting random calls that changed their lives forever. Sometimes, these calls come with devastating and heartbreaking news: a car wreck just occurred or someone passed away unexpectedly. At times, these life-changing events come via the media, like watching the Challenger space shuttle explode in 1986 after months of built-up excitement about putting a schoolteacher in space for the first time, or the attacks in New York on 9/11 as we helplessly watched the twin towers crumble to the ground. We all remember where we were when we got "the call" or saw these events.

The call that came for me on that day was from my friend Barry, who at the time, wanted to ask me a quick, spiritual question. Easy enough, I figured. His question was, "How do you deal with ongoing sin that you commit every day?" It seemed like a strange but simplistic question at the time, and I remember thinking that water skiing seemed like a much better topic to be thinking about. Spinning off of 1 John 1:9 (simply confess your sin and He is faithful and just to forgive us and cleanse us from unrighteousness) I said, "Well, when I pray at night, I just try to remember anything I did wrong that day, and just pray for forgiveness."

But he would not be easily satisfied with a quick answer: "What about all the sins you can't remember, the sins that only lasted a few seconds—a quick lust, a quick yelling at the guy who cut you off in traffic, the lakefront houses you enviously wished you had the past couple hours?" I remembered, before I answered, that Barry scored higher on the SAT than any person I have ever met, so I knew how my analytical friend thought. I hesitated for a few seconds and said, "Well, I just do a 'blanket' forgiveness prayer at night to cover all of those."

Even as those words came out of my mouth, it didn't seem right, but also in a different way, it seemed like the right answer. After all, I had been a Christian for almost twenty-five years at the time, and I was the director of the eighth-grade Sunday School class at church. Not only was I teaching at my church in that season, but I was obsessed with theology and accessing all the very best material I could find.

In contrast to most other teachers I was around, and because of my severe attention to detail from operating businesses, I turned a bedroom in my home into a spiritual library. I had every popular Christian book that had ever been written, hundreds of tracts from various Church sources, dozens of cassette-tape teaching series (yes, it was a while ago!), and years' worth of monthly publications from leading ministries. Bookshelves and tables filled the room, and friends always got a kick from walking in and trying to figure out what in the world I was doing with all that stuff! I explained to them that whatever the topic was next Sunday morning, I would grab all the best material and formulate my lesson plan. Most looked bewildered that I would go to all that trouble.

With our denominational backgrounds being the same, the call with Barry continued a little deeper into theology as he proceeded to tell me he had been studying the New Covenant and the new arrangement we had with God, on this side of the Cross. At the time, the New Covenant sounded like a boring topic, something from ancient days. What in the world could that have to do with forgiveness? A quick question turned into a forty-five-minute conversation, and even though I knew a lot about theology and the Bible, I had never fully understood until then just how much changed after the resurrection in how we relate to God, where we stood with God, and how God now views us as believers under the New Covenant.

The conversation led me into a spiritual, life-changing, twenty-year journey of redefining grace (God's unexplainable love), redefining forgiveness (a one-time event), redefining righteousness (being forever made right in God's eyes), and redefining justification (no other requirements needed because of a substitutionary death on the cross)—all facets of the New Covenant. Many Christians already knew this before me. How had I missed the biggest piece of the puzzle after so many years of being in a church environment? Denominational blindness would eventually be the answer, and many people who sit on a church pew are in the same boat.

That one call started ongoing email and phone correspondence with my friend and many other Christians that stretched for years, searching out just what was this New Covenant? How different was it from what was in place before the cross? Little did I know at the time that until you understand the New Covenant, you do not fully understand Christianity. Trying to view Christianity outside the context and scope of the New Covenant is like someone with reading glasses suddenly looking up and trying to view something from a distance without removing those glasses. Everything is blurry.

Yet, for those who wear distance glasses, everything becomes crystal clear. Every single theological position and every single verse in the Scriptures has to be viewed from the perspective of the New Covenant, or it will fully blur the meaning.

Grace vs. Penance

As we leave eight revealing chapters about the history of the Roman Catholic Church and its current condition, exposing events that Catholics would never guess had transpired, and seeing how the original, apostolic church was abandoned—having very few similarities with the Catholic Church of today—we stumble across grace. Catholics hear about the "graces" of God all the time in the Roman system, but how did Jesus, the early apostles, and the original catholic Church define grace (singular) that encompasses everything a Christian will ever need for life's journey? The search will reveal that there are no "graces"; there is only grace.

Growing up in the Christian faith, I became familiar with many Bible verses, but 1 John 1:9, which I quoted to my friend Barry about confessing sins, was a very important verse—it was needed above all the rest! I knew whatever I did wrong, I could just confess before I went to bed, gain all the forgiveness that was needed from a faithful God who was happy to give it, and I was content to go to sleep. We could start off the next day on good terms. Of course, I remember lying in bed racking my brain trying to remember everything I had done wrong that day. It wasn't an easy task. First, because I couldn't remember everything; and second, I was getting really sleepy and many prayers ended mid-sentence.

On the nights I did stay awake, there was still that little fear that if I couldn't remember all the sins that I had done, maybe He wouldn't forgive me of them, and that was my thinking process. Like many, I visualized God or one of His angel representatives standing at a blackboard with an eraser, and when I confessed a specific sin, it would be erased, and then I thought of another sin, and that one would be erased, then another and another.

Then, the next day, it would start all over again. He was up there writing and writing, and later, erasing and erasing. I straightened everything up with God every night. None of this daily cycle was in the Bible, but it seemed like the logical conclusion, and many times what is actually taught. We sin, and then there's this back-and-forth process going on: I'm forgiven, and now I'm not; I'm forgiven again, and now I'm not. One can just imagine this scene unfolding in Heaven: an unlimited number of super-massive computers monitored by angels, with a rolling list of sins scrolling too fast for the human eye to follow—billions upon billions of sins committed every minute of the day by Earth's inhabitants. This system would need enhanced software to erase and eliminate sins that are confessed and for those who "trickle into another Mass." It's a foolish theology that God would have no part in, and it would never allow Jesus to "rest" from His finished work.

Another visualization was even more fearful for me: Although all my sins were forgiven, when I arrived in Heaven there would be a massive video screen, and when it was my turn, I would walk up in front of thousands of witnesses; it was time for the "Jeff video." All my bad deeds were about to be on full display, and I would think, "Oh no, don't show that one!" It would be an embarrassing few hours, but I would have to go through it and suffer the humiliation, and at the end of the session God would say, "Don't worry, you're fully forgiven!" And I would think, "Well, that is great Lord, but now everyone knows!"

For Catholics, there is a different angle, and although there are some similar crossover theologies, it's unsurprisingly much more convoluted and complicated. We have to camp out much longer to understand the Catholic view of sin. Transgressions are distinguished and sorted into venial sins (those that are not that bad), and mortal or grave sins (those that will send you uncontrollably tumbling into hell if you do not clear them up). Instead of grabbing 1 John 1:9, Catholics grab one or two verses, plucked from its context, about the early apostles forgiving sins. They apply this to a priesthood action that doesn't exist in the New Covenant.

Catholics play the same confession game, and it is a sacrament in the Roman Catholic economy. This practice used to revolve around Lent, in preparation for Easter, from around the fifth century, but that was changed during the Fourth Lateran Council in 1215. Note the date, and that the change took place during the times of the Church's most corrupt popes in the Middle Ages. After the change, the penitent (reluctantly at times) ventured into the dark booth of the priest and proceed to go down a list of deeds done wrong.

All this is to receive an absolution (the green light from the priest that everything is OK now that he has pronounced forgiveness on behalf of Christ), and only after the confessor has proven genuine contrition (sorrow for their sins). However, the guilty as charged still has to participate in penance for the cycle to be complete.

This penance (making amends, or even better described as "self-punishment"), announced by the priest, can be a variety of made-up requirements. It might be anything from saying a certain number of "Our Fathers" and "Hail Marys" to repeating various prayers, fasting, doing charitable works, making amends with a victim, attending Mass more often, meditation, or even mowing the Church lawn. The priest just makes it up off-the-cuff and away goes the confessor to perform their duty.

Not to be overly critical, but I always found it humorous when people say a certain number of "Our Fathers" or "Hail Marys", as if the words coming out of their mouths repetitiously like a parrot have any effect at all in the reconciliation process with God.

Husband: "Honey, did the priest say ten and ten, or twenty and twenty– I've already forgotten."

Wife: "Just text him. I can't remember either. Try not to screw up next time and you won't have this problem!"

Husband: "Me screw up? If you hadn't opened your mouth and said what you did ..."

Wife: "Are you calling me a liar? Why don't you call the priest back up and go back to confession again for calling me names."

This repetitive rhetoric of phrases reminds me of when I was a kid. My mom would make me write a certain number of "sentences" as part of my punishment (penance) for doing wrong.

I will not curse again.

I will not curse again.

I will not curse again.

I would have to write these sentences 200 or 300 times, depending on what the offense was. My hand would certainly be cramping before I was done. One day my brother told me about carbon paper. I thought I had stumbled across a gold mine. I got multiple sheets and thought this would cut my workload in half in the future. Of course, what did I know at nine years old? My mom spotted the carbon copies in about one second and increased my punishment to 500 sentences!

One Catholic describes his experience as a kid:

> "I would go back to the pew, kneel and pray away [penance], usually as fast as possible, and go out into the world 'as pure as the driven snow' as the priest would say, because I was 'forgiven.' When you're a child this actually does make you feel good, lighter, freer because you've been told you're 'pure' again and God will love you. Sometimes, as a child, I would walk from the Church and hope to die right when I was 'purified' so I could go to heaven with a clean slate because I knew I was going to sin again, perhaps very shortly."[1]

To complicate the confession game even more, mortal sins (such as lust, greed, anger, pride, jealousy, selfishness, and drunkenness) must be addressed immediately in the Catholic world. This is because if there is even one unabsolved mortal sin before death, one is suddenly "dejustified" and no longer righteous in God's eyes. The list of mortal sins is quite long, but if committed, there is no Heaven or Purgatory; it's straight to the fiery pit. In fact, even deliberately and voluntarily dwelling on a sinful thought can be considered a mortal sin.

Effectively, you could walk to the kitchen for some nighttime ice cream—completely justified in God's eyes with the bliss of eternal life in your future—but an hour later, because of purposeful lusting during the latest Netflix show, you could spend eternity separated from all your family members and friends if this sin is not immediately addressed and "fixed" by a priest. To be clear on this unbelievable doctrine: if a thought you had was "voluntary" or "deliberate" (and dwelt upon) during the TV series you were watching (and not taken care of through confession), it's trillions of years separated from God. However, if that same segment or scene on TV merely generated a "fleeting" thought or "temptation" that you resisted, your place in Heaven is still secure (for now). All of this contrast in your future destination can happen just while sitting on the couch.

> "... to die in mortal sins without repenting and accepting God's merciful love means remaining separated from him forever by our own free choice" (CCC 1033).

Sadly, if you are a sixty-year-old guy who had raised an awesome family—kids could not have asked for a better father—you were an amazing, loving husband to your wife of forty years, participated in going to Mass thousands of times, known as the best employer in the community, spent decades of volunteering at the Church and leading people to Christ, you pray daily, are humble, honest, hard-working, with super character; but most importantly you have placed your faith and trust in Christ—watch out. If you purposely commit that mortal sin and do not get that dealt with, say goodbye for eternity, you maggot! And even if you do deal with your mortal sin, be ready, you have a lot of making up to do in Purgatory.

What if you commit a mortal sin but end up like Tom Hanks in *Castaway*, stranded for years? Where is a priest when you need one? Maybe you are out of the country and need to take care of a mortal sin—where is a priest when you need one? Are you sure you want to get on that airplane? If it crashes before you get to confession, it's "goodbye" forever. What if you committed a mortal sin and on the way to confession you have a car wreck and end up in a coma? Where's a priest when you need one? Catholics will have an explanation for all this, but there is nothing sacred about these man-made traditions.

In fact, theology has gotten so far off base in the Roman Catholic Church that it's hard to comprehend how disturbed the early apostles would be if they were able to see some of the developments. One example is Trent Horn's description of how to find out if you have committed a mortal sin: You simply go online!

> "One way to determine if you've committed a mortal sin is to conduct an 'examination of conscience'. These practical guides, which can be found online, ask a series of questions that help us see if we have committed a mortal sin."[2]

Incidentally, Horn reminds his readers that most churches offer confession on a certain day of the week, which can be found on the Church's website! One can only visualize kids gathered around the computer in their father's office:

"Dad, I really want you to go to Heaven with us when you die." The father replies, "Just a second kids; let me go *online* and see where I stand with God." The dad proceeds to surf the Internet only to find that he has violated something on the Catholic list of mortal sins. He then responds honestly to his kids, "Guys, according to the Internet, Daddy will not make it to Heaven with you if he dies this week because I did slip up and commit one very serious sin. I am working eleven-hour days, but first thing Monday morning—wait, they don't accept confessions on Mondays—first thing Tuesday morning, I will head over to the Church, round up a priest, and make everything right. Afterward, Daddy will be ready to join you (well, at least until another mortal sin drifts my way)."

In the Roman Catholic economy, this is what Jesus's sacrifice on the cross has been reduced to: going online to see if you're going to burn in the fiery furnace. It's simply horrible theology and would make the early apostles horror-struck if they knew what the Church has evolved into. The Roman Church believes in evolution, but this type of spiritual evolution of justification and forgiveness is pretty sad news.

One of the most misunderstood verses about forgiveness that Catholics grab to fit their agenda is found in the book of John:

> "If you forgive the sins of any, their sins have been forgiven them, if you retain the sins of any, they have been retained" (John 20:23 NKJV).

The Catholic Church's whole system regarding forgiveness pivots primarily around this single verse, taking it out of context, and ignoring dozens of scriptures that say that forgiveness has already been settled at the cross. The disciples, in their evangelism, forgiving or retaining sins meant they would pronounce someone as either forgiven or not, depending on if the Gospel message was received by the unbeliever. They were not forgiving or absolving someone of sins, they were "pronouncing" that an individual was forgiven by God. Paul said something similar in the book of Acts:

> "Therefore, my brothers, I want you to know that through Jesus the forgiveness of sins is <u>proclaimed</u> to you" (Acts 13:28).

Thompson, in his documentary, states the early church fathers knew this to be true as well. Clement, in his letter to the Corinthians, says:

> "The Lord, brethren, stands in need of nothing; and He desires nothing of anyone except that confession be made to Him."[3]

How did early Christians deal with sin? We see that they did not go to a priest to confess or be forgiven. The first-century Didache shows that they would instead engage in public confession of sins in the congregation:

> "In your gatherings, confess your transgression, and do not come for prayer with a guilty conscience." (Didache, 4:14)[4]

Patristic scholar J.N.D. Kelly notes:

> "With the dawn of the third century ... there are still no signs of a sacrament of private penance (i.e., confession to a priest, followed by absolution and the imposition of penance) such as Catholic Christendom knows today. The system that existed in

the Church at this time, and for centuries afterwards, was wholly public ..."[5]

Thompson concludes that even the Catechism has no hesitation about admitting the specific practice of confessing to a priest is a modern innovation that did not exist in the primitive Church:

"During the first centuries, the reconciliation of Christians who had committed particularly grave sins after their Baptism was tied to a rigorous discipline, according to which penitents had to do public penance ... During the seventh century, Irish missionaries, inspired by the Eastern monastic tradition, took to continental Europe the 'private' practice of penance ... From that time on, the sacrament has been performed in secret between penitent and priest. This new practice envisioned the possibility of repetition, and so opened the way to a regular frequenting of this sacrament."[6]

Catholic scholar Kenan Osborne also concedes:

"Major biblical scholars today, however, do not find either in the text or in the context of these passages, (Matthew 16:16 and 18:18; John 20:23), an account of an institution of a reconciliation ritual."[7]

Whether it was Catholics or Protestants making up their own system throughout the centuries, how did we cheapen grace and let it get so messed up? How did we let the unbelievable substitutionary death of Christ on the cross become such a minimalistic event? How did we miss the plan that God was accomplishing through sending Jesus? Why do we keep inserting ourselves into the equation of a finished event? Why do so many religious entities keep going back to the Old Covenant and embracing Judaic legalism? Do we even know the Jesus of the New Covenant?

In both systems, the thinking is that if we just confess, we get forgiven; if we confess, we make things right with God; if we confess, we have a clear conscience. "I made it right," we think. But did you know that Scripture doesn't teach that? The Bible teaches that if you are a Christian, your sins have already been forgiven. When Jesus died all of our sins were yet to come, and hanging on a cross He reached into the future and dragged all the sins that would ever be committed back through time and nailed them to the cross.

Once and for All

The moment you make the decision to repent (change your mind about the direction of your life), follow Him, trust Him, embrace Him, and fully believe that He came to die on a cross for the sins of mankind, you receive forgiveness once and for all.

It's all about Him and what He did; not us. It's about a new contract we entered with God (a New Covenant) in which He says, "I'm not going to remember your sins ever again" (Hebrews 8:12). It's all about a new arrangement, on this side of the cross, "I'm putting them behind my back and will remember them no more" (Isaiah 38:17). The Old Covenant advised everyone that a new way was coming. John the Baptist prepared the way as well: "It's not going to be like anything you have ever seen or heard." Throw everything you have ever been taught out the window and get ready for the finality of the cross.

Consequently, treating God like a teller machine—punch in the right code and you get the forgiveness slip, punch in the right code, get another forgiveness slip, confess to the priest, get another forgiveness slip—after a while is just meaningless, daunting, and drudgery. Our relationship with God is built on what He did, not on what we do every day. It's built on a one-time event on the cross, not our confession as we will see in the verses listed later on. To continue to have our own little system of relying on the useless pursuit of more forgiveness, announcing to Christ, "Your sacrifice was not enough so we will participate to help you out," is simply not accepting what Jesus has already completed on our behalf.

This "helping God" mentality minimizes the blood of Christ and what He accomplished in His mission. It's prideful and full of self-righteousness. Whenever we try to obtain more forgiveness, in some ways, we are not acknowledging the finality of the cross. As one pastor put it, "We can never do what God has done."

Something incredible happened at the cross. Many Christians have never truly grasped the magnitude of the exchange that took place. He took all of our unrighteousness (sin) and gave us His righteousness (holiness). If we could assimilate, comprehend, and understand that concept the Christian life would never be viewed the same again. He exchanged places with us on the cross. We deserved the penalty for sin, but He took it in our place. The only acceptable penalty for sin has always been death (Romans 6:23), not penance, not forgiveness slips from a priest, not a useless prayer at night.

"God made Him who had no sin to be sin for us, so that in Him we might become the righteousness of God" (2 Corinthians 5:21).

"... not having a righteousness of my own that comes from the law, but that which is through faith in Christ—the righteousness that comes from God and is by faith" (Philippians 3:9).

"For if, by the trespass of the one man, death reigned through that one man, how much more will those who receive God's abundant provision of grace and of the gift of righteousness reign in life through the one man, Jesus Christ." (Romans 5:17).

A whole book can be written on these verses alone, but as a Christian, can you just imagine the implications of what God did for us? As Christians, our spirits became righteous during the exchange at the cross. Not by our merit, not because of our behavior, not because we strive and work for it; God did everything on our behalf to give us His righteousness. He became sin and in doing so, He set us free from the bondage of sin. This was accomplished as an act and demonstration of His incredible love. Sin no longer has power over us. How is that possible?

When we try to grasp the truth of becoming the righteousness of Christ, we must remember what happened at the time of salvation. The Holy Spirit unzipped our bodies and came on in. Why does God see every single believer as holy and righteous? It only takes a few seconds to figure it out. He sees

His righteousness inside of us via the Holy Spirit. Our flesh? It can never improve. Our mind, will, and emotions? He can mature those over time. But what is our new position in Christ as believers?

> "And by that will we <u>have been made holy</u> through the sacrifice of the body of Jesus Christ <u>once for all</u>" (Hebrews 10:10).

The Catholic alternative to what Jesus ushered in is a man-made infusion version of Christianity that has no biblical basis. It requires mankind to continually earn righteousness and maintain righteousness in an ongoing justification—and here is the key—with absolutely no way to measure how you are doing. Pastor John Barnett illustrates by visualizing this form of Christianity as a patient with an IV stuck in their arm infusing them with righteousness every minute of the day. One is in complete bondage to that IV bag and stand, taking it every place they go for the rest of their life, and the medicine in the bag that they are being infused with is not even measurable in its effect.[8]

It's a sad way to live, but it's more than just sadness. It's a system of religion, not relationship. It's a system of human achievement versus the grace of God, a system of hoping family and friends will pray or contribute financially to reduce your time in a fictional Purgatory versus God giving us His righteousness in a great exchange.

God made a legal verdict of "acquittal" on our behalf. He does not "make" us justified; He declares us justified. "Abraham believed God, and it was credited to him as righteous" (James 2:2). He declares this justification at the time of salvation. Origen, one of the early church father, uses justification as a synonym for forgiveness, acquittal, pardon, and remission, and as a legal verdict of acquittal.[9] From the Heavenly Father's perspective, the trial is over; we have been found "not guilty."

In the Roman system, if you lose justification, you have to earn it back. Justification is impermanent: you can lose it over and over and over again. The believer still has to do something more to make amends for his sin: he must "make satisfaction" for his sins per the orders of the Church. Multiple different inadequacies jeopardize a Catholic's standing with God. The Church believes that "if you follow Catholic dogma, if you participate in the sacraments, if you attend the stations of the cross, if you practice confession, if you serve penance, if you honor the pope, if you follow the Ten Commandments, if you believe everything the Church proclaims, if you have extreme unction performed on you before you die, if you comply with all the restrictions in the Catechism, if you endure until the end, then there is a good chance you will make it to Heaven. But we have no idea how long you will be in Purgatory before you get there. It's our law, it's our works, it's our path that qualifies you for Heaven. We wish you good luck."

It's a tedious, discouraging, and threatening system of control. Who could ever want to be a part of something that our Heavenly Father would never condone? By adding sacramental and institutional works to Christ's perfect work you negate the cross and the resurrection for justification and you negate being righteous in God's eyes. You adopt a system that allows you to boast in your accomplishment, not God's free gift. Justification is a gift. Righteousness is a gift. One-time forgiveness is a gift. Eternal life is a gift. In the Roman Church, you cannot rely on the victorious work of Christ, you have to rely on human effort, and a lot of it. It's the pharisaical way that Jesus despised so much, and that's why the Roman Church, although it tries, does not monopolize a path to salvation.

The Roman Church rejects *sola fide* (faith alone) in Christ as the means to salvation. They add the unmeasurable element of works and human achievement to the equation. Yet Pope Benedict XVI says in his 2011 book, *Jesus of Nazareth*:

> "Paul places so much emphasis on the impossibility of justification on the basis of one's own morality. If, on the other hand, we should acknowledge that Paul in no way yields to moralism in this exhortation or in any sense believes his doctrine of justification through faith and not through works, it is equally clear that this doctrine of justification does not condemn man to passivity."[10]

Pope Benedict admits that Paul rejected justification on the basis of moral endeavor and taught that justification by faith apart from works is the message of the Scriptures (faith alone). Why can't the Roman Church just accept this reality? Why can't Christians just be allowed to do good works out of a genuine heart and not tie it in with the salvation process? Why can't they grasp what God accomplished?

Our new position in Christ is that we have been made holy and are fully justified. As Christians, we have been 100% completely forgiven. No more sacrifice is needed, no more sacrifice is available, no more forgiveness is available. We are complete in Christ; we are seen as perfect in Christ. There is no need to ever enter the dark booth again, no need to lay in bed at night trying to reconcile back to Christ when He has already reconciled the world back to Himself.

Could this conclusion come from grabbing a single verse and taking it out of context? On the contrary; it is the whole central theme of the Bible, the centerpiece of Christianity, and this was the plan all along for the redemption of mankind. Taste the amazing grace of Christ in its purest form:

> "I write to you dear children, because your sins have been forgiven on account of [Jesus] name" (1 John 2:12).

Our sins "have been" (past tense) forgiven, but how? On the action of a priest? On the action of contrition? On the act of penance? On the action of repetitions? On the action of a nightly prayer? On the action of our initiations? The answer is no, unless we want to contaminate the blood of Christ. We are forgiven "on account of His name." What an incredibly powerful verse of truth.

> "... that God was reconciling the world to Himself in Christ, not counting men's sins against them" (2 Corinthians 5:19).

I'm not sure there is a more powerful, definitive verse in the whole Bible. Reconciliation was necessary because we were separated from God as a result of sin, and therefore spiritually dead. God had two choices when He sent Jesus to the cross: to count our sins against us continually; or not to count our sins against us ever again. He chose not to hold us responsible.

> "Not only is this so, but we also rejoice in God through our Lord Jesus Christ, through whom we have now received reconciliation" (Romans 5:11).

What God initiated must have been successful. Reconciliation has been completed. We have now received it.

> "In Him we have redemption through his blood, the forgiveness of sins, in accordance with the riches of God's grace that he lavished on us with all wisdom and understanding" (Ephesians 1:7).

Redemption is not something we are going to get or something that we continually have to get. No, we have redemption right now. We don't get it; we have it! And not according to our confession, but because of His grace. He just saturated us with this gift. Amazing grace has the sweetest sound imaginable for a Christian.

> "When you were dead in your sins and in the uncircumcision of your sinful nature, God made you alive with Christ. He forgave us all our sins" (Colossians 2:13).

There is great satisfaction as a believer in knowing that all of our sins have been (past tense) forgiven.

> "... Look the lamb of God, who takes away the sin of the world!" (John 1:29).

God didn't just do away with sin, He did away with dealing with sin.

> "And where these have been forgiven, there is no longer any sacrifice for sin" (Hebrews 10:18).

Past tense is used again. Jesus has already forgiven the sins of the world. For Him to have to provide any more forgiveness of sin, He would have to come back down and go through the excruciating crucifixion all over again. Is Jesus going to do that? He's not. Jesus is next to the Father, having completed the mission of reconciliation and redemption. Over and over again, verse after verse, the Bible says that there is no longer any sacrifice left for sin.

"All the prophets testify about Him that <u>everyone</u> who <u>believes in Him, receives forgiveness of sins</u> through His name" (Acts 10:43).

What is the offer that is given to every person on the planet? Simply believe in Jesus, just as the 3,000 did the day Peter preached the very first sermon, and you will receive every benefit of permanent forgiveness.

Intellectual belief or intellectual assent to Jesus is not what saves someone. Praying a prayer ("repeat after me"), and signing on the bottom line does this either. There is no "easy peasy gospel." The truth that is taught in the New Testament, both through Jesus's teachings and the apostles, has a much deeper meaning than just a superficial belief.

Oftentimes, Catholics get stuck on and oppose phrases like "faith alone" (a super easy pathway into the kingdom) which goes fully against their "striving to obtain salvation" through a merited Roman system, but that is not the true meaning of belief and faith alone. It's a combination of faith, belief, trust, yielding, repentance (changing your mind), and accepting the fact that Jesus exchanged unrighteousness for righteousness, giving us a one-time, eternal forgiveness, and choosing to follow Christ (leaving everything else behind). The key here is a "genuine" faith and belief. A sincere change of heart.

It is during this time in a person's life that a true transformation takes place by faith. A person crosses over from living in darkness to living in the light of Christ. The power of God literally enters our hearts, minds, wills, emotions, and souls, driving out the death that sin held us hostage.

In other words, at this point, we have fully embraced God's grace. This is a journey that was started by God years ago in drawing us by His Spirit and bringing us to a point in our lives where we are drained and worn out from "self," exhausted from trying to live up to all the requirements (a fatiguing list) and are finally ready to exit the pilot's seat and allow Him to control our lives.

However, although we have taken that step of faith and trust in entering into a relationship with God, we have to understand that "total surrender," "total commitment," and "totally yielding our lives to God" are still very ambiguous terms. Those actions are not measurable on a chart or a gauge. Our human efforts are virtually worthless in God's eyes, but He does know a genuine heart. Salvation is a result of one's heart being sincere and coming to the conclusion of who Jesus is by faith, and wanting Him to be in the center of a person's life.

"Loving God with all your heart, mind, and soul" is not a measurable metric either. As Apologist James White points out: "Has anyone ever done that? Yes, Jesus. I need that righteousness to stand before Him and that's why He imputed (assigned and gave) that righteousness to me. The Christian message is: 'I have nothing to offer, I bring nothing to the table, I come empty-handed (not: "here's a little something I would like to offer— good works, my cooperation, my merit").'"[11] Jesus did the work for everything we will ever need. Jesus's work is presented to the Father, not our work. It's his accomplishment not ours.

The verses in the previous pages are too powerful to ignore. It would be easy to list just a few and move on, but looking at larger portions of the Scriptures solidifies the central theme: the theme of a one-time, permanent forgiveness because of the completed work of Christ. We don't need a confession booth or a nightly prayer to keep short accounts with God. There's no blackboard with a list of sins and an eraser to clean the slate again. It's already taken care of forever by His one-time sacrifice.

CHAPTER 10

Forgiveness: What Kind Does Jesus Offer?

One has to wonder what freedom there would be in forgiveness if it only lasted for fifteen minutes. I so clearly remember singing songs at Church proclaiming, "We have been forgiven, we have been forgiven," only to have the pastor call for Christians to come down to the altar to receive more forgiveness. However, all along, there was no more forgiveness available. There are no altar calls in the New Covenant. There was one altar, one sacrifice, and Jesus accomplished the goal.

The verses are beautiful; they are reassuring; Jesus took our place; we have been offered the most incredible gift. That gift of grace is sitting at your front door like an Amazon package if you are willing to open the door, grab and embrace it. The gift does have something in it when you open it. What's in the gift? It's a message from Christ, written in blood: "I have taken away all of your sin, once and for all." The message would never say, "I have taken away all your sin, once and for all, or at least for the next few minutes, or until you can round up a priest, or until you mess up again."

To grasp the true nature of this gift, it's helpful to understand the previous system before Jesus came. God gave Israel a system for obtaining forgiveness in the law of Moses in the Old Testament. The people were to confess their sins and bring a sin offering to the altar to obtain forgiveness. Annually, there was a Day of Atonement to do so. This system was an ongoing arrangement that could only reach backward into a person's past to forgive sin that had already been committed. All the verses of David, Nehemiah, and other Old Testament authors asking for forgiveness fall under this category. They were in a state of waiting for Messiah to come and die for their sins, once and for all. The animal sacrifices they made only covered (atoned for) their sins until Jesus could come and take them away.

Why is this important to understand? Because "The Lord's Prayer" taught under the Old Covenant, exactly where Jesus was before the cross, conveyed what was applicable at the time: "Forgive us our debts, as we forgive our debtors." The Old Covenant came and went and was replaced by the New Covenant that God ushered in immediately after the resurrection with a new message, a reverse from the Old Covenant, a replacement to The Lord's Prayer:

"... Forgiving each other; as the Lord has forgiven you ..." (Colossians 3:13 ESV).

Notice the nuance. Essentially, when Jesus taught The Lord's Prayer to His disciples, the people He taught it to were still in the same state as David and others: waiting for the Messiah to sacrifice Himself once and for all. They were still living under the Old Covenant. Listening to Jesus that day was a crowd of Jews, under the law of Moses, worshipping and sacrificing at the temple (totally appropriate) under a system of ongoing forgiveness by animal sacrifice that could only reach into the past, that "... can never, by the same sacrifices repeated endlessly year after year, make perfect those who draw near to worship" (Hebrews 10:1).

It was fitting for Jesus's disciples, at that point in time, and up to the cross, to ask often for God to forgive them for their sins, because the price for their sins had not yet been paid. Likewise, the kingdom had not yet come, and they had not been delivered from evil, so those were appropriate things to ask for in the Lord's Prayer also, because at that point those things had not been accomplished either.

Few Christians think about the fact that there were no "born again" people in existence when Jesus taught His disciples the Lord's Prayer. The New Covenant was not ushered in until the resurrection, and no one was born again until the Spirit was first given at Pentecost.

On this side of Christ's wonderful accomplishment, however, God is living in those who have been born again, we have been rescued from the dominion of darkness, and we possess, in Him, the forgiveness that He bought with His death, which is total and reaches into all of our futures.

"For he has rescued us from the dominion of darkness and brought us into the kingdom of the Son he loves, in whom <u>we have redemption, the forgiveness of sins</u>" (Colossians 1: 13-14).

Jesus taught an appropriate prayer to the Jews at the time—He was still on the scene, He still had not died for the sins of the world at that point. This gives total clarity on why He taught this prayer. Sins were still being atoned for before the cross, believers still had to ask for forgiveness. But after the resurrection Jesus ushered in a new way to relate to God, under the New Covenant, with a message that He has already forgiven us (past tense) as genuine believers, and therefore, we should forgive others (for our benefit, but not to receive forgiveness). The Lord's Prayer has been updated! Who updated it? Our Heavenly Father.

The Jews did not want to let go of their tradition. Even the apostles struggled with the transition, and this was evident when Paul journeyed back to Jerusalem and found that law and grace were being mixed together by the other apostles in Acts 15. He corrected them and wrote letters to various churches to correct them as well. They did not want to let go of the Old Covenant, the way of life they had always known. However, prophecy had come true: Jesus was the final sacrifice for sin, ushering in a new system of how we relate to God, removing the penalty for sin forever, and making the Old Covenant obsolete.

As Christians, we have to be able to discern between the law-based teaching Jesus did at that time, applicable to only the Jews before the cross and representing the majority of what is written in the four Gospels. This includes the Sermon on the Mount. The contrast to this law-based teaching is the new way of grace that would be acquired through faith that would apply to the whole world, but only after the resurrection. The Gentiles (most of us) were never under the Old Covenant, yet many Christian religions embrace the old system of the law and try to apply it to daily Christian living. The results are disastrous. The Roman Catholic Church leads the pack in this Old Covenant pursuit, yet God says we are not under that outdated system. The entire world, today, is living under the canopy of the New Covenant.

As either Catholics or Protestants, we all have to accept the will of God that was executed and that is currently in place, the New Covenant, with a message and a promise: "You have been permanently forgiven, and I now see you as righteous." It's not an option. It's not a choice. We were not consulted about the plan. The God that created the universe has permanently set in place the New Covenant. No priest is needed. No prayer begging for more forgiveness is needed, either.

"Be kind and compassionate to one another, forgiving each other, just as in Christ God forgave you" (Ephesians 4:32).

"Therefore, as one trespass led to condemnation for all men, so one act of righteousness leads to justification and life for all men. For as by the one man's disobedience the many were made sinners, so by the one man's obedience the many will be made righteous" (Romans 5:18-19 ESV).

"And if Christ has not been raised, your faith is futile; you are still in your sins" (1 Corinthians 15:17).

"... After he had provided purification for sins, he sat down at the right hand of the Majesty of heaven" (Hebrews 1:3).

"But you know that he appeared so that he might take away our sins ..." (1 John 3:5).

"But if anyone does not have them (a list of good qualities in the verses before), he is nearsighted and blind, and has forgotten that he has been cleansed from his past sins" (2 Peter 1:9).

Bob George, the author of *Classic Christianity* and *Faith that Pleases God* so eloquently states the reality, completion, and finality of the Cross:

"That all the sins we have ever committed; all the sins we will ever do in the future, were paid for in full by the death, burial and resurrection of Jesus Christ. He, forever, removed the penalty of sin. Afterwards, God made an announcement and proclamation that every single believer has been, and will continue to live up under the canopy of this type of forgiveness: permanent not temporary, complete not partial, finished not ongoing, applying to all sins not some, sins are forgotten not remembered.

"... the Bible says that all of our sins, in the past, today and in the future have already been judged. What was the verdict? Guilty. What was the penalty? Death. Was the penalty paid? Yes. Where? At the Cross. Who paid it? Jesus Christ. How much of it? All of it. How much did He leave for us to pay for? None of it. While hanging on the Cross, God reached into the future, and drug all of the sins we would ever commit back through time, nailing them to the cross."[1]

Here is the shocking revelation: There is no partial forgiveness offered on this side of the cross, just a one-time, permanent forgiveness at the time of salvation. We can only accept what God offers. We have no other alternative. As a result, sin is no longer being held against us! Sin can no longer separate us from God. He is no longer mad at us for sin. He took His anger out on Jesus at the cross. The sin issue between God and us is over.

We do not need to ask the pope or a priest or a pastor to forgive us of sin. In fact, under the system God put in place after Jesus rose from the dead, once we receive his one-time gift of forgiveness, it is no longer necessary to ask God for forgiveness either. Why? Because He has already dealt with our sin issue, He is resting, and there is no longer any forgiveness to receive. Would God get angry if a Christian were to ask for more forgiveness? Of course, not. His grace is completely able to cover errors in our thinking. However, He simply wants you to understand the full benefit of what was accomplished on the cross by Christ.

His gift of forgiveness and eternal life was final and complete and was never dependent upon anything we could do in the first place. There is nothing we can do to earn our way into Heaven, to earn God's favor on our life, or to ever obtain forgiveness on our own accord. We simply can't do it. He made it available as a free gift, no strings attached. He didn't just cover up our sins; He erased all of them completely.

Bob George makes the point that either we receive what God offers and have life, or we reject it and have death. We should no longer bring ourselves to tell God that Christ's death on the cross did not accomplish what He meant for it to by trying to earn our own righteousness.

Our new identity is in Christ, so although we will definitely sin, we are not in bondage to sin anymore. We actually have the power through the Holy Spirit to not be trapped by sin with no way to get out. It is important to understand that there is no more penalty or condemnation for sin:

> "Therefore, there is now no condemnation for those that are in Christ Jesus, because the law of the Spirit of life set me free from the law of sin and death" (Romans 8:1).

> "Whoever believes in Him is not condemned, but whoever does not believe stands condemned already because he has not believed in the name of God's one and only Son" (John 3:18).

Notice that Paul says there is "now" no condemnation. Until Jesus came to the Cross, mankind was in a big mess under the Old Covenant. Jesus didn't come to atone for our sins (sweeping them under the rug), He came to forever remove the penalty of and the dealing with sin. We definitely have earthly consequences when we sin, and they are extensive. A lost job because of dishonesty, a broken relationship because of unfaithfulness; and if you rob a bank, you are going to jail! However, amazing grace is that God has forever removed sin's spiritual penalty from us: eternal death and separation from Him.

Many Christian institutions are scared to death of teaching that Christians are permanently and completely forgiven from sin because that would seem to give the believer a green light to profusely and uncontrollably sin any time they want. However, there are major flaws with that thinking. The focus of a genuine Christian is *not* the fact that sin is no longer held against them so they are free to sin at will. Their focus, instead, is on Christ and growing in maturity.

Does anyone think a Christian feels good after doing something wrong? The Holy Spirit is inside of a believer like air in a balloon. "Hey, I wouldn't do that, you will not benefit from that, remember what happened the last time you gave in?" The Holy Spirit does not take naps inside of the believer. He is active every minute we are awake to encourage us not to sin, not to condemn us when we do.

Realistically, there isn't much difference in the Protestant and Catholic confession games that teach that with human effort and jumping through confession hoops, we are off the hook anyway. Thinking you are free to sin at liberty (since you are no longer under the penalty of sin because of grace) is the same concept as believing that if you do sin, you can just confess and get forgiveness from a priest or directly from God Himself. There is simply no difference between those errors in thinking.

Finally, it is an absolute insult to the power of God, and an insult to the miracle of transformation when we are born again, to subscribe to the thinking that the blood of Christ and our new life in Christ would motivate us to sin. Look what Paul says about that:

> "What then? Shall we sin because we are not under the law but under grace? By no means! Don't you know that when you offer yourselves to someone to obey him as slaves, you are slaves to the one whom you obey ... But thanks be to God that, though you used to be slaves to sin, you wholeheartedly obeyed the form of teaching to which you were entrusted. You have been set free from sin and have become slaves to righteousness" (Romans 6: 15-18).

> "Therefore, if anyone is in Christ, he is a new creation; the old has gone, the new has come! All this is from God, who reconciled us to himself through Christ" (2 Corinthians 5:17-18).

> "For the grace of God that brings salvation has appeared to all men. It teaches us to say 'No' to ungodliness and worldly passions, and to live self-controlled, upright and godly lives in this present age" (Titus 2:11-12).

Paul is saying that we are no longer held captive by sin; we are no longer in bondage to sin. Should believers think that living under grace permits them to sin anytime and as much as they want since they're forgiven already?

Never. Paul directly disputes the notion that as Christians we are going to be motivated to sin because grace has permanently removed the penalty. Trying to obtain forgiveness from a priest or any other means as a Christian is enslavement to an institution that is trying to control. Although it applies to Protestant churches as well, we have already seen the Roman Catholic Church and its attempt to exercise unwarranted authority.

This is why it is so important for Catholics not to be kept in the dark any longer by an institution that, for hundreds of years, banned believers from ever seeing these verses on grace. They hid the truth that reveals a different system than what was being taught. We are already forgiven and we are already righteous in God's sight because of our new identity in Christ (no Purgatory for us to bake a little longer is needed). He accepts us one hundred percent "as is" because of His accomplishment—His righteousness, not by our merit and behavior.

Confession as Christians

As mentioned, the Old Covenant required a blood sacrifice in the temple once a year by priests. The New Covenant did away with that system and replaced it with Jesus coming as the final, one-time blood sacrifice. He did away with the need to ever confess to a priest, or to make sacrifices, or to do anything to try to obtain forgiveness on one's own accord (such as visiting the confession booth or penance). Why? That system is obsolete and is no longer applicable.

We have to believe God's mission of reconciliation and redemption has been completed, or we call Him a liar. Too many Christians walk around doubting their salvation and wondering where they stand with God. Christ said your salvation is not dependent on you, it's dependent on Him and His faithfulness, not yours. Jesus Christ did for us what we couldn't do for ourselves. We didn't get what we deserved!

Jesus has taken away all my sin, full stop. Not, "but if I confess, he'll take it away again"—that would be a completely double-minded concept under the New Covenant.

Many Christians miss the most important gift that was ever given to mankind in favor of religious tradition or a single verse like 1 John 1:9 ("If we confess our sins, He is faithful to forgive us our sin and cleanse us from all unrighteousness"). When examining a verse like that, you simply have to understand the context. The Apostle John is writing a letter to the Church with a mixed crowd—like we have in today's congregations with Christians and non-Christians present. 1 John 1:9 is an invitation to *non-believers* to receive the free gift of forgiveness and salvation; John isn't offering Christians a bar of soap to clean themselves up. We know that from the verses right before and after it.

1 John 1:8 states, "If we claim to be without sin, we deceive ourselves and the truth is not in us." Here John is speaking to a non-believer who is claiming to be without sin. We know this because he says the truth (Jesus Christ) is not inside them. The truth (Jesus Christ), however, is inside of every believer.

1 John 1:10 states, "If we claim we have not sinned, we make him out to be a liar and his word has no place in our lives." This verse is a reiteration and continuation from 1 John 1:8. Christians do not claim we have not sinned; part of our salvation process was understanding that we were in desperate need of a Savior, and we placed our faith in the truth of the cross and resurrection. The verses found in 1 John 1:8-10 are *strictly* for non-believers as an invitation to receive Christ.

The greater context of the situation in this particular congregation is this: John was addressing Gnostics who were part of a group of people who denied the reality of sin. This was a problem with that assembly during that day. These Gnostics needed to confess in order to be cleansed and forgiven because they were not Christians, so John addressed them.

Dozens and dozens of scriptures indicate we have total, one-time, permanent forgiveness as Christians, that we are already righteous because of Christ, and that every Christian is a saint. Most of those verses have already been listed, but they have been grouped together on the last pages of this book for accessibility. So when we suddenly stumble across a verse that seems to contradict the completeness of forgiveness (and we interpret it to mean that more is still needed), it's worth spending the time to examine why there is an apparent conflict. We find after a cursory search that there is no conflict at all.

We simply have to look at the context and larger portions of the Scriptures; and most importantly, never forget the central theme of the Bible: Jesus came as a substitutionary sacrifice and did everything on our behalf to fulfill the righteous requirements for salvation with an invitation: will you put your trust and faith in this message of redemption? This was Peter's original message on opening day.

As Christians, it is totally appropriate to confess our sins to other believers (James 5:16) or to our Heavenly Father. Confessing is defined as agreeing with God about our wrongdoing. However, confessing is only for the purpose of communicating and working through the sin we are dealing with, not to obtain forgiveness. John absolutely forbids the idea that we are confessing for further forgiveness.

Here again, all through the New Testament, we see verses that apply to believers and some that apply to non-believers. There are hundreds of examples, but let's use Romans 10:13: "Everyone who calls on the name of the Lord will be saved." When I was thirteen years old, I had no interest in spiritual matters. This verse fully applied to my non-Christian life. At fourteen years old, in coming to the realization of who Jesus was, placing my faith and trust in Him, and accepting His death and resurrection into my life, I needed that verse. For the past forty-seven years, that verse has not applied to me. I no longer call on the name of the Lord to be saved; I am already saved.

John clears up any misunderstanding today's Christians might have on whether or not we have forgiveness or we need to get more forgiveness just fourteen verses later in 1 John 2:12: "I write to you, dear children (Christians), because your sins have been (past tense) forgiven on the account of His name (Jesus)."

If you are Protestant and have tagged along so far, you will likely admit that just about every church you have been a part of seems to teach that you have to ask God for more forgiveness if He is going to cover all of your recent sins, all hinged on one verse. Yet teachers, leaders, and millions of Christians who finally understand the New Covenant do not think that way. They finally realize the complete message of grace and our new arrangement on this side of the cross. Dr. Charles Stanley, probably the best-known Protestant pastor besides Billy Graham, wrote in his book *Forgiveness*:

"So which is it? Are our sins forgiven based on His grace and the death of Christ two thousand years ago, or our up-to-the-minute confession? We can add nothing to Christ's death that will gain for us any more forgiveness than we already have. After we are saved, the basis of our continuing forgiveness is still none other than the shed blood of Christ at Calvary. Yet many believe that all future forgiveness is conditional upon the proper confession of sins...This is what happens when we come to God confessing our sins—the confession does not persuade God to forgive us. He did that at the cross."[2]

Keep in mind that for fifty years, Dr. Stanley was part of a denomination that states that you have to obtain more forgiveness as a Christian,[3] yet in black and white, he personally states that the truth is there is no forgiveness left to receive. Dr. Stanley continues and describes confessing as agreeing with God and restoring our fellowship and intimacy with God, not asking for more forgiveness for sins we can't even keep up with.[4]

It's important for Christians to understand that any change in fellowship or intimacy is happening on our side, not God's. So, any separation from God because of sin is only in our minds, not God's response to our sin. Everyone sins quite frequently, sometimes unknowingly, but that does not mean one has to feel separated from God in their mind.

If I do sin, I have the option to chat with Him about it and ask Him to clear my conscience, claiming victory, again and again, in His final sacrifice. Many teachers declare something like, "As soon as you confess (not to get forgiveness, but to agree with God about your sin), instantly your fellowship with God is restored." However, that is not entirely correct.

To subscribe to that reasoning alludes to the idea that "God is mad at me for my sin, and there has been some sort of 'separation.'" But there is nothing that can separate us from God's love (Romans 8:38). He's never angry at us for sin. The truth is that Christians sin so much that we do not even acknowledge that anything is wrong with our fellowship most of the time. We can't even remember everything that we did erroneously. Sin is coming at us so fast that we can't keep up. We simply walk in the Spirit of God daily, and make the best decisions we can because of His Spirit living inside of us and the wisdom He has given us.

This is not splitting hairs. The Scripture isn't teaching, "Wait! You can confess to God and agree with Him about something you did wrong, but do not confess to get forgiveness—be careful of your word choice here." No, that is not the issue. The most important concept in all of the Scriptures is understanding our position in Christ, our new arrangement, His New Covenant, and His promise to us that we live in a state of forgiveness, twenty-four hours a day, seven days a week because of His sacrifice. However, behavior and frequency of sin can vacillate like the wind if we choose not to walk in the Spirit of God (Galatians 5:16). Chatting with our Heavenly Father about any sin we are struggling with is always appropriate and beneficial, but resting in His accomplished work is His gift of grace.

If you are Catholic, it is critical to understand this spiritual truth: Sacrifice and forgiveness are joined at the hip. If we do not need any more sacrifice, we do not need any more forgiveness. Forgiveness can only be achieved with a sacrifice. Jesus was the final sacrifice. The comprehension of what God has proclaimed to be true changes everything.

Confession to a priest for forgiveness is obsolete and not applicable to a believer on this side of the cross. The attempt of Catholics to obtain forgiveness for their venial sins in the Eucharist is unnecessary as well (we'll look closer at that in Chapter 13). When you understand that God only sees us as righteous and has already made us holy "in Him," there is no need for being purged or sanctified in the afterlife either; God already sees you as righteous and transformed. Our choices are either tradition or God's proclamation. One has to choose.

It Is Finished

There is nothing more refreshing than knowing that as Christians we live in a constant state of forgiveness with every breath we take. We cannot live in a state of forgiveness and unforgiveness at the same time. Those concepts are diametrically opposed. When you turn the light on in a dark room, the darkness is no longer the visible state. The darkness is gone. If you eat a giant Thanksgiving dinner and you have a stomach so full it hurts and feels like it is going to rupture, hunger is banished. It is not possible for fullness to exist in the presence of emptiness, and emptiness in the presence of fullness.

There is nothing logical or biblical about convincing someone that they are fully forgiven in Christ, only to have them be in a state of unforgiveness just hours later. We do not walk through the Christian life with our fingers crossed, thinking, "I hope I'm forgiven; I hope I'm forgiven." We walk in the finished work done at the cross. We can live in deception about being in a state of unforgiveness and be in bondage to sin, or enjoy the freedom we have in Christ. We can't have it both ways. You can't be forgiven and ask for more, you can't have salvation but with a time limit, you can't be justified only to have to work for justification. Not in God's economy; not in the New Covenant.

God directed his wrath over sin at Jesus in our place, at the cross, and He placed the full penalty and all of His justice for our sins on Jesus, and now there is no penalty left for us. Justice was served, and what is left is love in God-sized portions! He didn't condemn us, He condemned sin in us, accepting the full penalty Himself, leaving us totally acquitted.

Thinking that we are responsible for seeking out means to be forgiven is self-righteousness and pride in its truest form. Paul, who wrote half of the New Testament, talks about his struggles with sin but never asks God to forgive him. Instead, in Romans and throughout the other books he wrote, he talks about this unexplainable grace that goes "beyond our understanding" —a one-time sacrifice to provide forgiveness and eliminate our need to ever approach the throne for more.

Bob George makes a great observation that if there is no more sacrifice for sin—and without the shedding of blood there is no forgiveness of sin—what do we conclude about the death of Christ? We have to conclude that the sin issue is finished and amazingly, that is exactly what Jesus said from the cross.

What then do we do if we sin? We simply thank God that He has already forgiven us, agree with Him that sin never benefits us, and ask Him to please allow His Holy Spirit to give us the strength to resist temptation in the future.

As Christians, we have to stop focusing on sin. The Christian life isn't about sin, it's about Christ. Sin is no longer the stumbling block between God and man. The wages of sin was the death of Christ and that debt has been paid. His death on the Cross was sufficient. The sin issue between God and the believer is over. God's purpose was to take care of the sin problem once and for all between man and Himself through Jesus Christ, and no other way. Author Steve McVey writes,

> "So, are you forgiven or not? Saints, either He did it all or we're up the creek ... Have you forgotten that the new covenant promise from our faithful Lord is that our 'sins and (our) lawless deeds I will remember no more' (Heb. 10:17)? If He has chosen to remember them no more, why do we insist upon parading them before Him day after day?"[5]

In his book, George said it best:

> "Until you rest in the finality of the cross, you will never rejoice in the reality of the resurrection. There has been a proclamation of forgiveness—a public authoritative announcement and this is the announcement of God—that every single believer has been forgiven and is living under the canopy of God's continuous, unending, never-ending, eternal forgiveness."[6]

Christians can be very ingrained with certain traditions; they are hard to let go of. It is embedded in the minds of Catholics that you have to walk into a dark room and confess your sins, be absolved from your sins, and do penance for your sins. That system is obsolete. It's forever gone under the blood of Christ. Those are Old Covenant practices and they ignore the greatest events in history.

Charles Spurgeon observes:

> "According to this gracious covenant (The New Covenant), the Lord treats His people as if they had never sinned. Practically, He forgets all their trespasses. Sins of all kinds He treats as if they had never been; as if they were quite erased from His memory. O Miracle of Grace! His mercy works miracles which far transcend all other miracles. Our God ignores our sin now that the sacrifice of Jesus has ratified the covenant. We may rejoice in Him without

fear that He will be provoked to anger against us because of our iniquities. See! He puts us among the children; He accepts us as righteous; He takes delight in us as if we were perfectly holy. O my soul, what a promise is this! Believe it and be happy."[7]

Protestants, meanwhile, have to be willing to let go of thinking you have to keep "short accounts with God." Praying for forgiveness is not applicable on this side of the cross. Confessing your sins to God or one another is biblical, but praying for forgiveness is obsolete under the New Covenant of grace.

As a Catholic, to be aligned with God's plan for your life, you have to leave the Old Covenant behind, never walk into a gloomy confessional booth again, and accept your new position in Christ and enjoy true freedom. The Heavenly Father will never look at us again and see anything but fully forgiven believers who are fully righteous (in right standing with Him); believers who are fully justified on account of His name. Imagine the incredible implications if Catholics could fully embrace these truths from God. It will truly set you free from the enslavement of an institution. When you abandon self-effort, rules, regiments, and requirements, your Christian life will never be the same again. Rituals and repetitions do not give anyone forgiveness or life. Only faith in Christ does so.

Jesus said it was finished. Can we simply rest in His perfect forgiveness?

> "The author of Hebrews wants Christians to know that the entire Trinity agrees with Jesus's finished work. The Trinity is not divided about us. The Father, the Son, and the Spirit know that we are perfectly forgiven. This means that the Holy Spirit is not condemning us of sin. To the contrary, the Holy Spirit remembers our sins no longer (Hebrews 10:16-17). Hebrews teaches that one thing alone brings forgiveness: blood. Jesus shed His blood once, and as a result we are perfectly forgiven. Jesus did not need to suffer multiple times. His sacrifice was so sufficient that He only needed to die once. His death does not cover sins but removes them entirely. This is why Jesus returns without reference to sin" (Dr. Andrew Farley).[8]

CHAPTER 11

The Twofold Gospel

I remember being fourteen years old like it was yesterday. I had a great life. Our family lived on thirty-six beautiful acres in the country, we had a brand-new home with a swimming pool, rode horses on the miles of dirt roads, and raced friends through the green pastures; it was a complete blast. Exploring the woods and walking through the creeks with my 30/30 deer rifle was thrilling for someone my age, and I missed my share of curfews when the weather was good. I was in my fifth year of baseball on the county team; my brothers, several friends, and I played endless hours of basketball on a hoop that was nailed to a telephone pole just yards away from the house.

My parents had the *Notebook* type of marriage in the sense that they had an incredible connection and great communication, and we would see them sitting out in the pastures on one of the terraces in the afternoons, where they would talk for hours. I'm not sure life could have been any better for someone my age, except for the fact that I was empty inside, had an unexplainable fear that wouldn't go away, and would stare out the windows for hours trying to figure out why was I even here, and what was my purpose and place in this world? Unfortunately, this overwhelming and consuming feeling led me to wonder if maybe it would be better if I were dead—that would certainly alleviate the intense emotional pain I was feeling at the time. Puberty? It certainly was at play, but I felt completely dead inside.

The feelings were so intense that my appetite had just dwindled away. Of course, I did not know what was happening, so I did not share these internal secrets with anyone, and my parents thought something was physically wrong with me. They proceeded to take me to countless doctors who ran every test that was available in the '70s, but to no avail. There was nothing wrong with me physically. All the tests were perfect. I knew the results were going to come back with no conclusion and would not give my parents any satisfaction of finally figuring out what in the world was going on.

I was attending a Christian school at the time and my family attended the church that was affiliated with the school. My friends and I sat through hours of tedious, boring sermons and could only think about the service being over so we could throw the football in the parking lot, goof off, and enjoy hanging out. However, over the course of a couple of weeks, something started to change. Looking back, I cannot even remember what the exact messages were about during those few weeks, but I remember the pastor talking about how a relationship with Christ changes your life.

He taught that what was missing in someone's life who was not a Christian was the life of Christ and the Holy Spirit living inside the hearts and minds of a person, giving them meaning and purpose. He said that if someone is not a Christian, there is an empty vacuum inside their heart that could only be filled by the power of God. Wow, I was actually listening to every word he was saying; he had my attention.

It was April 7th, 1977, a Thursday night, when it happened. I was in my bedroom (not an emotional Church service or Christian summer camp) and could almost audibly hear God calling my name. It really is hard to describe in words, but I felt God inside my room leading me to start a relationship with him by surrendering my life, allowing him to take control, and receiving His Spirit inside of me. I remember kneeling by my bed and telling God that if He was real, I wanted Him to be a part of my life and I wanted to trust in Him. It was my first prayer, outside of childish prayers that had no context and only said with my mom before going to sleep as a kid.

Life of Christ

Although I knew the basics and was growing in Christ, it would be almost twenty-three years before I fully grasped what happened that night. I understood the good news that I was in great need of a Savior for the forgiveness of sins (once and for all), as discussed in the last two chapters, but there was something even more critical. I was also missing the life of Christ, the Spirit of the living, holy God, inside of me.

"I have been crucified with Christ, and I no longer live, but Christ lives inside of me" (Galatians" 2:20).

"If anyone acknowledges that Jesus is the Son of God, <u>God lives in him</u> and he in God" (1 John 4:15).

"... <u>God lives in us</u> and his love is made <u>complete</u> in us" (1 John 4:12).

Most Christians have heard of the importance of Christ dying on the cross for the forgiveness of the world, but the resurrection has been perceived by many as just a nice, chronological event that happened afterward. Yet that could not be further from the truth. At the cross is where forgiveness was provided, but we are left hopelessly in peril without the resurrection. We were also in desperate need of the life of Christ inside us.

Bob George uses a great analogy to describe and clearly demonstrate just what we were in need of before we became Christians:

> "Let's imagine that a man has died of ... cancer, for example ... if you had the power to save the man, how many problems would you have to solve? Two! You'd have to raise him to life, but you'd also have to cure his cancer ... what if you cured his cancer, but did nothing else? He would still be dead ... You'd just have a healthy dead man on your hands! ... On the other hand, what if you raised him to life without curing the cancer? ... He would just die again. Before God could give life to the dead, He had to totally eradicate the fatal disease that killed men—sin. So the cross was God's method of dealing with the disease called sin, and the resurrection of Christ was and is God's method of giving life to the dead!"[1]

Both the cause of death (sin) and the death itself (spiritual death during the fall of man) needed to be solved. Jesus died to permanently take away our sins, and He was resurrected so that He may give us His resurrected life. The cross took away the cause of our spiritual death so that it may not kill us again; and when we receive Christ's Spirit we gain life, allowing us to be born again. Note that the cross took away the sins of the whole world, and created the potential for everyone to be able to receive life, but that did not save everyone. It is those who receive that life through genuine faith and trust who are saved and become born again. Those who do not are cured of the cancer but are not cured of its effects (spiritual death).

Here are some key verses to understand these points:

"Therefore, just as sin entered the world through one man, and death through sin, and in this way death came to all men ..." (Romans 5:12).

"... You were dead in your transgressions and sins ..." (Ephesians 2:1).

"... no one can see the kingdom of God unless he is born again" (John 3:3).

"... The Son gives life to whom He is pleased to give it" (John 5:21).

"... I have come that they may have life ..." (John 10:10).

"... I am the way and the truth and the life ..." (John 14:6).

"... I am the resurrection and the life ..." (John 11:25).

"I am the bread of life" (John 6:48).

"But if Christ is in you ... your spirit is alive" (Romans 8:10).

"When Christ, who is your life ..." (Colossians 3:4).

"... This life is in the Son. He who has the Son has life, he who does not have the Son of God does not have life" (1 John 5:11-12).

What encouraging verses that clearly illustrate why a person who has not received the Spirit of Christ and has not been born again is so empty inside. We have no life! This is what I was experiencing as a teenager and what millions have experienced as well. I was dead inside, in need of Christ's Spirit inside of me. A doctor would have never given me that diagnosis, much less the proper prescription!

So, it's crucial not to try and "over-spiritualize" the Gospel of Jesus Christ. He did not make it complicated. It is not something that requires an institution to walk you through endless steps, a strategic process, different stages, complicated doctrine, checking all the boxes, only to end up engaging in a fatiguing list of maintaining your salvation. All of those agendas are meaningless and spiritually unhelpful and distractive. It's a sad and condemning theology that results when religious entities try to serve up a spiritual formula that, if mixed just right, could give you a little hope to make it to eternal life.

We have a simple twofold Gospel:

1. Total forgiveness was a necessary preparation; Jesus's death bought your forgiveness once and for all.
2. The giving of new life was God's ultimate goal; Jesus's life is what saves you.

Was Jesus successful? Did He accomplish His mission? Yes, He completed the will of the Father. Did He create a system that would keep the average individual from clearly understanding? Not in the least. Was complicated theology and a hierarchy needed to understand an elementary twofold Gospel? Absolutely not. Should there be a system where one must go through life presuming and hoping they did enough to obtain what He offered? Never! Christ did all the work, on our behalf, as a substitution, leaving us with the simple task of trusting in that accomplishment, placing our faith in His settled work.

In my bedroom that night, I only had one sincere, from the heart, surrendering faith prayer that changed me over from death into life. I became born again on that night. Not just because words were coming out of my mouth in a prayer, but the words represented that I was accepting the twofold mission that Jesus had accomplished, and I genuinely wanted Christ in my life. That was my only part. No priest was needed, no system was needed, there was no journey to salvation, righteousness, and justification, there were no rules or sacraments—I just needed the Spirit of God filling my life after I came to accept the simple Gospel.

> "I tell you the truth, whoever hears my word and believes him who sent me has eternal life and will not be condemned; he has crossed over from death to life" (John 5:24).

> "You diligently study the Scriptures because you think that by them you possess eternal life. These are the Scriptures that testify about me, yet you refuse to come to me to have life" (John 5:39).

> "I tell you the truth, he who believes has everlasting life" (John 6:47).

> "For if, when we were God's enemies (as non-believers), we were reconciled to him through the death of his Son, how much more, having been reconciled, shall we be saved through his life!" (Romans 5:10).

> "Everyone who believes that Jesus is the Christ is born of God, and everyone who loves the father loves his child as well" (1 John 5:1).

> "For you have been born again, not of perishable seed, but of imperishable, through the living and enduring word of God" (1 Peter 1:23).

Bob George talks about the benefit of erasing everything on the blackboard of our minds: erasing all the religious junk that has accumulated for decades, wiping the slate clean, and starting all over again with just Christ.[2] When we do this, the Gospel becomes crystal clear and free of man's self-interested, self-indulgent, and self-righteous obtainments. The easiest way to think about the Gospel is simply to ask, "What mission was God trying to accomplish in the first place by initiating the plan to send Christ to save us?"

If we answer that question properly, all the confusion about Christianity is gone in a flash. If we do not answer that question properly, we will remain trapped in a system of obtainment, trapped in an endlessly long list of things to do to become righteous (right standing with God) and maintain it. That's a fearful plight to go through life, with religious frustration beyond imagination and burn-out from working for salvation that was already accomplished, all the while hoping you punched in the right code to be justified and right in the eyes of God. It's a fruitless, prideful, and self-righteous exercise to adopt institutional proclamations that would never be condoned by our Heavenly Father.

Being born again does not just encompass a destination, but is indicative as to what has occurred because of a certain state we were in (being spiritually dead). We understand through the Scriptures that the wages of sin is death, and the Bible paints a clear picture that through Adam, all of mankind died not physically, but spiritually.

God determined to make a new creation and a new way of relating to Him through the New Covenant; God sent His Son to Earth to put on a human's body and accomplish a mission. Part of the mission was to tell God's people that a new way was coming and that they needed it in lieu of what they already had. That was not a popular message, and it led to an important part of the mission. Jesus was to die to take away the sins of the whole world. To atone for them? To sweep them under the rug? To just pay for them? No. To take them away, so that the only thing that could ever cause us to die spiritually again would be neutralized.

Jesus put in place His New Covenant, by which Hebrews and other scriptures clearly say we may draw near to God and experience His Spirit living inside of us—not for just a week, not for a few months, not until we really mess up with a "mortal" sin, but forever.

Good Works

The sins of the whole world have been taken away and are removed from between man and God. With that being the case, what is this arrangement God has in place to ensure and guarantee our salvation forever? Since the Bible clearly states we could never act or be good enough or engage in any type of work that will save us (Ephesians 2:8-9), our part is to have faith in Christ's completed and settled work.

When we do this, God applies to us all the forgiveness Christ earned on the cross, and we gain all the righteousness of Christ, His resurrected life. This all happens when Christ comes to live in us in the form of His Holy Spirit. All this is done by God after we respond to His invitation: *Faith and trust in Christ*. The "spiritually dead" problem disappears. It's a free gift, a debt paid in full. Spiritual life is once again restored.

This clearly answers the question of whether we have to add elements of good works and follow requirements and institutional regiments in order to be saved and have God's Spirit living inside of us. By the very nature of the events that God initiated on our behalf to restore life to us again, we do not. By God's own actions, He says that good works are not applicable to acquire or maintain salvation, and He is repulsed by our self-effort to do so because it is our attempt to negate everything Christ did.

Instead, good works are a reflection of our new identity in Christ, like sharing the Gospel, mission works, and other endeavors we do as a result of our love for God. These activities declare to the world that God is alive and active in our lives. Pastor and theologian Bob Bowman states:

> "We do not deny the importance of works or the necessity of works, but works does not support our standing with Christ or else grace is not grace."[3]

Good works are something that a true, genuine believer does automatically, not something required in order to acquire or maintain salvation. We do not need to be told to do them; we do not need to be threatened by a religious entity if we don't do them. We do them out of a grateful and excited heart for God. The thief on the cross next to Christ did not have a chance to participate in good works or participate in a regimented, ritualistic salvation process according to religion. He simply did exactly what was required to inherit eternal life: he placed his faith in God's work (Jesus's death and subsequent resurrection), not his own work (Luke 23:39-43).

We must never forget that participating in events, works, or religious acts (like the sacraments) will never make us "right" with God. God did everything to make us righteous and holy. Our part is faith in what Christ accomplished, His work, through the cross and through the resurrection. To grab one or two verses that seem to indicate the necessity of good works as an "essential part of the salvation process" is to ignore the context of book after book, chapter after chapter, and verse after verse of Paul and others explaining that our faith alone in Christ's work on the cross saves us. Paul spelled out the salvation process in detail, and good works are not a part of the plan. It's part of the "after-plan" that genuine Christians do good works as a reflection of salvation, not to obtain it.

If single verses are plucked out of context and misinterpreted by your church or spiritual leader (many times for the deceptive motive of control), that threatens your security, threatens your identity in Christ, your position in Christ, your status as God's child, your eternal destiny—they are tarnishing the blood of Christ. It's an insult to God's amazing grace. Caution: they teach a different Jesus than what the New Covenant conveys.

There are several paradoxes in the Scriptures and a few verses that seem to contradict each other, causing some believers to be confused. An example of that apparent conflict is with regard to faith alone in Christ, or faith in Christ plus works being necessary for salvation.

> "For it is by grace you have been saved, through faith—and this
> not from yourselves, it is the gift of God—not by works, so that
> no one can boast" (Ephesians 2:8).

When Paul wrote this verse, he painted a very clear picture of how salvation happens. We continue reading in the New Testament, and we suddenly find a verse that seems to present a conflict:

> "You see that a person is justified by what he does and not by
> faith alone" (James 2:24).

This verse in James seems to add a requirement to "faith alone" that Paul didn't add. What do we do with this conflict? In order to fully understand the apparent conflict, anyone reading verses 14 through 23 of James 2 will quickly realize that James is talking about someone with a dead type of faith, evidenced by there being no actions or spiritual fruit coming from that person's life.

James is teaching that a true Christian will engage in fruitful works because of their enthusiasm as a result of the Holy Spirit living inside of them. If you do not see any type of activity engaging in charity toward others, in a genuine Christian's life, they do not have the saving faith of Christ yet. That person is more than likely spiritually dead, not spiritually alive in Christ. They would still be a non-believer living in darkness, going through the motions.

James 2:24 describes a *non-believer* just as we saw 1 John 1:9 describe a *non-believer*. There is no conflict between Paul and James. "Faith in Christ" is the central theme of the Scriptures for salvation, and is the message of the New Covenant. James is stating that the test to see if you are a changed person (with Christ in your life) is evidence of good works. Works is a byproduct of faith, not a prerequisite for salvation.

Catholic apologists like Trent Horn give conflicting messages with regard to works being a part of the salvation process:

> "But no one can ever work himself out of hell any more than he could work himself into heaven."[4]

> "No matter how hard we try, none of us is 'good enough' to get to heaven on our own. That's why we need the free gift of God's grace ..."[5]

> "'By grace you have been saved not through works' (Ephesians 2:8): That's true!"[6]

> "There are no specific works that 'earn' our salvation."[7]

Anyone who fully comprehends the components of the New Covenant would be thrilled to read these comments by Horn, but the reality is: "so close, yet so far away." Right when Catholic leadership convinces someone that salvation is by faith in Christ and you cannot work your way into Heaven, under the Catholic umbrella the rain starts to penetrate. Horn, in conflict with his previously quoted comments, also says:

> "... works do play a role in the process of our salvation."[8]

"As long as a person remains in a state of grace, he will go to heaven after death ..."[9]

"... we merit [earn] our salvation by cooperating with God's grace to do the works he prepared for us ..."[10]

"God must do something to us after death in order to make us fit to spend eternal life with him."[11]

And with just a few more comments, so much for God's grace! It is interesting that all the quotes above come from the same author. Conflicting message? A misunderstanding of true grace? Absolutely.

A handful of misunderstood scriptures promulgated by the Church keep believers under their control and jurisdiction: "work out your own salvation with fear and trembling," "if we deliberately keep on sinning after we have received the knowledge of truth, no sacrifice of sins is left," "but he who endures to the end shall be saved," "if you continue in your faith ..." and a couple more. Christians have to understand that if you treat these as prerequisites or requirements to obtain eternal life, you will only live a fearful and sad Christian life. Paul is simply encouraging believers to live out their faith and demonstrate their salvation through actions and in a way that reflects their new life in Christ, not: "You better figure out this salvation thing with fear and trembling or you're doomed!" That theology and thinking is not only foolish, but conflicts with the whole New Testament.

As mentioned previously, the authors of the New Testament are speaking to a small Church that is comprised of believers and non-believers. Some verses in the Bible are directed to non-believers, some to believers.

Unfortunately, Catholics and many Protestants take a "prescriptive" view of these verses: the Christian is responsible for "enduring to the end," "bringing about our own salvation by performance and actions," "keeping faith until the end" with the thinking, "God will do what He can, but ultimately it's up to us" (all while never knowing if we fulfilled all the conditions). Apologist James White talks about this "prescriptive/descriptive misunderstanding of the Scriptures" in a lot of his debates. It's a disturbing view of the saving faith of Jesus Christ, who accomplished everything on our behalf to think we have this burden of maintaining our own salvation. Jesus is not a failed Savior. There is either perfect obedience to the law (which only Jesus pulled off), or we have to pull it off, resulting in us failing miserably. These verses that stumble so many believers into living in fear are descriptive, not prescriptive. The descriptive message is: this should be the way Christians live because of our new life in Christ, but not as a prerequisite to maintain salvation.

How do you determine if salvation is by faith alone in Christ, or if you have to participate, endure, cooperate, and merit your way and maintain your standing with Christ? Simply look at the central theme of the Scriptures. The message of grace, through faith in Christ, will come blasting in.

We can conclude this meaning because there are only a of couple verses comparable to the one listed in James (which are taken completely out of context), but then religious organizations inappropriately use them as fear tactics "if you do not comply." However, we have to remember that there are over 200 verses in the New Testament that clearly state that salvation is *solely* by sincere, genuine faith and trust in Christ and His fulfilled work. That's not a misprint. There are over 200 verses stating that permanent salvation is by faith alone in Christ's finished work, not by our participation, performance, or works. Many of those verses have already been quoted. Christ did the work for our salvation. We do not. We are new creatures in Christ and genuine believers are excited to influence and participate in making the world a better place because of our enthusiasm for the amazing privilege of being invited into God's story.

As genuine believers, can anything separate us from God? Catholic leaders like Horn, when talking about marriage, state, "Sin cannot undo what God has joined together. But grace can overcome sin." I totally agree with this observation (so far)! Yet it's sad that regarding our salvation (the most important topic any human being can experience) Horn agrees with the Catechism that unconfessed mortal sin *will* separate and "undo" you from God and cause you to be separated forever. My appeal to all Christians is don't buy into this fallacy. It's inaccurate and condemning theology.

"Who shall separate us from the love of Christ? ... For I am convinced that neither death, nor life, neither angels nor demons, neither the present nor the future, nor any powers, neither height nor depth, nor anything else in all creation, will be able to separate us from the love of God that is in Christ Jesus our Lord" (Romans 8:35-39).

"And this is the will of him who sent me, that I shall lose none of all that he has given me, but raise them up at the last day. For my Father's will is that everyone who looks to the Son and believes in him shall have eternal life, and I will raise him up at the last day" (John 6: 39-40).

"I give them eternal life, and they shall never perish; no one can snatch them out of my hand. My Father, who has given them to me, is greater than all; no one can snatch them out of my Father's hand. I and the Father are one" (John 10: 28-30).

"And you also were included in Christ when you heard the word of truth, the gospel of salvation. Having believed, you were marked in him with a seal, the promised Holy Spirit, who is a deposit guaranteeing our inheritance until the redemption of those who are God's possession ..." (Ephesians 1:13-14).

"... for God's gifts [of salvation] and his call are irrevocable" (Romans 11:29).

"I tell you the truth, he who believes has everlasting life" (John 6:47).

"Now when a man works, his wages are not credited to him as a gift, but as an obligation. However, to the man who does not work but trusts God who justifies the wicked, his faith is credited as righteousness" (Romans 4: 4-5).

"I write these things to you who believe in the name of the Son of God so that you may know that you have eternal life" (1 John 5:13).

The Roman Catholic Church does not want your salvation to be secure in Christ, it wants to be involved in controlling your salvation. Many Protestant faiths, likewise, teach that salvation can vanish like the wind if we do not keep forgiveness up to date. It's an absolute, disrespectful, slap in the face to God for those who embrace that false and deplorable message. It totally discredits the blood shed at the cross by our Savior. Christians should refuse such sacrilege.

As Christians we rejoice in doing good works and thrive on living godly lives—not to gain salvation, but to celebrate salvation. We were in need of forgiveness and we were in need of spiritual life (the life of Christ inside us), and He accomplished both: one through his death, the other by His resurrection. Our salvation is 100% secure "in Christ," but only because of Him; not because of our confession, accomplishments, achievements, behaviors, merits, or sinlessness.

It's the twofold Gospel that anyone can understand without a magisterium or an institution.

CHAPTER 12

A New Covenant, A New Promise

The message of the New Covenant, our new arrangement with God, is His promise to us on this side of the cross. A great exchange took place: He gave us His righteousness and He took on all of our unrighteousness. Jesus satisfied all the righteous requirements to please the Heavenly Father so we would not have the burden of doing so ourselves. The perfect, accomplished work of Jesus Christ satisfies God's holiness and provides for our sinfulness. His Spirit comes to live inside of us, and before that could happen, He had to prepare the way.

A holy God refuses to house Himself inside a dirty temple, so He had to forever, one time provide complete (not partial) forgiveness. Jesus said that the kingdom He was bringing into this world would not fit into old containers. Bob George describes the process with a food canning metaphor: "First, you clean and sanitize the jars, then you fill them."[1] The already accomplished forgiveness is a preparatory step, and the second birth (being born again) is receiving life by receiving the Spirit. This makes the process complete.

If we were not cleansed by being permanently forgiven, God's Spirit could not stand to live in us. The physical Church, the institutional, organized Church is not God's house or temple; God's new place of dwelling is inside the life of a believer. We never summon God down to perform any ritual because God is already present inside us.

Under the New Covenant, if we sin it does not drive God out of His temple because He has already made our spirits righteous and the temple pure. The flesh will mess up every day, every few hours, every few minutes—it's never-ending. The New Covenant reveals that the Spirit of God will never leave us again because the One who prepared us as His temple (for His dwelling) wasn't us; it was God, through Christ.

This is where religion is devoid of understanding the twofold Gospel. It's almost universal. Religion is always trying to work and merit its way into right standing with God, trying to participate in the salvation process, and following old traditions because unconditional grace still cannot be comprehended. However, God did not set the system up that way. Andy Stanley describes the scene:

> "As the Jews and Pharisees went down to hear John the Baptist preach, who always followed tradition, they learned that the days of reducing religion to tradition are over. A new way is coming and you need to be ready to change your minds about everything and learn what Jesus is up to when He shows up. John was warning them out of their apathy and their self-made religion that was so far off sync with what God was about to do."[2]

Churches often try to pour the "new wine" of Jesus into "old wineskins" (Old Covenant traditions), which ultimately destroys both. Jesus did not come to tweak something old, He came to establish something brand new. Too many churches try to mix the Old Covenant with the New Covenant. God clearly tells us that He ushered in a whole new system, a new way of relating to Him, and it was not a system of climbing the ladder of performance to try to get close enough for Him to say, "Well done."

It is not a sacramental system, it is not a sacrificial system, it is not a self-righteous system, it is not a self-effort system. It is grace, fully and completely extended to all who choose to believe and follow Him. Jesus climbed down the ladder and came to us. Not only did He come to us, He came with a specific mission: to fulfill all the requirements for us to be able to access God, to be in right standing with God, to be justified by God, and to be eternally secure with God.

Institutions have formulas; God has grace. Anything we do in an attempt to earn righteousness, earn salvation, or earn justification is not acceptable to God. When we hold out our hand and inform God, "Look what I would like to offer you, look at what I bring to the table," He is unable to receive what we offer. Why? Because the sacrifices of the Old Covenant no longer apply. If you are Catholic, you can read between the lines and start to see that the system of obtainment, endless repetitive prayers, checking all the boxes through perpetual sacraments, following Lent restrictions, priest involvement, and adhering to a hierarchy, and much more is all completely and fully rejected by God as any form of relationship with Him.

The Catholic List referenced throughout these pages is rejected by God with the message, "not applicable." God's desire for a Roman Catholic follower is to abandon all those practices, be released from all those requirements, and bask in the successful work of Christ.

Should you be participating in charity and good works because you are flowing in love and enthusiasm for Christ? Absolutely. But participating in those works in an effort to obtain something? Absolutely not. The moment we link our good works, behaviors, and religious pathway to salvation we are inserting ourselves into the equation of the crucifixion and the resurrection. This results in proclaiming that Christ was insufficient, and subsequently we enter the land of "not acceptable"—your good works will not obtain anything. It's dangerous theology, but it's exactly the theology of the Roman Catholic institution and many Protestant churches of today. God's invitation is to stop striving and learn the valuable lesson of yielding and resting in His accomplishment: His finished work.

Imagine how ridiculous it is for us to try to achieve salvation through our own accomplishments:

Bill: "Hey, Bob, I see that you are jumping up and down in the living room. What's up with that?"

Bob: "Well, I'm trying to jump to the moon."

Bill: "Oh, and how is that working out for you?"

Bob: "I'm not sure, but I'm really trying hard to get there."

Ten years later:

Bill: "Hey, Bob, I see you are still trying to jump to the moon. How is that going?"

Bob: "Well, I am a little closer than the last time you visited."

Bill: "Bob, do you think you will ever land on the moon by jumping?"

Bob: "Well … (studder) … maybe not, but I sure am going to try."

Bill: "Bob, no offense, you look like a fool!"

This is how irrational it is for a Christian to set a standard that has already been achieved by Christ. There is no better way to insult the reconciliation process initiated by God on our behalf—through the gruesome sacrifice of Christ on the cross and the subsequent resurrection—than to follow a system of obtaining righteousness (right standing with God) through human effort. He made a public announcement that the great exchange was completed and that we are already in right standing with Him—all because of His unexplainable grace. How hopeless it must be to hear that you need to do better and do more, all while there is no assurance that even that will be good enough.

Many teachers who understand grace state that if they only had one opportunity to preach a single message, the topic would be the New Covenant."[3] When we understand the critical components of this new promise God made to mankind (on this side of the cross), Christianity becomes crystal clear. So far, we have looked at the two most critical aspects of the New Covenant: the permanency of forgiveness and the Spirit of God living inside of every believer making us alive in Christ, creating our non-changing status of "right in God's eyes."

Old vs. New

Although the full Gospel message has already been presented, the final part of the journey concludes with a contrast of the Old Covenant and the New Covenant, looking at life-changing and amazing scriptures to substantiate the difference. This is what I missed when I got the call years ago asking me if I really knew just what Jesus did about our sin problem. It is key to the discovery of the life of Christ living inside the believer, the hallmark of the New Covenant, the new way we relate to God, on this side of the cross.

This understanding turns the lightbulb on in a way that makes many confusing verses in the Bible suddenly clear. The dividing line in the expedition of all mankind is the cross and resurrection. Before the resurrection: Old Covenant; after the resurrection: New Covenant. Matthew, Mark, Luke, and John: Old Covenant while Jesus was alive; New Covenant as soon as He rose again. Before understanding this divide, many verses and concepts blended together for the average believer, but now armed with this information, the central theme of the Scriptures makes sense!

As we look at the New Covenant it is essential to understand that all the requirements of the Old Covenant do not apply after the resurrection. We see this verified when Hebrews gives the example of a will. We all know it is necessary for someone to die in order to execute a will. A will is never processed or probated while someone is alive.

> "In the case of a will, it is necessary to prove the death of the one who made it, because a will is in force only when somebody has died; it never takes effect while the one who made it is living" (Hebrews 9:16-17).

Likewise, for an individual to show up in an attorney's office with a stack of old wills and inform them, "I think I want to use every one of these—I spent a lot of time planning my final wishes in all the documents you see." The attorney in charge would quickly remind their client that the only will that has any legal precedence is the one you see on the very top, the one signed and dated just a couple of months ago. Only the most recent one is valid; you can toss the others in the fireplace.

The New Covenant is the executed will on this side of the cross. For Catholics or any denomination attempting to blend law and grace—to blend the covenants together—they make the mistake of misinterpreting Jesus's harsh words to the Pharisees and Jews of His day (with their endless commandments where perfect adherence was the only acceptable manner) and will only become frustrated, exhausted, and bewildered.

Jesus showed up on the scene challenging pharisaical Judaism, announcing a new system. He steamrolled over the Pharisees and their attempt to keep the 613 Jewish laws. Christ knew that they were not capable of keeping the law and He was brilliant in communicating that they didn't need to have that burden anymore. Jesus was the only one capable of fulfilling the law once and for all.

Contrast the two ideas for entering into the kingdom of God. One is to keep every single commandment, and if you stumble even one time—one mistake, one flaw—you are guilty of all of the commandments and cannot enter into God's kingdom. The other path is Jesus coming to satisfy all the righteous requirements Himself, alleviating us of that horrible duty (which was set up for failure by divine purpose), where the only thing remaining for a person to enter the kingdom is to have faith and trust in His completed work.

In light of that truth, the words that Jesus taught make sense. When the rich young ruler approached Jesus and asked what to do to inherit eternal life, Jesus told him to sell all his possessions and perfectly keep the law. If the young ruler had complied and said that he had sold all his possessions, Jesus would have kept giving him instructions until he went away frustrated. Jesus wanted to show that righteousness based on keeping the law requires one to perfectly perform everything God has commanded. The truth is no one, whether a believer or non-believer, (through any amount of effort, obedience, good intentions, or good works) can ingratiate themselves with God. Not even for a moment.

We see this same strategy used by Jesus in the Sermon on the Mount. How many times as a Christian have you heard this sermon described as "the beautiful love message" or "God's love instruction to us" or "the greatest sermon ever preached." No, it was not exactly a love instruction. Not when you see what Jesus was up to. But yes, it was the greatest sermon ever preached, just not in the way one might think. "Follow the law perfectly or you're guilty of every crime imaginable," was the message. Jesus not only gave impossible commands in His earlier teachings, but set the bar even higher with the Sermon on the Mount. "If you even lust you are guilty of adultery," (a sin punishable by death under Jewish law). Oh boy!

If you randomly pick up the Bible as a believer and do not understand that Jesus was challenging the Jewish system in this sermon, you will leave the message sad, hopeless, and frustrated because the standard is too high. You will leave like the young, rich ruler: sad and disappointed that perfection was the requirement. However, the good news in the message is that there is one other option Christ offers: "Let me fulfill all those requirements for you and give you the most incredible gift that has ever been given in all of creation: My perfect grace. I will achieve the keeping of those impossible commands." Suddenly and enthusiastically, He has everyone's attention with that promise!

For those who do not agree and want to follow the exact commandments conveyed in The Sermon on the Mount, let's take a moment and put that to the test:

> "If your right eye causes you to sin, gouge it out and throw it away. It is better for you to lose one part of your body than for your whole body to be thrown in hell" (Matthew 5:29).

> "And if your right hand causes you to sin, cut it off and throw it away" (Matthew 5:30).

Imagine your priest or pastor saying, "Good morning, everyone, today we will be doing something a little different, and I apologize in advance that we did not start this sooner. We certainly have not been good law keepers, but that is about to change. We will be implementing the commands from The Sermon on the Mount and taking steps to guarantee our entrance into Heaven. I would like Richard to come forward this morning. Richard has had a big problem with lusting, and this morning I'm going to initiate something that will give Richard a better chance of getting through the pearly gates. We've all read Matthew 5:29, and now it's time to do something about it. If someone can hand me the scalpel, I'm going to cut Richard's eye out. It's going to get a little messy, but the end result will be quite beneficial. Parents you might want to remove the kids at this point in the service. Or, if you want to prepare them for what's ahead for them, please feel free to keep them in the room.

"In the meantime, Steve, I would like for you to come down forward. Steve has had issues slapping his wife and can't seem to get this under control. Based on Matthew 5:30 we are about to resolve this once and for all. If someone would be so kind as to pass me the rotary saw, we are going to remove only the right hand for now. For those of you who want to take that first step in your journey to the kingdom, please come forward and state which body part you want to be dismembered. Better one body part removed than your whole body burn in hell!"

Is this radical? Not according to Jesus, who was speaking just as face-tiously. It's totally biblical, right? Do we omit these verses from the Bible and just turn a "blind eye" (pun intended)? Absolutely not. Why? Because Jesus didn't want us to saw off body parts to keep us out of hell. He said to do it to make a point, but he doesn't want us to do it. Here is what Jesus was really saying: "If you want to follow the law, you better follow it without ever doing a single thing wrong the rest of your life, or you are guilty of breaking all the laws and you will be condemned. Your system will never get you into My kingdom."

Jesus made it crystal clear that if you try to follow "laws" to get yourself into His kingdom, you will fail miserably. "If you are going through a religious, regimented, Church-demanding, law-keeping system to get into My kingdom, you will never make it." The law was put in place so we would be so frustrated in our inability to follow it, that we finally stop trying. Of course, only Christ can keep those rigid commands. We certainly cannot. And God said, "Look, I am going to relieve you from the obligation of ever having to follow these rules and requirements again. I'm dying on a cross and taking those requirements with Me. Your role? Leave your old life behind, and follow Me. Trust in Me. Believe in Me. Embrace Me. Have faith in Me. Walk in the Spirit of Christ."

See, the truth is that Jesus's Sermon on the Mount was preached to demonstrate our *inability* to meet God's standard. Jesus would ultimately be the end of these requirements.

> "All who rely on observing the law (the Ten Commandments, Old-Covenant Jewish traditions, etc.) are under a curse, for it is written: 'cursed is everyone who does not continue to do everything written in the Book of Law" (Galatians 3:10).

> "Christ is the end of the Law so that there may be righteousness for everyone who believes" (Romans 10:4).

> "Therefore no one will be declared righteous in his sight by observing the law; rather, through the law we become conscious of sin" (Romans 3:20).

"Having cancelled the written code (the Law), with its regulations, that was against us and that stood opposed to us; he took it away, <u>nailing it to the cross</u>" (Colossians 2:14).

"... for <u>if</u> a law had been given that could impart life, then righteousness would certainly have come by the law" (Galatians 3:21).

"Before this faith came (in Jesus Christ) we were <u>held prisoners by the law</u>, locked up until faith should be revealed. So the law was put in charge to lead us to Christ that <u>we might be justified</u> (made right in God's eyes) <u>by faith</u>. Now that faith (Jesus) has come, we are no longer under the supervision of the law" (Galatians 3:23-25).

If you are searching for the Ten Commandments, I have a GPS pin on their location: they are still hanging on the cross. If you are on a mission to follow the specifics of the Sermon on the Mount, here is their permanent location: they are still hanging on the cross. If you have been given a long list of fatiguing, sacramental instructions by an institution on obtaining salvation, those teachings are hanging on the cross too. If you live in constant fear and have no idea where you stand with God, those emotions and confusion are hanging on the cross. If you are concerned about dwelling in a mysterious Purgatory for an undetermined amount of time (waiting to be fully sanctified and righteous before entering Heaven), that false doctrine and dogma was developed centuries after the original Gospel and is likewise hanging on the cross.

As Christians, we are not to be held prisoners of these "systems of requirements" ever again. Do the Ten Commandments give us guidance to affect our minds in making wise decisions and choices? Sure. Are we under their condemning authority? Raise your hand if you would like to be; the punishment for not following them is death! I will take a pass on that one. We've been set free from the Ten Commandments because of a better system He put in place: the promise of the New Covenant.

We have to be able to see that the New Covenant that now governs our lives is far different than what was in place before. The Bible is crystal clear that the Old Covenant (the Law) was just a shadow of things to come. In a room full of close friends and family, we do not embrace and greet their shadow. That is not the real thing. Their shadow is just a reflection of the reality.

Jesus Christ is our only hope. The Law was a shadow; Christ is the real deal. When He came onto the scene, He changed everything. The Old Covenant is gone; the New Covenant is in place. We will see why that is so critical to understand, but let's look at the departure, once and for all, from the Old Covenant:

> "But now, by dying to what once bound us (rules and regulations), we have been released from the law so that we serve in the new way of the Spirit, and not in the old way of the written code [the Ten Commandments]" (Romans 7:6).

> "I found that the very commandment (i.e., Sermon on the Mount) that was intended to bring life actually brought death. For sin, seizing the opportunity afforded by the commandment, deceived me, and through the commandment put me to death" (Romans 7:10).

> "But the ministry Jesus has received is as superior to theirs as the covenant of which he is mediator is superior to the old one, and it is founded on better promises" (Hebrews 8:6).

> "For if there had been nothing wrong with that first covenant, no place would have been sought for another" (Hebrews 8:7).

> "He has made us competent as ministers of a New Covenant—not of the letter but of the Spirit; for the letter kills, but the Spirit gives life" (2 Corinthians 3:6).

> "But when the time had fully come, God sent His Son, born of a woman, born under law, to redeem those under law, that we might receive the full rights of sons" (Galatians 4:4-5).

"But if you are led by the Spirit, you are not under the law" (Galatians 5:18).

"Clearly no one is justified before God by the law, because, 'the righteous will live by faith.' The law is not based on faith; on the contrary, 'the man who does these things will live by them.' Christ redeemed us from the curse of the law by becoming a curse for us ..." (Galatians 3:11-13).

"Through the law I died to the law so that I might live for God" (Galatians 2:19).

"You foolish Galatians! Who has bewitched you? Before your very eyes Jesus Christ was clearly portrayed as crucified. I would like to learn just one thing from you: Did you receive the Spirit by observing the law, or by believing what you heard? Are you so foolish? After beginning with the Spirit, are you now trying to attain your goal by human effort? Have you suffered so much for nothing—if it really was for nothing? Does God give you his Spirit and work miracles among you because you observe the law, or because you believe what you heard?" (Galatians 3:1-5).

"The former regulation is set aside because it was weak and useless (for the law made nothing perfect), and a better hope is introduced (Jesus Christ), by which we draw near to God" (Hebrews 7:18).

"Because of this oath (promise), Jesus has become the guarantee of a better covenant" (Hebrews 7:22).

"By calling this covenant "new", he has made the first one obsolete; and what is obsolete and aging will soon disappear" (Hebrews 8:13).

"For Christ did not enter a man-made sanctuary that was only a copy of the true one; he entered heaven itself, now to appear for us in God's presence. Nor did he enter heaven to offer himself again and again, the way the high priest enters the Most Holy Place every year with blood that is not his own" (Hebrews 9:24-25).

Why all the emphasis on the fact that a New Covenant is now in place? Why list so many verses about it? Many Christians do not know we are under a new arrangement with God. Most do not know that He has made a promise on this side of the cross, and any attempt to mingle the two covenants together will leave one completely frustrated and flustered.

The importance of this understanding is to identify religious teachings that try to implement their own arrangement with God. The red flags are waving when you recognize this error. When you are giving a "pathway" to salvation you are in the wrong covenant. When you are told that a priest has the power to absolve you from sin, you are in the wrong covenant. When you are told that your self-effort and participation in the salvation process are necessary, you are in the wrong covenant. When you are told that you have to spend time in a fictional Purgatory to be righteous enough to enter the kingdom, you are in the wrong covenant. When you are told that praying to another mediator besides Christ is an option, you are in the wrong covenant. When works, requirements, and sacraments are added to faith and become the "combined condition" necessary to make it to Heaven, you are in the wrong covenant.

A true Christian cannot remain in the Old Covenant, and God has announced that any actions you engage in under the old system are worthless for salvation. They count for nothing. A big fat zero. Nobody will ever gain God's acceptance and love under a system that is obsolete. It truly is a spiritual treadmill going nowhere. It's spiritual bondage. Only the truth of the New Covenant can set someone free.

We do not have a sabbath day anymore; as Christians, we live in a "sabbath rest" every single day, and God's Spirit does God's work through us as we "rest" in His accomplishment, and as we walk in the Spirit (yielding to Him as we journey through life). How do I, as a born-again person, relate to God in this New Covenant? By faith in His work, not by my own works.

It is the message of the Scriptures and the heart of the Gospel. We can never reform ourselves enough to satisfy God's standard of perfection, and to say, "We are going to work for righteousness on our own accord," is to put ourselves under the law where we can only miserably fail. We can never make ourselves more righteous, more sanctified, more holy, more redeemed, more justified, or more saved. Instead, we simply yield to God's desire to mature our mind, will, and emotions through our experiences in life.

God has rescued us from religion. He has rescued us from legalism. He has rescued us from the bondage of a religious institution. We do not live the Christian life according to rules, but according to a person: Jesus Christ. God is not a scorekeeper. God loves us, He likes us, He approves of us, just the way we are in Christ. There is nothing we can add to what Christ has done. God wants to strip away religion so our dependence stays on Him. When a church tries to combine law and grace, or combine the New Covenant and the Old Covenant, it completely nullifies grace.

> "For this reason Christ is the mediator of a new covenant, that those who are called may receive the promised eternal inheritance—now that he has died as a ransom to set them free from the sins committed under the first covenant" (Hebrews 9:15-16).

> "For all have sinned and fall short of the glory of God, and are justified freely by his grace through the redemption that came by Christ Jesus" (Romans 3:23-24).

> "However, to the one who does not work but trusts God who justifies the wicked, his faith is credited as righteousness" (Romans 4:5).

The scriptures in the last three chapters tell the story far better than any words I could possibly muster together. The verses proclaiming "this righteousness from God comes through faith in Jesus Christ to all who believe" and we are "justified freely by His grace through the redemption that came by Christ Jesus" (Romans 3:21-26) are simply amazing. Salvation has always been about God doing the reconciling, God giving us His righteousness, and God providing justification on account of His work, not ours. When will Christians finally rest from their duty to obtain and perform?

310 | WHEN THE ROMAN BOUGH BREAKS

Here is a chart that depicts some of the differences between the Old Covenant (which only applied to a unique group of people at the time, in a specific place on earth) and the New Covenant (which applies to the entire world). How disturbing it is to watch legalistic institutions adapt to the Old Covenant, dragging those practices from the past into the modern Church. Tithing, food restrictions, and priestly duties, to name a few. Where is your church on the chart that God has declared to be active on this side of the cross?

Old Covenant (Righteousness by the Law)	New Covenant (Righteousness of Christ)
Blood of animals	Blood of Christ
Written on stone	Written on hearts
Shadow to come	Reality of Christ
Has an end	Has no end
Law of Moses	Law of Christ
Law of works	Law of faith
Law of sin and death	Law of spirit and life
Spiritually dead	Alive in Christ
Condemned by the law	Christ fulfilled the law
Legalism	Freedom in Christ
No "born-again" people	Spiritually "born-again"
Not reconciled to God	Reconciliation completed by Christ
Annual atonement	One-time sacrifice
Sins are remembered	Sins are forgotten
Sins held against people	No eternal condemnation from sin
Partial forgiveness	Complete, permanent, total, one-time forgiveness
Priest was needed	Jesus is the one high priest
Powerless to save	Powerful to save
Self-effort	Faith, trust, belief, follow Him
No solution	Christ is the solution

No freedom	Freedom in Christ
Unexecuted will	Executed will
Striving to please God	Yielding to the Holy Spirit
Animal blood	Christ's blood
Multiple steps to God	One step to God
Multiple mediators	One mediator (Christ)
Mankind is waiting	Reconciliation, justification, and forgiveness are complete
No security	Eternal security based on His finished work
In process	It is finished

The Old Covenant simply cannot be blended with the New Covenant. Law and grace cannot coexist. You have to choose one or the other. To choose both is to be "double-minded and unstable in all your ways" (James 1:8). Teachers of God's true grace have always stated it with clarity: Law requires; grace does not; law punishes; grace pardons; law convicts, grace declares "not guilty"; law points a finger, grace is open arms; law frowns in disapproval, grace smiles with eyes sparkling.

This is not a situation in which God messed up the first covenant and is making corrections. It's not as though the first had faults in it, so He had to make a new one. God intentionally put the Old Covenant in place at the time that He chose to. He knew mankind would never measure up to the standard that was required, but Jesus would. This was all part of the plan to redeem mankind.

Unfortunately and because we live in a fallen world, shortly after the New Covenant was put in place, some spiritual leaders began trying to implement food restrictions and engage in estranged teachings not part of the original Gospel. Pastor Trent Shoemake gives a simple, cursory glance at the New Covenant in uncovering this simple formula:

Jesus + Nothing = Something

Jesus + Something = Nothing[4]

This message has to be heard at a deafening decibel: You lose Jesus when you attempt to add something to His perfection. True faith is in Jesus plus

nothing. If you add anything to the perfect, all-sufficient, completed and finished work of Christ, it discredits the Savior and nullifies grace.

If you are Catholic, the Roman Church and all its hoops to jump through
have been a big part of your religious experience, just like observances at the
temple for the Jews. That system is gone. Everything is brand new. Everyone
was warned that something was about to change, and it was like nothing
anyone had ever seen. It was not based on Jewish traditions anymore, it was
based on Christ, plus nothing.

Paganism, politics, legalism, and monarchies came along and blended with
Christianity in the Roman system with the message: "You need to come to
Mass, you need to come to our building, you need to come to our altar, you
need continual forgiveness, you need to maintain justification, you have multiple steps to perform for salvation, you need to stay really busy with works,
you need to stay busy with constant parroted repetitions, you need to honor
the sacraments, you need to be perfect before you can be in the presence of
God, you need more of Jesus inside of you through the Eucharist. Come do it
our way." My friends, that system is gone.

> "What then shall we say? That the Gentiles (that's us) who did
> not pursue righteousness, have obtained it, a righteousness that is
> by faith; but Israel, who pursued a law of righteousness, has not
> attained it. Why not? Because they pursued it not by faith but as
> if it were by works. They stumbled over the 'stumbling stone'"
> (Romans 9:30-32).

> "There remains, then, a Sabbath rest for the people of God; for
> anyone who enters God's rest also rests from his own work, just
> as God did from his. Let us, therefore, make every effort to enter
> that rest ..." (Hebrews 4:9-11).

The encouraging invitation from God is to simply receive His extended
grace (singular), not graces. The message from God is: "Please do not participate in sacrifices in the temple anymore. Adapt to the new promise, embrace
My new arrangement." He has given us the Holy Spirit as part of the New

Covenant made possible for us by the blood of Christ. Which covenant are you going to choose?

> "Then they asked him, 'What must we do to do the works God requires?' Jesus answered, 'The work of God is this: to believe in the one he has sent'" (John 6: 28-29).

> "But when the kindness and love of God our Savior appeared, he saved us, not because of righteous things we had done, but because of his mercy. He saved us through the washing of rebirth and renewal by the Holy Spirit, whom he poured out on us generously through Jesus Christ our Savior, so that, having been justified by his grace, we might become heirs having the hope of eternal life" (Titus 3:4-7).

The previous four chapters in this book have unfolded the whole Gospel. As Christians, we live in a New Covenant, our sins are permanently forgiven, Christ only sees us as righteous, justified, and holy because of His achievement, and now we simply walk in His Spirit. This is all based on God's promise of how He chose to relate to us on this side of the cross. This is the arrangement He has chosen.

Bob George, in his book *A Scriptural Journey to Discover the Grace of God*, spells out a believer's options:

1. Either Jesus did it all or He did nothing at all.
2. God's grace is either total or it is not grace at all.
3. Either all of our sins are forgiven or none of them are forgiven.
4. Either all of our sins have been taken away or none of them have been taken away.
5. Eternal life lasts forever or it is not eternal life.
6. Either it is finished or it is not finished.
7. Either we have been cleansed of all our unrighteousness or we have not been cleansed of any of our unrighteousness.
8. Either we have been reconciled to God or we have never been reconciled to God.

We simply can't have it both ways. God accomplished His mission.[5]

PART V

THE EUCHARIST

CHAPTER 13

The Truth About the Eucharist

A s Christians, we have a very serious consideration. This consideration is for both Catholics and Protestants alike, according to Pastor John Barnett: how do we get righteousness, paid for by Jesus's death, to the life of an individual? The previous four chapters have clearly shown that in the New Covenant, righteousness (being made right in the eyes of God) is a result of our faith in His work and performance, not by anything we accomplish.

We contribute nothing to the equation; we are completely dependent on the reconciliation plan that God put in place. This acknowledges that we are not adding anything to the original Gospel but simply agreeing that Jesus did everything needed on our behalf. It's the grace message that is so incredible, and those who understand it cannot stop celebrating it.

I worshipped in Protestant churches for decades and never remotely learned what has been revealed in the last few chapters concerning the New Covenant. Many of these truths of the New Covenant seem to be absent in Roman Catholicism as well. There are many books written to debate specific theological positions with both Catholic and Protestant assumptions, but those discussions are almost unnecessary with the realization of the New Covenant. However, because it is so critical for a Catholic Christian to understand their position in Christ on this side of the cross under a New Covenant with God, I do want to address the most critical sacrament of the Roman Catholic Church: the Eucharist. It is crucial to examine this dogma of the Church in light of the New Covenant.

This is a very sensitive topic for the average Catholic attendee, but one still has to decide what is more important: loyalty to an institution and its assertions (especially the Church described in the first eight chapters) or the honesty and freedom that come from embracing the truth Christ gave us under the New Covenant. Let's take the final journey in this book and decide: who do we serve, and what is really being accomplished in one's participation of communion?

The Claims of the Eucharist

At the very heart and soul of the Roman Catholic belief system is participation in the Holy Eucharist, also known by many other names such as Holy Communion, Eucharist Assembly, Holy Sacrifice, Most Blessed Sacrament, the Lord's Supper and Holy Mass. Without hesitation, Catholics defend this sacrament with every fiber of their being, and I believe the hearts and minds of those doing so are primarily pure and wholesome. I admire and commend Catholics for their loyalty and dedication, even if we might differ in our interpretation of aspects of the Eucharist. More importantly, there are critical components of the Mass that create a vast conflict with the New Covenant and are not in alignment with what the early Church taught.

Because this sacrament is extremely important to Catholics, it is not my intention to try to decimate something that they sincerely believe to be true. My sole purpose and motive is to take the truths that have been discussed in the past few chapters and look through the lens of the New Covenant while examining what is practiced in the Catholic Church concerning this topic.

It is imperative for all Christians to seek out the truth, and in doing so, it's important for Catholics to look at several aspects of the Eucharist, especially concerning the sacrificial portion, the forgiveness perspective, and the role a priest has in performing "magic powers."

If you were to ask a hundred Catholics to give a full explanation of what the Eucharist entails, more than likely, just a few would be able to scratch the surface of a comprehensive description. They could respond that the bread and wine turn into the body and blood of Christ, and quote phrases like, "The real presence of Christ in the Eucharist." Beyond that is a very shallow knowledge of the actual belief system. I know this because I have been in discussions with numerous Catholics on forums, and they never advance beyond the brief description above. I do not fault this, but it is an interesting observation.

As simple as Jesus and the apostles made it, many Catholics have no idea that it took twenty-three pages in the Catechism to assimilate and dissect the full meaning of the Eucharist and are not familiar with its many aspects.

To dive in, as most Catholics know, the Church strongly encourages the faithful to receive the Holy Eucharist on Sundays, feast days, or even daily (CCC 1389). They require Catholics to fast for an hour before going to Mass (Canon 919), and all "grave" sins have to be dealt with before participating (Canon 916). Of course, no one worries about the "venial sins" (the simple ones) because the consumption of the bread and wine (seen as the body and blood of Christ) will wipe those away according to Roman teaching. The latter of these topics will be addressed a little later.

In keeping with the changing policies of the Roman Catholic Church, it is worth noting that participation in Holy Communion used to be annual. Many Catholics are probably not aware of that. As important as the emphasis is today on taking it more frequently, it was not done like that for most of the history of the Church. After almost 1,900 years, and only under Pius X (about 100 years ago) was it changed from annually to weekly or daily.[1] Other "random" changes by Pius included the change from fasting after midnight to just an hour before the taking of the Eucharist, and the minimum age to consume the Lord's Supper moving from around twelve or fourteen years old down to seven years old. The issue is not that there is anything inherently wrong with any one of these changes, but they represent verifications that the Church historically announces a policy change with no scriptural reference (which is common), and it becomes non-optional for Catholic followers. Yet, the Church functioned without many of these proclamations for 1,000 years or more because those certain beliefs and policies were not in place. "Do as we say, we are in charge" is essentially all a Catholic follower needs to understand, and the subsequent compliance thereof. The same decisions were made in developing and proclaiming the doctrines on The Catholic List. Those were not a part of the patristic Church, but were proclamations that "this is what we believe now," and this becomes the basis for many of the red flags that surface regarding the Roman system.

Only an ordained priest or bishop in the Catholic landscape can administer the Eucharist (CCC 1411). This is interesting because, apparently, no one was in charge of administering the Eucharist in the original catholic Church. Catholic scholar Richard P. McBrien admits,

> "It is not clear, however, that anyone in particular was commissioned to preside over the Eucharist in the beginning. Indeed, there is no compelling evidence that [the apostles] presided when they were present, or that a chain of ordination from Apostles to bishop to priest was required for presiding."[2]

As we look further into Eucharist doctrine, the basic premise at the heart of this sacrament comes from taking these verses in the Bible literally instead of metaphorically:

> "Jesus said to them, 'I tell you the truth, unless you eat the flesh of the Son of Man and drink his blood, you have no life in you. Whoever eats my flesh and drinks my blood has eternal life, and I will raise him up at the last day. For my flesh is real food indeed, and my blood is real drink. Whoever eats my flesh and drinks my blood remains in me, and I in him. Just as the living Father sent me and I live because of the Father, so the one who feeds on me will live because of me'" (John 6:53-57).

The actual process of changing the bread and wine into the physical body and blood of Christ is called "transubstantiation," a dogma that was only ratified as official at the Fourth Lateran Council in 1215, and that also required every Christian to go to confession and communion at least once a year.[3] Here again, for over 1,000 years, it was not a dogma of the Church. The claim from some Catholic leaders, to apparently soften the image of cannibalism, is that the bread and wine do not visibly transform into the body and blood of Christ but become the "substance" of the body and blood of Christ. This is a slightly different terminology from how transubstantiation has often been described by many Catholics over the years: that the moment you open your mouth and start to chew and swallow, the bread and wine turn into the actual physical flesh and blood of Christ. But that is the true belief in what happens during the Eucharist. In fact, Catholic.com states that the elements "actually" change to real flesh and blood: "According to Transubstantiation, the bread and wine are actually transformed into the actual body, blood ... of Christ, and only the appearances of bread and wine remain." The word "substance" seems to be carefully chosen so as not to project a gross visualization through consuming actual flesh and blood.

Of course, this begs obvious and silly questions if the bread and wine actually turn into the flesh and blood of Christ. How many calories was it? Was it raw or cooked? Is the flesh and blood going through the digestive system and being assimilated into nutrition? If we were to hire a surgeon to cut open a willing volunteer's stomach after consuming the Eucharist, are we going to find consumed flesh and blood, or are we going to find bread and wine? To verify authenticity, did a person's blood alcohol level remain the same since the wine was turned into blood? But make no mistake—the view of the Roman Church is that the bread and wine do transform into the "actual" body and blood of Christ.

Apologist Gavin Ortlund points out that transubstantiation is a departure from the early church fathers, and the word "substance" can be defined in multiple different ways and has been over the years. He states,

> "There is no change that happens. It's forcing an action through dogmatic action that simply doesn't exist. Substance of the bread, remains bread. Why? Because it doesn't need to change. Nothing is being accomplished by the elements changing. It has no bearing or influence over the Gospel of Christ ..."[4]

Another claim in the Catholic liturgy is that the Eucharist sacrifice is:

> "... offered for the faithful departed who have died in Christ but are not yet wholly purified, so that they may be able to enter the light and peace of Christ. By offering to God our supplications for those who have fallen asleep, if they have sinned, we ... offer Christ sacrificed for the sins of all, and so render favorable, for them and for us" (CCC 1371).

Of course, this teaching is a departure from anything you will find in the New Testament, but the Catechism is viewed as the gospel according to the Church. In other words, Christians who are hanging out in Purgatory are yelling out, "Hey, what are you doing to get me out of here!" Catholic priests often express the summary of the Christian life that fits this portion of the Eucharist: "We are all on a long journey to perfection." Of course, in earlier chapters, we saw where this ever-changing doctrine of Purgatory was derived, how it developed, and has been redefined over time. A claim that was mentioned earlier is the wiping away of venial sins through the process of the Eucharist. Here is how it is explained in the Catechism:

> "Holy Communion separates us from sin. The Eucharist cannot unite us to Christ without at the same time cleansing us from past sins and preserving us from future sins. If, as often as his blood is poured out, it is poured for the forgiveness of sins, I should always receive it, so that it may always forgive my sins. Because I always sin, I should always have a remedy ... The Eucharist is offered in reparation for the sins of the living" (CCC 1393).

This concept of the Eucharist forgiving sin is a critical miscalculation (as we have seen in the last 4 chapters) and will be addressed again shortly. Another important feature of the Eucharist is its ability to move a believer a little closer to being complete and righteous in Christ:

> "That moves us to an ever more complete participation in our redeemer's sacrifice which we celebrate in the Eucharist" (CCC 1372).

> "Then we all rise together and offer prayers for ourselves ... and for all others, wherever they may be, so that we may be found righteous by our life and actions, and faithful to the commandments, so as to obtain eternal salvation" (CCC 1345).

Additional restrictions on participating in the Eucharist, besides abstaining due to an unconfessed mortal sin, are described:

> "We call this food Eucharist, and no one may take part in it unless he believes that what we teach is true, has received thanksgiving, has received baptism for the forgiveness of sins and new birth, and lives in keeping with what Christ taught" (CCC 1327).

The Church also makes the assertion and restriction that the Eucharist can only be offered in select places: churches consecrated and blessed according to Cath- olic canon law (the Roman Catholic or Eastern Orthodox Church), and only a bishop, priest, or deacon can administer this sacrament.

> "Only those churches whose bishops were ordained in the unbroken historical line back to the apostles can claim to have the valid sacrament of orders, with its three level of bishop, priest, and deacon. Therefore, only those churches (i.e., Catholic and Orthodox) have the valid Eucharist as Christ intended."[5]

Obviously, hundreds of millions of non-Catholic Christians who have awesome relationships with the Heavenly Father, through Jesus Christ, with the indwelling Holy Spirit, desire to participate in remembering the incredible sacrifice on the cross and the miracle of the resurrection through communion. But the message that is alluded to from the Catholic Church is: "Don't waste your time, it's useless if you are outside of our system." The Roman Church proudly announces and reserves that if you are a non-Catholic in attendance of a Catholic Church service, you are not eligible to participate in Holy Communion.[6] Gavin Ortlund uses an example that in many concentration camps, the bread and wine was slipped into the facility and, at the appropriate time, the signal was given and communion would commence. No priest or consecration or formal mass was applicable—but there is no doubt, the participation was a legitimate communion.[7] One can imagine a non-Catholic being out of town with a desire to stop by a church for prayer and communion (if it's available), and a Catholic Church is the only option in the area. The person might be allowed to warm up a pew and pray, but if you want to participate in remembering the awesome sacrifice of Christ for the redemption of mankind, even as a Christian, the message from the Catholic priest is: You can keep heading down the road. A shady practice from the Roman-ruled Church? Readers will have to decide.

One of the many controversial ideas of the Eucharist is its sacrificial nature. In his book, Trent Horn states:

"Therefore, through the new Passover the Eucharist would make Christ's sacrifice present for all future believers...That Christians believed the Eucharist was a sacrifice for God is also evident in Paul's teaching to the Corinthians...Catholics agree that Christ was sacrificed *once* on the Cross and no longer has to suffer or offer a bloody sacrifice ... But this does not mean that Christ, in his glorified body, does not continue to offer himself as a living sacrifice to the Father just as we offer ourselves to God...If Christ were a 'priest forever', it would follow that Christ always fulfills his priestly duty by offering his one sacrifice to the Father on our behalf ... But we've shown that Hebrews acknowledges the existence of multiple, unbloody heavenly sacrifices."[8]

The Catechism quotes St. Augustine: "The church continues to reproduce this sacrifice in the sacrament of the altar" (CCC 1372).

Two more interesting quotes spotlight the sacrificial nature of the Eucharist:

"The Eucharist is thus a sacrifice because it re-presents the sacrifice of the cross, because it is its memorial and because it applies its fruit" (CCC 1366).

"Because it is the memorial of Christ's Passover, the Eucharist is also a sacrifice. In the Eucharist Christ gives us the very body, which he gave up for us on the cross, the very blood which he 'poured out for many for the forgiveness of sins'" (CCC 1362).

"The sacrifice of Christ and the sacrifice of the Eucharist are one single sacrifice" (CCC 1367).

I will address these last few aspects of the Eucharist a little later in the Chapter. This is a lot of information to digest, but it's important to have an accurate view of this teaching when looking at the contrast between the Roman Catholic view and the true meaning of the New Covenant promise. In summary, but not comprehensively, the participation in the Eucharist makes these claims:

1. To receive the Lord Himself
2. To re-present the one sacrifice on the Cross over again
3. To receive the forgiveness of venial sins
4. To have power to accelerate those stuck in Purgatory
5. To journey toward completeness in Christ
6. To journey toward becoming more righteous
7. To work toward salvation
8. To participate per the commands of Christ
9. To deepen the communion with Christ and others
10. To engage in a form of worship

In addition to these specific Eucharist affirmations, the Roman Church claims that these have been the universal teachings of the Church since the beginning and all church fathers affirmed these doctrines. For example, the Council of Trent claimed transubstantiation was taught by "all our forefathers."[9] The Council also claimed that transubstantiation "has ever been a firm belief in the Church of God."[10] Scott Hahn also claims,

> "The clergy, teachers, and defenders of the early Church were united in their concern to preserve the Eucharist doctrines: the Real Presence of Jesus's body and blood under the appearance of bread and wine."[11]

However, both the Council of Trent and Scott Hahn are incorrect. In his documentary on the Catholic Church, Thompson uncovers several of the following points: The early Church was mixed in its view of the body and blood of Christ being a literal representation during the Eucharist. Augustine, who is quoted above, was a renowned theologian and one of the most famous fathers of the Latin Church, states,

> "If the sentence ... seems to enjoin a crime or vice ... it is figurative. 'Except ye eat the flesh of the Son of man,' says Christ, 'and drink His blood, ye have no life in you.' This seems to enjoin a crime or a vice; it is therefore a figure ..."[12]

In addition to Augustine, Eusebius of Caesarea, another early church father, emphasizes that not only is the body and blood of Christ "symbolic" in the Eucharist, but the whole purpose of the Eucharist was a sacrifice of praise, not an actual sacrifice. He also confirms that in the Eucharist we are thanking Christ for salvation (not trying to achieve it). He writes,

> "Having then received the memory of this sacrifice to celebrate upon the Table by means of the symbols of His body and His saving blood ... 'from the rising of the sun even unto its setting My name has been glorified among the nations; and in every place incense is offered unto my name, and a pure sacrifice.' We sacrifice then to the supreme God a sacrifice of praise ... Celebrating the memory of the great sacrifice ..."[13]

Ignatius, in a letter to the Romans, speaks of Jesus's blood as incorruptible love and eternal life,[14] and to the Philadelphians, he says the flesh of Jesus is the Gospel,[15] and in his letter to the Trallians, he says Jesus's flesh is faith and his blood is love.[16]

Ignatius felt that the body and blood of Jesus Christ were simply symbols of love and faith and the food for eternal life was represented in those spiritual attributes.

In his magnum opus, *History of the Christian Church*, historian Philip Schaff documents the four views the early church held in regard to the way in which Christ was associated with the bread and wine:

> "You had, one, the mystical view of Ignatius, Justin Martyr, Irenaeus, and Cyril of Jerusalem, which said the body and blood of Jesus are mystically in union with the elements leading to a sort of repetition of the incarnation, though no change in substance actually takes place as in later Romanism. Two, the symbolic view of Tertullian, Cyprian, Eusebius, Gregory Nazianzen, Macarius, the Elder, Theodoret, Augustine, and Gelasius, which said the Eucharist symbolizes the body and blood of Jesus and is a commemoration. Three, the allegorical or spiritual view of Clement of Alexandria, Origen, and Athanasius, which said the believer receives

the spiritual but not physical blood in life of Jesus at the Mass. And four, the literalistic view of Hilary, Ambrose, and Gaudentius, which affirmed the bread and wine as being the literal transformed body and blood of Jesus, which is similar to the modern Roman Catholic system. Thus, the Roman view is in the minority, while the symbolic and mystical views seem to be the most primitive and popular."[17]

Tertullian, as just one example mentioned above, is very clear in refuting that the Eucharist was not to be perceived as being the literal body and blood of Christ:

"Now, because they thought His discourse was harsh and intolerable, supposing that He had really and literally enjoined them to eat his flesh, He, with the view of ordering the state of salvation as a spiritual thing, set out with the principle, 'It is the spirit that quickeneth;' and then added, 'The flesh profiteth nothing,' meaning, of course, to the giving of life. He likewise called His flesh by the same appellation; because, too, the Word had become flesh, we ought therefore to desire Him in order that we may have life, and to devour Him with the ear, and to ruminate on Him with the understanding, and to digest Him by faith."[18]

Unlike the Roman claim, research obviously proves that the Church was *not* united in believing that the wine and bread transform into the body and blood of Christ—either literally or by substance. As is the pattern of many Catholic defenders, there is a hope that Catholic attendees will not do any extensive investigation. Why is this the case? Why all the misinformation throughout the pages of books by Catholic spokespeople? The answer could be that when you examine encyclopedias' worth of early letters from the patristic fathers of the primitive catholic Church, it fully conflicts with what the Roman Catholic Church proclaims. It shines the spotlight on the Roman Catholic Church changing the Gospel of the original catholic Church, and that would not be a popular realization. It appears that the overwhelming reason that the Roman Catholic claim has to be made (that the early church fathers were on board with this perspective of the Eucharist) is to maintain and justify the need for a priestly sacramental system. In fact, we see that the apostles didn't have a priestly sacramental system. The patristic fathers didn't have one either. This priestly sacramental organism was not part of the early catholic Church. It's a stunning revelation to wake up in the Roman Catholic system and realize that relying on a priest to dispense and administer the Eucharist (through the mechanism of transubstantiation) is something that would be totally foreign to everyone from the earlier centuries, and especially during apostolic times.

Not only were the majority of early church fathers in opposition to the view of Jesus's body and blood being literal in the Eucharist, but they had a clear understanding that every individual who seeks to have eternal life achieves this by faith and belief in Christ. No processes. Jesus is the food and drink we need for eternal life—will you trust and follow Him?

Although it is beyond the capacity of this book to examine every single aspect of the Mass and the twenty-three long pages of explanations in the Catechism, it is critical to bring these teachings into the New Covenant and see how they measure up. Do the teachings of the Eucharist match the biblical story on this side of the cross? Does the Eucharist blend the Old Covenant and the New Covenant together, or is it in alignment with the new arrangement God promised us?

The Eucharist in the New Covenant

What was the intention of Christ regarding His body and blood? As many can already see, there is a glaring contradiction to the story unfolded in the past few chapters and what has been disclosed, in a quick glance, about the Catholic Eucharist.

In fairness, as a Catholic exercising proper due diligence in seeking out the truth, it's important to consider the realities of the New Covenant presented in the Scriptures and deliberate on the apparent fact that there has been a departure from the apostolic deposit in the teachings of the Holy Eucharist by the Roman Catholic Church.

Before we begin to look at some additional opposing views regarding aspects of the Eucharist, in light of the New Covenant, Catholics should be concerned about the continual threats from the Roman Catholic Church toward its members. It seems to be standard protocol throughout Catholic liturgy. As mentioned earlier in the book, the Church has a super long list of anathemas (damnations) they have been pronouncing for centuries, most coming from popes and a dysfunctional magisterium. Although the Bible explicitly says, "there is no condemnation to those that are in Christ Jesus" (Romans 8:1), and dozens of verses substantiating the same promise, the Roman Catholic Church attempts to override those scriptures to bring condemnation.

For example, those who do not attend Mass on Sundays (except for "Church-stated acceptable reasons") are in mortal danger of hellfire. That is not only a serious accusation, but very dysfunctional theology. Catholic.com confirms this as well and starts off in full stride with one of these erroneous threats to everyone's eternal security concerning the Eucharist in quoting the Catechism:

> "For Catholics, the Holy Eucharist / Catholic Mass is considered the most important and highest form of prayer. In fact, attending Mass is an obligation, under penalty of mortal sin, each Sunday and on certain other Holy Days of Obligation" (CCC 2281).

Keep in mind that any unconfessed mortal sin results in eternity in hell for an individual according to Roman Catholic rules. It's the very opposite of the New Covenant teaching of complete forgiveness that God ushered in Himself through Jesus Christ. So, if you are Catholic and decide to skip Mass, kick your feet up on the couch one Sunday and watch a movie or some football, and do not take care of that mortal sin in time, you are doomed to hell for eternity. Literally, by hanging out in your own living room on a Sunday, your eternal presence with your Heavenly Father is jeopardized forever. It takes a moment to realize just how awful that corrupt teaching is, yet it has to be accepted by the attendees. Many Catholics interviewed dispute this teaching, but if you contest that one, what else with the Church is suspicious or questionable?

The Catholic Church has tried to soften the impact of all these anathemas (a curse by ecclesiastical authority), but they have never been rescinded.

Indeed, if one understands the magisterium of the Church, how could they ever be rescinded? According to the Church, these anathemas are as authoritative as the Scriptures, which cannot be altered, and there are entirely too many to list.

I think it is fair to say the moment a church threatens the redemption, reconciliation, and justification accomplishments that Jesus Christ gruesomely died for, giving life to anyone willing to follow Him, is the moment to reassess with whom your loyalty lies. If one accepted every teaching of the Roman Catholic Church, they still should reconsider embracing Catholicism because of endless and baseless threats to one's security. Especially with the doctrine of "mortal sin" that can wipe out eternity for a Catholic in a matter of seconds. It's a horrendous and unacceptable threat and an extreme Church error to teach that one mortal sin, and you are no longer reconciled to God. If so, "justifying" baptism (in the Catholic world) is a complete waste of time because if unconfessed mortal sin is not addressed by a Catholic, there is no eternal life, regardless of being baptized.

The Church simply cannot play God and has no power to announce anyone's eternal destiny. Under the New Covenant, our identity and security are in Christ, not in a Church's liturgy. We are His children, His saints, and our salvation is based on what He did, not on what we do or don't do according to a religious institution. Our security is based on God's promises, not a church's threat. It's a blasphemous pronouncement to threaten Christians with a "death sentence" if one does not obey their commands. It's quite disturbing and should not be accepted by any educated, critically-thinking Catholic. This is another hallmark of ecclesiastical control, and there are not many pronouncements more in conflict with new-covenant teaching than the Church's anathemas.

As we get into the specifics of the Catholic version of the Eucharist, we find something shocking. The most disturbing aspect of Holy Communion in researching transubstantiation (the process of a priest magically turning the bread and wine into the body and blood of Christ) is depicted in a quote by Father John O'Brien. With an earned PhD, he is a renowned Catholic scholar and the author of over forty books. He is highly recognized by the Catholic

Church. Here is his description of a priest performing Mass and initiating transubstantiation:

> "When the priest announces the tremendous words of consecration, he reaches up into the heavens, brings Christ down from His throne, and places Him upon our altar to be offered up again as the victim for the sins of man. It is a power greater than that of saints and angels. The priest speaks and lo! Christ, the eternal and omnipotent God, bows his head in humble obedience to the priest's command ... For the priest is and should be another Christ."[19]

This quote is so disturbing that when I was sharing this with one of my friends, he was not even able to respond. He was so sickened by this ungodly quote after I read it that, after a moment of silence, he said he would just call me back later. When I first read the quote, I remember a nauseating feeling in my stomach. I could feel the Spirit of God, so alive inside of me, rejecting this horrendous and sacrilegious portrayal.

I wondered, does anyone believe that the omnipotent Creator of the universe bows His head to a priest and responds after getting called down from Heaven? In addition, the idea that a priest is "another Christ" seems disconcerting, appalling, and extremely blasphemous. Did O'Brien actually think that any of this could ever happen or be accepted into mainline belief?

Theologian and scholar Dr. James White responded to O'Brien's remarks:

> "In speaking on Roman Catholicism's grotesque perversion of scriptural truth ... Though I have quoted these words many times in my debates, always to great effect upon anyone who is biblically oriented, my Roman Catholic opponents have never repudiated the words. They have had little comment to offer ... the true nature of the Roman religion is exposed by them."[20]

It should be noted that O'Brien's quote is from a book he wrote in 1938 and is not the "official" position of the Catholic Church. However, in practice, the priest *does* perform similarly to O'Brien's claims, seen in the mere necessity of a priest being needed to turn the wafer and wine into the body and blood of Christ. The perception that many Catholics have expressed in the past about the Eucharist seems very parallel to O'Brien's claim. Nevertheless, when I think of the priest holding up the wafer in demonstration of the actual body of Christ in the Eucharist, I can only think of the verse:

> "At that time if anyone says to you, 'Look here is the Christ!'... do not believe him" (Matthew 24:23).

We can know Jesus does not come down daily to deal with sin in the Eucharist because Scripture says He does not:

> "... so Christ was sacrificed once to take away the sins of many people; and he will appear a second time [at the end of time], not to bear sin, but to bring salvation to those who are waiting for him" (Hebrews 9:28).

Jesus is not coming again until the end of time. He does not come down daily as being locally present or by substance, because He remains at the right hand of the Father. Catholic teachers do agree about Him not being "locally present," which seems a contradiction with transubstantiation. The logic seems to be: "He's not here 'locally' but His body and blood are sure flowing down my esophagus." The truth is if Jesus were to come, He would have nothing to do but enjoy a Church picnic with Southern cooking. He is fully finished dealing with the sin issue. It's all over.

In looking at the sacrificial nature of the Eucharist, we see somewhat of a play on words. "The sacrifice of Christ and the sacrifice of the Eucharist are one single sacrifice" as announced by the Church, but O'Brien declares, "and places Him upon our altar to be offered up again as the victim of the sins of man." Catholic scholars and the Catechism can provide justifications that the sacrifice they are performing during the Eucharist is one and the same, but if you are offering Christ on an altar over and over again, you are not "re-presenting," you are "re-sacrificing" Christ over and over again. How can the Eucharist and the sacrifice of Christ be one single sacrifice when the Eucharist "sacrifice" is taking place thousands of times per day? I believe Catholic teachers will stick with that narrative, but it's simply not a logical explanation. It's an exegesis that keeps the priest in the middle of the equation.

The truth is that the sacrificial system is over. Jesus is not offering sacrifices in Heaven as Trent Horn declares, but affirming to the Heavenly Father that His one sacrifice completed the mission. We do not need to emulate or try to repeat the crucifixion again. Christ is no longer on the cross (as depicted on the crucifix riddled throughout the Catholic landscape). The Church tries to get around this doctrinal fallacy by declaring that Christ is offered in an "unbloody manner" during the Eucharist (CCC 1367), totally missing the point that Christ is not to *ever* be offered again. As pointed out in a Servus Christi Ministries podcast on the Eucharist: how can you have an "unbloody" sacrifice when the wine is actually been turned into the "actual" blood of Christ? He states, "It's a doctrine that doesn't work, because it self-contradicts."[21] The podcast also brings up the observation that if Jesus was not talking metaphorically about His body and blood being eaten, then this would be the reality:

> "When Jesus was in the presence of His disciples, He takes the bread, He clones Himself in the form of bread, sacrifices or kills Himself in His own hands and then watches His disciples cannibalize Him ... That's what is taught ... and then does the same thing with His blood ... [And therefore] according to the Roman Catholic Church, Jesus was sacrificed the night before He was sacrificed"[22]

It's imperative for all Christians to understand that we are now in a New Covenant. The cross is empty, the tomb is empty, and Christians should refuse to try to force Christ back on the cross again, only to have Him come down from Heaven to repeat sacrifices over again (either bloody or unbloody). Why can't Jesus's words, "It is finished," be honored?

> "Unlike the other high priest, [Christ] does not need to offer sacrifices day after day, first for his own sins, and then for the sins of the people. He sacrifices for the sins once for all when he offered himself" (Hebrews 7:27).

> "But only the high priest entered the inner room, and that only once a year, and never without blood, which he offered for

himself and for the sins the peoples had committed in ignorance. The Holy Spirit was showing by this that the way into the Most Holy Place had not been disclosed as long as the first tabernacle was still standing. This is an illustration for the present time, indicating that the gifts and sacrifices being offered were not able to clear the conscience of the worshipper. They are only a matter of food and drink and various ceremonial washings—external regulations applying only until the time of the new order" (Hebrews 9: 7-10).

"When Christ came as high priest of the good things that are already here, he went through the greater and more perfect tabernacle that is not man-made … He did not enter by means of the blood of goats and calves; but he entered the Most Holy Place once and for all by his own blood, having obtained eternal redemption" (Hebrews 9:11-12).

"When he had received the drink, Jesus said, 'It is finished.' With that, He bowed His head and gave up His spirit" (John 19:30).

The priesthood and its sacrificial system applied to the Old Covenant. There are no priests in the New Covenant because Christ is now and forever the one High Priest, and He does not bow His head to anyone. There are no magical powers a Catholic priest can perform, there is no ability to turn bread and wine into the body and blood of Christ. Jesus is not coming again until the end of time. He is not going to show up for the Eucharist per the command of a priest. It is over! The sacrificial system is over forever. The postulation that the priest is doing anything supernatural is total deception, placing a person in the wrong covenant, just as with a priest absolving one of sins, as we saw a few chapters back.

Here is what the Roman Catholic scholar Raymond Brown says regarding the Church's later development of the Eucharist as a Christian sacrifice:

"One has reason to doubt that [the author of Hebrews] would have been enthusiastic about such a development."[23]

The Apostles only knew of one sacrifice, one event of atonement; any attempt to accomplish this daily would be totally foreign to all the leaders of the early Church.

Real Presence

I want to circle back around and continue the discussion of the real presence of Christ in the Eucharist. It could be confusing and bewildering to anyone researching and trying to understand this concept that Christ, Himself, is either spiritually present while taking Holy Communion or that through the process of Transubstantiation (the Roman Catholic view) that the elements (bread and wine) actually turn into the physical body and blood of Christ. The recent survey of Catholics confirms this to be true. That confusion alone seems to indicate that institutions have not only done a poor job in explaining their perspectives on this topic, but have tried to make a "simple request by Jesus" much more complicated than it should be. It's a venturing away, once again, from something that was supposed to be easily understandable. Religion is notorious for doing that. Catholic.com shares the survey, done in 2019 by the Pew Research Center on how its members view the real presence of Jesus in communion, that shows just how far off base most Catholics are from what their Church teaches:

> "A new survey shows that most people who say they're Catholic think that the Eucharist is just a symbol of Christ's body ... In fact, nearly seven in ten Catholics [70%] ... say they personally believe that during the Catholic mass, the bread and wine used in communion are symbols of the body and blood of Jesus Christ."[24]

The article did go on to state that for those who participate in the Eucharist weekly, that percentage drops, as regular attendees seem to be more informed of what the Church actually teaches. Yet, this still shows that a huge number of Catholic members are not on board with their own ecclesiastical teachings. Recall that this was also true with the 80% who were not on board with the massively destructive celibacy law. There is evidence, and apparently a pattern emerging, that quite a number of Catholics have seen through the smokescreens of the Roman Church and its numerous errors, including doctrinal teachings. Hopefully, because of what was disclosed in the first eight chapters, this represents a sign in a positive direction that a high number of Catholic members have a desire to return to the teaching of the original catholic Church.

There are about five different views on "Real Presence", but before commenting more on the Catholic view, I want to highlight one other view that is held prominently in the Protestant arena (mostly reformed Baptists and others), and that is the "Spiritual Presence" view. Here is a general summary of that view as expressed in a teaching session by Reformed Apologist Gavin Ortlund:

> The definition of Real Presence in this view is that the substance of the bread and wine remain bread and wine, but there is still an "act" of sorts taking place. This act is not that Jesus is "locally or carnally" present, but is "truly and substantially" present, in and through the elements—a climactic expression of our union with Christ. The reception by which Christ is taken is not the stomach, but the soul. The participation is not mechanical, but a faith action by a believer. The participation creates intimacy with Christ. Feasting on Christ and all the benefits of his death. One example given is sticking an iron rod in a fire where it takes on a union with the fire but still remains an iron rod. The benefits mentioned do not include forgiveness of sins of any kind (venial or mortal) under the Spiritual Presence view.[25]

Although both views acknowledge the Real Presence of Christ in communion, transubstantiation takes it to a whole new level within the sacramental system changing the actual elements, giving job security to the priest. We saw earlier in that there were a lot of mixed patristic views regarding Real Presence, and especially transformation of the elements into the "actual" flesh and blood, leaving the Roman Catholic view in the minority. However, to take it one step further, even among those that recognized the "actual body and blood" interpretation there was not a priestly consecration anywhere in view. Once again, that is not readily acknowledged by the Roman

Church and it becomes embarrassing in proclaiming "unity from the beginning" when Roman Catholic scholars know this not to be true.

Although I respect the Real Presence view expressed by both sides, I still think that based on the components of the New Covenant (and its finished accomplishment) the Memorial view is what Christ had in mind. I use the example that if three people were sitting side by side at a Church service, each with a separate view of what transpires during communion (a Memorial view, a Spiritual Presence view, and a Transubstantiation view), what just happened after communion was taken? The bread and wine is consumed and then the event is over. For the Memorialist, he paused before taking communion and reflected on just how thankful he was for the sacrifice of Christ, and ended his experience with gratitude and a grateful heart. For the Spiritual Presence guy, he probably did something similar and (in his mind) became the rod inserted into the fire where he was in union with Christ, but seconds later he still remains on the pew next to the Memorialist. Is the Spiritually Presence guy on fire, or does he seem electrically charged, or is he uncontrollably jumping up and down? Is he glowing like Charlton Heston as Moses in the movie *The Ten Commandments*? Although he was previously told that he just "received all the benefits of Christ," didn't we all receive the benefits of Christ at the time of salvation? I certainly did, so what really changed or happened other than a grateful heart? The New Covenant confirms we already received all the benefits we will get at the time of salvation (as seen in the past four chapters). Did both believers become more "intimate" with Christ during that communion event? Sure, I would not argue with that idea, but having a "Real Presence" view didn't give that person a benefit more than what would be expected by the Memorialist.

For the third person in this example, let's pretend that a priest was there and did "dispense" this sacrament with the claim of actual flesh and blood going into his system. What did the person receiving it specifically gain? He might erroneously think he was forgiven of venial sins, but outside of the context of that unbiblical idea, is this person glowing, or appearing to be electrically charged, or showing any apparent signs that anything changed? Or are all three participants going to just leave church and head off to lunch feeling gratitude in their hearts?

I have always hesitated and felt discomfort at church services where they want to "call God down" to perform a certain function. Whether priests serving up the sacrifice again and again, or Baptists singing for the "Holy Spirit to fall down on me," or Pentecostals feeling incomplete until someone jumps a pew in the Spirit.

The Catholic Church and others emphasize the presence of Christ in the Eucharist, but the Holy Spirit dwells inside us. Jesus specifically said He was going away but would leave us a Counselor who would "be with you forever—the Spirit of truth." (John 14:16-17). He lives inside us! How can we possibly distinguish Jesus (who remains and stays at the right hand of the Father) being present in the Eucharist from the Holy Spirit living inside of every believer? We are "in Christ;" He is "in us" already. You can't get any closer or more intimate than that. Why would Jesus suddenly need to appear at communion for us to have the "real presence of Him" when He has been with us the whole time? Augustine confirms this truth as well:

> "But in respect of the flesh He assumed as the Word ... 'ye will not have Him always.' And why? Because He ... ascended into heaven and is no longer here. He is there, indeed, sitting at the right hand of the Father; and He is here also, having never withdrawn the presence of His glory. In other words, in respect of His divine presence we always have Christ ... In this respect the Church enjoyed His presence only for a few days; now it possesses Him by faith, without seeing Him ..."[26]

This is why it is critical to look at the New Covenant's perspective on what Christ was trying to communicate to the disciples with this new promise and covenant He was going to usher in, because Christians are often victims of Church inertia. "We've always done it this way, we were told to do it this way, we're going to do it this way." And this precipitates the very message of this book: to sound the alarm that everything has changed! We are no longer under a traditional old system. The New Covenant has painted a different story than before, unlike anyone anticipated, and it was so radical it was rejected by the Jews, resulting in the crucifixion of Jesus under God's divine plan the whole time.

We have to look at why we are doing this act of Holy Communion at all. The answer is a known phrase by all: "In remembrance of Him." Three different times in the Catechism, the phrase "Do this in remembrance of me" is acknowledged (CCC 1339, 1356, 1371). The New Covenant's purpose of the Eucharist is done at that moment; but unfortunately, the Catechism expands on this phrase. Just a few paragraphs later the Catechism accepts the literal interpretation of Jesus's words in John 6:53-58 ("Whoever eats my flesh and drinks my blood has eternal life,"), and applies actions that are being accomplished that are not scripturally supported (the forgiveness of venial sins, a re-presentation of a sacrifice, and more).

How do we know that this is a metaphor and not a literal command? One cannot just grab a few isolated verses without looking at the whole context of the topic. Christians have to acknowledge the verses in the same chapter that come before this teaching:

> "Then Jesus declared, 'I am the bread of life. He who comes to me (not he who eats me) will never go hungry, and he who believes in me (not he who drinks me) will never be thirsty" (John 6:35).

> "I tell you the truth, he who believes has everlasting life. I am the bread of life" (John 6:47-48).

> "The Spirit gives life; the flesh counts for nothing. The words I have spoken to you are spirit and they are life. Yet there are some of you who [still] do not believe ..." (John 6:63-64).

Jesus is saying that He is the pathway into the kingdom. The Spirit of Jesus is the bread. The Spirit of Jesus is the drink. The flesh counts for nothing! *Believe in Him* and you will never thirst or be hungry again. Look at what Jesus said—only a few verses before the section the Roman Catholic Church takes literally—about consuming the literal body and blood of Christ:

> "For my Father's will is that everyone who looks to the Son and believes in him shall have eternal life, and I will raise him up at the last day" (John 6:40).

Eating and drinking Jesus at the Eucharist is not going to result in forgiveness or eternal life, despite the Church's claim in the Catechism. Believing in Jesus is going to give one forgiveness and eternal life. We see this truth before the confusing "eat my flesh and drink my blood" verses, and we see it afterward as well. As mentioned before, there are over 200 verses in the Bible that confirm the reality of the verse above.

Eating the flesh of Jesus and drinking His blood is a type of metaphor that is repeated all throughout the Scriptures:

> "Destroy this temple, and in three days, I will raise it up" (John 2:14-16).

> "... Finally two came forward and declared, 'This fellow said, "I am able to destroy the temple of God and rebuild it in three days."' Then the high priest stood up and said to Jesus, 'are you not going to answer? What is this testimony that these men are bringing against you?' But Jesus remained silent." (Matthew 26:60-63).

> "'How can a man be born when he is old?' Nicodemus asked. 'Surely he cannot enter a second time into his mother's womb to be born!' ... Jesus answered ... 'You must not be surprised at my saying, "You must be born again"' ... 'How can this be?' Nicodemus asked" (John 3:4-9).

> "Jesus answered her, 'If you knew the gift of God and who it is that asks you for a drink, you would have asked him and he would have given you living water.' Sir, the woman said, you have nothing to draw with and the well is deep ... Jesus answered, 'Everyone who drinks this water will be thirsty again, but whoever drinks the water I give him will never thirst'" (John 4:10-13).

> "I am the gate" (John 10:7).

> "I am the vine" (John 15:5).

> "You are the salt of the earth" (Matthew 5:13).

There are numerous examples of Jesus using metaphors all throughout the New Testament. Jesus Himself said, "Though I have been speaking figuratively ..."(Matthew 16:25), so it was very common for Him to teach using this method. The context in which He is doing this regarding the Eucharist is that He is life, He is the food we need, He is the drink we need, but always in the context that "whoever comes to Me, whoever believes in Me, whoever has faith in Me will gain this life." Jesus was present when He told his disciples that "whosoever eats my body or drinks my blood will have eternal life." None of the disciples started chewing on Jesus's arm or cutting Him with a sword to obtain blood. This acceptance of a literal interpretation would have been cannibalism, a violation of the Old Covenant Law which strictly forbade the consumption of flesh and blood. At the time of this gathering with His disciples, Jesus was fulfilling the Old Covenant perfectly, not disregarding it.

Catholic apologist and author Tim Staples argues that if Jesus was speaking metaphorically about flesh and blood being bread and wine, then He would have corrected the Jews who were grumbling and not understanding Him.[27] His assumption is based on instances where Jesus does explain His teachings more clearly while using metaphors. However, Staples is incorrect that Jesus provided these explanations every time. The verses above clearly show Jesus's metaphorical teachings with no follow-up explanation ("But Jesus remained silent"), yet we know Jesus was not a gate, we know Jesus was not a vine, we know a temple cannot be built in three days, and we know it's impossible to drink water a single time and not thirst again. So, the argument Staples made is not accurate, as anyone can clearly see.

Jesus spells out for us what is required for eternal life and the message is contained within these announcements: belief in Him, come to Him. Look at just a few of the other supporting verses that tell us how to get eternal life. None of these require the Eucharist because that is only to be done "in remembrance" of the redemption event.

> "Whoever believes in the Son has eternal life, but whoever rejects the Son will not see life ..." (John 3:36).

"I write these things to you who believe in the name of the Son of God so that you may know that you have eternal life" (1 John 5:13).

"Yet to all who received Him, to those who believed in his name, he gave the right to become children of God" (John 1:12).

"And you also were also included in Christ when you heard the word of truth, the gospel of your salvation. Having believed, you were marked in him with a seal, the promised Holy Spirit, who is a deposit guaranteeing our inheritance ..." (Ephesians 1:13).

"This righteousness from God comes through faith in Jesus Christ to all who believe ... and are justified freely by his grace through the redemption that came by Christ Jesus" (Romans 3:22).

"... Sirs, what must I do to be saved? [Paul and Silas] replied, 'Believe in the Lord Jesus, and you will be saved'" (Acts 16:30-31).

"I am not ashamed of the gospel, because it is the power of God for the salvation of everyone who believes ..." (Romans 1:16).

"For the wages (penalty) of sin is death, but the gift of God is eternal life in Christ Jesus our Lord" (Romans 6:23).

It's always been about grace. It's always been a gift. It's always been about a guarantee. The blood of Christ secures our position. He maintains our standing as His children. It cannot be taken away. We are marked with a seal. He will never deny or reject our citizenship. Eternal life is protected—not by our actions or participation in the Eucharist but by his action on the cross. The apostles knew that participating in a communion celebration would not remove sin, because Jesus is already resting from dealing with sin. In the Roman Church economy, participating in the Eucharist daily or weekly is just a reminder that sin is still being held against the believer, instead of reminding of the finished work done, one time, by Christ.

Jesus Christ honors His Word. God has concluded dealing with our sin. He is done dealing with mortal sins, He is done dealing with grave sins, He is done dealing with venial sins. There are no threats on the table from Jesus Christ for those who have received His one-time forgiveness and righteousness. He is able to save completely and unconditionally.

The Roman Catholic Church, in the past centuries, was willing to murder to keep these truths from the common man. The Scriptures were not allowed in the hands of anyone and was placed on the list of "forbidden books" because they knew the central theme of the Scripture is about a New Covenant and a new way to relate to God on this side of the cross, eliminating the need for a monarchial organization with a hierarchy and a priestly sacramental system.

We not only have the life of Christ living inside of us via the Holy Spirit, but our reservations in Heaven cannot be canceled. Why would the Catholic Church keep this information secret from its followers? It can be continually answered in one word: control. Create a path, a system, a process, a journey to eternity that has to go solely through you, and you have ultimate control over others. The Roman system has strategically developed a platform of enslaving Catholics to the priest from the time they are born until death, but even after that. The priest is needed for Infant Baptism, Confirmation, Reconciliation, Eucharist, Marriage, Holy Orders, Anointing the Sick and even for Prayers at Mass to get loved ones out of Purgatory sooner. Yet, sacraments seem to be "hand-picked" by the Church. Why just pick a few? How about casting out demons, or multiplying food, or healing lepers, or raising the dead like Jesus did? Does the Church only choose what a priest could succeed at with no spiritual power necessary? For millions of Christians that live outside that system, a priest is simply never needed.

The truth of the New Covenant conflicts with the Eucharist claim that we need more of Jesus inside of us, more righteousness, more justification, more forgiveness, another sacrifice, and that we are in danger of eternal flames if we do not follow the Church's teachings, that we have to be on the "pilgrimage to perfection" by following regiments to really make it to God.

Instead, Jesus and the writings within the New Covenant say there is no "journey to perfection." Faith in Christ alone completely saves, and this genuine faith, belief, and trust will be evident in a believer's fruit and good works. That will be the evidence, but not required "in conjunction with faith." Jesus challenged that old system of self-effort and self-righteousness, making the claim that those "religious doers" are the people who will not make it into His kingdom. Steve McVey states in his book *Grace Rules*:

> "Teach a man who he is in Christ and he can't be stopped from godly activity. Try to control him through rules, and you set him up for spiritual ruin."[28]

The contrary truth to the bread and wine turning into the body and blood of Christ is so simple, and it's baffling how the Catholic Church has missed this spiritual revelation: We already have Jesus inside us. We can't get any more of Him inside us. We are completely full. There is no room left. We already have His righteousness. We already have justification. We already have forgiveness, and it's on the account of His sacrifice, not our confession or participation in the Eucharist. Jesus finished what He started and did all the work Himself. The completed work of Jesus saves us; not our participation.

The Church cannot legitimately claim the concept of Purgatory as a place to get cleaned up (like going through a car wash) before entering God's presence because Jesus did everything necessary on our behalf for salvation, and now He sees us as 100% holy. He is now at the right hand of the Father resting, not providing more forgiveness, not providing more sacrifices, not coming down at the command of a priest, not appearing in any elements, not waiting for us to be cleaned up; we are already perfect in the eyes of God. We have His righteousness inside of us.

> "But now a righteousness from God, apart from the law, has been made known, to which the Law and Prophets testify. This righteousness from God comes through faith in Jesus Christ to all who believe" (Romans 3:21-22).

> "I do not set aside the grace of God, for if righteousness could be gained through the law, Christ died for nothing!" (Galatians 2:21).

It's the most incredible news mankind could have ever imagined. From a sincere heart, if we place our faith and trust in Christ, He will forever see us as righteous and forgiven. Nothing else is required. That's the definition of grace. Amazing grace. Unlimited grace. Unconditional grace. Sustaining grace. Grace with no strings attached. Grace with no contingencies. Grace that has set us free. Grace that does not require. The Roman Church does not believe this. They have set out to "control" grace by their commands, never allowing a believer to ever have peace and assurance. As apologist James White has brought to light, "you can go to mass 50,000 times, but it will not perfect you-—in fact, under Catholic theology you still might be eternally lost and eternally condemned ... Jesus didn't finish the work of Redemption"[29]

It's a sad system of threats by an institution that attempts to hold grace hostage, and it is an affront to Christianity. It's a system that forces Christ back on the cross to perpetually deal with sin, still not providing any peace for its followers as indicated in a quote from Ludwig Ott in *Fundamentals of Catholic Dogma*: "Without a super revelation from God no one can know with certainty that they have fulfilled all the conditions that are necessary for achieving justification."[30]

Daily, the Catholic Eucharist is denying the sufficiency of Christ. Don't let it do that anymore. Don't let an institution rob you of peace, joy, and the assurance of your salvation by insisting that you need more of what Christ has fully given already. Holy Communion can only be done properly with this being the whole of it: "Do this in remembrance of me" (Luke 22:19, 1 Corinthians 11:24). The Eucharist has no other power to offer. Participating in the Eucharist does not remove sin or provide justification because the blood of Christ has already done so. McVey continues:

> "God has closed the book on your sins. We owe God nothing
> for our sin. He chose to carry the weight of our offense against
> Him to the cross, and to release us from all obligation toward
> Him. Jesus satisfied God's demand for justice to be carried out,
> and the Father has chosen to totally release you from all debt
> to Him. Believers stand before God in complete forgiveness. A

Christian's faulty belief about forgiveness will necessitate that he constantly focus on himself. Where law rules, one is preoccupied with his own behavior, while grace causes us to be preoccupied with Jesus."[31]

Author Mike Gendron states:

"One of the miracles that took place at Calvary was when Jesus gave up His Spirit, the veil, separating the holy of holies from sinful man was torn open from top to bottom, showing through faith and the shed blood of Jesus, we have direct access to the Father. We no longer need priests offering sacrifices that can never take away sin, because Jesus Christ, the perfect High Priest, offered Himself, the perfect sacrifice, to a perfect God, who demands perfection, and then He cries out, 'It is finished.' We have direct access to the Father, from one mediator, the Lord Jesus Christ—nobody else is qualified to mediate between God and man."[32]

I know this is a very sensitive topic for Catholics caught in the Roman system, but the truth is that certain aspects of the Catholic Eucharist and its components are old news. To be more specific: Old Covenant, obsolete news. Resting in what Jesus has accomplished will be the most freeing realization of one's entire Christian journey. Jesus Christ has set us free from the Old Covenant requirements and all the aspects of the Eucharist except for praise and thanksgiving in remembrance of Him. Law and grace do not mix, Christ and an institution (in opposition to Christ's triumphant work at Calvary) do not mix either. I encourage Catholics to continue in *remembering* Christ's sacrifice by participating in the Eucharist, but in the New Covenant way. The Roman version of the Eucharist is no longer applicable on this side of the cross. We no longer need to appease an angry God. We no longer need to be "infused" with grace; God has permanently and completely ascribed, assigned, and declared that we *have* His grace. A priest is no longer needed. One can simply have communion in the privacy of their own home or in the quietness of a Church pew, away from a sacrificial altar that no longer exists.

An Invitation to Catholics

Although this book has been focused on the broken Roman Catholic system, I cannot emphasize enough my support and adoration for individual Roman Catholics. Most I have met, as mentioned earlier, are incredible, loyal Christians who have found Christ in the midst of the chaos and man-made requirements, and thrive in walking in His Spirit. The hearts of the ones I have encountered are gracious and genuine, and I trust them in my very closest circle of friends.

However, it's deeply disturbing that most Catholic followers have no idea the extent of the atrocities that have unfolded in 1,700 years of this Roman system. It's a history that is not indicative of just a bad period or a few decades, but centuries and centuries of embarrassing and unacceptable tragedies and behaviors.

I also believe most Catholics have no idea of how much has changed, been added to, or taken away from the original Gospel of the New Covenant and the simplicity of its message. Unfortunately, Catholic followers primarily hold on to just a handful of phrases that have trapped them in this system of control which threatens their eternal security and misrepresents the blood of Christ:

- There is only one true Church and the Roman Catholic Church is it.
- Obey, believe, and do everything the Church tells you to do or risk damnation.
- Peter was the first pope and there has been an honorable line of successors ever since.
- Peter got the keys to the kingdom.
- The Roman Catholic Church acknowledges the magisterium (headed by the pope), Sacred Tradition, and the Scriptures as equal sources of authority.

- Believers have to maintain their salvation and endure until the end if they are going to make it into Heaven.
- Catholics need constant forgiveness, more righteousness, and continual justification. The Eucharist, confession to a priest, performing good works, and other sacraments are the vehicles to accomplish that.
- Purgatory will more than likely be a stopping place for most believers, who will need to be fully purified, sanctified, and holy before entering the pearly gates.

There are many more phrases that Catholics are taught to honor, but these are some primary ones that Catholic apologists and the Roman Church espouse and defend. However, there is so much more to the story than hanging a belief system on a handful of worn-out phrases that have been concocted by a secular magisterium and monarch popes. The belief system promulgated by the Roman Catholic Church doesn't match what the early apostles or the early church fathers believed. The proof is available for anyone to research.

One of the more difficult parts of writing this book has been being limited to sharing only a fraction of the documented facts that show how out of sync this institution is with the behaviors and actions of Christ and the early apostles. When I was researching the murderous campaigns committed by the Roman Catholic Church, I could only select a few stories to share (there are hundreds). When I was exposing the popes for their corruption and evil, I could only share just a portion of their history. When I was recounting the global pandemic of pedophile priests, I was not able to cover the thousands of individual stories of shattered lives, and children who were never able to live a normal life after the horrendous rape and sexual abuse by these clerics. When I was describing the Vatican, primarily informed by the comprehensive book written by Martel, I only scoured a small portion of the dirty window in order to glance inside.

Catholic apologists like Scott Hahn, Trent Horn, Jimmy Akin, and many more have not been forthcoming with their omission of these horrendous truths about the Roman Catholic Church. If asked, they minimize the history and dismiss the persons and events as an exception to the rule. This is proven over and over again by simply researching what these profile leaders say about the past and watching the deferral, downplay, and minimization. It's simply not honest.

I sincerely believe that every single person who has ever left an affiliation where they followed Christ and were convinced to follow the path of the Roman Catholic Church did not do the research that is available to uncover its true past. On day one of researching sources for this book, I was sincerely open-minded and very curious about what I was going to find as I dove into the history of the Church. Would the Roman Catholic Church be acquitted from things that I have heard most of my Christian life?

Unfortunately, it has been to the contrary: the deeper I dove the darker the Roman system became, and everything in this book (which is such a very small fraction of the complete magnitude of the past) is historically documented and put together based on sound biblical exegesis. This dark past did not emerge from Protestant propaganda. Instead, it is simply the history of the Roman Catholic Church, admitted by every *honest* Catholic scholar and apologist. Even more important than the Church's dark side is that they changed the simple message of Christ and what was taught in the early catholic Church. However, the message of Christ is not changeable, it doesn't evolve.

Here is something to consider: The more tasks we are "required" to do to be in good standing with God (as promulgated through the Roman Catholic faith), the more we rely on human effort to maintain our salvation. This steals the glory away from God. However, when we come to the end of ourselves and realize we are barely part of the equation in God's story, all the focus goes on Him. It is pure pride to tell God we will assist Him in the reconciliation, redemption, justification, forgiveness, and salvation process.

God does not want us focused on keeping commandments, doing endless procedures, checking boxes, and trying to work our way to Heaven through a church program or system. There is no way to earn right standing with God, there is no way to please God with enough effort, or to impress God by keeping all the rules. We simply live the Christian life by yielding to His Spirit (who lives inside of us). We acknowledge that He did everything on our behalf to reconcile us back to Him, which paved the way to eternal life through faith and trust and belief in His finished work: a one-time sacrifice never to be repeated again.

There is wonderful news if you are Catholic and have followed along so far: There is no more pressure and stress about performing. If you skip Mass one week to go to the Sunday football game and bond with your son, it's not a mortal sin. You never have to walk into the dark booth of a priest ever again to confess and get your absolution and penance instructions—Christ has *already* absolved you once and forever at the cross, satisfying the requirements of penance. It's finished.

Instead of rushing home just in time to say the Rosary at 7:00 pm, you can relax and just chat with your Heavenly Father when you have time later that night. It will certainly not be easy to say goodbye to Mary and the Rosary, but the freedom you will experience later will be amazing! Catholics have to realize that Mary is not omnipresent, she's not omnipotent, she's not omniscient. Mary fulfilled her role as the mother of our Lord in His humanity, not the mother of God. She's never heard a single Hail Mary or prayer and would be appalled if she knew Christians were attempting to do so. The mumbling and repetition and rhetoric can stop with peace of mind and no guilt.

At first, it will be shocking to the system because Mary is supposed to be the "soft version" of God, but she's not. To even envision Mary telling God, "Calm down—I got this," is extremely irreverent. God is not flawed. The Heavenly Father, through Jesus Christ, extended all the grace toward humanity that He will ever extend. It was complete. It was successful. Mary disappears after Acts. Paul let her go, and subsequent early Church leaders let her go as well. She doesn't mediate. She plays no part in the salvation of man. The Scriptures prove this to be true. She primarily re-emerges hundreds of years after the resurrection as the Roman Catholic Church broke away from its roots and started generating The Catholic List. You can rest in peace at night knowing that you will never diminish the role of Jesus Christ ever again. His mission to reconcile, provide redemption, and solely mediate between you and the Father is unchangeable.

I have been a Christian for almost fifty years, and words cannot express the freedom of not being in bondage to a system, to live the Christian life with no threats of damnation from a spiritual monarchy. It is pure joy to wake up every day and simply live the Christian life, going through the journey in a way that exemplifies following Christ just as He requested. The Holy Spirit gives us the power to do this. It's amazing grace that is reckoned and enjoyed with no contingencies or righteous requirements to accomplish in order to obtain salvation, no infused salvation or IVs stuck in your arm, no guessing, no fear of a place to get cleaned up before entering Heaven. Christ did everything on your behalf. He was successful in that mission. It's the most incredible intervention that has ever happened.

Believers should understand that the Church is a movement, not a system of control. The Church has one High Priest, not a hierarchy with magic powers. Jesus offers a promise and a new way on this side of the cross, that says, "Jesus did it all." The Catechism is the never-ending, fatiguing rule book; the New Covenant is the message, "It is finished." It is past time to stop competing with the New Covenant.

Fear tactics will certainly be used to get you to never leave the institution. The Church will say that salvation is based on one continuing in their faith and enduring until the end (the Roman way), and promising never to condemn the Church's teachings, or you will be at extreme risk. These proclamations are not true. The Roman Catholic Church should not exert authority over anyone and has the wrong spiritual instructions. Spider webs are difficult to escape from, but embracing Christ with no religion and controlling entity will be life-changing.

The Roman Catholic Church is not an institution that has blossomed into an oak tree from an acorn, as apologists say in trying to explain the evolution of The Catholic List. Their history has been exposed, yet they have the audacity to pronounce damnations. Its followers should refuse to be threatened by contingencies and condemnations anymore. They changed the Gospel and presented a new Jesus that the early Church would not recognize—a Jesus who bows His head to a priest, dismissing that He created the universe. It's a true tragedy that the wholesomeness and purity of the early Church have disappeared from the Catholic landscape.

True beauty is not in breath-taking cathedrals, participating in the Eucharist, or in the Roman Catholic faith. True beauty is in knowing that Jesus accomplished everything on the cross on our behalf, setting us free from the bondage of rules, regulations, and regiments, permanently removing the penalty from sin, and giving us His righteousness and life by dwelling within us. That's true beauty.

Is the Roman Catholic Church the "one, holy, catholic, and apostolic Church of Jesus Christ"? This entire book has answered that question. I encourage Roman Catholics not to be in bondage to that single phrase that is espoused by the Church in justifying the actions and doctrinal developments of its liturgy. Following rituals and requirements and commands from a catechism does not give a person life. Life is in the true definition of Church: the message about the resurrection declaring that Jesus reconciled the world back to Himself, not counting sins against mankind. Are you willing to put your faith and trust in this message? If so, follow Christ, and enjoy the freedom of never having your standing with God ever compromised or threatened again.

I've been asked before in forums, "When did your Church start"? As a non-Catholic, I can confidently say that my Church started in AD 33 because I follow the apostolic teachings and the authentic teachings of the first century, catholic Church. A return to the early catholic Church means to be fully immersed in the assurance, knowledge, grace, and freedom of what was proclaimed from the onset. Committing to just a couple weeks of asking your Heavenly Father what the truth is (away from Church influence) will certainly give you the direction that is needed. If you truly want to be distinguished as Catholic, if you truly want to embrace the first, original, one true, holy, apostolic church of Jesus Christ, one must return to the original catholic (universal) Church that only taught the truth of the New Covenant of grace that God ushered in. Trying to obtain and maintain your own salvation is not only dangerous theology in opposition to the Scriptures, but it sets the believer up for failure. Jesus made it understandable for all of us. It's a gift. It's grace unmerited. Will you simply follow Him?

A Word to Protestant and Catholic Parents

I remember being in love for the first time when I was in my early twenties. I attended a super small private school, and we only had twenty-eight students in my class. Unfortunately for me, there were twenty guys and only eight girls! As a result, there were virtually no girls to date, and all the cute ones were linked with the football jocks of the day. It was only later, after attending a local college, that I met a girl that I was crazy excited about.

I had noticed attractive girls from a distance since I was twelve years old, but finally, I developed an infatuation on the highest level. At first, we went out on the boat occasionally with her two brothers, one of whom had been in my high school class. One day, her brothers were not able to go to the lake, so it was just me and her. It was thrilling. I guess she liked me a little too because we had our first kiss. I thought heaven had finally arrived on earth!

Everything was much more innocent back then, lacking the modern desensitization we have today through millions of images and depravity everywhere we look. I still can envision riding in the car that day on the way to take her back home, and we were holding hands. I looked down near the gear shift and saw my hand embraced in hers, and I could not believe this was actually happening. As a young, naive Christian, sex was not even in the equation, but I sure do remember all the exciting making-out times, the hugs, and the dates to fun places. I was in love with every part of her.

About six months later I had my first heartbreak, as I was not the only guy going after this cute girl. I remember as that was happening, I had the feeling that I would do anything not to lose her. Real life had its own way of moving us on to the next stage, and that exciting segment of my life, at least for the moment, was coming to a close. It was devastating.

As either a Catholic Christian or a Protestant Christian, it is essential to always apply honesty to every single area of our lives. It is highly common for Catholics and Protestants to date one another, and as the relationship gets more serious, the spiritual direction of the future marriage becomes an issue of concern. Because of the extreme, legalistic, inflexibility of the Roman

Catholic Church, most of the time the Protestant guy or girl—because of pressure from the other side—caves in and "converts" to Catholicism.

I can't tell you how many times over the years I have heard similar comments from Catholic parents stating, "Hey, did you hear? Bill is going to become a Catholic." I always chuckle inside, because Bill has zero desire to convert and become Catholic; Bill wants your daughter. Bill is forced to fake it and will pretend to check all the boxes and jump through all the hurdles because he has no choice. I've seen this over and over again. Bill is forced to become an actor. How do we know this is true? Just in the mere statistics that state for every Protestant that leaves their Church to become Catholic, seven Catholics leave to become Protestant. This antiquated canon law of Catholics having to marry Catholics puts undue pressure on a Catholic son or daughter.

This pressure from family, which really becomes an unspoken ultimatum, is extremely dishonest, unethical, and borders on coercion from parents who engage in these practices. Bill has a Protestant background. All his family is Protestant, he does not want to switch except in the rarest of cases. But what choice does he have? He's in love. He will do anything not to lose the girl. Of course he is willing to "superficially" convert.

This same principle applies to Protestant parents who apply the same pressure on their children's potential spouse to come over to their side, although this is the exception, not the rule. Regardless of your opinions of the other side, this conversation should happen with teenagers well before their dating encounters take place.

As written throughout the pages of this book, nobody should be "converting" to anything but a relationship with Christ. Whenever I hear someone say they are "converting" to this religion now, it sounds like they are joining a cult. It's silly and meaningless. Catholic and Protestant labels should be a distant memory for all born-again Christians.

The acceptance of the New Covenant and its truths unfolded in these chapters eliminates the problem of mixed marriages. When Christians finally come to the reality of the arrangement we have with God on this side of the cross, we should all be on the same page spiritually. We follow Jesus free of rules, regiments, and requirements from a controlling and threatening establishment.

Are parents willing to sell their souls to a religious institution, as opposed to doing what is in the best interest of their children? I would certainly hope not; but if so, not only is that unwise but is in direct opposition to the will of God and the message of the New Testament. Conflicts between Catholics and Protestants evaporate when the truths of the New Covenant are realized. My encouragement to parents and all young adults is to embrace the New Covenant and leave required religions in the wind. It will not take long for these pious, archaic obligations to blow away forever, eliminating the endless stress of differing spiritual backgrounds.

The Power of the Scriptures

If you were to take all the words in this book, none would be more important than the life-changing message in the infallible, inherent, Word of God. Many Catholics that leave the Church do so in the discovery that they can exchange religious regiments and a works-based salvation for a relationship with Christ through simple faith. They come to the realization that grace doesn't flow through a sacramental system or through Mary or a priest or dead saints, but only through Christ. They turn from placing their trust in an institution to placing it in the Savior. The Scriptures that were shared throughout the pages of this book tell the story and will set you free. Pause after each one and really think about the meaning. The Holy Spirit will reveal the truth.

Forgiveness

"I write to you dear children, because your sins have been forgiven on account of His (Jesus) name" (1 John 2:12).

"God was reconciling the world to Himself in Christ, not counting men's sins against them" (2 Corinthians 5:19).

"God made Him who had no sin to be sin for us, so that in Him, we might become the righteousness of God" (2 Corinthians 5:21).

"In Him we have redemption through His blood, the forgiveness of sins, in accordance with the riches of God's grace that he lavished on us with all wisdom and understanding" (Ephesians 1:7).

"When you were dead in your sins and in your sinful nature, God made you alive with Christ. He forgave us all our sins, having cancelled the written code with its regulations, that was against us and that stood opposed to us; He took it away, nailing it to the cross" (Colossians 2:13-14).

"But if anyone does not have them, he is near-sighted and blind, and has forgotten that he has been cleansed from past sins" (2 Peter 1: 9).

"Look the lamb of God, who takes away the sin of the world" (John 1:29).

"And where these have been forgiven, there is no longer any sacrifice for sin" (Hebrews 10:18).

"All the prophets testify about Him that everyone who believes in Him, receives forgiveness of sins through His name" (Acts 10:43).

"But you know that he appeared so that He might take away our sins" (1 John 3:5).

"Forgive others as the Lord forgave you" (Colossians 3:13).

"Be kind and compassionate to one another, forgiving each other, just as "in Christ" God forgave you" (Ephesians 4:32).

"So then as through one transgression there resulted condemnation to all men, even so through one act of righteousness there resulted justification of life to all men. For as through the one man's disobedience the many were made sinners, even so through the obedience of the One the many will be made righteous" (Romans 5: 18-19).

"And if Christ has not been raised, your faith is futile; you are still in your sins" (1 Corinthians 15:17).

"For He has rescued us from the dominion of darkness and brought us into the kingdom of the Son he loves, in whom we have redemption, the forgiveness of sins" (Colossians 1:13-14).

"After He had provided purification for sins, He sat down at the right hand of the majesty of heaven" (Hebrews 1:3).

"Therefore, if anyone is in Christ, he is a new creation; the old has gone, the new has come! All this is from God, who reconciled us to himself through Christ" (2 Corinthians 5:17-18).

"Christ is the end of the Law so that there may be righteousness for everyone who believes" (Romans 10:4).

"Day after day every priest stands and performs his religious duties; again and again he offers the same sacrifices, which can never take away sins. But when Jesus had offered for all time one sacrifice for sins, he sat down at the right hand of God...because by one sacrifice he has made perfect forever those who are the holy ones (Christians)" (Hebrews 10: 11-14).

"Their sins and lawless acts I will remember no more" (Hebrews 10:17).

"And where these have been forgiven, there is no longer any sacrifice for sin" (Hebrews 10:18).

"... not having a righteousness of my own that comes from the law, but that which is through faith in Christ- the righteousness that comes from God and is by faith" (Philippians 3:9).

"Not only is this so, but we also rejoice in God through our Lord Jesus Christ, through whom we have now received reconciliation" (Romans 5:11).

"In Him we have redemption through his blood, the forgiveness of sins, in accordance with the riches of God's grace that he lavished on us with all wisdom and understanding" (Ephesians 1:7).

"Later, knowing that all was now completed, and so that the Scripture would be fulfilled...When he had received the drink, Jesus said, 'It is finished'" (John 19: 28-30).

"In fact, the law requires that nearly everything be cleansed with blood, and <u>without the shedding of blood there is no for-giveness</u>" (Hebrews 9:22).

"Unlike the other high priests, He (Christ) does not need to offer sacrifices day after day, first for his own sins, and then for the sins of the people. He sacrificed for their sins <u>once</u> and for all when he offered himself" (Hebrews 7:27).

Saved By Grace

"But because of His great love for us, God, who is rich in mercy, made us alive with Christ even when we were dead in transgressions- it is by grace you have been saved. And God raised us up with Christ and seated us with him in the heavenly realms in Christ Jesus" (Ephesians 2:4-6).

"Not only is this so, but we also rejoice in God through our Lord Jesus Christ, through whom we have now received reconcil-iation" (Romans 5: 11).

"For it is by grace you have been saved, through faith- and this not from yourselves, it is the gift of God- not by works, so that no one can boast" (Ephesians 2:8).

"And if by grace, then it is no longer by works; if it were, grace would no longer be grace" (Romans 11:6).

"But to the one who does not work, but believes in Him who justifies the ungodly, his <u>faith is reckoned as righteousness</u>" (Romans 4:5).

"There remains, then, a Sabbath-rest for the people of God; for anyone who enters God's rest also rests from his own work, just as God did from his. Let us, therefore, make every effort to enter that rest" (Hebrews 4: 9-11).

"For if, by the trespass of the one man, death reigned through that one man, how much more will those who receive God's abundant provision of grace and of the gift of righteousness reign in life through the one man, Jesus Christ" (Romans 5:17).

"Everyone who calls on the name of the Lord will be saved" (Romans 10:13).

"For if, when we were God's enemies (as non-believers), we were reconciled to him through the death of his Son, how much more, having been reconciled, shall we be saved through his life" (Romans 5:10)!

"What then shall we say? That the Gentiles who did not pursue righteousness, have obtained it, a righteousness that is by faith; but Israel, who pursued a law of righteousness, has not attained it. Why not? Because they pursued it not by faith but as if it were by works. They stumbled over the 'stumbling stone'" (Romans 9:30-32).

"I am not ashamed of the gospel, because it is the power of God for the salvation of everyone who believes" (Romans 1:16).

"For the wages (penalty) of sin is death, but the gift of God is eternal life in Christ Jesus our Lord" (Romans 6:23).

"But now a righteousness from God, apart from the law, has been known, to which the Law and Prophets testify. This righteousness from God comes through faith in Jesus Christ to all who believe" (Romans 3:21-22).

"For all have sinned and fall short of the glory of God, and are justified freely by his grace through the redemption that came by Christ Jesus" (Romans 3:23-24).

"Whoever believes in Him is not condemned, but whoever does not believe stands condemned already because he has not believed in the name of God's one and only Son" (John 3:18).

"... if anyone acknowledges that Jesus is the Son of God, God lives in him and he is in God" (1 John 4:15)

"God lives in us and his love is made complete in us" (1 John 4:12).

"This life is in the Son. He who has the Son has life, he who does not have the Son of God does not have life" (1 John 5: 11-12).

"I tell you the truth, whoever hears my words and believes him who sent me has eternal life and will not be condemned; he has crossed over from death to life" (John 5:24).

"You diligently study the Scriptures because you think by them you possess eternal life. These are the Scriptures that testify about me, yet you refuse to come to me to have life" (John 5:39).

"I tell you the truth, he who believes has everlasting life" (John 6:47).

"Everyone who believes that Jesus is the Christ is born of God" (1 John 5:1).

"Then they asked him, "What must we do to do the works God requires? Jesus answered, 'The work of God is this: to believe in the one he has sent'" (John 6:28-29).

"Then Jesus declared, "I am the bread of life. He who comes to me (not he who eats me) will never go hungry, and he who believes in me (not he who drinks me) will never be thirsty" (John 6:35).

"The Spirit gives life; the flesh counts for nothing. The words I have spoken to you are spirit and they are life. Yet there are some of you who (still) do not believe" (John 6:63-64).

"For my Father's will is that everyone who looks to the Son and believes in him shall have eternal life, and I will raise him up at the last day" (John 6:40).

"Whoever believes in the Son has eternal life, but whoever rejects the Son will not see life" (John 3:36).

"I write these things to you who believe in the name of the Son of God so that you may know that you have eternal life" (1 John 5:13).

"Yet to all who received Him, to those who believed in his name, he gave the right to become children of God" (John 1:12).

"For God so loved the world that He gave His one and only son that whosoever shall believe in him shall not perish, but have eternal life" (John 3:16).

"And you also were included in Christ when you heard the word of truth, the gospel of your salvation. Having believed, you were marked with a seal, the promised Holy Spirit, who is a deposit guaranteeing our inheritance" (Ephesians 1:13).

"... 'Sirs, what must I do to be saved?' (Paul and Silas) replied, 'Believe in the Lord Jesus, and you will be saved'" (Acts 16:30-31).

"For you have been born again, not of perishable seed, but of imperishable, through the living and enduring word for God" (1 Peter 1:23).

"But when the kindness and love of God our Savior appeared, he saved us, not because of righteous things we had done, but because of his mercy. He saved us through the washing and rebirth and renewal by the Holy Spirit, whom he poured out on us generously through Jesus Christ our Savior, so that having been justified by his grace, we might become heirs having the hope of eternal life" (Titus 3:4-7).

"You foolish Galatians! Who has bewitched you? Before your very eyes Jesus Christ was clearly portrayed as crucified. I would like to learn just one thing from you: Did you receive the Spirit by observing the law, or by believing what you heard? Are you so foolish? After beginning with the Spirit, are you trying to attain your goal by human effort? Have you suffered so much for nothing" (Galatians 3:1-4)?

"I do not set aside the grace of God, for if righteousness could be gained through the law, Christ died for nothing" (Galatians 2:21)!

"As Jesus went on from there, he saw a man named Matthew sitting at the tax collector's booth. Jesus said, 'follow me', he told him, and Matthew got up and followed him" (Matthew 9:9).

"Peter got up and addressed them...'Brothers, you know that some time ago God made a choice among you that the Gentiles might hear from my lips the message of the gospel and believe. God, who knows the heart, showed that he accepted them by giving the Holy Spirit to them, just as he did to us. He made no distinction between us and them, for he purified their hearts by faith. Now then, why do you try to test God by putting on the necks of the disciples a yoke that neither we nor our fathers have been able to bear? No! We believe it is through the grace of our Lord Jesus that we are saved, just as they are" (Acts 15:7-11).

James spoke: "It is my judgment, therefore, that we should not make it difficult for the Gentiles who are turning to God" (Acts 15:19).

"'The time has come', he said. 'The kingdom of God is near. Repent and believe the good news'" (Mark 1:15)!

"But these are written that you may believe that Jesus is the Christ, the Son of God, and that by believing you may have life in his name" (John 20:31).

"Salvation is found in no one else, for there is no other name under heaven given to men by which we must be saved" (Acts 4:12).

Jesus said, "I told you that you would die in your sins; if you do not believe that I am the one I claim to be" (John 8:24).

"For in Christ all the fullness of the Deity lives in bodily form, and you have been given fullness in Christ" (Colossians 2:9).

"... the word is near you; it is in your mouth and in your heart, that is, the word of faith we are proclaiming: That if you confess with your mouth, Jesus is Lord, and believe in your heart that God raised him from the dead, you will be saved. For it is with your heart that you believe and are justified, and it is with your mouth that you confess and are saved" (Romans 10:8-10).

"But as many as has received Him, to them, he gave the right to become children of God even to those who believe on his name" (1 John 1:12).

"Therefore, He is able to save completely those who come to God through Him, because he always lives to intercede for them" (Hebrews 7:25).

New Covenant

"He has made us competent as ministers of a New Covenant-not of the letter but of the Spirit; for the letter kills; but the Spirit gives life" (2 Corinthians 3:6).

"All who rely on observing the law (10 Commandments, etc.) are under a curse, for it is written: 'cursed is everyone who does not continue to do everything written in the book of law" (Galatians 3:10).

"For the law was given through Moses; grace and truth came through Jesus Christ" (John 1:17).

"Do not think that I have come to abolish the Law or the Prophets; I have not come to abolish them, but to fulfill them" (Matthew 5:17).

"But now, by dying to what once bound us (rules and regulations), we have been released from the law so that we serve in the new way of the Spirit, and not in the old way of the written code (10 Commandments, laws, etc.)" (Romans 7:6).

"When Christ came as high priest of the good things that are already here, he went through the greater and more perfect tabernacle that is not man-made...He did not enter by means of the blood of goats and calves; but he entered the Most Holy place once and for all by His own blood, having obtained eternal redemption" (Hebrews 9: 11-12).

"For this reason Christ is the mediator of a new covenant, that those who are called may receive the promise eternal inheritance- now that he has died as a ransom to set them free from the sins committed under the first covenant (old covenant). In the case of a will, it is necessary to prove the death of the one who made it, because a will is in force only when somebody has died; it never takes place while the one who made it is living" (Hebrews 9:15-17).

"I found that the very commandment(s) that was intended to bring life actually brought forth death. For sin, seizing the opportunity afforded by the commandment, deceived me, and through the commandment(s) put me to death" (Romans 7: 10).

"Therefore no one will be declared righteous in his sight by observing the law; rather, through the law we become conscious of sin" (Romans 3:20).

"What, then, was the purpose of the law? It was added because of transgression until the Seed (Jesus) to whom the promise referred had come" (Galatians 3:19).

"For if a law had been given that could impart life, then righteousness would certainly have come by the law" (Galatians 3:21).

"Before this faith came (Jesus Christ) we were held prisoners by the law, locked up until faith should be revealed. So the law was put in charge to lead us to Christ that we might be justified (made right in God's eyes) by faith. Now that Faith (Jesus) has come, we are no longer under the supervision of the law (10 Commandments, etc.)" (Galatians 3:23-25).

"But the ministry Jesus has received is as superior to theirs as the covenant of which he is mediator is superior to the old one, and it is founded on better promises" (Hebrews 8:6).

"For if there had been nothing wrong with that first covenant, no place would have been sought for another" (Hebrews 8:7).

"The sting of death is sin, and the power of sin is the law. But thanks be to God! He gives us victory through our Lord Jesus Christ" (1 Corinthians 15:56).

"Such confidence as this is ours through Christ before God. Not that we are competent in ourselves to claim anything for ourselves, but our competence comes from God. He has made us competent as ministers of a new covenant- not of the letter but of the Spirit; for the letter kills, but the Spirit gives life" (2 Corinthians 3: 4-6).

"Now if the ministry that brought death, which was engraved in letters on stone, came with glory, so that the Israelites could not look steadily at the face of Moses because of its glory, fading though it was, will not the ministry of the Spirit be even more glorious? If the ministry that condemns men is glorious, how much more glorious is the ministry that brings righteousness" (2 Corinthians 3: 7-9).

"We proclaim Him, admonishing and teaching everyone with all wisdom, so that we may present everyone perfect in Christ" (Colossians 1:28).

"See to it that no one takes you captive through hollow and deceptive philosophy, which depends on human traditions and the basic principles of this world rather than on Christ" (Colossians 2:8).

"Since you died with Christ to the basic principles of this world, why, as though you still belonged to it, do you submit to its rules: Do not handle! Do not taste! Do not touch!"? These are all destined to perish with use, because they are based on human commands and teachings. Such regulations indeed have an appearance of wisdom, with their self-imposed worship, their false humility and their harsh treatment of the body, but they lack any value in restraining sensual indulgence" (Colossians 2: 20-23).

"Having cancelled the written code (10 Commandments), with its regulations, that was against us and that stood opposed to us, He took it away, nailing it to the cross" (Colossians 2:14).

"I want you to know, brothers, that the gospel I preached is not something that man made up. I did not receive it from any man, nor was I taught it; rather, I received it by revelation from Jesus Christ" (Galatians 1: 11).

"But when the time had fully come, God sent his son, born of a woman, born under law, to redeem those under the law, that we might receive the full rights of sons" (Galatians 4:4-5).

"It is for freedom that Christ has set us free. Stand firm, then, and do not let yourselves be burdened again by a yoke of slavery" (Galatians 5:1).

"But if you are led by the spirit, you are not under the law (10 Commandments, etc.)" (Galatians 5:18).

"Clearly no one is justified before God by the law, because, 'The righteous will live by faith'. The law is not based on faith; on the contrary, 'the man who does these things will live by them.' Christ redeemed us from the curse of the law by becoming a curse for us" (Galatians 3: 11-13).

"Know that a man is not justified by observing the law, but by faith in Jesus Christ. So we, too, have put our faith in Christ Jesus that we may be justified by faith in Christ and not by observing the law, because by observing the law no one will be justified" (Galatians 2:16).

"Through the law I died to the law so that I might live for God" (Galatians 2:19).

"You foolish Galatians! Who has bewitched you? Before your very eyes Jesus Christ was clearly portrayed as crucified. I would like to learn just one thing from you: Did you receive the Spirit by observing the law, or by believing what you heard? Are you so foolish? After beginning with the Spirit, are you now trying to attain your goal by human effort? Have you suffered so much for nothing- if it really was for nothing? Does God give you a Spirit and work miracles among you because you observe the law, or because you believe what you heard" (Galatians 3: 1-4)?

"For the grace of God that brings salvation has appeared to all men. It teaches us to say "No" to ungodliness and worldly passions, and to live self-controlled, upright and godly lives in this present age, while we wait for the blessed hope- the glorious appearing of our great God and Savior, Jesus Christ, who gave himself to redeem us" (Titus 2: 11-14).

"For when there is a change of the priesthood, there must also be a change of the law" (Hebrews 7:12).

"You show that you are a letter from Christ, the result of our ministry, written not with ink but with the Spirit of the living God, not on tablets of stone, but on tablets of human hearts" (Hebrews 3:3).

"The former regulation (10 Commandments, law) is set aside because it was weak and useless for the law made nothing perfect, and a better hope is introduced, by which we draw near to God (Jesus Christ)" (Hebrews 7:18).

"Because of this oath (promise), Jesus has become the guarantee of a better covenant" (Hebrews 7:22).

"But God did find fault with the people (under the old covenant) and said, ' The time is coming, declares the Lord, when I will make a new covenant with the house of Israel and with the house of Judah. It will not be like the covenant I made with their forefathers when I took them by the hand to lead them out of Egypt, because they did not remain faithful to my covenant, and I turned away from them, declares the Lord.' This is now the covenant I will make with the house of Israel after that time. I will put my laws in their minds and write them on their hearts" (Hebrews 8: 8-10).

"No longer will a man teach his neighbor, or a man his brother, saying, 'know the Lord', because they will all know me, from the least of them to the greatest. For I will forgive their wickedness and will remember their sins no more" (Hebrews 8: 11-12).

"By calling this covenant "new", he has made the first one obsolete; and what is obsolete and aging will soon disappear" (Hebrews 8:13).

"But only the high priest entered the inner room, and that only once a year, and never without blood, which he offered for himself and for the sins the people had committed in ignorance. The Holy Spirit was showing by this that the way into the Most Holy Place had not yet been disclosed as long as the first tabernacle was still standing. This is an illustration for the present time, indicating that the gifts and sacrifices being offered were not able to clear the conscience of the worshiper. They are only a

matter of food and drink and various ceremonial washings- external regulations applying only until the time of the new covenant"
(Hebrews 9: 7-10).

"For Christ did not enter a man-made sanctuary that was only
a copy of the true one; he entered heaven itself, now to appear
for us in God's presence. Nor did he enter heaven to offer himself
again and again, the way the high priests enters the Most Holy
Place every year with blood that is not his own. Then Christ
would have had to suffer many times since the creation of the
world. But now he has appeared once and for all at the end of the
ages to do away with sin by the sacrifice of himself...so Christ was
sacrificed once to take away the sins of many people; and he will
appear a second time, not to bear sin, but to bring salvation to
those who believe" (Hebrews 9:24-28).

"The law (10 Commandments, etc.) is only a shadow of the
good things that are coming- not the realities themselves. For this
reason the law (rules and regulations) can never, by the same sacrifice repeated endlessly year after year, make perfect those who
draw near to worship. If it could, would they not have stopped
being offered? For the worshippers would have been cleansed
once and for all, and would no longer have felt guilty for their
sins. But those sacrifices are an annual reminder of sins, because
it is impossible for the blood of bull and goats to take away sin"
(Hebrews 10: 1-4).

"First he said, 'sacrifices and offerings, burnt offerings and sin
offerings you did not desire, nor were you pleased with them'
(although the law required them to be made). Then he said, 'Here
am I, I have come to do your will. He sets aside the first (covenant) to establish the second (covenant). And by that will we
have been made holy through the sacrifice of the body of Jesus
Christ once and for all" (Hebrews 10: 8-10).

"In the same way, after the supper he took the cup, saying, 'this cup is the <u>New Covenant</u> in my <u>blood</u>, which is poured out for you" (Luke 22:20).

"For when we were controlled by the sinful nature, the sinful passions <u>aroused by the law were at work in our bodies</u>, so that we bore fruit for death" (Romans 7:5).

"For what the law was powerless to do in that it was weakened by the sinful nature, God did by sending his own son in the likeness of sinful man to be a sin offering. And so he condemned sin in sinful man, in order that the righteous requirements of the law might be fully met in us, who do not live according to the sinful nature but according to the Spirit" (Romans 8: 3-4).

"For sin shall not be your master, because you are not under law, but under grace. What then? Shall we sin because we are not under law but under grace? By no means" (Romans 6: 14-15)!

"You have been set free from sin and have become slaves to righteousness" (Romans 6: 18).

Security in Christ

"Therefore, there is now no condemnation for those who are in Christ Jesus, because through Christ Jesus the law of the Spirit of life set me free from the law of sin and death" (Romans 8:1).

"For you died, and your life is now hidden with Christ in God. When Christ, who is your life, appears, then you also will appear with Him in glory" (Colossians 3:2-4).

"My sheep listen to my voice; I know them, and they follow me. I give them eternal life; and they shall never perish; no one can snatch them out of my hand" (John 10:28).

"And you also were included in Christ when you heard the word of truth, the gospel of your salvation. Having believed, you were marked in him with a seal, the promised Holy Spirit, who is a deposit guaranteeing our inheritance" (Ephesians 1:13-14).

"You have not received a spirit of slavery again, but you have received a spirit of adoption as sons by which we cry out, 'Abba Father!'. The spirit Himself bears witness with our spirit that we are children of God" (Romans 8:15-16).

"Now it is God who makes both us and you stand firm in Christ. He anointed us, set His seal of ownership on us, and put His Spirit in our hearts as a deposit guaranteeing what is to come" (2 Corinthians 1:21-22).

"For I am convinced that neither death, nor life, neither angels, nor demons, neither height nor depth, not anything else in creation, will be able to separate us (believers) from the love of God that is in Christ Jesus our Lord" (Romans 8:38).

God Lives Inside Believers and Teaches Us

"I have been crucified with Christ, and I no longer live, but Christ lives inside of me" (Galatians 2:20).

"...I will put my laws in their minds and write them on their hearts. I will be their God, and they will be my people. No longer will a man teach his neighbor, or a man his brother, saying, 'Know the Lord' because they will all know me, from the least of them to the greatest" (Hebrews 8:10-11).

"For the word of God is living and active. Sharper than any double-edge sword, it penetrates even to the dividing soul and spirit, joints and marrow; it judges the thoughts and attitudes of the heart" (Hebrews 4:12).

"And I will ask the Father, and he will give you another Counselor to be with you forever- the Spirit of truth. The world cannot accept him, because it neither sees him nor knows him. But you know him (Holy Spirit), for he lives with you and will be in you" (John 14: 16-17).

"But the Counselor, the Holy Spirit, whom the father will send in my name, will teach you all things and will remind you of everything I have said to you" (John 14:26).

"You show that you are from Christ, the result of our minis-try, written not with ink but with the Spirit of the living God, not on tablets of stone but on tablets of human hearts" (2 Corinthians 3:3).

"For who has known the mind of the Lord that he may instruct him? But we have the mind of Christ" (I Corinthians 2:16).

"... for we are the temple of the living God" (2 Corinthians 6:16).

"For prophecy never had its origin in the will of man, but men spoke from God as they were carried along by the Holy Spirit" (2 Peter 1:21).

"... and how from infancy you have known the holy Scriptures, which are able to make you wise for salvation through faith in Christ Jesus. All Scripture is God-breathed and is useful for teach-ing, rebuking, correcting, and training in righteousness, so that the man of God may be thoroughly equipped" (2 Timothy 3:15-17).

"For there is one God and one mediator between God and men, the man Christ Jesus" (1 Timothy 2:5).

Sources

1517.org, "The Christian History Almanac", January 27, 2021.

ABC News, "The Hidden Children of the Catholic Church | Foreign Correspondent", YouTube.com.

Akin, Jimmy, "Scripture Commentary Recommendation", jimmyakin.com.

Alphahistory.com, "1501: Pope Alexander VI Likes to Watch".

Armellini, Alvise, "Argentine child abuse victims urge Pope Francis to hear their grievances", *Reuters*, March 9, 2023.

Associated Press, "Landmark Pennsylvania grand jury report finds more than 300 predator priests sexually abused children", as quoted on *Yahoo! News*, August 14, 2018.

Barnett, John, Calvary Bible Church, "Q&A What is the Catholic Church? Where did the early Church go? What Church did Jesus start?", YouTube.com.

Bavinck, Herman, *Reformed Dogmatics: Holy Spirit, Church and New Creation, Volume 4*, trans. John Vriend, ed., John Bolt, Baker Academic, 2008.

Beggarsallreformation.blogspot.com, "What was Augustine 'Retracting' on Peter, on the Rock, and Matthew 16?".

Bertuzzi, Cameron, "Do Bad Popes Count Against the Truth of Catholicism?", Capturing Christianity, YouTube.com, 2020.

Bloggerpriest.com, "Did the Catholic Church prohibit Bible reading", January, 2011.

Britannica.com, "Paul III".

Britannica.com, "Paul IV".

CAnswersTV, "Vatican System: List of Murdered Popes, 75 Popes Approved Torture, Murder, Burning at the Stake", YouTube.com, 2015.

Catholic.com, "Did the church begin in AD 30 or 33?"

Catholicplanet.org, "First Vatican Council, Chapter III, 1869, 1870".

CBS Sunday Morning, "Gay Priests: Breaking the Silence", YouTube.com.

Chamberlin, Russell, *The Bad Popes*, Sutton Publishing, 1969 and 2023.

Chappell, Paul, "Massacred for the Faith: A Faith Worth Dying For" Ministry127.com, January 23, 2012.

Christi, Servus, "The Catholic Church: Masterpiece of Deception", YouTube.com, 2020.

Code of Canon Law, Vatican.va.

Complicitclergy.com, "Pope Francis appoints Pro-Abortion, Pro-LGBT friend as founding member of New Vatican Institute".

Conroy, Helen, *Forgotten Women: In Convents*, Kessinger Publishing, 2010.

Corbet, Sylvie, "French report: 330,000 children victims of church sex abuse", *AP News*, October 5, 2021.

Corpuschristiphx.org, "The Three Sources of Church Authority", 2020.

Cozzens, Donald B., *The Changing Face of the Priesthood*, The Liturgical Press, Minnesota, 2000.

Cyril of Alexandria, *Commentary on John, A Library of Fathers of the Holy Catholic Church, Vol. 48*, Trans. Thomas Randell, London: Walter Smith, 1885, vol. 2, book XII, chapter XIX.

Demony, Catarina and Miguel Pereira, "Child abuse found in Portugal Catholic Church is 'tip of iceberg', commission says", *Reuters*, February 13, 2023."

Dias, Elizabeth, "'It Is Not a Closet. It Is a Cage.' Gay Catholic Priests Speak Out", *The New York Times*, February 17, 2019.

Donuhue, William, "Catholic Church's issue homosexuality, not pedophilia", *The Washington Post*, archived from the original on July 23, 2010.

Duffy, Eamon, *Saints and Sinners: A History of the Popes*, 2nd Edition, Yale University Press, 2002.

Edward, Raymond Brown, John P. Meier, *Antioch and Rome: New Testament Cradles of Catholic Christianity*, Paulist Press, 1983.

Engel, Randy, *The Rite of Sodomy: Homosexuality and the Roman Catholic Church*, New Engel Publishing, 2006.

Fargodiocese.net, "Why are non-Catholics but baptized Christians not to receive the Eucharist?"

Farley, Andrew, "Book of Hebrews", Biblecommentary.org,

Fradd, Matt, "Gavin Ortlund vs. Trent Horn: Is Sola Scriptura true?", YouTube.com, 2023.

Fradd, Matt, "I stopped defending Pope Francis w/ Joe Heschmeyer", YouTube.com, 2020.

Fradd, Matt, "The Worst Pope Ever! w/ Jimmy Akin", YouTube.com, 2024.

Fradd, Matt, "Why Bad Popes Don't Disprove the Papacy w/ Scott Hahn and Cameron Bertuzzi", YouTube.com, 2022.

Gendron, Mike, "Ex-Catholic Exposes the Twisted Teachings of the Catholic Church", YouTube.com, 2023.

Gendron, Mike, "Proclaiming the Gospel Ministry", email publication.

Gendron, Mike, various sermons.

George, Bob, "The New Covenant", YouTube.com.

George, Bob, *A Scriptural Journey to Discover the Grace of God*, The Classic Christianity Conference, Texas, 1999.

George, Bob, *Classic Christianity*, Harvest House Publishers, 1989.

George, Bob, *Faith that Pleases God*, Harvest House Publishers, 2001.

Gibbons, James, *The Faith of Our Fathers*, Tan Books, 1980.

Goodstein, Laurie, "Catholic order Jolted by Reports That Its founder Led a Double Life", *The New York Times*, February 4, 2009.

Gosepl Simplicity, "Baptist-Catholic Dialogue on the Eucharist (w/ Dr. Gavin Ortlund and Dr. Brett Salked)", YouTube.com, 2022.

Gracegems.org, "Wicked Popes!"

Green, Toby, *Inquisition: The Reign of Fear*, St. Martin's Press, 2007.

Hahn, Scott, *The Lamb's Supper: The Mass as Heaven on Earth*, Random House LLC, 2002.

Herman, Luc and Paul Moreira, "The Church: A Code of Silence", Java Films, YouTube.com.

Hernández, María, "In Chile, justice eludes victims of Catholic clergy sex abuse years after the crisis exploded", *AP News*, September 19, 2023.

Historyskills.com, "The worst popes in the history of the Catholic Church".

Homework.study.com, "Crusades and Inquisitions".

Horn, Trent, "Debate: Is the Doctrine of Purgatory true? (Horn vs. White)", YouTube.com, 2024.

Horn, Trent, "Protestantism is winning (and the Lessons for Catholics)", Catholic.com, April 14, 2025.

Horn, Trent, "Why 70% of Catholics Deny Christ's Real Presence in the Eucharist", Catholic.com, August 15, 2019.

Horn, Trent, *The Case for Catholicism*, Ignatius Press, 2017.

Horn, Trent, *Why We're Catholic*, Catholic Answers, Inc., 2017.

Huang, Justin, "Corrupt Popes", The Justice Measure, October 18, 2015.

Intelligence Squared, "A List of Apologies from the Catholic Church – Christopher Hitchens", YouTube.com, 2022.

Johnson, Kathy, "(Catholic) Scott Hahn vs. (Protestant) Bowman Salvation debate #1 of 3", YouTube.com.

Jstor.org, "Crusades".

Kann, Drew, "Eight of the worst popes in church history", CNN.com, April 15, 2018.

Keating, Karl, *What Catholics Really Believe: Setting the Record Straight*, Servant Publications,1992.

Kelly, J.N.D., *Early Christian Doctrines: Revised Edition*, Harper-One, 1978.

Kirchgaessner, Stephanie, "Pope Francis' words on clergy sex abuse ring hollow for some survivors", *The Guardian*, September 27, 2015.

Lauer, Claudia, Associated Press, and Meghan Hoyer, "Almost 1700 priest and clergy accused of sex abuse are unsupervised", *NBC News*, October 4, 2019.

MacArthur, John, "The Scandal of the Priesthood", YouTube.com.

Mampieri, Martina, *Living under the Evil Pope*, Brill, 2019, introduction.

Martel, Frederic, *In The Closet of the Vatican: Power, Homosexuality, Hypocrisy*, Bloomsbury Publishing Plc, 2019.

McBrien, Richard P., *Catholicism: Catholicism: Completely revised and updated*, HarperOne, 1994.

McVey, Steve, "Forgiven … forever?", Grace Walk Ministries, Atlanta.

McVey, Steve, *Grace Rules*, Harvest House Publishers, 1998.

Meneolawgroup.com

Murphy, Cullen, *God's Jury*, Mariner Books, 2013.

Neyrey, Jerome, "St. Peter", ed. Richard P. McBrien, *The HarperCollins Encyclopedia of Catholicism*, HarperCollins Publishers, 1995.

Onepeterfive.com, "Pope Benedict IX was a 'devil from hell'".

Ortlund, Gavin, "A Baptist Case for Real Presence in the Eucharist", YouTube.com, 2023.

Ortlund, Gavin, "Intense Discussion on the Papacy (Cordial Catholic x Gospel Simplicity Crossover)", Gospel Simplicity, YouTube.com, 2021.

Ortlund, Gavin, "Pope Vigilius: A Challenge to Vatican I", April 23, 2023, YouTube.com.

Ortlund, Gavin, "Purgatory: A Protestant Perspective", YouTube.com, 2021.

Ortlund, Gavin, "Sola Scriptura Defended", YouTube.com, 2021.

Ortlund, Gavin, "Why I don't Accept the Papacy", YouTube.com, 2021.

Osborne, Kenan, *Reconciliation*, ed. Richard P. McBrien, *The HarperCollins Encyclopedia of Catholicism*, Harper-Collins Publishers, 1995.

Oxford Dictionary, "unblemished".

Pannenberg, Wolfhart, *Systematic Theology Volume 3*, trans. Geoffrey W. Bromiley, Wm. B. Eerdmans Publishing, 1998.

Pew Research Center, "Americans See Catholic Clergy Sex Abuse as an Ongoing Problem", June 11, 2019.".

Pope Leo XII, "Providentissimus Deus", 1893.

Popehistory.com, "Pope Julius III".

Premm, Matthias, *Dogmatic Theology for the Laity*, Tan Books & Publishers Inc., 1982.

Quijano, Elaine and Betty Chin, "Pope Leo XIV takes helm of Catholic Church amid a priest shortage in the U.S.", CBS News, May 16, 2025.

Rahner, Karl, *Theological Investigations*, Volume 10, Herder and Herder, 1973.

Ralph, Brenda Lewis, *A Dark History: The Popes: Vice, Murder, and Corruption in the Vatican*, Metro Books, 2011.

Ratzinger, Joseph, *Jesus of Nazareth*, Ignatius Press, 2011.

Researchgate.net

Riley, John, various sermons, Metro Bible Study, Atlanta.

Save the Children, "Eyes That Fail to See: The sexual abuse of children in Spain and failures in the system", September 2017, https://resourcecentre.savethechildren.net/pdf/eyes_that_fail_to_see_executivesummary.pdf.

Schaff, Philip and Henry Wace, ed., *A Select Library of the Nicene and Post-Nicene Fathers of the Christian Church*, Christian Literature Publishing Co., 1896-1900.

Schaff, Philip, *History of the Christian Church, Volume 5*, Hendrickson Publishers, 2011.

Schroeder, Rev. H.J., *The Canons and Decrees of the Council of Trent, Fourth Session, Decree Concerning the Canonical Scriptures*, O.P., Translator, Tan Books, 1978.

Shaw, Christine, *Julius II: The Warrior Pope*, Wiley-Blackwell; 1997, Editor's comments, Amazon.com.

Shelly, Bruce, *Church History in Plain Language, 5th Edition*, Zondervan, 2021.

Shoemake, Trent, "New Covenant in Hebrews", McDonough Christian Church, Georgia.

Sola Media, "Defending Sola Scriptura in the Church Fathers/Michael Horton Responds to Trent Horn", YouTube.com, 2025.

Southern Baptist Convention, Statement of Faith.

Spurgeon, Charles, *Faith's Checkbook*, July 23 entry, Whitaker House, 1993.

Stanley, Alessandra, "Pope asks forgiveness for errors of the church over 2000 years", *The New York Times*, March 13, 2000.

Stanley, Andy, "The Big Church", Part 1.

Stanley, Charles, *The Gift of Forgiveness*, Thomas Nelson Publishers, 1991.

Staples, Tim, *Nuts and Bolts*, Basilica Press, 2007.

Stravinskas, Peter M.J., *The Catholic Church and The Bible*, 2nd ed., Ignatius Press, 1996.

Studysmarter.co.uk

Svendsen, Eric, *Evangelical Answers*, Reformation Press, 1999.

Svendsen, Eric, *Upon this Slippery Rock*, Calvary Press, 2002.

The Apologetic Dog, "Roman Catholic Mass Debate/Dr. James White vs. Joe Heschmeyer", YouTube.com, 2025.

The Canons and Decrees of the Council of Trent, trans. H. J. Schroeder, Tan Books and Publishers, 1978.

The Catechism of the Catholic Church, DoubleDay, 1994.

Thecollector.com, "10 Terrible Catholic Popes".

Thestar.com, "Argentine justice's apartments used by prostitutes".

Thevaticantickets.com

Thompson, Keith, "The Errors of the Roman Catholic Church", YouTube.com, 2021.

Thomsett, Michael C., *The Inquisition: A History*, McFarland & Company, Inc., Publishers, 2010.

Tierney, Brian, *Origins of Papal Infallibility, 1150-1350*, Leiden: Brill, 2022.

Usccb.org

Vaticancitytours.it, "Paul IV".

Vaticancitytours.it, "Who were the worst Popes in history?"

Vitello, Paul, "For Catholics, a Door to Absolution Is Reopened", *The New York Times*, February 10, 2009.

VOA News, "Investigation: 400,000 May Have Suffered Sexual Abuse from Spain's Clergy, Lay People", October 28, 2023.

Walker, Williston, *A History of the Christian Church, Fourth Edition*, Scribner, 1985.

Web.stanford.edu, "Julius Excluded from Heaven by Erasmus," January 2014.

Westminster Confession of Faith.

White, James, "Oh That Those Who Follow Rome Would Know the Finished Work of Christ!", Alpha and Omega Ministries, aomin.org, September. 11, 2009 and other sermons.

Wikipedia.org, "Bernard Francis Law".

Wikipedia.org, "French Wars of Religion".

Wikipedia.org, "History of the Papacy".

Wikipedia.org, "John Geoghan".

Wikipedia.org, "John XXIII".

Wikipedia.org, "Julius III".

Wikipedia.org, "North American Man/Boy Love Association".

Wikipedia.org, "Papal Infallibility".

Wikipedia.org, "Paul IV".

Wikipedia.org, "Pius IX", "Edgardo Mortara".

Wikipedia.org, "Pope Sergius III".

Wikipedia.org, "Pope Urban VI".

Wikipedia.org, "Vatican".

Williams, Peter, *Catholic Principles for Interpreting Scripture*, Gregorian & Biblical Book Shop, 2001.

Wilson, Derek, *Out of the Storm: The Life and Legacy of Martin Luther*, Hutchisson, 2007.

Endnotes

Chapter 1 – The Pope: How Did It Go So Wrong?

1. Catholic.com, "Did the church begin in AD 30 or 33?"
2. Bruce Shelly, *Church History in Plain Language, 5th Edition*, Zondervan, 2021, page 169.
3. Ibid., 173.
4. Ibid., 151.
5. Bruce Shelly, *Church History in Plain Language,*129.
6. Eamon Duffy, *Saints and Sinners: A History of the Popes*, 2nd Edition, Yale University Press, 2002, page 13, 2.
7. Ibid., 21.
8. Ibid., 9-10.
9. Ibid., 42.
10. Jerome Neyrey, "St. Peter", ed. Richard P. McBrien, *The Harper Collins Encyclopedia of Catholicism*, HarperCollins Publishers, 1995, page 193.
11. Gavin Ortlund, "Pope Vigilius: A Challenge to Vatican I", April 23, 2023, YouTube.com.
12. Ibid., Vatican One, Pastor Aeternus 4
13. Gavin Ortlund, "Pope Vigilius: A Challenge to Vatican I".
14. Ibid.
15. Bruce Shelly, *Church History in Plain Language*, 266-267.
16. Brenda Ralph Lewis, *A Dark History: The Popes: Vice, Murder, and Corruption in the Vatican*, Metro Books, 2011, page 125.
17. En.wikipedia.org, "History of the Papacy".
18. Eamon Duffy, *Saints and Sinners*, 274.
19. Ibid., 118.
20. Ibid., 73.
21. Ibid.,110.
22. Catechism of the Catholic Church (CCC 882).
23. Eamon Duffy, *Saints and Sinners*, 20.
24. Ibid., 33.
25. Ibid., 37-38.
26. Ibid., 54-56.
27. Ibid., 57.
28. Ibid., 98.
29. Ibid., 90.
30. Brenda Ralph Lewis, *A Dark History: The Popes*, 15-17.
31. Ibid., 18.
32. Ibid., 10.
33. Ibid., 20.

34. Ibid., 20.
35. Philip Schaff, *History of the Christian Church, Volume 4*, Hendrickson Publishers, 2011, page 284.
36. Brenda Ralph Lewis, *A Dark History: The Popes*, 19.
37. En.wikipedia.org, "Pope Sergius III".
38. Ibid.
39. Russell Chamberlin, *The Bad Popes*, Sutton Publishing, 1969 and 2023, page 43.
40. Brenda Ralph Lewis, *A Dark History: The Popes*, 32.
41. Ibid., 32.
42. Russell Chamberlin, *The Bad Popes*, 43.
43. Brenda Ralph Lewis, *A Dark History: The Popes*, 10.
44. Eamon Duffy, *Saints and Sinners*, 106.
45. Brenda Ralph Lewis, *A Dark History: The Popes*, 10.
46. Russell Chamberlin, *The Bad Popes*, 66.
47. Brenda Ralph Lewis, *A Dark History: The Popes*, 13.
48. Ibid.
49. Ibid.
50. Ibid.
51. Onepeterfive.com, "Pope Benedict IX was a 'devil from hell'".
52. Brenda Ralph Lewis, *A Dark History: The Popes*, 13.
53. Eamon Duffy, *Saints and Sinners*, 118.
54. Ibid., 140.
55. Ibid, 156.
56. Russell Chamberlin, *The Bad Popes*, 88.
57. Brenda Ralph Lewis, *A Dark History: The Popes*, 35.
58. Russell Chamberlin, *The Bad Popes*, 95.
59. Vaticancitytours.it, "Who were the worst Popes in history?"
60. Russell Chamberlin, *The Bad Popes*, 87-111.
61. Bruce Shelly, *Church History in Plain Language*, 263.
62. En.wikipedia.org, "Pope Urban VI".
63. Russell Chamberlin, *The Bad Popes*, 142.
64. Ibid., 136-145.
65. Thecollector.com.
66. Web.stanford.edu, "Julius Excluded from Heaven by Erasmus," January 2014.
67. Christine Shaw, *Julius II: The Warrior Pope*, Wiley-Blackwell; 1997, Editor's comments, Amazon.com.
68. Vaticancitytours.it, "Who were the worst popes in history?"
69. Ibid.
70. Brenda Ralph Lewis, *A Dark History: The Popes*, 119.
71. Russell Chamberlin, *The Bad Popes*, 168.
72. Ibid., 211.
73. Brenda Ralph Lewis, *A Dark History: The Popes*, 108-112.

74. Ibid.,113.
75. Ibid., 133.
76. Alphahistory.com, "1501: Pope Alexander VI Likes to Watch".
77. Brenda Ralph Lewis, *A Dark History: The Popes*, 129.
78. Popehistory.com.
79. Eamon Duffy, *Saints and Sinners*, 177.
80. Ibid., 194.
81. Matt Fradd, "Why Bad Popes Don't Disprove the Papacy w/ Scott Hahn and Cameron Bertuzzi".
82. Alessandra Stanley, "Pope asks forgiveness for errors of the church over 2000 years", *The New York Times*, March 13, 2000.

Chapter 2 – The Pope: Murder, Deception, and Denial

1. Keith Thompson, "The Errors of the Roman Catholic Church", YouTube.com, 2021.
2. Eamon Duffy, *Saints and Sinners*, 177.
3. Russell Chamberlin, *The Bad Popes*, 220.
4. Vaticancitytours.it, "Who were the worst popes in history?"
5. Trent Horn, *Why We're Catholic*, Catholic Answers, Inc., 2017, page 150.
6. Eamon Duffy, *Saints and Sinners*, 194, 200, 197
7. Ibid., 201.
8. Bruce Shelly, *Church History in Plain Language*, 264.
9. Ibid., 286.
10. Eamon Duffy, *Saints and Sinners*, 167.
11. Thecollector.com, "10 Terrible Catholic Popes".
12. Drew Kann, "Eight of the worst popes in church history", CNN.com, April 15, 2018.
13. Historyskills.com, "The worst popes in the history of the Catholic Church".
14. Gracegems.org, "Wicked Popes!"
15. Studysmarter.co.uk
16. Brenda Ralph Lewis, *A Dark History: The Popes*, 163.
17. Britannica.com, "Paul III".
18. Popehistory.com, "Pope Julius III".
19. En.wikipedia.org, "Julius III".
20. Ibid.
21. Vaticancitytours.it, "Paul IV".
22. Martina Mampieri, *Living under the Evil Pope*, Brill, 2019, introduction.
23. En.wikipedia.org, "Paul IV".
24. Britannica.com, "Paul IV".
25. Eamon Duffy, *Saints and Sinners*, 219.
26. Ibid., 75.
27. Russell Chamberlin, *The Bad Popes*, 11.
28. Brenda Ralph Lewis, *A Dark History: The Popes*, 103.

29. Ibid.,127.
30. Eamon Duffy, *Saints and Sinners*, 154.
31. Ibid., 232
32. Brenda Ralph Lewis, *A Dark History: The Popes*, 66.
33. Ibid., 92, 100.
34. Ibid., 118.
35. Ibid., 181.
36. Eamon Duffy, *Saints and Sinners*, 318.
37. Brenda Ralph Lewis, *A Dark History: The Popes*, 217.
38. En.wikipedia.org, "Pius IX", "Edgardo Mortara".
39. En.wikipedia.org, "John XXIII".
40. Gracegems.org, "Wicked Popes!"
41. Ibid.
42. Eamon Duffy, *Saints and Sinners*, 204-205
43. Ibid., 216
44. Ibid., 233
45. Ibid., 237
46. Ibid., 266
47. Ibid., 337
48. Gracegems.org, "Wicked Popes!"
49. Cullen Murphy, *God's Jury*, Mariner Books, 2013, page 6.
50. Ibid, 15.
51. Ibid.
52. Ibid.
53. Jstor.org, "Crusades".
54. Ibid.
55. Homework.study.com, "Crusades and Inquisitions".
56. Jstor.org, "Crusades".
57. Ibid.
58. Keith Thompson, "The Errors of the Roman Catholic Church".
59. *Innocent III*, Ep., XI. 230; Migne, 215, 1546, quoted in Philip Schaff, *History of the Christian Church, Volume 5*, Hendrickson Publishers, 2011, page 510n.1.
60. Keith Thompson, "The Errors of the Roman Catholic Church".
61. *Lucius III*, Ad abolendum, 1184, quoted in Michael C. Thomsett, *The Inquisition: A History*, McFarland & Company, Inc., Publishers, 2010, page 13.
62. Dr. Paul Chappell, "Massacred for the Faith: A Faith Worth Dying For" Ministry127.com, January 23, 2012.
63. Philip Schaff, *History of the Christian Church, Volume 5*, 528.
64. Bruce Shelly, *Church History in Plain Language*, 309.
65. En.wikipedia.org, "French Wars of Religion".
66. Keith Thompson, "The Errors of the Roman Catholic Church".
67. Ibid.

68. Ibid.
69. Williston Walker, *A History of the Christian Church, Fourth Edition*, Scribner, 1985, page 40.
70. Keith Thompson, "The Errors of the Roman Catholic Church".
71. Ibid.
72. Toby Green, *Inquisition: The Reign of Fear*, St. Martin's Press, 2007, page 8-9.
73. Brenda Ralph Lewis, *A Dark History: The Popes*, 116.
74. Cullen Murphy, *God's Jury*, 11.
75. Paul Vitello, "For Catholics, a Door to Absolution Is Reopened", *The New York Times*, February 10, 2009.
76. Usccb.org
77. James White, various sermons.
78. 1517.org, "The Christian History Almanac", January 27, 2021.
79. Greek Orthodox Archdiocese of America, as quoted in Gavin Ortlund, "Purgatory: A Protestant Perspective", YouTube.com, 2022.
80. Tertullian Against Marcion, 4.34, ibid.
81. Cyril of Alexandria, *Commentary on John, A Library of Fathers of the Holy Catholic Church, Vol. 48*, Trans. Thomas Randell, London: Walter Smith, 1885, vol. 2, book XII, chapter XIX, page 638.
82. John Chrysostom, Homily 3 on Philippians, as quoted in Gavin Ortlund, "Purgatory: A Protestant Perspective".
83. Gavin Ortlund, "Purgatory: A Protestant Perspective".
84. Bruce Shelly, *Church History in Plain Language*, 226.
85. Ibid.
86. Ibid.
87. Ibid., 227.
88. Cameron Bertuzzi, "Do Bad Popes Count Against the Truth of Catholicism?", Capturing Christianity, YouTube.com, 2020.
89. Matt Fradd, "Why Bad Popes Don't Disprove the Papacy w/ Scott Hahn and Cameron Bertuzzi", YouTube.com, 2022.
90. Trent Horn, *The Case for Catholicism*, Ignatius Press, 2017, page 114.
91. Matt Fradd, "The Worst Pope Ever! w/ Jimmy Akin", YouTube.com, 2024.
92. Justin Huang, "Corrupt Popes", The Justice Measure, October 18, 2015.
93. "Vatican System: List of Murdered Popes, 75 Popes Approved Torture, Murder, Burning at the Stake", CAnswersTV, YouTube.com, 2015.
94. Catholicplanet.org, "First Vatican Council, Chapter III, 1869, 1870".

Chapter 3 – The Pope: Never Bow Down

1. Trent Horn, *The Case for Catholicism*, 100.
2. Ambrose, *On the Holy Spirit*, Book III, Ch.14.94, as quoted in Keith Thompson, "The Errors of the Roman Catholic Church".
3. Trent Horn, *The Case for Catholicism*, 100.

4. Ibid., 101.
5. Gavin Ortlund, "Why I don't Accept the Papacy", YouTube.com, 2021.
6. Richard P. McBrien, *Catholicism: Completely revised and updated*, HarperCollins, 1994, page 753.
7. Wolfhart Pannenberg, *Systematic Theology Volume 3*, trans. Geoffrey W. Bromiley, Wm. B. Eerdmans Publishing, 1998, page 249.
8. Eamon Duffy, *Saints and Sinners*, 6.
9. Gavin Ortlund, "Intense Discussion on the Papacy (Cordial Catholic x Gospel Simplicity Crossover)", Gospel Simplicity, YouTube.com, 2021.
10. Keith Thompson, "The Errors of the Roman Catholic Church".
11. Herman Bavinck, *Reformed Dogmatics: Holy Spirit, Church and New Creation, Volume 4*, trans. John Vriend, ed., John Bolt, Baker Academic, 2008, page 365.
12. Jerome Neyrey, "St. Peter", ed. Richard P. McBrien, *The HarperCollins Encyclopedia of Catholicism*, HarperCollins Publishers, 1995. Page 993, as quoted in Keith Thompson, "The Errors of the Roman Catholic Church".
13. Beggarsallreformation.blogspot.com, "What was Augustine 'Retracting' on Peter, on the Rock, and Matthew 16?", ibid.
14. St. Augustine, *Retractions*, Book 1, Chapter 21. A.D. 427, ibid.
15. *A Library of the Fathers of the Holy Catholic Church*, Parker, 1884, *Homilies of S. John Chrysostom on the Gospel of St. Matthew*, Homily 54.3 as quoted in William Webster, *Roman Catholic Tradition: Claims and Contradictions*, Christian Resources, 1999, page 29, ibid.
16. Commentary on Isaiah IV.2, M.P.G. Vol. 70, Col. 940, as quoted in William Webster, *Roman Catholic Tradition: Claims and Contradictions*, 29, ibid.
17. Gavin Ortlund, "Why I don't Accept the Papacy".
18. Ibid.
19. Ibid.
20. William Webster, *Roman Catholic Tradition: Claims and Contradictions*, 29, as quoted in Keith Thompson, "The Errors of the Roman Catholic Church".
21. Johann Joseph Ignaz Von Döllinger and Johannes Huber, *The Pope and the Council*, Roberts, 1869, p 74 as quoted in William Webster, *Roman Catholic Tradition: Claims and Contradictions*, 30, ibid.
22. Gavin Ortlund, "Why I don't Accept the Papacy".
23. Eamon Duffy, *Saints and Sinners*, 23.
24. Westminster Confessions of Faith, 25.6.
25. Trent Horn, *The Case for Catholicism*, 114.
26. Ibid., 116.
27. Ibid., 118.
28. En.wikipedia.org, "Papal Infallibility".
29. Eamon Duffy, *Saints and Sinners*, 353.
30. Mike Gendron, "Ex-Catholic Exposes the Twisted Teachings of the Catholic Church", YouTube.com, 2023.
31. Trent Horn, *The Case for Catholicism*, 139.

32. Ibid., 131.
33. Ibid., 131, 133.
34. Gavin Ortlund, "Pope Vigilius: A Challenge to Vatican I".
35. Gavin Ortlund, "Intense Discussion on the Papacy (Cordial Catholic x Gospel Simplicity Crossover)".
36. Brian Tierney, *Origins of Papal Infallibility, 1150-1350*, Leiden: Brill, 2022, page 281.
37. Gavin Ortlund, "Pope Vigilius: A Challenge to Vatican I".
38. Karl Keating, *What Catholics Really Believe: Setting the Record Straight*, Servant Publications,1992, page 14.
39. Trent Horn, *The Case for Catholicism*, 95.
40. Gavin Ortlund, "Intense Discussion on the Papacy (Cordial Catholic x Gospel Simplicity Crossover)"
41. Ibid., 126.
42. Complicitclergy.com, "Pope Francis appoints Pro-Abortion, Pro-LGBT friend as founding member of New Vatican Institute".
43. Thestar.com, "Argentine justice's apartments used by prostitutes".
44. Matt Fradd, "I stopped defending Pope Francis w/ Joe Heschmeyer", YouTube.com, 2020.

Chapter 4 – The Early Church: A Movement, Not a Hierarchy

1. Eamon Duffy, *Saints and Sinners*, 9.
2. Andy Stanley, "The Big Church", Part 1.
3. Ibid., Part 4.
4. Ibid., Part 1.
5. Ibid., Part 5
6. Ibid, Part 1
7. Council of Trent, 1545-1564 as quoted by Bloggerpriest.com, "Did the Catholic Church prohibit Bible reading", January, 2011.
8. "Gavin Ortlund vs. Trent Horn: Is Sola Scriptura true?", Matt Fradd, YouTube.com, 2023.
9. Bruce Shelly, *Church History in Plain Language*, 274.
10. Ibid., 275.
11. Ibid., 277.
12. Ibid., 278.
13. Ibid., 279.
14. Matthias Premm, *Dogmatic Theology for the Laity*, Tan Books & Publishers Inc., 1982.
15. Matt Fradd, "Why Bad Popes Don't Disprove the Papacy w/ Scott Hahn and Cameron Bertuzzi".
16. Trent Horn, *Why We're Catholic*, 88.

Chapter 5 – The Roman Catholic Church: Endless Apologies

1. Bruce Shelly, *Church History in Plain Language*, Contents.
2. Eamon Duffy, *Saints and Sinners*, 25.
3. Bruce Shelly, *Church History in Plain Language*, 123.
4. Ibid.
5. Ibid., 124.
6. "A List of Apologies from the Catholic Church – Christopher Hitchens", Intelligence Squared, YouTube.com.
7. Bruce Shelly, *Church History in Plain Language*, 230-231.
8. Ibid., 231.
9. Ibid., 232.
10. Trent Horn, *The Case for Catholicism*, 129.
11. Oxford Dictionary, "unblemished".
12. Westminster Confession of Faith, 1:10 as quoted in Keith Thompson, "The Errors of the Roman Catholic Church".
13. Corpuschristiphx.org, "The Three Sources of Church Authority", 2020, ibid.
14. Hippolytus, Against Noetus, Ch. 4, ibid.
15. Cyril of Jerusalem, Catechetical Lectures, ibid.
16. Irenaeus, *Against Heresies*, 3.1.1, ibid.
17. Ibid., 1.8.1.
18. Ibid., 2.27.2.
19. John Chrysostom, *Homilies on Second Corinthians*, Homily 13 as quoted in Keith Thompson, "The Errors of the Roman Catholic Church".
20. Athanasius, *Against the Heathen*, Part 1.1, ibid.
21. Ambrose, *Of the Christian Faith*, Book I, Ch. 2, 516, ibid.
22. Ambrose, *On the Duties of the Clergy*, Book I, Ch. 23, 102, ibid.
23. Ambrose, *Theological and Dogmatics Works, The Sacraments of the Incarnation of our Lord*, Chapter 3, P.224, ibid.
24. Philip Schaff and Henry Wace, *Nicene and Post-Nicene Fathers, Second series: Volume V, Philosophical Works, On the Soul and the Resurrection*, Peabody: Hendrikson,1995, page 439, as quoted in William Webster, *Roman Catholic Tradition: Claims and Contradictions*, Christian Resources, WA, 1999, ibid.
25. Clement of Alexandria, "Stromateis, V1.15.125.3", as quoted in "Defending Sola Scriptura in the Church Fathers/Michael Horton Responds to Trent Horn", Sola Media, YouTube.com, March 26th, 2025.
26. Basil the Great, "Letter 189 [to Eustathius]", ibid.
27. Basil the Great, "Letter to Jerome", ibid.
28. Augustine, "Letter 82 [to Jerome]", ibid.
29. Augustine, "On the Unity of the Church 4.7", as quoted in Gavin Ortlund, "Sola Scriptura Defended", YouTube.com, 2021.
30. Rev. H.J. Schroeder, *The Canons and Decrees of the Council of Trent, Fourth Session, Decree Concerning the Canonical Scriptures*, O.P., Translator,

Rockford, Tan, 1978, page 17, as quoted in Keith Thompson, "The Errors of the Roman Catholic Church".

31. James Gibbons, *The Faith of Our Fathers*, TAN Books, 1980, page 72-73, ibid.

32. Pope Leo XII, "Providentissimus Deus", 1893, ibid.

33. *Commentary on John XXI*. 24-25, paragraph 2656, ibid.

34. "Gavin Ortlund vs. Trent Horn: Is Sola Scriptura True?"

35. Ibid.

36. Ibid.

37. Ibid.

38. Ibid.

39. Servus Christi, "The Catholic Church: Masterpiece of Deception", YouTube.com, 2020.

40. Ibid.

41. "Defending Sola Scriptura in the Church Fathers/Michael Horton Responds to Trent Horn", Sola Media, YouTube.com, March 26th, 2025.

42. Ibid.

43. Karl Rahner, *Theological Investigations*, Volume 10, Herder and Herder, 1973, page 108, as quoted in Keith Thompson, "The Errors of the Roman Catholic Church".

44. Eric Svendsen, *Evangelical Answers*, Reformation Press, 1999, page 122, ibid.

45. Gavin Ortlund, "Intense Discussion on the Papacy (Cordial Catholic x Gospel Simplicity Crossover)".

46. Eamon Duffy, *Saints and Sinners*, 14

47. Gavin Ortlund, "Intense Discussion on the Papacy (Cordial Catholic x Gospel Simplicity Crossover)".

48. Peter M.J. Stravinskas, *The Catholic Church and The Bible*, 2nd ed., Ignatius Press, 1996, page 8, as quoted in Keith Thompson, "The Errors of the Roman Catholic Church".

49. Peter Williams, *Catholic Principles for Interpreting Scripture*, Gregorian & Biblical Book Shop, 2001, page 155, ibid.

50. Trent Horn, "Debate: Is the Doctrine of Purgatory true? (Horn vs. White)", YouTube.com, 2024.

51. Jimmy Akin, *Scripture Commentary Recommendation*, jimmyakin.com, as quoted in Keith Thompson, "The Errors of the Roman Catholic Church".

52. Trent Horn, "Debate: Is the Doctrine of Purgatory true? (Horn vs. White)".

53. "Roman Catholic Mass Debate/Dr. James White vs. Joe Heschmeyer", The Apologetic Dog, YouTube.com, 2025.

54. Eric Svendsen, *Upon this Slippery Rock*, Calvary Press, 2002, page 60-61, as quoted in Keith Thompson, "The Errors of the Roman Catholic Church".

55. Ibid., 61-62.

56. John Riley, various sermons, Metro Bible Study, Atlanta.

Chapter 6 – Catholic Priests: It's Worse Than You Think

1. William Webster, *Roman Catholic Tradition: Claims and Contradictions*, as quoted in Keith Thompson, "The Errors of the Roman Catholic Church".
2. Keith Thompson, "The Errors of the Roman Catholic Church".
3. Jerome, *Commentary on Titus 1:5*, as quoted in Keith Thompson, "The Errors of the Roman Catholic Church".
4. Code of Canon Law, Book II, Canon 277, Vatican.va.
5. John MacArthur, "The Scandal of the Priesthood", YouTube.com.
6. Ibid.
7. Elizabeth Dias, "'It Is Not a Closet. It Is a Cage.' Gay Catholic Priests Speak Out", *The New York Times*, February 17, 2019.
8. Donald B Cozzens, *The Changing Face of the Priesthood*, The Liturgical Press, Minnesota, 2000. Page 99.
9. John MacArthur, "The Scandal of the Priesthood".
10. Ibid.
11. Ibid.
12. Ibid.
13. Meneolawgroup.com
14. Ibid.
15. Ibid.
16. Stephanie Kirchgaessner, "Pope Francis' words on clergy sex abuse ring hollow for some survivors", *The Guardian*, September 27, 2015.
17. En.wikipedia.org, "Bernard Francis Law".
18. En.wikipedia.org, "John Geoghan".
19. En.wikipedia.org, "North American Man/Boy Love Association".
20. Claudia Lauer, Associated Press, and Meghan Hoyer, "Almost 1700 priest and clergy accused of sex abuse are unsupervised", *NBC News*, October 4, 2019.
21. Associated Press, "Landmark Pennsylvania grand jury report finds more than 300 predator priests sexually abused children", as quoted on *Yahoo! News*, August 14, 2018.
22. Trent Horn, *Why We're Catholic*, 131.
23. Pew Research Center, "Americans See Catholic Clergy Sex Abuse as an Ongoing Problem", June 11, 2019.".
24. VOA News, "Investigation: 400,000 May Have Suffered Sexual Abuse from Spain's Clergy, Lay People", October 28, 2023.
25. Sylvie Corbet, "French report: 330,000 children victims of church sex abuse", *AP News*, October 5, 2021.
26. Ibid.
27. Catarina Demony and Miguel Pereira, "Child abuse found in Portugal Catholic Church is 'tip of iceberg', commission says", *Reuters*, February 13, 2023.".

28. María Hernández, "In Chile, justice eludes victims of Catholic clergy sex abuse years after the crisis exploded", *AP News*, September 19, 2023.

29. Alvise Armellini, "Argentine child abuse victims urge Pope Francis to hear their grievances", *Reuters*, March 9, 2023.

30. Derek Wilson, *Out of the Storm: The Life and Legacy of Martin Luther*, Hutchisson, 2007. This allegation was made in the pamphlet Warnunge D. Martini Luther/An seine lieben Deudschen, Wittenberg, 1531, as quoted in en.wikipedia.org, "Catholic Church Sexual abuse Cases".

31. Trent Horn, *Why We're Catholic*, 108.

Chapter 7 – Catholic Priests: Have the Talk

1. Researchgate.net

2. Donuhue, William, "Catholic Church's issue homosexuality, not pedophilia", *The Washington Post*, archived from the original on July 23, 2010. Retrieved December 4, 2010, as quoted in en.wikipedia.org, "Catholic Church Sexual Abuse Cases".

3. Engel, Randy, *The Rite of Sodomy: Homosexuality and the Roman Catholic Church*, New Engel Publishing, 2006.

4. Trent Horn, *Why We're Catholic*, 132.

5. Ibid., 135.

6. Save the Children, "Eyes That Fail to See: The sexual abuse of children in Spain and failures in the system", September 2017, https://resourcecentre.savethechildren.net/pdf/ eyes_that_fail_to_see_executivesummary.pdf.

7. John MacArthur, "Scandal of the Priesthood".

8. Mike Gendron, various sermons.

9. Bruce Shelly, *Church History in Plain Language*, 151.

10. Eamon Duffy, *Saints and Sinners*, 201.

11. CBS Sunday Morning, "Gay Priests: Breaking the Silence", YouTube.com.

12. Elaine Quijano and Betty Chin, "Pope Leo XIV takes helm of Catholic Church amid a priest shortage in the U.S.", CBS News, May 16, 2025.

13. Eamon Duffy, *Saints and Sinners*, 365.

14. ABC News, The Hidden Children of the Catholic Church | Foreign Correspondent", YouTube.com.

15. Elizabeth Dias, "'It Is Not a Closet. It Is a Cage.' Gay Catholic Priests Speak Out", *The New York Times*, February 17, 2019.

16. John MacArthur, "Scandal of the Priesthood".

17. Ibid.

18. Helen Conroy, *Forgotten Women: In Convents*, Kessinger Publishing, 2010.

19. Jon Schlosberg, Lindsey Griswold, Haley Yamada, Janice McDonald, and Steve Osonsame, July 27, 2022, ABC News Report as seen on Trent Horn, "Protestantism is winning (and the lessons for Catholics)", YouTube.com, 2025.

20. John MacArthur, "Scandal of the Priesthood".

Chapter 8 – The Vatican: A Homosexual Paradise

1. En.wikipedia.org, "Vatican".
2. Thevaticantickets.com
3. Frederic Martel, *In The Closet of the Vatican: Power, Homosexuality, Hypocrisy,* Bloomsbury Publishing Plc, 2019, page VII.
4. Ibid., IX.
5. Ibid., X.
6. Ibid., VIII.
7. Ibid., 5, 8, 10, 34, 469, 92, 537, 459.
8. Ibid., 14.
9. Ibid., 18.
10. Ibid. P 18
11. Ibid, 309.
12. Ibid., 30.
13. Ibid., 47.
14. Ibid., 49.
15. Ibid., 42-43.
16. Ibid., 60.
17. Ibid., 68
18. Ibid., Book Cover.
19. Ibid., 70-71.
20. Eric Sammons, Crisis Magazine, as quoted in Trent Horn, "Protestantism is winning (and the Lessons for Catholics)", Catholic.com.
21. Ibid.
22. Trent Horn, "Protestantism is winning (and the Lessons for Catholics)", Catholic.com.
23. Real Stories, Luc Herman and Paul Moreira, "The Church: A Code of Silence", Java Films, YouTube.com.
24. Ibid.
25. Ibid.
26. Laurie Goodstein, "Catholic order Jolted by Reports That Its founder Led a Double Life", *The New York Times*, February 4, 2009.
27. Frederic Martel, *In The Closet of the Vatican*, 231-239.
28. Ibid., 126.
29. Ibid., 129, 134, 139, 143, 145
30. Ibid., 269.
31. Ibid., 300-301.
32. Ibid., 529.
33. Ibid., 513-514.
34. Ibid., 478.
35. Ibid., 470.

Chapter 9 – Forgiveness: It Really Is Finished

1. Quora.com, Random Forum
2. Trent Horn, *Why We're Catholic*, 213.
3. Clement, "Letter to the Corinthians", 52, as quoted in Keith Thompson, "The Errors of the Roman Catholic Church".
4. Keith Thompson, "The Errors of the Roman Catholic Church".
5. J.N.D. Kelly, *Early Christian Doctrines: Revised Edition*, Harper-One, 1978, page 216, as quoted in Keith Thompson, "The Errors of the Roman Catholic Church".
6. *The Catechism of the Catholic Church*, DoubleDay, 1994, par. 1447, p.403, ibid.
7. Kenan Osborne, *Reconciliation*, ed. Richard P. McBrien, *The HarperCollins Encyclopedia of Catholicism*, Harper-Collins Publishers, 1995, page 1083, ibid.
8. Pastor John Barnett, Calvary Bible Church, "Q&A What is the Catholic Church? Where did the early Church go? What Church did Jesus start?", YouTube.com.
9. Origen, *Commentary on the Epistle to the Romans*, 3.9.4., as quoted in Keith Thompson, "The Errors of the Roman Catholic Church".
10. Joseph Ratzinger, *Jesus of Nazareth*, Ignatius Press, 2011, page 236-237, ibid.
11. Trent Horn, "Debate: Is the Doctrine of Purgatory true? (Horn vs. White)".

Chapter 10 – Forgiveness: What Kind does Jesus offer?

1. Bob George, combined quotes from: *Faith that Pleases God, Classic Christianity,* and *A Scriptural Journey to Discover the Grace of God*, Bob George Ministries.
2. Charles Stanley, *The Gift of Forgiveness*, Thomas Nelson Publishers, 1991, page 94-95, 98.
3. Southern Baptist Convention, Statement of Faith.
4. Charles Stanley, *The Gift of Forgiveness*, 93, 97.
5. Dr. Steve McVey, "Forgiven … forever?", Grace Walk Ministries, Atlanta.
6. Bob George, *A Scriptural Journey to Discover the Grace of God*, The Classic Christianity Conference, Texas, 1999, page 42.
7. Charles Spurgeon, *Faith's Checkbook*, July 23 entry, Whitaker House, 1993.
8. Andrew Farley, "Book of Hebrews", Biblecommentary.org,

Chapter 11 – The Twofold Gospel

1. Bob George, *Classic Christianity*, Harvest House Publishers, 1989, page 68.
2. Bob George, *Faith that Pleases God*, Harvest House Publishers, 2001, page 30.

3. "(Catholic) Scott Hahn vs. (Protestant) Bowman Salvation debate #1 of 3", YouTube.com.
4. Trent Horn, *Why We're Catholic*, 198.
5. Ibid., 201.
6. Ibid., 140-141.
7. Ibid., 142.
8. Ibid., 141.
9. Ibid., 141.
10. Ibid., 142.
11. Ibid., 145.

Chapter 12 – A New Covenant, A New Promise

1. Bob George, *Classic Christianity*, 59.
2. Andy Stanley, "The Big Church", Part 1.
3. Bob George, "The New Covenant", YouTube.com.
4. Pastor Trent Shoemake, "New Covenant in Hebrews", McDonough Christian Church, Georgia.
5. Bob George, *A Scriptural Journey to Discover the Grace of God*, The Classic Christianity Conference, Texas, 1999, page 40-41.

Chapter 13 – The Truth about the Eucharist

1. "Baptist-Catholic Dialogue on the Eucharist (w/ Dr. Gavin Ortlund and Dr. Brett Salked)", Gosepl Simplicity, YouTube.com, 2022.
2. Richard P. McBrien, *Catholicism: Catholicism: Completely revised and updated*, HarperOne, 1994, page 866-867, as quoted in Keith Thompson, "The Errors of the Roman Catholic Church".
3. Eamon Duffy, *Saints and Sinners*, 148
4. "Baptist-Catholic Dialogue on the Eucharist (w/ Dr. Gavin Ortlund and Dr. Brett Salked)".
5. Fargodiocese.net, "Why are non-Catholics but baptized Christians not to receive the Eucharist?"
6. Code of Canon Law, Book IV, Canon 844, §1, Vatican.va.
7. Gavin Ortlund, "A Baptist Case for Real Presence in the Eucharist", YouTube.com, 2023.
8. Trent Horn, *The Case for Catholicism*, 162-163, 165.
9. *The Canons and Decrees of the Council of Trent*, trans. H. J. Schroeder, Tan Books and Publishers, 1978, page 73, as quoted in YouTube.com, "The Errors of the Roman Catholic Church", Keith Thompson, 2021.
10. Ibid., Chapter 4, p. 75

11. Scott Hahn, *The Lamb's Supper: The Mass as Heaven on Earth*, Random House LLC, 2002, p.30, as quoted in Keith Thompson, "The Errors of the Roman Catholic Church".

12. Philip Schaff, *Nicene and Post-Nicene Fathers*, Grand Rapids: Eerdmans, 1956, *Volume II, St. Augustin, On Christian Doctrine III*, 16.24, page 563; *Volume VII, Homilies on the Gospel of St. John*, Homily 50.13, page 282-282, as quoted in William Webster, *Roman Catholic Tradition: Claims and Contradictions*, Christian Resources, Inc. WA., 1999, page 57, ibid.

13. *Demonstratio Evangelicu* I.x.28-38. Cited in Darwell Stone, *A History of the Doctrine of the Eucharist*, Longmans, Green, 1909, Volume I, page 110-111, as quoted in William Webster, *Roman Catholic Tradition: Claims and Contradictions*, 59.

14. Ignatius, *Letter to the Romans*, 7, as quoted in Keith Thompson, "The Errors of the Roman Catholic Church".

15. Ignatius, *Letter to the Philadelphians*, 5, ibid.

16. Ignatius, *Letter to the Trallians*, 8, ibid.

17. Keith Thompson, "The Errors of the Roman Catholic Church".

18. Tertullian, *On the Resurrection of the Flesh*, xxxviii, as quoted in Keith Thompson, "The Errors of the Roman Catholic Church".

19. James White, "Oh That Those Who Follow Rome Would Know the Finished Work of Christ!", Alpha and Omega Ministries, aomin.org, September. 11th, 2009.

20. Ibid.

21. Servus Christi, "The Catholic Church: Masterpiece of Deception".

22. Ibid.

23. Raymond Edward Brown, John P. Meier, *Antioch and Rome: New Testament Cradles of Catholic Christianity*, Paulist Press, 1983, page 171, as quoted in Keith Thompson, "The Errors of the Roman Catholic Church".

24. Trent Horn, "Why 70% of Catholics Deny Christ's Real Presence in the Eucharist", Catholic.com, August 15, 2019.

25. Gavin Ortlund, "A Baptist Case for Real Presence in the Eucharist".

26. Philip Schaff, *Nicene and Post-Nicene Fathers*, Eerdmans, 1956, Volume II, *St. Augustin, On Christian Doctrine III*, 16.24, page 563; Volume VII, *Homilies on the Gospel of St. John*, Homily 50.13, page 282-282, as quoted in William Webster, *Roman Catholic Tradition: Claims and Contradictions*, 57.

27. Tim Staples, *Nuts and Bolts*, Basilica Press, 2007, page 33 as quoted in Keith Thompson, "The Errors of the Roman Catholic Church".

28. Steve McVey, *Grace Rules*, Harvest House Publishers, 1998, page 88.

29. "Roman Catholic Mass Debate/Dr. James White vs. Joe Heschmeyer".

30. Ibid.

31. Steve McVey, *Grace Rules*, 148-149, 154.

32. Mike Gendron, "Proclaiming the Gospel Ministry", email publication.

Acknowledgments

As I reflect on all the incredible people who have shaped my faith over the decades, the list quickly grows long. For me, it begins with the privilege of having Christian parents in a more wholesome time. They kept my brothers and me involved in Church and lived out the Christian principles that shaped my foundation. They taught us honesty and integrity, free from the influence of the modern media engines of today. My friends and I often talk about how lucky we were to grow up before Facebook, Instagram, cell phones, and even the Internet. It allowed us to grow rich in the aspects of life that were most important without negative and secular influence.

Each church I was involved with taught me something a little different about being a Christian. One denomination focused more on worship, while others concentrated on living out the daily Christian life with a regular quiet time. Each one, although theologically diverse, and at times ignoring the Scriptures on many of the details, provided another layer of my experience, helping to assimilate biblical truths and pave a pathway for my life's journey.

In my earlier years, I attended Metro Bible Study and 722, non-denominational Bible studies consisting of both Catholics and Protestants. These midweek meetings had over 2,000 people in attendance, and we engaged in awesome worship times and detailed Bible studies presented by a renowned Bible teacher. These meetings I attended in my twenties and thirties were incidental in shaping how I think and live as a Christian, and how to apply biblical principles to operating the small businesses I would be connected with later.

After the elementary foundations were laid, my discovery of the New Covenant (explored in Chapters 9 through 12) was the biggest shift in my spiritual understanding. I grew up with the knowledge that God was all about love and grace, but what He accomplished was far more comprehensive and complete than I had ever imagined. I extend a special thanks to my friend Barry who filled in many of the final missing pieces that I would use for my Christian journey. My subsequent study of grace would not only be eye-opening, but has become life-changing.

Likewise, I thank all of my close Christian friends over the years (and there are many), who in their own separate ways helped mold my thinking process and provided great role models, allowing me to have a healthy balance in my Christian perspective. We had endless dialogues on theology, and we all learned a little more each time.

All thanks and honor to God, who waited until the right time to expose me to His message of the New Covenant—His ultimate gift of grace that has allowed me to live these past decades in total freedom and total assurance that I have been permanently forgiven and sealed by Him, confident He satisfied all the righteous requirements through Christ for salvation. God is certainly patient, and will even use our involvement in churches that are not theologically correct to work out His purposes in our lives.

After discovering the truth, I can say with assurance that the Christian life is pretty dang amazing when living in the realities of His finished work!

Special thanks to my editor, Benjamin Kelley, who demonstrated extreme professionalism, patience and perseverance in his endless edits, phone calls, emails, and video chats in dealing with my obsessive nature! His insights were of incredible value for such a complicated and tedious topic.

And to all the authors of books and video productions that were used as valuable resources to substantiate all the data needed to put a book with this magnitude together in an accurate and orderly manner. These people include, but are not limited to:

Bob George	Keith Thompson
Steve McVey	Cullen Murphy
Andy Stanley	Eamon Duffy
Bruce Shelly	Gavin Ortlund
Brenda Lewis	James White
Philip Schaff	John MacArthur
Russell Chamberlin	Frederic Martel
John Barnett	Mike Gendron

About the Author

Jeff Nottingham has studied biblical theology for over thirty years and is a former writer for *The Good Life Newsletter*. A graduate of Gordon State College, Jeff is a retired businessman and lay leader, having taught middle and high school Sunday school classes in Fayetteville, Georgia for fourteen years. He enjoys performing piano concerts for assisted living residents and flying friends and family on local excursions from his fly-in community in south Atlanta.

The author welcomes your questions or comments at
jeffnottingham8@proton.me